Chaucer's Verse Art in its European Context

MEDIEVAL AND RENAISSANCE
TEXTS AND STUDIES

VOLUME 513

Chaucer's Verse Art in its European Context

Martin J. Duffell

ARIZONA CENTER FOR MEDIEVAL
ACMRS
AND RENAISSANCE STUDIES

Tempe, Arizona
2018

A generous contribution to support the publication of this volume was provided by The Pakis Family Foundation.

THE ARIZONA CENTER FOR
MEDIEVAL & RENAISSANCE
STUDIES

Published by ACMRS (Arizona Center for Medieval and Renaissance Studies)
Tempe, Arizona

Cover Illustration:
This portrait of Dante by Sandro Botticelli dates from 1495 and that of Shakespeare from the first folio of 1623. The portrait of Chaucer was also painted at some time during the first quarter of the seventeenth century.

∞
This book is made to last. It is set in Adobe Caslon Pro,
smyth-sewn and printed on acid-free paper to library specifications.
Printed in the United States of America

To Dawn

Contents

Foreword

In the late twentieth century and the early twenty-first, cultural theory has assumed an importance in literary criticism that would have surprised scholars of earlier times. In the case of Chaucer studies, this importance can be justified on the grounds that Chaucer was as obsessed by sex, class, race, power, and violence as the modern audience. But, he was also obsessed by other issues that have faded in Western consciousness, things like honor, virtue, faith, purity, courtesy, guilt, and penitence. These have attracted less attention among modern critics, but they emphasize that Chaucer's cultural values were those of his times: they were not unique in his society. This lack of uniqueness is common to most of the content of his poetry: he told hundreds of tales, hardly any of them of his own invention.

The feature of Chaucer's poetry that is most distinctive is not its content but its form. First, Chaucer dared to compose in the newly respectable English when his friend Gower hid behind the established status of Latin and French. Chaucer played no small part in making his East Midlands dialect (the *English* of Stratford atte Bowe) the language first of England, then North America, and then the world. And secondly he crafted verses that became the canonical forms of written poetry in that language. His verse craft, unlike his social attitudes and his stories, was highly original: his longer line, in particular, had many features found in no other poet or language.

So much was written about Chaucer's metrics in earlier centuries that most twenty-first-century literary scholars shy away from the subject, particularly since many English departments now regard meter as too difficult a subject for undergraduates. This belief must be a delusion, however, because in English public schools thirteen-year-old children still learn to compose perfectly adequate Ancient Greek quantitative verse. Another factor in the modern neglect of Chaucer's metrics is a vague feeling among teachers that all the questions on Chaucer's meter have now been answered. But the truth is that they haven't, and a host of issues are hotly disputed by specialists in this area. The unresolved questions include:

> How does Chaucer's versifying relate to modern theories of linguistic rhythm?

How far did the differences between English, French, Latin, and Italian phonology influence versifying in the four languages known to Chaucer?

Could Chaucer have been aware of such influence?

Did Chaucer compose in French before turning to English?

Was Chaucer's versifying influenced by earlier English verse?

Should his shorter lines be regarded as the first iambic tetrameters?

Where did his longer line come from?

When did he first employ it?

Is that longer line more than a crude precursor to the canonical iambic pentameter?

Did Chaucer's verse designs change during the thirty years of his poetic career?

Did Gower do more than copy Chaucer's verse designs?

Why did Chaucer's Scots followers capture his longer line so well?

Why did his English followers lose the knack for more than a century?

What were those English poets' metrical intentions?

Which sixteenth-century English poets helped recover Chaucer's longer line?

Why has the popularity of Chaucer's longer line proved so enduring?

This book sets out to answer all these questions, and to counter the charges that metrics is difficult and outmoded. In that cause it will employ a number of modern theories of rhythm and meter, and it will test its conclusions with established statistical tools wherever possible.

Acknowledgement

I wish to thank Donka Minkova, Christopher McCully, Derek Attridge, and Dominique Billy for the important contributions they have made to this volume, and Robert Bjork, Roy Rukkila, and Todd Halvorsen for the care and patience with which they have prepared it for publication.

Abbreviations

Chauncer's Works

AA	*Anelida and Arcite*
BD	*Book of the Duchess*
CT	*Canterbury Tales*
GP	General Prologue
HF	*House of Fame*
KT	Knight's Tale
LGW	*Legend of Good Women*
PF	*Parliament of Fowls*
PT	Pardoner's Tale
RT	Reeve's Tale
ST	Tale of Sir Thopas
TC	*Troilus and Criseyde*
PP	Parson's Prologue

Other Poets' Works

CA	*Confessio Amantis*
CB	*Cinkant Balades*
IPP	*In Praise of Peace*
LOL	*Life of Our Lady*
MO	*Mirour de l'Omme*
OA	*L'Orloge amoureus*
O & N	*The Owl and the Nightengale*
PL	*Paradise Lost*
RR	*Roman de la Rose*
T	*Traité*

Other Abbreviations

AN	Anglo-Norman
a-verse	first hemistich in OE or ME
b-verse	second hemistich in OE or ME
L1	mother-tongue
M	consistuent of ME alliterative foot
ME	Middle English
OE	Old English
OT	Optimality Theory
PT	Parametric Theory
R1	first reading language
SMP	Stress Maximum Principle
s	stronger element in contrast
s^w	left-strong binary foot
w	weaker element in contrast

1
Rhythm and Language

The twenty-first century's first president of the Modern Humanities Research Association reminded his audience that poetry is important because 'reading and writing poetry it is the most remarkable thing that humans do with their most distinctive property, language.'[1] The *Oxford English Dictionary* defines *poetry* as follows:[2]

> Literary work in which special intensity is given to the expression of feelings and ideas by the use of distinctive style and rhythm.

The key word here is *rhythm*, because this book aims to give its readers a broader yet deeper understanding of the rhythms found in Chaucer's poetry, in order to support the claim that Chaucer raised the craft of versifying in English to an art.

This book's first three chapters explain what modern research tells us about the nature of rhythm, the choice of rhythms poets have when they versify, and the structure of lines of English verse. Four of the remaining chapters are devoted to rhythms Chaucer found in the poetry (of four languages) that he knew. The remainder of the book is shared between a detailed analysis of how Chaucer and his friend Gower developed a new mode of versifying between 1368 and 1400, and an investigation of what happened to Chaucer's new longer line in the centuries that followed.

The Physics of Rhythm

The most concise definition of *rhythm* is "the repetition of an event in time," and the essential components of rhythm are *events*, their *number*, and the *intervals* between them.[3] A single event repeated at regular intervals produces what is

---

[1] For this speech, see Smith, 2000.

[2] See Pearsall, 1998: 1430. French dictionaries employ almost exactly the same terms to define *poésie*; see, for example, Davau, Cohen, & Lallemand, 1972.

[3] Dictionaries expand this definition from acoustic physics to: "rhythm: a regularly recurring sequence of events, actions, or processes"; see Pearsall, 1998: 1593.

termed a *simple primary* rhythm, and examples might include the human pulse or the ticking of a clock. When two events are repeated in conjunction it is termed a *complex secondary rhythm.*[4] The clear difference between the two can be exemplified by human locomotion, where hopping on one leg produces a simple primary rhythm (hop-hop-hop), and walking a complex secondary rhythm (left-right-left-right).

The human fetus becomes addicted to rhythm in the womb, rocked for nine months by the mother's bipedal locomotion, lapped by her waters, reassured by her respiration, and sustained by the pumping of her blood in tiny vessels. When the neonate finally emerges into the light, every rhythmic mechanism springs into action: first comes breathing, then suckling, and then the echo of a smile; and afterwards come crawling, walking, running, and jumping; singing, drumming, dancing, and at some point swimming, which reminds us of our first home. Rhythm is a deep-seated habit that we break only when we die.[5]

The human mind, like life, seeks complexity: a clock's ticking may produce a simple rhythm, but listeners don't always perceive it as such. For centuries clocks have been constructed to go 'tick-tick,' yet in most listeners' experience (and in the conventional wisdom) they go 'tick-tock.'[6] Whenever people produce rhythms they tend to display this tendency of increasing complexity as they gain confidence: a tap-dancer, having mastered *threes* (three taps on every contact with the floor), attempts *fours*; and a drummer tries out ever more complicated routines. We should not therefore be surprised if the history of versifying shows the same tendency towards complexity.

The regularity of repetition, like the 'tick' and the 'tock,' is to some extent a product of the human mind: we sometimes perceive as regular events that when measured objectively with laboratory instruments prove not to be so. Regularity may be thought of as a continuum: at some point in a series of events becoming more regular we perceive rhythm. We derive pleasure from regularity, but only up to a point: many people enjoy drum solos, but few can bear the sound of a pneumatic drill for very long. What makes the drum solo more interesting is the potential for change that the human drummer has and the drill has not: the ability to punctuate a major regularity with minor irregularities in the quantity and quality of sound produced.

The subtle interplay of regularity and variety will be a recurring motif in this volume.

The human appetite for complexity also affects rhythmic intervals: if we introduce a longer interval in a primary rhythm, a different type of rhythm results, a *complex primary rhythm.* For example, in delivering blows to a nail with a hammer I might leave a longer interval after every third blow

[4] See Chatman, 1965: 29.

[5] For biological rhythms, see Widmaier, Raff, and Strang, 2010.

[6] See Potter et al., 2003: 103–9.

(tap-tap-tap—tap-tap-tap—tap-tap-tap). This, in effect, creates a new event, a *trio* of blows with short intervals between them, as well as a new interval (the longer one after every third blow). And complex primary rhythms appear to be more attractive than simple ones to minds that are themselves complex structures seeking stimulation.

The grouping of events to produce a different event raises an interesting question: how many events can be grouped in this way to produce a new event? Psychologists have shown that human beings *subitize* very small numbers, that is they perceive them as entities: just as to commuters a single bus is an entity, so a pair of buses (which, for scientific reasons, are much more likely to turn up) is also an entity.[7] Similarly a trio of buses and, for some people, a quartet is an entity. But beyond that we have to count, which is a very different process from subitizing. An obvious linguistic example of human mental processes recognizing no more than three categories occurs in the grammars of the oldest Indo-European languages: three numbers differentiate noun and adjective forms, singular, dual, and plural; and three persons differentiate pronoun and verb forms, first, second and third.[8] In theory, grammars could contain special forms for groups of four, or forms for combinations of first, second, and third persons, but in fact they do not.

It does seem, however, that people learn to count numbers beyond three rapidly and intuitively within certain limits, and the psychologist George A. Miller argued that those limits are "the magical number seven plus or minus two."[9] He had noted this first in laboratory experiments into how many gradations of salinity and how many different stimuli the human senses can learn to recognize. On reflection, however, he found that many commonplace pieces of knowledge supported his conclusion. Thus, in many cultures the continuum of the rainbow is perceived as seven colors, and the continuum of fundamental frequencies is perceived as seven distinct notes. And, on a more mundane level, which we can verify by our own personal research, tap-dancers can perfect a series of seven taps but not a series of ten.[10]

In the next chapter I shall try to demonstrate that these psychological factors combine with linguistic factors in determining the choices poets have available when they versify, but before doing so I want to explore another equally important constraint on the process of crafting verse: the nature of linguistic rhythm.

---

7 See Hurford, 1987: 93–97.

8 For duals in Sanskrit, see Whitney, 1962: 26; for duals in Greek, see Palmer, 1980: 5.

9 See Miller, 1956: 81–97.

10 See Hartley, 2007.

Linguistic Rhythm

One of the most important advances in the study of phonology in the late-twentieth century was a logically rigorous explanation of linguistic rhythm, and the branch of linguistics that the discovery spawned is known as *metrical phonology.*[11] Metrical phonology builds on basic concepts that have become well established, but which are worth recapitulating here.

Phonologists describe speech as a stream or chain of sounds that are either vowels or consonants. Laboratory equipment shows this chain to resemble a wave with peaks and troughs.[12] The speech chain can be broken down into *phonemes*, the smallest units of sound that can distinguish meaning: thus *b*, *c*, and *r* are phonemes because they distinguish the words *bat*, *cat*, and *rat*; and *a* is a phoneme because it distinguishes *cat* from *cot*, and *rat* from *rot*. The phonemes *a* and *o* are vowels, which are said to be more *sonorous* because they are louder and have a lower fundamental frequency than consonants like *b*, *c*, and *r*. Vowels are merely vibrations of the vocal chords with different exit strategies; consonants involve other organs of speech such as teeth, lips, and tongue. Vowels in combination are known as *diphthongs* (two) and *triphthongs* (three), while consonants in combination are known as *clusters*.

In English we represent phonemes by the twenty-six letters of the Roman alphabet, but English speakers employ at least forty-four different phonemes.[13] As a result many letters have to stand for more than one phoneme, and some phonemes are represented by more than one letter. Linguistics has provided a tool to solve this problem of orthographic inaccuracy which besets every written language: an international phonetic alphabet (IPA) that enables phonemes in any language to be captured much more accurately.[14] I shall not employ the IPA for the examples I give in this volume because its chief interest is in the poetic use of what are termed the *suprasegmental features* of language (such as *stress* and *syllabification*, and to a lesser extent *syllable weight*), rather than in the segmental features (such as *rhyme* and *alliteration*).[15] I can easily indicate these suprasegmental features by a few typographical devices added to the normal orthography.

Written English is an unsatisfactory guide to these three features because many of its letters perform conventional functions. Thus, double consonants in English are not two phonemes but simply indicate the quality of the preceding vowel, as when they distinguish between *matting* and *mating.*[16] Many times the final *e* is present for the same purpose, as when distinguishing the sound of the

[11] See Hogg and McCully, 1987 and Hayes, 1995.

[12] For spectograms of speech, see O'Connor, 1973: 63–65 and 161 (Plates 1–13).

[13] See Aitchison, 1978: 50–51.

[14] For IPA, see Lord, 1974: 128–36.

[15] For suprasegmentals, see Crystal, 1985: 276.

[16] See Crystal, 2012: passim.

vowel in *cut* from the sound of that in *cute*. Sometimes they are simply historical relics that are not pronounced at all, like those in *have* and *come*. I shall therefore need to employ typographical conventions to identify the number of syllables in a line and its stress contour, and I shall explain the notation used when I present my first example.

There is one English phoneme for which IPA has a symbol and the Roman alphabet does not, and that is the sound termed *schwa* (denoted by the symbol ə in IPA). Many short, unstressed vowels in English are reduced to this minimal sound. Thus, in US English the second syllable of the word *missile* becomes schwa, whereas in UK English a *missal* is something quite different. In unstressed syllables all the English vowels, still written *a, e, i, o,* or *u*, are subject to reduction in this way.[17] Schwa has a big part to play later in this volume, but most of its concerns will not be with segments of the speech chain, but with suprasegmental features.

The suprasegmental that people identify most easily is the syllable, a unit that is difficult to isolate in the laboratory, but which speakers of a language recognize intuitively. This can be seen in the uniform way that English speakers observe syllable boundaries when inserting expletives into polysyllabic words. It is not clear why the human mind can recognize something that laboratory instruments cannot, but it does.

A syllable consists of a peak of sonority (a vowel or diphthong) plus any consonants that can be attached to it, but the process of attachment is fluid: in continuous speech final consonants of words get *re-syllabified* with any vowel that opens the next word. Thus "Give a dog a bone" appears more like "Gi-va-do-gabone." Despite this fluidity, works on phonology generally agree in anatomizing the syllable as in Figure 1:[18]

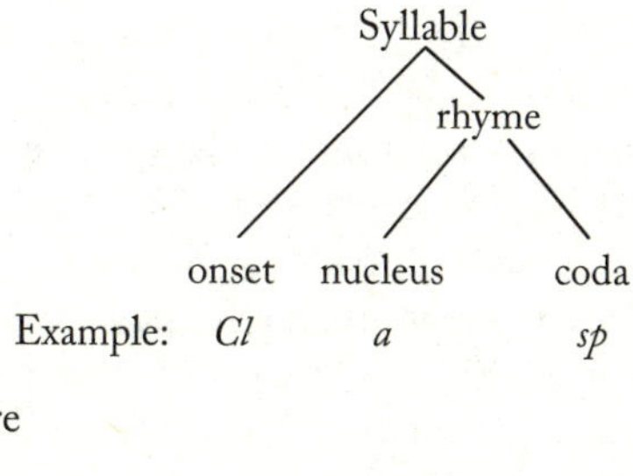

Fig.1: Syllable Structure

Note that some syllables lack an onset (for example, the word *on*), some lack a coda (for example, the word *go*), and others lack both (for example, the word *I*).

Since two thirds of the components of the syllable are optional, clearly all syllables are not equal, and the differences in structure are reflected in the fact

[17] See Crystal, 1985: 296–97.

[18] See Hogg and McCully, 1987: 35–41.

that some syllables occupy more time in delivery than others. Classical authors referred to this distinction as one of syllable *length*, but modern linguists prefer to refer to it as one of *weight*, of *heavy* syllables versus *light*. The difference in weight resides in the rhyme part of the syllable: a syllable is heavy if it has a *branching* rhyme, that is, (a) if it has a coda that can't be re-syllabified, or (b) if its nucleus is a long vowel or diphthong; otherwise it is light.[19] Whether a syllable has an onset or not does not affect syllable weight. Thus the example of continuous speech given above, "Gi-va-do-ga-bone," is four light syllables followed by a heavy one.

The Ancient Greeks perceived a heavy syllable as having the duration of two light ones and modern linguistic researchers accept this hypothesis; thus they employ the Greek term for the duration of a light syllable, one *mora*, and Anglicize its plural as two *moras* for the duration of a heavy syllable. Moras seem to belong in pairs in English, where all lexical words contain at least two moras and the only one-mora monosyllables are grammatical words like *a* and *the*. This ratio of 2:1 causes problems in perception, and Morse code, an artificial language used in telegraphy, demonstrates this. In this code, short sounds called dots (•) and long ones called dashes (—) represent letters of the Roman alphabet; and there is a standard interval between sounds in the same letter, and a longer interval between letters in the same word. By careful experiment the code's inventor found that dashes needed to be three times as long as dots to prevent confusion at the message's destination, and intervals between words three times as long as those within them. A ratio of 2:1 was not sufficient to avoid confusion.

Thus it is, that the speakers of some languages can detect the difference between heavy and light syllables (with their ratio of 2:1) intuitively, while those of other languages cannot. This can be seen most clearly in Latin, where in Classical times poets could base their rhythms on syllable weight and their audiences could appreciate them; but by about AD 300 the Empire's poets could no longer versify correctly in this way.[20] In modern European languages two different habits of speech militate against a clear recognition of differences in syllable weight: the speakers of some languages, such as English, tend to equalize the length of time between peaks of stress in their utterances, known as *stress-timing*; and speakers of others, such as French, tend to equalize the time taken in delivery of all syllables (*syllable-timing*).[21] This makes it difficult for poets to imitate the versification of one language in another, a problem that greatly affects the subject of this book.

English syllables, however, contain a contrast that is much more salient than that between the language's heavy and light syllables: the *stress* contrast. Languages like English have what is known as a *dynamic accent*: in delivery some syllables are stressed, which is to say that they are made longer, and louder, and have a different

---

[19] See Hayes, 1995: 50–54.

[20] See Lote, 1939: 219 25.

[21] See Giegerich, 1980 and Roach, 1982.

pitch (fundamental frequency) contour from others.[22] Stress shares an important property with phonemes: it can distinguish meaning; stress separates *incite* from *insight* in the same way that the initial phonemes distinguish *rat* from *cat*.

Metrical phonology describes the rhythm of the English language in terms of stress: the contrast between stressed and unstressed syllables produces a complex secondary rhythm. Binary contrasts in linguistics are described in terms of strength: a stronger element contrasts with a weaker one, and stress contrasts are either left-strong (s^w) as in *insight*, or right-strong (w^s) as in *incite*. For convenience linguistic researchers employ the traditional term *trochee* for a left-strong and the term *iamb* for a right-strong contrast, and use the term *foot* to describe a unit containing such a contrast. Researchers into metrical phonology have discovered only three types of linguistic rhythm in the many languages they have studied: the first is a rhythm of *syllabic trochees*, the second one of *moraic* trochees, and the third one of *iambs*.[23] English has a rhythm of the second type: it is a *moraic trochaic language* and, as noted above, a *mora* is the unit that represents the duration of a light syllable.

Moraic theory explains much that is otherwise inexplicable in English phonology, including the weight-rule for monosyllables, the position of stress in longer words, and the indifference of lines of verse to an extra post-tonic syllable. In his analysis of linguistic rhythm Bruce Hayes employs a simple notation for moraic feet: *x* denotes a strong mora, a point (.) denotes a weak one, and parentheses enclose each foot. Figure 2 below shows the moraic structure of some sample words and phrases using Hayes's notation:[24]

(a) Break, break, break	*(b) Pretty Polly Parrot*	*(c) heavily*
(x .) (x .) (x .)	(x .) (x .) (x .)	(x .) .
(d) Sunset Park Zoo	*(e) quaintly*	*(f) immensely*
(x.)(x.) (x .) (x .)	(x .) .	. (x .) .

Fig. 2: Moraic Structure

In Figure 2 (a), (b), and (d) the example contains a regular moraic trochaic rhythm, but the examples in (c), (e) and (f) contain un-footed (weak, or single) moras. These un-footed moras are of two types. The word-final ones are *extrametrical* (literally, outside the rhythm) like the final mora of 2(c) above. The others are known as *degenerate* feet, like the initial mora of 2(f).[25]

---

[22] See Hayes, 1995: 5–7.

[23] See Hayes, 1995: 63–69.

[24] See Hayes, 1995: 40–41.

[25] See Hayes, 1995: 56–60 (for extrametricality) and 86 (for degenerate feet).

Since English speakers do not intuitively recognize syllable weight the most obvious result of the language's trochaic rhythm lies in the stress relationships among syllables and within words and phrases. Metrical phonologists argue that stress is hierarchical, as shown in Figure 3 below.

level			
word	x	x	x
syllable	x	x x	x x
mora	(x .)	(x .)	(x .) .
	(a) break	(b) pretty	(c) weighty

level			
word	x	x	x
syllable	x x	x x	x x
mora	. (x .)	(x .) (x .)	(x .)(x .)
	(d) rejoice	(e) playground	(f) dis-rupt

Fig. 3: Stress Hierarchy within Words

The three levels at which strong/weak contrasts are shown are the *mora*, the *syllable*, and the *word*. Word 3(a) is a lexical monosyllable; 3(b) is a disyllable with two light syllables; 3(c) has a heavy syllable followed by a light one; 3(d) has a light syllable followed by a heavy one; and both 3(e) and 3(f) have two heavy syllables. The examples with two syllables also contain a stress contrast (strong / weak). Note that in English most nouns, adjectives, and adverbs are *left-strong* at word level, like the words *pretty* in 3(b) and *playground* in 3(e), which are both [s^w], or *heavily* [s^w w]. Prefixed words, on the other hand, are usually *right-strong* like *rejoice* in 3(d) and *disrupt* in 3(f), which are both [w^s].

For many years scholars argued over how many levels of stress there were in English, two (stress and non-stress), three (primary, secondary, and non-stress), or more.[26] Metrical phonology shows that the number of levels is variable depending on size of the utterance, and that within both words and phrases, stress forms a hierarchy. Bruce Hayes illustrates how phrasal stress operates in English by a grid in which the symbol *x* shows each of the levels of stress, and Figure 4 below illustrates how this hierarchy works in some of the phrases examined in Figure 2. The lowest level of the grid is that of moras, and the next is that of syllables, while the higher levels are those of relative stress within the phrase.[27]

[26] For a four-level theory of English stress, see Trager and Smith, 1951. For the first use of this example, see Hayes, 1995: 18–21.

[27] For a more detailed analysis of phrasal stress, see Hayes, 1995: 35–37.

			x					x	
level	x		x	x				x	
phrase	x		x	x		x		x	
syllable	x	x	x	x	x	x	x	x	x
mora	x .	x .	x .	x	.	x	.	x	.
	(a) *Break, break, break*			(b) *Pretty Polly Parrot*					

level							
phrase							x
phrase			x	x			x
word	x		x	x		x	x
syllable	x	x	x	x	x	x	x
mora	x.	x.	x.	x.	x.	x.	x.
	(c) *Sun-set Park*			(d) *Sun-set Park Zoo*			

Fig. 4: Phrasal Stress Grids

Figure 4 demonstrates a number of important features of stress in English: the first is that phrasal stress is right-strong: the right-most stressed syllable receives most stress in delivery. The second is that the complex secondary rhythm at mora level is transmitted to higher levels so that stress peaks and troughs offer binary contrasts at every level. The third feature is that phrasal stress may change the relative prominence of syllables: thus in 4(c) 'Park' has more stress than 'Sun-,' but in 4(d) the principal phrasal stress on 'Zoo' has promoted the stress on the word 'Sun-' and demoted that on 'Park.' And, in 4(a) the stress on the second 'break' can be demoted in rapid speech to ensure alternation rather than clash in the stress profile. Finally, Figure 4 shows that the intervals between stress peaks in phrases is most often one syllable (termed duple time), as in 4(a) and 4(c), or two (termed triple time), as in 4(d). And, when the interval between two stress peaks is three syllables the middle syllable tends to become a minor peak of stress.

Figure 4 also illustrates the fact that the number of levels of stress in English utterances depends on the complexity of the utterance: thus 4(d) has four levels above the moraic and 4(c) only three. Yet probably the most important point made by the examples in Figure 4 is that in English stress is less stable than syllable weight. Thus, in 4(c) *park* has more stress than *sun*, while in the longer phrase in 4(d) that relationship is reversed. This is so even though syllable weight in English is less stable than in Classical Latin or Ancient Greek. Thus, the first syllable of *rejoice* in 3(d) is light in some people's pronunciations, and the word *word* is a heavy syllable in Scotland, where the *r* is pronounced, but a light one in England, although not light enough to be reduced to schwa. Although light syllables may become heavy by position, even in languages where speakers are sensitive to syllable weight, heavy syllables become light only in special conditions, such as careless speech or regional variation. But stress relationships in English often vary from one syntactic structure to the next.

Metrical phonologists describe this variability as resulting from the *rhythm rule*, or *Move X*.[28] In words like *sixteen*, the second syllable usually receives more stress in delivery than the first, if only to distinguish it more clearly from *sixty*. But the property of strength (relative stress) shifts according to context: thus in *sixteen tons* the disyllable is left-strong, but in *sweet sixteen* the same word is right-strong. Here, as throughout this volume, bold typeface indicates the strong syllable of a polysyllabic word and underlining indicates other peaks of stress. That stress is less stable than weight raises doubts about the long-established tradition of explaining English meter in Ancient Greek terms. And, as I shall show in a later chapter, the variability of stress was even greater in Middle English than in Modern.

In summary, metrical phonology has shown that every utterance in the English language contains a complex secondary rhythm at the deep level of the mora. Middle English was also undoubtedly a moraic trochaic language, as were Old French, Medieval Latin, and Italian, the other languages with which Chaucer was familiar. This rhythm affects the way poets versify in those languages, as does the wide variation in the strength of their trochaic pulse.[29] The second great achievement of metrical phonology is to show that stress assignment is a dynamic process and not an assembly line for two components labeled indelibly "stressed" and "unstressed."

Finally, the discovery that all English utterances are metrical (in the sense that they have a regular rhythm) has forced specialists in versification to move over: in modern linguistics, *meter* is a property of language, and the special property of verse is now termed *poetic meter*.[30] The next chapter will be devoted to that subject and the choices that poets have when they try to create a distinctive rhythm.

[28] For restrictions on the rhythm rule, see Hayes, 1995: 382–91.

[29] See Hayes, 1995: 91–92 and 117–18.

[30] For the use of the term *poetic meter*, see Hanson, 1995 and Hanson and Kiparsky, 1996.

2
Poetic Rhythm

The modern discovery of the metrical properties of all speech has led metrists to accept the clumsier term *poetic meter* where for centuries the word *meter* was sufficient. But the fact that all language is rhythmic forces us to recognize the difference between *linguistic rhythm* and *poetic rhythm*. Linguistic rhythm is a phonological given: all English utterances consist of a series of moraic trochees interspersed with un-footed moras. But poetic rhythm is a cultural construct: poetic meter superimposes on language an artificial structure, an artificial regularity at any level of the prosodic hierarchy that the poet chooses.

The term meter is derived from the Greek word *μέτρον*, meaning a measure, and by measuring out their language poets can make its rhythms much more regular than those of normal speech. They can choose to measure any discernible amount of linguistic material and, by repeating it, create rhythm. The linguistic units available to poets for rhythmic purposes vary greatly in size (and by language), and they are listed in Figure 1 below in descending size order:

Utterance
|
Phrase
|
Word
|
Foot
|
Syllable
|
Mora
|
Phoneme

Fig. 1: Sources of Poetic Rhythm

The poet can choose to repeat any one (or more) of these linguistic units in his or her verse, making it a perceptible rhythmic event. The remainder of this chapter is devoted to an attempt to draw up a comprehensive list of types of poetic rhythm. To my knowledge this has not been attempted before, but it has a place in this volume because Chaucer's poetry is rich in rhythms of many types and, in his versifying, he chose judiciously between the types of rhythm that he found in the poetry of his English and Continental European predecessors. I shall examine how each of the levels in the prosodic hierarchy can provide poetic rhythm, and I shall tackle them in ascending order of importance to the subject of this volume. In this way I shall be able to move from the least to the most complex and controversial.

Moraic Rhythms

Poets of the Japanese language create a primary poetic rhythm by making the individual mora their repeated event, but this is only possible because that language lacks stress and has very few heavy syllables, which are recognized as double syllables by speakers.[1] Note that the moraic rhythms of Japanese verse are complex primary rhythms and line length is therefore restricted to Miller's "magical number," and most lines contain either five or seven moras. Poets of the Indo-European languages have only ever used secondary moraic rhythms: Sanskrit, Ancient Greek, and Classical Latin poets employed repeating groups of three or four moras with implicit binary contrasts.[2] This quantitative verse was almost certainly known to Chaucer and is discussed briefly under the headings 'Ictic' and 'Foot-Based Rhythms,' below.

Verbal Rhythms

Because of re-syllabification and the fact that speech is a continuous stream the peaks of sonority in an utterance are more salient than the word boundaries. This means that only in slow deliveries, or in repetitions of the same word, will the number of words be immediately obvious. Nevertheless, words have been used as rhythmic events in many different cultures; thus some Australian aborigine chants have lines consisting of three words, and spells in many languages sometimes repeat three words.[3] The most obvious regularity of some passages in the oldest Latin meter, the Saturnian, is also that the lines contain five lexi-

[1] For Japanese moraic verse, see Bownas, 1964; for examples of Japanese verse in Roman script, see Henderson, 1958.

[2] For Sanskrit versification, see Greene and Cushman, 2012: 687–89. For mora counting in Classical Latin, see Gildersleeve and Lodge, 1953.

[3] For word-based Native Australian chants, see Bowra, 1963: 32.

cal words.[4] In Medieval Latin, too, some versifiers seem to have been counting words rather than syllables.[5]

The relevance of verbal rhythms to English poetry lies in the fact that the meter of Old English verse seems to have originated in Germanic lines of four words.[6] Thus Geoffrey Russom has argued convincingly that the rhythmic events in the lines of *Beowulf* equate to the word configurations possible in the language.[7] The number of lexical words in each line of an inflected language like Old English is obviously equal to the number of primary stresses, and it is easy to see how counting stress peaks could evolve from counting words. Note that the verbal rhythms I have discussed are primary rhythms and, although it would be feasible for a poet to create a secondary verbal rhythm (for example, by contrasting monosyllables with longer words), I know of no actual case of this happening.

Phrasal Rhythms

In the interests of brevity I shall use the term *phrasal rhythm* (three English syllables rather than eight Latin ones) to describe repetitions at the highest levels of the prosodic hierarchy. The repetition of whole utterances with similar phrasal, semantic, or syntactic structures is very ancient, and the easiest place to find it is in the Bible. This is because Ancient Semitic verse employed such rhythms and the Bible's translators have usually rendered the original Hebrew phrase by phrase. Well-known and loved examples of this form of rhythm from the King James Bible include:

(1) Refrain thy voice from weeping, // and thine eyes from tears.
(Jeremiah, 31: 16)

(2) All the rivers run into the sea; // yet the sea is not full;
unto the place from whence the rivers come // thither they return again.
(Ecclesiastes, 1: 7)

This technical term for this form of rhythm is *parallelismus membrorum* and it is of several types.[8] The basic *phonic* (sound-based) rhythm in these verses is one in which the events are phrases, matching, complementing, or contrasting with one

[4] For the surviving texts in the Saturnian meter, see Koster, 1929; for a synopsis of rival interpretations of this meter, see Cole, 1969.

[5] For Medieval Latin verse in which words were the repeated events, see Norberg, 1958: 131–33.

[6] For the earliest surviving Germanic line of four stresses, see Russom, 1998: 1; for a discussion of the relative salience of word-boundaries and primary stresses in languages with strong word stress, see Duffell, 2004: 80–83.

[7] For word-feet, see Russom, 1987: 11–24.

[8] For *parallelismus membrorum*, see Greene and Cushman, 2012: 997–98.

another. But there are also *semantic rhythms* matching and contrasting meaning, *syntactic rhythms* doing likewise with grammar, and lexical *rhythms*, in which the events are words, either repeated, as in 'sea / sea,' or in the synonyms 'weeping' / 'tears.' These non-phonic rhythms have been studied more closely in modern times because they are the staple of many poets' free verse.[9]

There are limitations to our perception of phrasal repetitions: we recognize the rhythm of two, three, or even four phrases, but when many more are involved the phrases have to be simple, and have to repeat a great deal more than the phrasal structure. There is a rare example of multi-phrase parallelism in Ecclesiastes 3: 2–8, where there are twenty repetitions of the phrase "a time to" + verb phrase, beginning:

> (3) A time to be born, and a time to die; // a time to plant, and a time to pluck up that which is planted;

Another sign of weakness in the phrase as a rhythmic event is that it came to be reinforced both in the original Hebrew, where words became events as well as phrases, and in English, where peaks of stress tended to provide a rhythm. This use of phrasal combined with other rhythms can be seen in many European meters, where many lines are divisible into two phrases, or *cola*, including those of the Old English *Beowulf*, the Latin Goliardic meter, and French lines of ten and twelve syllables.[10] Chaucer's longer line almost always exhibits a two-or three-phrase structure, as in the brilliant translation of the Latin saw, "Vita brevis, ars longa," which opens *The Parliament of Fowls*:[11]

> (4) The <u>lyf</u> so <u>short</u>, // the <u>craft</u> so <u>long</u> to <u>ler</u>ne

Such a combination of phrasal with accentual rhythm can be found in many English poems of subsequent centuries.

Phonemic Rhythms

Phonemes also offer rhythmic potential. There are hundreds of phonemes in most texts and any two phonemes are either identical or not, so when two syllables are compared each of the syllable's three components may reflect this sameness or difference. There are technical terms for the different permutations of phoneme

---

[9] For non-phonic rhythm in free verse, see Utrera, 2010: 145–72.

[10] For *Beowulf*, see Wrenn and Bolton, 1988; for Goliardic meter, see Greene and Cushman, 2012: 574; for caesura in longer French lines, see Kastner, 1903: 82–101..

[11] Unless otherwise stated, references to Chaucer's work in this volume are to Benson, 1988.

repetition within the syllable, and I list them below in Figure 2 together with the constituents that the two syllables concerned share, O (onset), N (nucleus), and C (coda):[12]

N = *assonance*;	O = *alliteration*;	C = *consonance*;
O + N = *reverse rhyme*;	N + C = *rhyme*;	O + C = *cynghanedd*;
O + N + C: *full repetition*;	none of the above: *non-repetition*.	

Fig. 2: Types of Phoneme Repetition

Note that rhyme represents a subset of assonance and reverse rhyme a subset of alliteration. In assonance the syllable concerned may, or may not, have a coda (thus *go* assonates with *bone*); and in alliteration all the syllables concerned may lack an onset (thus *eagles* alliterates with *are*, as if there were a zero consonant that can alliterate like any other phoneme).[13] Rhyme between stressed syllables is described as *strong*, but its variants include *weak rhyme*, when unstressed syllable are rhymed (as in *catcher / daughter*); *mixed rhyme*, when a stressed syllable is rhymed with an unstressed (as in *insight / delight*); *pararhyme*, when the repetition is imprecise (as in *clasp / fast*); and *eye-rhyme*, when orthography offers a repetition that is missing in the phonology (as in *love / prove*).[14]

Ancient Greek and Roman poets used phoneme repetition (both rhyme and alliteration) occasionally, but medieval Romance poets used it systematically. Old English poets, however, used alliteration systematically, and it was Welsh bards who combined alliteration with consonance to produce *cynghanedd*, as its name indicates.[15] Some English poets continued to use systematic alliteration even after the Norman Conquest, when systematic rhyme came to England, and some Middle English poems preserve the older alliteration in their long lines, while borrowing the French practice of rhyme in their short ones.[16]

In English, rhyme may involve one, two, or three syllables: the monosyllabic rhyme of *bat* with *mat* is termed *masculine* rhyme; the disyllabic rhyme of *matter* with *batter* is termed *feminine* rhyme; but there is no specific term in English for the trisyllabic rhyme of *medicate* with *dedicate*. Trisyllabic rhyme cannot occur in French, where stress falls on the final or penultimate syllable of words, but French poets and audiences relish full repetition, known as *rime riche*, which

[12] For this paradigm of phoneme repetition, see Duffell, 2008a: 12–13; for a history of rhyme, see Greene and Cushman, 2012: 1182–92.

[13] For the alliteration of zero onsets, see Kiparsky, 1973: 240–41.

[14] For the classification of rhyme in English, see Schipper, 1910: 270–78.

[15] For phoneme repetition in Old Welsh verse, see Williams, 1973: 15.

[16] For Middle English verse employing both alliteration and rhyme see Kennedy, 2000b: 127–56.

is generally too rich for modern English ears.[17] In English, trisyllabic rhymes appear mostly in humorous verse, such as limericks, where the more outrageous the rhyme, the better it is (thus a young lady from *Tottenham* is likely to have had no manners, or else to have *forgotten 'em*). Although even the earliest Arabic poets employed two-syllable, or *feminine*, rhymes, when rhyme first became systematic in Europe (in Latin) it was invariably *masculine*.[18] But when medieval French poets began to employ systematic assonance, and later rhyme, they too included feminine lines.[19] In later centuries many French poets made a point of alternating masculine and feminine rhymes in their poems.[20]

Syllabic Rhythms

The most important rhythmic unit in European versification is undoubtedly the syllable. Many writers have argued that counting syllables is both the normal and original form of versifying in the Indo-European languages, even though the oldest verse in any Indo-European language, *The Song of Ullikummi*, is in a phrasal measure.[21] Many scholars attribute this to the influence of verse in neighboring Semitic languages. Certainly, the oldest verse in Sanskrit and Old Iranian is purely syllabic, but syllable boundaries, like word boundaries, are less salient than features such as stress, pitch change, or duration.[22] Ancient Greek poets counted syllables, but those of even the earliest surviving Greek poems are regulated by weight: certain positions in the line must contain a heavy syllable and certain others a light. Since, over time, Sanskrit verse also developed a sensitivity to syllable weight, it is probable that Greek verse was at first purely syllabic. In both languages lines might have a fixed number of syllables or a fixed number of moras (in Sanskrit *matras*).[23]

In his *History of European Versification*, M. L. Gasparov is able to instance examples of syllabic verse in many of Europe's languages, but the syllabic verse of Western Europe probably has its origin in Latin hymns.[24] The rhythm of the earliest of these hymns was a primary one, based purely upon the number of syllables, of any type, in the line, but when poets began composing in French

[17] For the French predilection for *rime riche*, see Kastner, 1903: 49–55.

[18] See Beare, 1957: 197 and Brittain, 1957: 288.

[19] For feminine assonances in the *La Chanson de Roland* (c. 1100), see Woledge, 1961: 8–10.

[20] For rhyme alternation in French, see Kastner, 1903: 63–66.

[21] For the case that the earliest Indo-European verse was syllabic, see Meillet, 1923; for the *Song of Ullikummi*, see West, 1973: 182.

[22] For Old Iranian versification, see Pighi, 1970: 5–8.

[23] For Sanskrit meters based upon matras, see Greene and Cushman, 2012: 688.

[24] For syllabic versifying across Europe, see Gasparov, 1996: 119–65 and 210–37.

they ensured that every line ended in a syllable with phrasal stress. This produced a secondary rhythm in which, for example, seven syllables without such a stress could be contrasted with one syllable with it. Although it is thus stress-syllabic (syllabo-tonic), as compared with the purely syllabic verse of Early Sanskrit or of Latin hymns, most scholars have continued to refer to French verse as syllabic.[25]

French verse also supports the hypothesis that humans can learn to recognize only up to 7 ± 2 stimuli: French lines of more than eight syllables are always divided by a *caesura* into *hemistichs*. Thus the French line of 12 syllables, is actually a line of 6 + 6, and its secondary rhythm is usually reinforced by making it a line of 6 unrhymed + 6 rhymed syllables. This mode of versifying is peculiarly suited to the French language, where word stress soon disappeared, leaving the language's phrase-final stress extremely salient.[26] This mode of versifying was imitated in all the neighboring Romance languages that fell under French literary influence.[27] In some of those languages the presence of word stress hindered the imitation.

Here it should be noted that there are two ways of counting syllables in languages that have dynamic accent. The first, or *rhythmic*, way is to count syllables up to and including the last stress in the line, ignoring any line-final post-tonic syllables; the human ear can count syllables rapidly and intuitively in this way, at least up to the number eight. The second, *anti-rhythmic*, way is to count all syllables, and this is easier for the eye than the ear. French poets, helped by the fact that their only post-tonic syllables were *e-atones* (schwas) that gradually became *e-muets* (that is, deleted), seized upon the rhythmic mode of counting. The poets of some other Romance languages (including the French of England, Anglo-Norman) wavered between the rhythmic and anti-rhythmic modes.[28]

In modern times some poets writing in English, most notably Marianne Moore and W. H. Auden, have tried to introduce syllabic verse.[29] They have chosen the anti-rhythmic mode and in some poems ignored the intuitive limit of eight syllables. As a result their syllabic verse has to be checked on the fingers or the page for regularity, a burden for which their editors are sometimes inadequate.[30]

---

[25] For the earliest French verse, see Duffell, 2007: 53–54.

[26] For the loss of word stress in French, see Ewert, 1943: 47–48.

[27] For syllabic meters in other Romance languages in imitation of French, see Duffell, 2007: 58–61 and 96–104.

[28] For syllabic meters in Anglo-Norman, see Duffell, 2005: 103–25.

[29] For modern anti-rhythmic syllabic verse, see Moore, 1967: passim and Auden, 1966: 166–70.

[30] For a demonstration of the difficulty posed by the anti-rhythmic counting of syllables, see the error ('round' for 'around') in the quotation of Moore's lines provided by Hobsbaum, 1996: 78.

Ictic Rhythms

In languages with strong word stress and a tendency towards stress timing in delivery there is something much more obvious in any line than the total number of syllables, and that is the number of peaks of stress. These are often called *ictic* syllables or *beats*, and Germanic verse soon evolved from lines of four words to lines of four beats. These beats were emphasized by an alliterative pattern and lines were divided into 2 + 2 beats by having different alliterative patterns (the most common combination being + + alliteration followed by + - alliteration).[31] English poets have continued to employ these native rhythms based on beats, especially for folk poetry, often adding alliteration, but sometimes not. The following examples are lines of four beats alternating with three; the first pair are from the Scottish ballad *Sir Patrick Spens*, which was first recorded in the sixteenth century, but probably composed in the thirteenth. The second pair are from the nineteenth century and open a short poem by Tennyson in the same meter:[32]

(5) O, Where will I get a **skil**ly **skip**per (1. 3)
(6) Will sail this good ship of mine? (l. 4)
(7) Break, break, break, (1. 1)
(8) And I would that my tongue could **ut**ter (l. 3)

In these, as in all my examples, I mark prominence peaks in two different ways, the strong syllables of polysyllabic words by bold typeface and monosyllables by underlining.

Note that the intervals between beats are irregular they contain 2–1–1–2–2–1 syllables in (5) and (6) and 0–0–2–2–1 in (7) and (8). In neither case is the interval between beats sufficiently regular to be regarded as a second event. This is a primary rhythm on the verge of becoming secondary: it requires only the standardization of the number of syllables in between beats to to convert the rhythm into a complex rhythm of beats and offbeats, rather like the upbeats and downbeats of music.[33]

---

31 See Russom, 1987: 13; for an alternative analysis Old English verse based entirely upon alliterative patterns, see Fabb and Halle, 2008: 263–67.

32 For 'Break, break, break,' see Tennyson, 1965: 116; for the ballad *Sir Patrick Spens*, see Graves, 1957: 17.

33 For beats in music, see Griffiths, 2004: 21.

Foot-Based Rhythms

Ancient Greek metrics was a branch of musical theory and Greek poets perceived the upbeats and downbeats of sung verse as constituting *feet* (two of which constituted a *metron*).[34] Greek quantitative feet consisted of two or more syllables in contrast, one ictic, others non-ictic. Those syllables were of either one mora or two, and passages of verse were said to be in the *Aeolian* mode if their lines were isosyllabic, and in the *Ionic* mode if they were iso-moraic. Ionic verse can be exemplified by the most highly esteemed of the Classical meters, the dactylic hexameter.[35] This was a line of twenty-four (6 x 4) moras, in which the last two feet were most strictly regulated, as in the opening line of Virgil's *Aeneid*; it ends '[**prī**mus ab] [ōrīs],' and here I mark the foot boundaries by brackets.[36] Note that each of these feet contains four moras when the final -b of the first is resyllabified and that the foot-initial syllables are accented.

At the close of the nineteenth century W. W. Skeat suggested that it would prove productive to analyze English verse in terms of *syntagmatic feet*, that is, by recognizing foot-boundaries, as in my scansion of a line from Tennyson's *In Memoriam*:[37]

(9) [The **seasons**] [bring] [the flower] [**again**] (1. 65)

Unfortunately, this system produces a mixed bag of feet in every type of English line, a series of events that are not repeated, and therefore it fails to distinguish between meters with very different rhythms. Although Robert Bridges tried to popularize syntagmatic metrics in the early years of the twentieth century, modern researchers have concluded that this *lexical bracketing* is parallel to, rather than part of, poetic meter.[38]

Much more important is the fact that most English poets eventually regularized the intervals between the beats in their verse, and English metrists soon settled on a foot-based analysis for this complex secondary rhythm. By combining beats with the material between them they coined the term *accentual feet* and borrowed Greek terms to describe them. The line in example (9) thus became a

[34] For a full list of Ancient Greek feet, see Gildersleeve and Lodge, 1953: 456–57.

[35] For Ionic meters, see Gasparov, 1996: 65–87. Note that attempts at composing quantitative verse in English have a long history; see Attridge, 1974.

[36] This line from Virgil's *Aeneid* is numbered 1e in Hirtzel, 1900.

[37] For his new proposal (syntagmatic metrics), see Skeat, 1898; for the quoted line from *In Memoriam AHH*, see Tennyson, 1965: 231.

[38] Robert Bridges argued for a syntagmatic analysis of English verse in his study of Milton's prosody; see Bridges, 1921.

line of four iambs, like most of the lines in Tennyson's poem, which is therefore described as being in iambic tetrameters:

(9)b [The **sea**][sons <u>bring</u>] [the <u>flower</u>] [**again**]

Modern linguistic metrics has also found it descriptively useful to apply this *metrical bracketing,* and metrists define accentual feet as rhythmic contrasts between syllables.[39] Most modern writers on meter argue that poetic feet have a maximum of three syllables, and that the Ancient Greeks were able to employ longer feet only because they were dealing in weight, not stress.[40] Modern metrical analysis confines accentual feet to five configurations: the iambs [w^s] and trochees [s^w] of linguistic rhythm plus the three types of ternary feet shown in Figure 3.

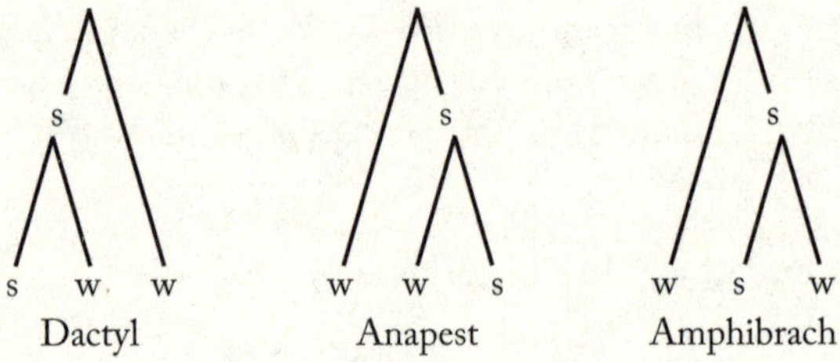

Fig. 3: Trisyllabic Poetic Feet

Note that the third of these is highly controversial: some writers, such as Kiparsky and Piera have argued for it, but many modern linguists disagree; certainly, there were no amphibrachic meters in Classical verse.[41] Greek quantitative feet, however, included such monsters as the *choriamb* (two heavy syllables separated

[39] For the modern use of the term *bracketing*, see Kiparsky,1977.

[40] For the maximum size of accentual feet, see Prince, 1989: passim, Fabb, 2002: 51, and Fabb and Halle, 2008: 7. The five types of accentual feet retain their Greek Names in modern linguistics: the word iamb is derived from the Ancient Greek for 'attack,' and the word trochee from the word for 'run'; the metaphor involved seems to be that of a chariot, which runs downhill but requires force to go uphill. The word anapest, which derives from a word meaning a 'delayed attack' (literally, a 'counter-strike'), draws upon the same metaphor. The word dactyl, however, is based on a simile (Greek: 'finger'), while amphibrach comes from the Greek for 'short on both sides.' See Liddell and Scott, 1968: 59, 156, 173, 374, and 821.

[41] The detailed case for the amphibrach is made by Piera, 1980: 71–75; the case that ternary feet are binary divisions of binary feet and part of an overall hierarchical structure is made by Prince, 1989: 45–56.

by two light) and the *molossus* (three heavy syllables), but the identification of accentual feet with binary stress contrasts precludes both of these.[42]

Modern writers on poetic meter disagree on the importance of feet in the rhythm of English verse. In many English poems it is impossible to be sure whether such feet would be trochaic or iambic, and if all English lines are to be analyzed in terms of feet then the existence of monosyllabic feet must be recognized. I shall return to this subject in Chapter 3, but the immediate lesson to be drawn from this is that some English lines are better explained by the concepts of the syllabic foot and metrical bracketing than others. We should, perhaps, be especially wary of accepting a foot-based analysis of English lines in a period when French influence was very strong, since almost all French metrists emphatically deny that the foot has any relevance to the versification of their language.[43] I shall therefore employ the concept of the foot in this volume with care, and check its validity for each type of verse that I analyze.

The Rhythms of Free Verse

The advent of free verse in Europe towards the end of the nineteenth century focused attention on less obvious types of rhythm that had been latent in poetry. The free verse of Eliot undoubtedly contained ictic rhythms, but later poets developed other types of rhythm.[44] One was a new type of linear rhythm in which lines contrasted with one another, often violently, rather than matching.[45] A second was syllabic verse based on anti-rhythmic counting (see above); a third was verse in which non-phonic rhythms, based on semantics or syntax, provided the events (also known as *internal* rhythms).[46] But English verse of all types has long held such rhythms, so we should not be surprised to encounter them in Chaucer's poetry.

To sum up, poetic rhythm (the repetition of events in time) and poetic meter (the measuring out of language in order to make its rhythms more regular) are complex, but this complexity is something that poets have sought, and audiences have enjoyed. It is clear from the foregoing analysis that poets have a wide choice of sources of rhythm with which to woo, seduce, and satisfy their audiences. Rhythm

[42] Some scholars doubt whether Latin poets ever employed choriambs; see Gildersleeve and Lodge, 1953: 479.

[43] For the orthodox view that stress plays no part within French lines, see Kastner, 1903: 1 and passim; a minority of metrists, however, has argued that there are rhythmic subdivisions within the cola of French lines; see, for example, Pensom, 2000.

[44] For an analysis of rhythm in Eliot's *The Waste Land*, see Duffell, 2012.

[45] For a discussion of linear contrasts in free verse, see Hobsbaum, 1996: 103–17 and Duffell, 2010: 25.

[46] Note that free verse in which the only rhythm common to all the lines is non-phonic often contains isolated lines with regular phonic rhythms; see Utrera, 2010: 146–47.

can make poets' words more meaningful, convincing, and memorable, and there are many types of poetic rhythms. In the next chapter I shall move on to the variety of ways that critics have tried to detect and define poets' metrical intentions, and to describe the form that rhythm takes in their work.

3
Design and Instance

Versification is, above all else, something that people do. It is behavior, and the people who do it include songwriters, entertainers, and greetings-card producers.[1] Some versifiers, however, attempt the 'special intensity in the expression of feelings and ideas' that forms part of the dictionary definition of poetry, and they are called *poets*. The word is derived from the Ancient Greek *ποιητής*, which translates precisely into the old Scottish term *makar*. The things that poets make are called *poems*; texts in which they employ language and rhythm in a special way. Although the nineteenth and twentieth centuries saw a vogue for *prose poems*, poems are usually in *verse*, which is a *stylization* of language; a special use of the same linguistic material that goes to make normal speech and written prose.

The most concise definition of this stylization is that of John Lotz, "Verse is numerically regulated language."[2] *Numerically regulated* implies that something in the language is being counted and the distinguishing feature of verse is that it has, in addition to syntactic structure, a quite different structure based upon lines. Nigel Fabb neatly defines the *line* as the unit that stretches from where the counting begins to where it ends.[3] Normally the lines in a poem match one another: the poet who counts to ten keeps counting to ten; but in *free verse* the poet is free to make the next line any length that produces the desired aesthetic effect. And there are always two ways to regulate units numerically: the poet can make them either the same, or different.[4] Until the advent of free verse poets, for the most part, settled for lines with major similarities and minor differences, they crafted regular, but not too regular, lines. The feature that regular and free verse have in common is that the poet, consciously or intuitively, designs the lines, and builds them into a poem.

---

[1] The entertainer Pam Ayres, currently the UK's best-selling versifier, explicitly denies being a poet; see Ayres, 2008: 10.

[2] See Lotz, 1960: 135.

[3] See Fabb, 2002: 48–49.

[4] See Duffell, 2010: 10.

Poem Design

There are three levels of organization in this process, termed *poem design*, *strophe design*, and *verse design*.[5] The simplest form of poem design is known as *stichic* verse: the poem consists of lines that match one another in their numerical regulation, with no intervening grouping. In contrast, *strophic* verse groups lines, which need not all match, into a series of matching sub-units or strophes.

Most long stichic poems are divided into *Books,* passages of convenient length to be read at a sitting. In medieval Europe, however, people believed that God had given the universe a perfect structure, and ambitious poets attempted to do the same with their longer poems. Dante's epic, the *Commedia*, is a prime example.[6] The poem is divided into three books each of which contains thirty-three *cantos*, except the first, which also has a prefatory canto, bringing the total to 100. The number three is the divine number (the number of the Trinity), and a hundred is the perfect number, the square of ten (the number of digits God gave his greatest creation, man). Dante's poem is thus an ingenious imitation of God's universe. An equally ingenious poem design is that of the fifteenth-century Spanish epic by Juan de Mena entitled *Laberinto de Fortuna*.[7] It appears at first to have a random number of lines and stanzas, but modern scholars have discovered that those numbers are very sophisticated exercises in numerology.[8] Chaucer's poem designs, with one exception, which I shall discuss in Chapter 12), are simple by comparison.

The medieval obsession with numbers and order extended to prose as well as verse: in Boccaccio's *Decameron* each of ten fugitives from the Black Death tells a story on each of ten days, making a total of 100 stories.[9] Chaucer, in contrast, seems to have had no regular structure in mind for the *Canterbury Tales*, and is inconsistent even in his stated intentions. The Host's suggestion in the General Prologue, that every pilgrim might tell four tales, conflicts with his expectation in the Parson's Prologue of one tale per pilgrim. In theory, one tale from each pilgrim and two from Chaucer (one aborted) would have given the round number thirty, but as the work stands the role of five of the pilgrims is limited to providing a cook with a story of East-End low life that we shall never hear.

There is one point in the *Canterbury Tales* where medieval numerology plays a role in poem design, and that is in The Tale of Sir Thopas, (*ST*). This

---

[5] I employ the Greek term *strophe* in this volume rather than its Italian synonym stanza because the adjective *stanzaic* has no antonym as simple and brief as the disyllabic *stichic*.

[6] For Dante's *Commedia*, see Petrocchi, 1975.

[7] For Mena's *Laberinto*, see Kerkhof, 1995.

[8] Mena's poem has 2,736 lines and 297 strophes, by digital addition: 2 + 7 + 3 + 6 = 18 and 1 + 8 = 9, while 2 + 9 + 7 = 18 and 1 + 8 = 9. For a modern scientific account of medieval numerology, see Burge, 2001.

[9] For Boccaccio's *Decameron*, see Rossi, 1982.

tale is designed to peter out, and to be cut off unceremoniously by the Host. Chaucer constructs *ST* around the number nine, the card of death in the fortune-teller's pack. Its three *fits* contain a diminishing number of strophes: (2 x 9) + (1 x 9) + ($^1/_2$ x 9), an indication that it was doomed from the start, like Achilles' pursuit of the tortoise in the Paradox of Zeno. But the Tale itself is a joke, since it parodies the type of content and form that Chaucer rejects in his versifying; its subject and style are those of the Middle English metrical romances, where perilous adventures have to compete with obtrusive rhymes.[10] Chaucer must have known a lot about numerology but, unlike Dante and Mena, he rarely designed a poem around it.

The House of Fame and *Anelida and Arcite* were both also unfinished, as was the *Legend of Good Women*, which tails off in the middle of the ninth legend. In the case of the last work, the brilliant new idea of telling stories within a pilgrimage framework probably led Chaucer to set it aside. A pilgrimage offered a far more varied setting than Ovid's collection of missives. In the case of his earlier unfinished works, Chaucer had the excuse that he was a busy civil servant, and later a Member of Parliament, so pressure of other work probably caused him to abandon some literary projects; and in the case of *The Canterbury Tales*, no author can predict when death will interrupt his labors. Chaucer was a far better finisher when he had a deadline: in *An ABC* he successfully reached the letter Z, and the *Parliament of Fowls* was, thankfully, completed by Saint Valentine's Day. And, doubtless, John of Gaunt's servant did not dare keep the most powerful man in the land waiting for *The Book of the Duchess*.

Overall, it is difficult to make a case that Chaucer was a master of the craft of poem design or, indeed, that it bothered him very much. But if the architecture of his long poems was pretty chaotic, his approach to further subdivision of his work was more consistent.

Strophe Design

A binary division can also be applied to poetic genre. There are stories to tell and songs to sing, and this affects poem structure; the lines of lyrics are usually grouped in verses while those of narrative poems are not. This is doubtless because musical audiences enjoy whistling or humming the catchiest tunes they have heard performed, and songwriters exploit this by repeating those tunes a number of times in their compositions. While narrative verse is usually *stichic*, an unbroken series of similar lines, lyric verse is usually *strophic*. Note that strophes are enclosures: they usually contain a fixed number of lines, whereas stichic verse imposes no such restriction.

[10] For tail-rhyme romances, see Gray, 1986: 163–69.

The shortest strophe form is the couplet, which is of ancient pedigree, having been employed in some of the earliest known verse in China, India, Persia, and the Mediterranean world.[11] Ancient Greek and Roman poets composed vast numbers of elegiac couplets, strophes in which a line of six quantitative feet was followed by a line of five.[12] In a series of couplets the first line sets up an expectation that the second fulfills, and in Greek and Roman couplets that expectation was of a shorter line. Classical elegiac couplets had a wide emotional range, from the poignancy of an epitaph to the provocation of a sexual invitation. They could also be very funny, and Ovid liked to joke about their structure.[13] Couplets are instant in their effect: they can bring quick laughs, easy tears, swift succor, and sudden rushes of blood to the parts that other strophe designs cannot reach.

Roman poets used rhyme (usually of unaccented syllables) as an occasional ornament, but their medieval successors adopted first assonance and then rhyme to seal the couplet's promise, and this enabled them to link two lines of the same length as surely as a regular alternation of line length.[14] The design of the Classical elegiac couplet allows enjambment within couplets, but not between them, and this feature was largely retained in the medieval rhymed couplet. Medieval poets employ these rhymed couplets in long sequences (known as *rimes plates*), but there was a new contrast between the couplet's lines: the first was free to introduce a new rhyme to which the second was chained.[15] This made couplets more enclosed than ever: their rhyme sharing cut them off from their fellows.

In more complex strophes poets match the lines in the same position in each strophe. In Classical verse the matching was in terms of line length and rhythm, and the Greek poet Pindar composed some of the most elaborate strophes in the Classical world; such a composition was called an *Ode*, and this title has since appeared over many English poems, some of which have tried to match the complexity of the Greek design.[16] The most elaborate strophe design in English

---

[11] For the earliest couplets, see Greene and Cushman, 2012: 310–11.

[12] For the couplets of *The Greek Anthology* translated into English, see Jay, 1973.

[13] Ovid suggests that Cupid stole one of his verse's feet to prevent him writing heroic poetry (for which only hexameters were employed); and later in the same work he teases Elegeia, the personification of the elegy, for having one foot shorter than the other. See *Amores*, I, 1: 3–4 and III, 1: 7–8 in Kenney, 1961.

[14] For the history of rhyme in Europe, see Greene and Cushman, 2012: 1182–91.

[15] For *rimes plates*, see Kastner, 1903: 67.

[16] For an analysis of Pindar's meter, see Itsumi, 2009. Pindar gave his odes something like sonata form: instead of *exposition*, *development*, and *recapitulation*, his odes consisted of *strophe*, *catastrophe*, and *epode*. Some English poets have attempted to capture this ternary division in their odes: Shelley's *Ode to Heaven* is divided between three spirits, and the rhyme scheme of Keats's odes subdivides each strophe into three. Keats goes one better than Shelley by giving the strophes of most of his odes ten lines, like Pindar's most famous ode, *The First Pythian* . For Shelley's ode, see Hutchinson, 1935: 72; for Keats's ten-line odes, see Stillinger, 1979: 369–77.

is probably that of Dryden's poem *Alexander's Feast* (1697), where everything changes from strophe to strophe: the line length, the rhythm, and the accompanying musical instrument.[17]

Some of the earliest European dictionaries were of rhymes and, if we compare them with modern English rhyming dictionaries, we can see that fourteenth-century poets of the Romance languages had more rhymes available than their English counterparts.[18] Medieval poets employed a vast number of different strophe designs, and modern scholars have produced *Repertoires* cataloguing them for each of the medieval Romance literatures.[19] These catalogs follow the long-established practice of using letters of the Roman alphabet to denote rhymes, and they use capital letters to denote lines where much more than the rhyme is repeated. I shall adopt these practices in this volume, and I shall also try to make rhyme schemes easier for readers to identify by extra space between groups of lines.

I give below the rhyme schemes of two widely used medieval set forms using my notation; Chaucer was familiar with both these designs from his reading of French and Italian poetry.

(a) Eight-line variant of French *ballade* meter: abab bcbc
(b) Eight-line Italian form known as *ottava rima*: ababab cc

When authors of *Repertoires* also need to indicate line lengths, they do this by placing Arabic numerals beneath each rhyme letter to denote the number of syllables in the line.[20] In this notation the first thirteen strophes of *ST* would appear as:

(c) (I–XIII) a a b a a b
8 8 6 8 8 6

I shall follow this practice only for strophes containing lines of different lengths. And, since the number of letters in a rhyme scheme indicates a strophe's length, I shall find little need to use the technical terms for the number of lines in a strophe, only some of which are in general use.

---

17 For Dryden's *Alexander's Feast*, see Hammond and Hopkins, 2005.

18 Thus, for example, the Medieval Catalan rhyming dictionary in Casa Homs, 1956 contains far more entries than the Modern English rhyming dictionary in Stillman, 1966.

19 For the first of these catalogs, which covered the work of the Occitan troubadours, see Frank, 1953–57.

20 Gómez Bravo, 1998 lists 2, 251 strophe designs in Castilian *cancionero* verse this way.

Verse Design

As noted above, the definitive feature of versifying is crafting lines, and modern linguistics terms this feature *verse design*. This term has the advantage of differentiating the two meanings of *a poet's line*: his or her meter and an individual line based upon that design known as a *verse instance*. A vast amount has been written and published upon the subject of English verse design, but until fifty years ago many of the contributions to the debate lacked logical rigor.[21] The chief problem was a confusion between the properties of quantitative and accentual feet, and I shall outline that problem before I turn to its modern solution.

Quantitative Feet and Accentual Feet

So great was the prestige of Classical Greece and Rome that until the middle of the twentieth century analogies with quantitative metrics dominated the discussion of English poetic meter.[22] The upside of this situation was that English speakers gained a vocabulary with which to describe rhythm; the downside was that some of the analogies were false. In comparison with stress, syllable weight is a stable entity: heavy syllables, at least, remain heavy in all contexts, and weight variation by position follows invariable rules. But stress, as shown in Chapter 1 of this volume, is relative, hierarchical, and, to some extent, mobile. This difference makes some terms and concepts in traditional English metrics invalid and redundant. More importantly, it leads to some of the subtleties of crafting verse in English being missed.

The first traditional fallacy of English metrics is that there exist the accentual equivalents of level quantitative feet: *spondees*, two heavy syllables, and *pyrrhics*, two light syllables. The poet Robert Pinsky perceptively notes that he cannot imagine what a level accentual foot sounds like in English, and modern linguistic research supports him.[23] Since accentual feet are contrasts, if there is no contrast there is no foot. Unfortunately, however, many modern scholars cling to traditional terms: thus in the best known modern study of Shakespeare's metrics George Wright uses the terms *spondees* and *pyrrhics* throughout his research findings.[24] And in a very

---

[21] For a late example of an analysis that refused to recognize the relative nature of stress, see Epstein and Hawkes, 1959.

[22] For two early-twentieth-century examples of the pseudo–Ancient-Greek analysis of English verse, see Saintsbury, 1906–10 and Schipper, 1910.

[23] See Pinsky, 1998: 65.

[24] See Wright, 1988.

recent volume of essays on the performance of Chaucer's verse all the writers on meter cling to the same tradition.[25]

Some writers have gone further in trying to proliferate English accentual feet so as to rival those of Ancient Greek verse. Perhaps the most extreme case is the actor Stephen Fry, who hypothesizes accentual *molossi* (feet of three consecutive level syllables).[26] His examples include W. S. Gilbert's "short, sharp shock," and Tennyson's "Break, break, break," which other writers scan as two feet and three. The first of Fry's examples thus has an iambic rhythm in its phrase, "a <u>short</u>, sharp <u>shock</u>," and the second is three monosyllabic feet, "[<u>Break</u>], [<u>break</u>], [<u>break</u>]." Consecutive lexical monosyllables are very common in English but, because stress is relative and mobile, consecutive syllables in the same phrase do not carry equal stress, and consecutive lexical monosyllables in different phrases become separate feet. It is clear from this that false analogies can lead to faulty analysis, and in this volume I shall use the Greek terms for only the five configurations of stress illustrated in Figure 3 of Chapter 2. Moreover, I shall not assume that a foot-based analysis is valid for every type of English poetic meter.

It was in the 1960s that researchers began to realize that stress is relative, hierarchical, and mobile: the first step was Seymour Chatman's identification of eleven levels of stress in the long word *antidisestablishmentarianism*.[27] A further step was the definitive article by Mark Liberman and Alan Prince, which showed that the only feature of stress listeners recognize in English speech is whether a syllable has more stress than its neighbors.[28] Finally Bruce Hayes showed that stress in English is a hierarchy with many levels and that stress shifts.[29] And if stress is relative and unstable then dividing syllables into two fixed classes, stressed and unstressed, is a simplification. From that realization a modern linguistic metrics was born.

Linguistic Metrics

The quest for a metrics that reflected recent advances in linguistics began with Roman Jakobson, who clarified a number of concepts and coined a set of terms that enabled linguists to analyze poetic meter with greater precision.[30] His first achievement was to disambiguate the word *line*, which had previously been used

---

[25] See, for example, the articles in Yager and Morse Gagné, 2013, the focus of which is on the performance of Chaucer's lines. Nevertheless, its authors' neglect of modern analyses of their structure illustrates my point.

[26] See Fry, 2005: 86–87.

[27] See Chatman, 1965: 13.

[28] See Liberman and Prince, 1977.

[29] See Hayes, 1995: 25–26.

[30] See Jakobson, 1960.

promiscuously to describe a meter, a specific line, or a performance of a line. Jakobson's terms separated actual lines of verse, which became *verse instances*, from the abstraction that was also called meter, which became *verse design*, while individual performances of a verse instance became *delivery instances*.

These terms depict the versifying process as the poet's adopting a design, crafting lines to match it, and offering them to readers as performance opportunities. Verse analysts, however, have to go through the reverse of this process, recognizing the common denominator of all meaningful delivery instances as the verse instance, and inferring the verse design from the instances based upon it.[31] Since few poets have ever left notes explaining their verse design, writers on poetic meter have to work hard in this cause, and they often disagree. In particular, they must be sure that they are analyzing the verse instance and not their own preferred delivery of it, and I shall try to remain aware of delivery alternatives throughout this volume.

That performances vary is shown by the history of the theater: Edmund Kean (b. c. 1790–d. 1833) changed the fashion on the English stage when he began to employ a natural speech delivery for iambic pentameters rather than the scanning delivery of his predecessors.[32] The variability of deliveries begs the question of *delivery design*: what was the delivery intended by the poet? We know that, when they made the first recordings of English poetry at the end of the nineteenth century, both Tennyson and Browning gave scanning deliveries.[33] But when a poet is asked to perform, he performs; at the moment of composition, however, the design is probably secondary to the meaning. The poet makes the line meaningful and the performer decides the delivery.

Linguists working in the USA were among the first to adopt Jakobson's terms and concepts, and much of the work they have done has come to be classed under the heading *generative theory*.

Generative Metrics

Generative metrics began as a quest for universal rules that would generate only metrical utterances, on the model of the rules Noam Chomsky had proposed for grammar.[34] The first step was to define verse design more clearly, and generative metrists argue that it is composed of two elements: a *template*, a blueprint or pattern in the poet's mind, and a set of *correspondence rules* for determining what

[31] See Chatman, 1965: 96.

[32] See Drabble, 1985: 526.

[33] These recording are now available on the internet; the website details are: www.poetryarchive.org/poetryarchive/singlepoet.

[34] See Chomsky, 1957.

type of linguistic material in verse instances could correspond to each element in the template.

One of the first major exercises in generative metrics was Morris Halle's and Samuel Keyser's new theory of the *iambic pentameter* (1966–67).[35] These two authors proposed a template for the meter containing ten positions alternating weak-strong, thus:

1	2	3	4	5	6	7	8	9	10
w	s	w	s	w	s	w	s	w	s

They also proposed a categorical correspondence rule, which they termed the *stress maximum principle* (SMP): this prohibited stress maxima (syllables with more stress than both their neighbors) appearing in weak positions. Halle and Keyser's original analysis was of Chaucer's verse, but this presents linguistic complications that I shall examine in detail later in this volume. I shall therefore illustrate SMP here by two lines from Shakespeare's sonnets:[36]

(1) Lilies that fester <u>smell</u> far <u>worse</u> than <u>weeds</u> (Sonnet 94, 14)
(2) <u>Be</u>, as thy presence <u>is</u>, gracious and <u>kind</u> (Sonnet 10, 11)

At this stage Halle and Keyser accepted stress as a zero-sum property and regarded all lexical words as stressed in every context; by this definition there is a stressed (lexical) monosyllable in a weak position in each of these lines. However, neither is a stress maximum, because the stress on 'far' in (1) is lower than that on 'worse,' and the stress on 'Be' in (2) lacks a second neighbor. Similarly, the stress on the first syllable of 'gracious' is equaled by that on the phrase-final 'is,' and that on the first syllable of 'Lilies' does not have two neighbors. Both lines are thus metrical iambic pentameters. Note that SMP does not specify that every strong position must be occupied by a stress maximum.

A number of scholars published criticisms of Halle and Keyser's theory, pointing out the deficiencies of SMP, and making many students of literature wary of this new linguistic metrics.[37] In 1971 Halle and Keyser mounted a spirited defense of their theory that emphasized other proposals in their first paper, which were more normative and less categorical. For example, they redefined SMP as "a prohibition of major stresses flanked by two unstressed syllables in the same syntactic constituent." This defense described lines that deviated from an iambic norm as more *complex*, rather non-metrical, and emphasized elements in the original paper that it described as *tension metric*, that is the presence of lines

[35] See Halle and Keyser, 1966–67.

[36] All references to Shakespeare's work in this volume are to Alexander, 1958.

[37] The barrage of criticism included: Wimsatt, 1969–70, Magnuson and Ryder, 1969–70, and Gaylord, 1976–77.

that contrast with the template rather than matching it.[38] The theory thus became more accurate, but many literature departments were never reconciled to it, hence the recent examples of literary scholars clinging to older theories noted above.[39]

In its final form SMP offers a logically rigorous test of whether a line is stress-syllabic and iambic, and I shall employ it in the present volume for that purpose. There are a few apparent exceptions among the iambic pentameters of major poets, but they are usually explicable as attempts at humor or special effects; for example, the well-known line that opens one of Keats's sonnets:[40]

(3) How **many** <u>bards</u> gild the **lap**ses of **time**

The words 'the lapses' in positions 6–7–8 violate SMP, and Keats was deliberately departing from the iambic norm in order to match his meter to his meaning: the line lapses from duple time (stresses on every second syllable) into triple time (stresses on every third).

Another scholar whose work was essential to the development of generative metrics was Paul Kiparsky, who published a number of papers culminating in his 1996 collaboration with Kristin Hanson, "A Parametric Theory of Poetic Meter."[41] *Parametric theory* (PT) differed from SMP in many respects. First, it emphasized the role of the *foot*, a grouping of syllables containing a binary contrast between a weaker and a stronger element, and PT included what it terms *metrical bracketing* in its description of the iambic pentameter's template, thus:

1	2	3	4	5
w^s	w^s	w^s	w^s	w^s

Secondly, it replaced *rules* with the term *constraints* to emphasize their flexibility. But, most importantly, PT argued that just five features (*parameters*) define all verse designs: (1) *position number*, (2) *orientation*, (3) *position size*, (4) *prominence site*, and (5) *prominence type*.

PT characterizes the parameters of the strict iambic pentameter as follows: (1) positions: ten; (2) orientation: right strong; (3) position size: one syllable; (4) prominence site: weak positions; (5) prominence type: syllable *strength*. That is, *strong* syllables (those with primary stress in polysyllabic words) are constrained from appearing in weak positions. The reason why only strong syllables are affected is because they have a fixed relationship with their neighbors which

---

[38] See Halle and Keyser, 1971–72.

[39] The standing of generative metrics among literary scholars in the present century can be seen from Gaylord, 2001, where Halle and Keyser's article is included but appears to have had very little influence on the ideas or vocabulary of subsequent writers.

[40] See Stillinger, 1978: 63.

[41] See Kiparsky, 1977, Hanson, 1995, and Hanson and Kiparsky, 1996.

is lexically determined. PT recognizes that certain pairs of monosyllables (*clitic* pairs) also have a fixed stress relationship (for example, *the boy*, *but he*, and *had fled*), and that these pairs are the phonological equivalents of disyllables, but PT's constraints against strong syllables in weak positions are not absolute; they allow two exceptions.

For these exceptions PT retains the traditional term *inversions*, so called because s^w in the instance corresponds to w^s in the template. The first exception is that inversion may occur when it follows a line boundary or a major syntactic phrase boundary (termed the *closure principle).*[42] In examples (1) and (2) above 'Lilies' and 'gracious' follow major syntactic boundaries: the first, a sentence boundary; the second, a phrase boundary. The second exception is that some poets allow inversion elsewhere in the line provided the two syllables involved are in the same word as well as the same foot (as in 'lapses' in (3) above). This last exception PT terms the *bracketing condition*, which it defines as: 'providing the *mismatch* in *metrical bracketing* does not coincide with a *mismatch* in *lexical bracketing*.' This provision is a prime example of how unwieldy the specialized vocabulary of generative metrics can become.[43]

Beneath the jargon, however, PT has many merits, not the least being its conciseness: it offers five parameters for all meters, and one constraint in the English iambic pentameter (against strong syllables in weak positions), to which there are two exceptions (the closure principle and the bracketing condition). The austerity of PT's provisions compensates for the prodigality of its terminology, and I shall employ it in this volume as a test for whether the verse of other times and languages can be classified as stress-syllabic.

Constraints on Strong Positions in the Iambic Pentameter

One of the weaknesses of PT is that pointed out by Nigel Fabb: "it underdetermines,"[44] PT says nothing about the contents of strong positions in the iambic pentameter, and nothing about the role of syntactic boundaries, and yet both are far from random in this meter.[45] PT sidesteps the question of the contents of strong positions by making the prominence-site parameter of the iambic pentameter weak ones. Almost half the syllables in English texts are either strong or are lexical monosyllables, and so it is a corollary of PT's constraint

[42] The *closure principle* states that the openings of both poems and lines are less strictly regulated than their closes; it was first proposed by Smith, 1968.

[43] See Duffell, 2002a: 175–79.

[44] See Fabb, 2001: 780.

[45] For the non-random distribution of word boundaries in the iambic pentameter, see Duffell, 2002b.

on syllable strength in weak positions in this meter that the majority of strong positions will contain strong syllables or monosyllables. Marina Tarlinskaja, who calculated the size of that majority for samples of verse by three poets, Chaucer, Shakespeare, and Milton, showed that the percentage varied by individual position.[46] For position 10 it averaged close to 100 percent, for position 4 it was just over 86 percent, and for position 6 it was 75 percent.

My own research has broadly confirmed her figures, but also revealed an anomaly: that the combination of position 4 and position 6 stress seems far from random. If this combination were random, both positions would contain stress in just over 65 percent of lines and neither would contain stress in over 3 percent of lines. My analysis confirmed that the first of these expectations was fully met, but I could find no line that lacked stress in both position 4 and position 6. Since my total sample of iambic pentameters was 10,000, it should have contained over 300 such lines; but there were none.[47] This at first appears surprising, because it is easy to construct lines that lack stress in both position 4 and position 6, such as the following:

4 6
(4)* He **per**ished and if on a**no**ther day
4 6
(5)* But **help**less as when in in**ten**sive care

These lines can be delivered so as to sound like iambic pentameters only by artificially stressing one of the grammatical syllables in positions 4 and 6. To borrow the language of generative metrics, any normal delivery of this line lacks *rhythmic adequacy*: it is not sufficiently iambic. From this I would argue that there is a constraint on strong positions in the iambic pentameter in addition to the one requiring stress in position 10 and allowing that stress to be followed by a post-tonic syllable. I term it the *cumulative stress constraint*: it prohibits both positions 4 and 6 in an iambic pentameter being filled by syllables that do not normally become peaks of stress. To put it more simply, if position 4 does not contain stress, than position 6 must do so.[48] Information technology may eventually discover,

---

[46] Tarlinskaja's statistics are quoted, but not correlated, by Youmans and Li, 2002.

[47] The figure of just over 3 percent is simply 14 percent of 25 percent, the proportion of lines lacking stress in position 4 times the proportion lacking it in position 6 (according to Tarlinskaja). The details of my thirty-four 300-line samples are given in Duffell, 2002b: 302n13, and, 2008a: 240–54.

[48] My cumulative constraint probably reflects a linguistic constraint against three consecutive unstressed syllables in English. Thus in most deliveries of my examples *(4) and *(5) 'if' and 'when' become minor peaks of stress, thus violating SMP (because they are stress maxima in weak positions).

and quantify, violations of this cumulative stress constraint, but in the meantime I shall regard it as a defining feature of the English iambic pentameter.[49]

Monosyllabic Constraints

In his early work Kiparsky identified monosyllables as being exceptional items in stress-syllabic verse design, and PT deals with this problem by identifying strength as the prominence type in English verse. PT includes *clitic groups*, such as 'the boy,' 'but he,' and 'had fled' in its definition of a *phonological word*, because they have a stress relationship not determined by context. But many consecutive monosyllables do not form such groups. English is a highly monosyllabic language: monosyllables provide well over 70 percent of words (as units) in normal English speech, in prose, and in verse texts.[50] And, since a large majority of disyllables in English are trochaic, monosyllables are the chief source of natural iambs in English.

Many iambic pentameter lines are entirely monosyllabic, and poets can use such lines to emphasize the verse template to their audience. For example, Shakespeare closes a number of sonnets, including 18, 26, and 43, with a monosyllabic couplet, as in Sonnet 18, quoted below:

(6) So <u>long</u> as <u>men</u> can <u>breathe</u> or <u>eyes</u> can <u>see</u> Sonnet 18, 13
(7) So <u>long</u> lives <u>this</u>, and <u>this</u> gives <u>life</u> to <u>thee</u>

This couplet follows twelve lines that contain a fair amount of tension and so its regularity provides a contrast. In both of these lines lexical monosyllables provide stress maxima in all the strong positions.

Monosyllables provide a great deal of rhythmic variety in English stress-syllabic verse, as can be seen in the following two examples; they represent what I consider the most natural deliveries of the verse instances that open Shakespeare's Sonnet 116, and I give the positions of the line's stress peaks in parentheses:

(8) <u>Let</u> me <u>not</u> to the **mar**riage of true <u>minds</u> (1 3 6 10)
(9) Ad**mit** impedi<u>ments</u>. <u>Love</u> is not <u>love</u> (2 4 7 10)

---

[49] I am indebted to Derek Attridge for pointing out that F. T. Prince first noted the operation of my cumulative stress constraint in Milton's *PL*. In, 1954 Prince concluded that Milton's meter was the *endecasillabo*, not the iambic pentameter, but in, 1962 he reversed this judgment (see Prince, 1954). The only other earlier reference to this constraint I can find is the statement that Shakespeare "did not allow consecutive pyrrhics" (Wright, 1988: 54).There is some evidence, however, that other poets occasionally allow both positions 2 and 4 to lack stress in their iambic pentameters; see Duffell, 2008a: 170.

[50] Tarlinskaja found that almost 80 percent of words in her samples of English verse were monosyllables; see Tarlinskaja, 1976: 13. For the percentage in the iambic pentameters of individual poets, see Duffell, 2002b: 305

The rhythms of the two lines are strikingly different, but most readers can also detect a possible, and still meaningful, scanning delivery (w^s w^s w^s w^s w^s) in both. As noted above, a verse instance is the common denominator of all meaningful delivery instances, and one of the subtleties of well-crafted stress-syllabic verse is this interplay between a natural delivery and a scanning delivery.[51] Note that the chief invariables in delivery are the peaks of stress in position 6 of example (8) and position 4 of example (9). This confirms the importance of the cumulative stress constraint in this meter.

To summarize this volume's stance in relation to generative metrics, both SMP and PT are valuable tools in assessing lines of verse (in any language) and deciding how close they come to the iambic pentameter norm. I shall employ both SMP and PT in the chapters that follow, and I shall also test decasyllabic lines against the cumulative stress constraint, and look for evidence of its origins. But such a process will identify only what lines have in common; at least as important are the ways in which they differ. In order to appreciate Chaucer's contribution to the history of European versifying I shall need to delve much deeper into the structure of lines.

Recent Developments in Generative Theory

There are three recent developments in generative theory that I shall mention briefly here. The first is the use in metrical analysis of *optimality theory*, which argues that language outputs are governed not so much by rules as by *ranked constraints*.[52] The constraints of optimality theory are hierarchical, and any constraint may be relaxed when it comes into conflict with a higher-ranking constraint. One of the first attempts to apply optimality theory to English historical metrics was that by Paul Getty in his analysis of *Beowulf*, which argued for a continuity between that poem's meter and modern trochaic meters.[53] Subsequent analyses of OE and ME verse employing optimality theory have proved even

---

[51] Pairs of monosyllables can be assimilated to the meter in the reader's mind; in the words of Ad Putter (2015: 4), "The established meter will dispose us to hear what we expect to hear."

[52] The pioneering works in optimality theory were Prince and Smolensky, 1991 and McCarthy and Prince, 1993. For the application of optimality theory to metrics, see Hammond, 1997.

[53] The highest-ranking constraint according to Getty, 2002 was that OE lines should accommodate the entire lexicon of a language. This is simply a restatement of the *principle of fit*, first proposed by Hanson and Kiparsky, 1996: 294 and 325.

more productive, and I shall employ optimality theory as a supplement to my own analysis in this volume.[54]

The second development in generative metrics was Fabb and Halle's radically new theory of poetic meter based on bracketing pairs and trios of syllables.[55] This bracketing was hierarchical and it produced a metrical grid with up to four levels which descended like a subterranean car park. The immediate response of other generative metrists was negative: they admired the theory's elegance but questioned whether it offered any new insights into poetic meter.[56] One of the new theory's chief merits is its universal scope: it attempts to explain every type of meter in every language as a bracketing of syllables. In this endeavor Fabb and Halle have mixed success, and in several cases their theory fails to convince: its analysis of Old English meter is superficial (identifying nothing but alliterative patterns); its labeling of Homer's meter as *loose trochaic* conflicts with Classical poets' intuitive perceptions; and its approach to Ancient Hebrew meters is eccentric (concentrating on one Psalm). For all this theory's ingenuity, therefore, I do not propose to use it in this volume.

The third development is that of hierarchical hypotheses to explain meters: using tree diagrams for this purpose dates back to 1980, and Carlos Piera, Bruce Hayes, Kristin Hanson, Gilbert Youmans, Xingzhong Li, Nigel Fabb, and Morris Halle have all contributed to the development of hierarchical models.[57] These authors, however, disagree on the hierarchical structure of the iambic pentameter, and in later chapters of this volume I shall examine and, hopefully, resolve some of that disagreement.

Statistical Methods and Rhythmic Theory

Generative theory has dominated the debate on poetic meter in most university linguistics departments, but it is not the only new brand of metrics launched in the last fifty years, nor the only one to boast a linguistic approach. Russian metrists have long combined linguistic analysis with statistical methods in analyzing Russian verse, and in the mid-1970s Marina Tarlinskaja showed that the use

---

[54] In Chapter 5 I shall summarize the main features of OE and ME alliterative meters using the optimality-theory-based analyses of McCully and Hilles, 2005 and Minkova, 2009. And in Chapter 14 I shall use optimality theory to contrast the metrics Gower and Lydgate

[55] For the chief differences between this theory and traditional metrics, see Fabb and Halle, 2008: 23–26.

[56] See Kiparsky, 2009 and Riad, 2010.

[57] See Piera, 1980: 37–39; this structure is supported by Hayes, 1983 and Hanson, 1996. In contrast, see Youmans and Li, 2002: 153, also Fabb and Halle, 2008: 11–20. Piera's structure is given as Figure 4 of Chapter 10 of this volume.

of statistical methods could deepen our knowledge of versifying in English.[58] In particular she drew attention to the relationship between syllabically regular and irregular meters.

Tarlinskaja argued that meters of an intermediate type bridged the gap between accentual and stress-syllabic meters in English, and she demonstrated that such intermediate meters have continued to play a major role in English poetry. Since there is no concise English term for these intermediate meters she called them by the Russian term *dol'niki*, which I shall anglicize to *dolniks*. Poets employing these meters count not syllables but *ictuses*, rhythmic beats, and allow the (*inter-ictic*) intervals between them to vary in size between zero and two syllables. Although Tarlinskaja's data was based on an outdated four-level theory of English stress, it was so comprehensive that writers are still making use of it in the twenty-first century.[59] Her theme of giving rhythmic beats priority over syllables in metrical analysis was taken up by Derek Attridge, who has published a series of works on poetic meter and rhythm over the last thirty years.[60]

Attridge's theory offers an explanation of versifying in English that covers both syllabically regular and irregular meters, and I have deliberately postponed my analysis of Shakespeare's dramatic iambic pentameter until I could do so with his aid. Attridge's analysis of poetic rhythm in English is much closer to musical theory than is Tarlinskaja's, and he employs the terms *beats* and *offbeats* (echoing the *downbeats* and *upbeats* of music) rather than ictuses and inter-ictic intervals.[61] Peaks of stress, for the most part, provide the beats, and the syllables that lie between them provide the offbeats, which are normally *single* (containing one syllable), *double* (containing two), or *implied* (zero syllables). Lines of English verse normally contain the same number of beats, but Attridge also argues that the last beat may be *unrealized* in some lines, as in English common measure, which gives it an aesthetically attractive combination of four- and three-beat lines.

When poets limit the size of offbeats in a given poem's lines to one syllable, regular verse results, and when they do not dolniks usually result. Although Middle English alliterative poets stretched the inter-ictic intervals in their long lines to three or even four syllables, English accentual verse is normally dolnik verse.[62] The following lines by Tennyson, already quoted, illustrate Attridge's theory, the three-ictic dolnik, and the artistic use of stress clash:

---

[58] See Tarlinskaja, 1976; for Russian precedents for Tarlinskaja's statistical analysis of English verse, see Duffell, 2002a: 175–76.

[59] Youmans and Li, 2002 brings together Tarlinskaja's statistics and those of Li, 1995.

[60] The first of these works was Attridge, 1982, the most recent Attridge, 2013.

[61] For the theory of musical beats, see Griffiths, 2006: 21.

[62] Russian poets have also employed ictic meters, termed *taktoviks*, with between zero and three syllables in each interval; see Tarlinskaja, 1993: 13.

(10) Break, break, break,
ô B ô B ô B (B)
(11) On thy cold, gray stones, O Sea!
ŏ B o B o B (B)

Here I supplement my usual bold typeface and underlining with Attridge's notation: B for a beat, (B) for an unrealized beat, o for a single offbeat, ŏ for a double offbeat, and ô for an implied offbeat. This scansion shows that Tennyson's lines contain four beats, one of which is unrealized in even-numbered lines, and that offbeats vary from zero to two syllables, making the meter a dolnik.

Attridge scans syllabically regular verse in the same way, as in the following examples already analyzed using different theories:

(1) Lilies that **fester** smell far worse than weeds
ô B ŏ B o B o B o B
(2) Be, as thy **presence** is, **gracious** and kind
ô B ŏ B o B ô B ŏ B

These examples show that what gives English meters syllabic regularity is what Attridge terms *compensation*: any double offbeat must be balanced by an implied offbeat. Similarly, what makes English meters irregular is the lack of compensation. This distinction captures the difference between the iambic pentameters of Shakespeare's sonnets, in which double offbeats are balanced by implied offbeats, and those of his plays, where there is no such compensation.

According to rhythmic theory, English verse templates consist of a number of beats, and poet's correspondence rules consist mainly of the size of the intervals (n syllables) between beats; this gives the metric typology shown in Figure 1, where n represents the size of intervals in syllables:

Size	*Type*
n = 0–2	dolnik verse
n = 2	triple-time verse
n = 1	duple-time verse

Fig. 1: English Metric Typology

According to this theory, whether duple-time verse is iambic or trochaic (and whether triple-time is anapestic or dactylic) depends on whether the poet opens the line with an offbeat: the rhythm of a poem may thus vary from line to line, as in Milton's *L'Allegro* and *Il Penseroso*.[63]

Attridge's theory of English verse design is comprehensive, elegant in its simplicity, and psychologically plausible. It is much easier for poets to count beats than

[63] For these two poems, see Leonard, 1998: 21–30.

syllables, because beats are fewer and far more salient than syllable boundaries. In most respects Attridge's theory is also historically credible: it explains why the least regular verse came first in English and the most regular last, and why four-beat verse came before five-beat. Yet, in one important historical respect his theory leaves grave doubts: the hypothesis of compensation. In order to remain isosyllabic lines do need to balance double offbeats with implied ones, but this doesn't seem a credible account of how such regular verse developed.

One of the earliest composers of iambic pentameters in Modern English, Sir Philip Sidney, described versifying largely in terms of counting syllables; and the earliest theorist, George Gascoigne, wrote that if there were such things in English as feet they must all be spondees.[64] I do not think that the concept of compensation occurred either to that generation, or to the vast number of poets who have employed that meter since. It seems much more likely that five stress contrasts between pairs of syllables (some of those contrasts sharp, others muted) were their immediate aim.

Attridge is also on much safer ground when he dissects four-beat verse than when he transfers his conclusions to five-beat. Unrealized fourth beats account well for common measure, but I have doubts about the applicability of the principle to five and six beat verse. When Sidney composed *Astrophel and Stella* he was clearly torn between the newly fashionable French *alexandrin* and the Italian *endecasillabo*, but the latter won out.[65] If six- and five-beat lines have a special rhythmic relationship, then Elizabethan poets might have been expected to experiment with couplets that exploit it, because of their similarity to Latin elegiacs, but I have so far found no example. On balance, therefore, Attridge's theory appears to be the best analysis of irregular verse in English, but positions and feet seem to be a better explanation of the syllabically regular.[66]

Conclusion

In the course of this volume I shall examine a wide variety of verse instances and try to infer their designs. I hope to identify some as influences on Chaucer's versifying and I shall use others for comparison. Only in this way can I demonstrate his innovations and improvements and the extent of his achievement. In the course of this exercise I shall employ many of the analytic tools discussed in this chapter; they will include terms from traditional English metrics; the tests of metricality provided by SMP and PT; the cumulative stress constraint;

---

[64] For Sidney's theorizing, see Farren, 2008; for Gascoigne's, see Dorsten, 1966.

[65] For alexandrines in *Astrophel and Stella*, see Bullett, 1947: 173 and 175.

[66] Hayes and MacEachern, 1998 divides verse into 'song-verse' (intended for singing) and 'art-verse' (intended for reading). It may be that song-verse is best described in terms of beats, while art-verse is best described in terms of positions.

optimality theory in general; Tarlinskaja's concept of the dolnik, and Attridge's concept of beats; and, finally, a great deal of statistical analysis.

In this volume I shall compare dozens of verse texts and to base that comparison upon analyses of the entire text is impractical, since many of them contain several thousand lines. I have therefore based my comparisons upon samples, and by trial and error I found that 300-line samples usually yield statistically significant differences in different poets' use of the same meter. Statisticians measure *samples* in order to estimate the contents of *universes* (for example, they question thousands of voters on their intentions in order to forecast how millions will actually vote)[67]. The extent to which a result based on a sample may differ from the result for the universe simply because the sample is atypical (known as *sampling error*) can be calculated, using a hypothesis known as that of *normal distribution*. This hypothesis posits that a difference of 2σ (two *standard errors*) between how often two features occur in a sample has a 95 percent chance of reflecting a difference in the universe, and that a difference of 3σ has a 99 percent chance.[68]

The conceptual framework of my method is a simple one: the universe of a meter is the infinite number of verse instances that could be generated by its verse design, and the 300 lines I analyze are samples sufficient to reveal significant differences between any two verse designs.

---

[67] Fortunately, my research will not be subject to *questionnaire design error*, which invalidated the pre-election polls in the UK in, 1970, 1997, and, 2015. In those cases design error invited respondents to lie about their intentions,

[68] The formula for calculating a standard error (σ) is as follows:

$$\sigma = \pm \sqrt{\frac{(a \times b)}{(a + b)}}$$

where a and b are the number of occurrences of each of the two features in the sample (for example, voters for and against the existing government).

4
Versifying in France

No documentary evidence of Chaucer's education has survived, but the circumstantial evidence from his career is overwhelming. He must have received the Latin and French education that was normal for rich boys in the middle of the fourteenth century, and he must have become fluent enough in French to impress as a page in royal courts.[1] These courts also drew a variety of people from all over France, ranging from very distinguished personages to common entertainers. The courtiers' ample leisure time was spent singing, dancing, flirting, fighting, and reading and writing poems in French.[2] Poets had been versifying in French for 500 years and over that time had developed a large number of forms, conventions, and techniques, and a good courtier went to some pains to learn them. It is possible that Chaucer first versified in French (a subject to which I shall return in Chapter 9), but his work in English shows that he was familiar with a large number of French poems. This chapter will, therefore, examine the features of French versifying that seem to have a parallel in Chaucer's practice.

The Latin of Gaul and the French Language

Until late in the ninth century literate French poets versified in Latin and the illiterate ones have left no records of their labors. The Latin in which these French poets composed was not very different from that studied in schools and colleges today. This classical, or literary, Latin was a highly conservative variety of the language that an educated elite approximated in their speech between roughly 200 AD and 200 BC (that is, when they weren't trying to distance themselves

[1] Although English had become established as the language of instruction in schools by 1385, fluency in French was still mandatory at New College Oxford in 1340; see Davies, 1999: 362–64.

[2] Henri Plantagenet's accession to the English throne in 1154 was followed by a vast influx of courtiers from his many French possessions, and his sons spent much of their time in France: the English court's adoption of the Francien dialect (the French of Paris) made French royal brides feel at home, and allowed courtiers to pursue careers on both sides of *La Manche*; see Davies, 1999: 281–82.

even further from the common people by using Greek). Popular Latin, which developed over the centuries into the modern Romance languages, was very different.[3] We know this from surviving inscriptions, from the dialogue of low characters in Latin drama, from scribes' spelling mistakes, and from occasional written references to incorrect speech. Most of the differences between Classical Latin and the Romance languages were prefigured in popular Latin, which also varied considerably between the empire's regions.[4]

The Romans were so in awe of Greek culture that from the beginning of the Classical period they imported into their own literary language the versifying practices of Ancient Greece. This was a considerable achievement since Latin had a higher proportion of heavy syllables, and a different type of accent (dynamic rather than melodic).[5] Nevertheless, Roman poets mastered the art of versifying based on syllable weight and the frequent use of triple-time rhythms requiring many light syllables. Traces of Latin's dynamic accent, however, can be found in this versifying, particularly at the close of lines. Thus, the final two feet of the Latin dactylic hexameter, the most prestigious of meters, almost always have the same accentual as durational pattern (S w w S s).[6]

In the Greek *quantitative* mode of versifying, some meters regulated syllable numbers, but they all regulated syllable weight. Poets versifying this way produced complex secondary rhythms not by alternating heavy and light syllables, but by repeating two events, *ictus* and *non-ictus* (Attridge's beats and offbeats). Ictus fell on a single syllable, usually a heavy one, and when the line was sung it coincided with the musical downbeat. We do not know for certain how ictus was marked in recitation but, since pitch change and duration were employed in Ancient Greek for other purposes, the obvious feature is volume: speakers probably emphasized ictic syllables by making them louder. The other repeated element in the rhythm, non-ictus, comprised the syllables, which might vary in number, that lay in the inter-ictic intervals.

Somewhere around AD 300 Roman poets and audiences lost the ability to distinguish long and short vowels (and as a result heavy and light syllables)

---

[3] See Alkire and Rosen, 2010: 37–40.

[4] How the two most geographically remote variants of popular Latin became modern Portuguese and Romanian is described in detail in Alkire and Rosen, 2010: 209–86.

[5] In the eighteenth and nineteenth centuries many European scholars subscribed to the view that Classical Latin accent had been *melodic* (that is based entirely on changes in fundamental frequency), because Latin authors uncritically translated descriptions of accent from Greek. Twentieth-century scholars, however, found good reasons to doubt that Latin accent was melodic (see, for example, Ewert, 1943: 29–32, Elcock, 1960: 51, and Allen, 1973: 154), and today linguists have no hesitation in describing Latin accent as *stress* (see, for example, Alkire and Rosen, 2010: 5–24).

[6] Note that when Greek accent changed from melodic to dynamic in the second century AD Greek poets began to take the same accentual precautions; see Palmer, 1954: 214.

intuitively.[7] Thus many Latin poems of that period contain false quantities, and eventually composing quantitatively in Latin became the preserve of scholars who had learned which vowels were long and which were short from careful study. This scholarly mode of versifying endured for centuries, and among the most skilled of its exponents were Walter of Chatillon (b. Lille, 1135–d. c. 1200), France's most influential twelfth-century poet, and John Gower (b. c. 1335–d. 1408), the polyglot poet of fourteenth-century England and close friend of Geoffrey Chaucer.[8]

Robbed of wide audiences who could appreciate quantitative verse, Medieval Latin poets turned first to counting syllables, using isosyllabic Classical verse forms, but ignoring quantities. Christian hymns are among the earliest surviving verse texts of this type, and many of these hymns have a very simple verse design that ignores accent as well as syllable weight. The only rhythm within their lines is thus the primary rhythm produced by a series of undifferentiated events – syllables.[9] However, it must be emphasized that these were written syllables that may have been pronounced only when sung since much of the surviving verse is that of hymns.

That these compositions were verse for the eye and not the ear is shown by the poet's treatment of adjacent vowels: every written vowel was counted as a syllable. In the Classical period Latin poets had *elided* ('struck out') word-final vowels when they preceded word-initial ones, in this way avoiding *hiatus* ('yawning') in the speech stream. Some Medieval Latin poets avoided such adjacent vowels altogether, while others allowed hiatus both between and within words, so that one note of the music was allocated to every written vowel.[10]

Medieval Latin poets compensated for the lack of ictic or quantitative rhythms in their lines by employing systematic phonetic repetition. Classical Latin poets had sometimes rhymed unaccented syllables, but combining such repetition with stress had far greater impact. However, combining stress and rhyme in Latin presents a problem: the only words accented on their final syllable are monosyllables, and few of them rhyme. The solution that medieval poets found was at first to place syllables with secondary accents at line ends and stress them heavily, and later to employ feminine rhymes, which gave a distinctive trochaic close to the line.[11]

---

[7] For examples of false quantities at this date, see Lote, 1939: 219–38.

[8] For Gautier de Châtillon's *Alexandreis*, see Migne, 1844: cols 459–74; for Gower's Latin poetry see Macaulay, 1901.

[9] For an early example of a hymn versified in this way, see Walpole, 1922: 47.

[10] See, for example, Prudentius, *Hymn XXX*, 1.28 in Walpole, 1922: 147.

[11] In Medieval Latin masculine rhymes occur much earlier than feminine rhymes; the latter first appear in poems composed soon after AD 1100; see Brittain, 1937: 197 and Beare, 1957: 288.

While some Medieval Latin poets were content to have iambic rhythms, as in *anima*, or trochaic ones, as in *locuturi*, only at line ends, others extended them throughout the line. Subsequently by the twelfth century, the Latin poets of France were employing not only syllable count and rhyme, but also a measure of accentual regulation; that is, they regularized the position in the line of all, or at least most, accented syllables.This can be seen in the following examples from a strophe that opens one of the poems by Walter of Chatillon.[12]

(1) Tanto viro locuturi	[1er 3^{e} 5^{e} 7^{e}]
(2) studeamus esse puri,	[1er 3^{e} 5^{e} 7^{e}]
(3) set et loqui sobrie,	[3^{e} 5^{e} 7^{e}]
(4) carum care venerari,	[1er 3^{e} 5^{e} 7^{e}]
(5) et ut simus caro cari,	[3^{e} 5^{e} 7^{e}]
(6) careamus carie.	[1er 3^{e} 5^{e} 7^{e}]

("Before speaking to such a man we must endeavor to be pure, but in order to speak well, to show such a dear man respect, and to be dear to him, we must be without spot.")

I give here the position of accented syllables in the line in brackets, using French ordinal numerals (for example, '8e' for *huitième*, and '10e' for *dixième*). In these examples, the only unstressed syllables in odd-numbered positions are line-initial monosyllables, like many in Longfellow's *Song of Hiawatha*. So, without hesitation, we can classify this meter as a trochaic tetrameter that allows both masculine (*catalectic*) and feminine lines. The widespread circulation of stress-syllabic poems in Latin was clearly an influence on its development in English, as I shall explain in the next chapter. However, when the poets of France first began to versify in their mother tongue, they had both syllabic and stress-syllabic Latin models available. Moreover, many of the earliest French poems were translations of Latin originals.

Versifying in French

To understand the transition from versifying in Latin to versifying in French, it is necessary to appreciate the linguistic differences involved. The first reference to the French language is in the records of the Council of Tours (813), where priests were exhorted to start preaching in French because their congregations could

[12] Here and elsewhere I employ the French convention of enclosing in brackets the language's ordinal numbers (1er, 2^{e} etc.) in order to emphasize the position of syllables capable of bearing stress. These lines (1–6) are from Walter of Chatillon's *Carmen I*; the full text of Walter's *Carmina* can be found at www.thelatinlibary.com/walter.html. For many other examples of stress-syllabic Medieval Latin verse, see Raby, 1934.

no longer understand Latin.[13] Old French, however, was probably spoken long before that date, and the French public's loss of the ability to understand Latin sermons probably had a political cause. In the 780s the Emperor Charlemagne entrusted Alcuin of York with reforming the language of the Church throughout his empire, and this forced the clergy to pronounce every syllable in the written texts, just as English Christians did.[14] Until then priests might write, 'Pater Noster,' but they could deliver the phrase to a lay audience as something more like the modern French 'Père Nôtre.'

Thus, there may have been a long period during which Latin was a logographic convention for Early Romance, one that facilitated written communications throughout Western Christendom.[15] This convention died out in France from the ninth century, when a few pioneers tried to represent their everyday speech phonetically; the first medieval texts that we recognize as French may therefore represent a relatively well-developed stage of the spoken language. The earliest prose text we have in phonetic French dates from around 840 and the earliest poem from the 880s. Both manuscripts also contain German texts, and their authors employed phonetic scripts for both languages.[16]

There were many differences between popular Latin and Classical Latin, either as affected by the educated elite of the Roman Empire or as interpreted by the English clergy. These differences embraced both phonology and morphology, and they grew greater as tendencies within the popular language were accelerated by the arrival in the western empire of Germanic peoples.[17] With the fall of that empire, local differences in popular Latin were further widened by the loss of a unified administrative system and by the erection of new political boundaries. Many of the subsequent changes in popular Latin were distinctive to the region of Northern Gaul, and from this the French language emerged.[18]

Some of these changes were of special importance to versifiers: they included the loss or reduction to schwa of post-tonic syllables; the loss of other unstressed syllables by syncope; a resultant plethora of stressed monosyllables; the gradual

---

[13] See Elcock, 1960: 341–45.

[14] For Alcuin, see Allott, 1974.

[15] See Wright, 1982 and 1994: 165–80. Modern English speakers are familiar with logographic convention: UK English speakers pronounce *Leicester* and *Scarborough*, as if they were *Lesteh* and *Scarbreh*. In the same way literate Early Romance speakers could read, "reges et feminae," and say "reis e femmes."

[16] For a comparison of the Old French in the *Strasburg Oaths* and the *Ludwigslied*, see Ewert, 1943: 352–354. For linguistic analysis of the *Strasburg Oaths*, see Alkire and Rosen, 2010: 323–26.

[17] For a detailed analysis of the changes in phonology that led to modern French, Italian, and Spanish, see Alkire and Rosen, 2010: 5–94.

[18] For the general and external history of the French language, see Ewert, 1943: 1–21 and Alkire and Rosen, 2010: 317–31.

weakening of word stress, leaving only salient phrase-final stresses that could be emphasized by rhyme; the development of a syllable-timed delivery that leveled out both weight and stress; and the eventual loss of final schwas in normal speech. These changes reinforced one another to produce a very distinctive language that is oxytonic, syllable-timed, and lacks word stress. The eventual mode of versifying in French reflects all these linguistic factors.[19]

Accentual Regulation in Old French Verse

Today, French poets craft their lines so as to ensure that line-final (and in longer meters hemistich-final) syllables have stress, but the earliest surviving poems in the language show some signs of accentual regulation within the line. The first is the *Sainte Eulalie*, which can be dated to 881 or 882 and is in the Picard-Walloon dialect and consists of fourteen assonating couplets plus a final half line.[20] Its lines vary from eight to thirteen syllables in length and its first hemistichs are even more irregular, varying between four and nine syllables. Most French scholars have interpreted the poem as a *sequence*, a Latin form in which the lines of each assonating couplet had the same syllable count, but this requires the emendation of five of the couplets, without any other justification, in order to regularize them.[21]

Some scholars, however, have found accentual regularity in the *Sainte Eulalie*.[22] The first twenty-eight of the poem's lines are divided into two hemistichs, and twenty-one of them have two clear peaks of stress in each hemistich. The seven lines that do not subdivide so as to give 2 + 2 stress peaks have a third stress peak in the first hemistich. Moreover, the overwhelming majority of the intervals between stress peaks contain exactly two syllables. The closes of lines are particularly regular in this respect: twenty out of twenty-eight lines have a final hemistich with a disyllabic interval between its two stress peaks. By my calculation, the odds against seven consecutive disyllabic intervals appearing by chance in a text are about 600:1. The case that this regularity is the result of verse design, rather than linguistic accident, is consequently very strong.

The inclusion of lines with an additional stress peak is a feature of the Medieval Castilian *Cantar de Mio Cid* and of poems in Middle English strong-stress meter.[23] In both meters, this extra peak is a common form of tension, and read-

---

[19] Alkire and Rosen make no mention of these suprasegmental features of French phonology, which perhaps emphasizes the gulf between literary studies and linguistics among today's students.

[20] The text of *Sainte Eulalie* given here is that of Aspland, 1979.

[21] See, for example, Lote, 1939: 118–20.

[22] See Paris, 1875: 108, Purczinsky1965–66: 271–75, and Duffell, 1999: 81–107.

[23] See Duffell, 2007: 76 and 2008a: 60.

ers of the *Sainte Eulalie* would not have to go far to find a local example of verse in this meter: the *Ludwigslied*, the poem that ensured the manuscript's survival. This German poem is an anomaly; it combines an ancient Germanic folk genre, the *preislied*, with rhyming couplets, but its two- and three-beat half-lines are as syllabically irregular as those of *Sainte Eulalie.*

These similarities, together with the fact that the two poems are in the same hand, led Julius Purcinsky to conclude that *Sainte Eulalie* and the *Ludwigslied* shared the same author.[24] Nevertheless, we should beware of assuming that the poem is a one-off experiment in composing in French by a German. The scribe may have included a French version of the Latin sequence in order to ensure that something in French was included in a German tribute to a French king. The only thing we know for certain is that no other poem in the same meter has survived: the *Sainte Eulalie* could thus be the only written record of a long-established oral mode of versifying. The point of most metrical significance about the *Sainte Eulalie* is that word stress in ninth-century French was strong enough to form part of a poet's verse design. The case that this was the result of having a German author would be stronger were there no other evidence of accentual regulation in Old French.

The Earliest surviving French *octosyllabes* are to be found in two poems in a manuscript in Clermont dating from c. 980.[25] The *Passion de Clermont* is clearly a local product, but the *Vie de Saint Léger*, which tells the story of a bishop of Autun, was almost certainly composed in Burgundy. The lines of these two poems are a favorite Latin line length, eight syllables, and the *Vie de Saint Léger* begins thus:

(7) **Do**mine Deu de**vemps** lau**der,**	[1er 4e 6e 8e]
(8) Et a sos sancz ho**nor** por**ter.**	[4e 6e 8e]
(9) In su' a**mor** can**tomps** dels sanz,	[4e 6e 8e]
(10) Quoe por lui **au**grent granz a·**anz;**	[4e 6e 8e]
(11) Et or est temps et si est biens	[2e 4e 8e]
(12) Quoe nos can**tumps** de sant Leth**gier.**	[2e 4e 6e 8e]

("Let us praise the Lord God and honor his saints. For love of Him let us sing the praises of the saints who were his champions; and now is a good time for us to sing of Saint Léger.")

Clearly, strong syllables and stressed monosyllables appear only in even-numbered positions (other than 1er) in these lines. They are, consequently, as iambic as those of Walter's Latin poem (quoted in (1)–(6) above) were trochaic. SMP would describe them as having no stress maxima in odd-numbered positions; PT would argue that the correspondence rules allow no strong syllables in weak

[24] See Purczinsky, 1965–66: 271.

[25] For the text of these two poems, see Henry, 1953: 6–13.

positions other than colon-initial ones (sanctioned by the closure principal). The earliest surviving *octosyllabes* are therefore iambic tetrameters.

At this point in time French word stress must have been strong enough for poets to regulate it in their versifying. What other poets could do in Latin, the authors of these two poems were able to do in French. But this mode of versifying seems to have died out in French just as Walter of Chatillon was showing his fellow clerics the potential of accentually regular verse in Latin. The same monasteries pumped out hagiographic and epic narrative in both languages, but for their own kind the age's poets produced subtle stress-syllabic Latin verse and for the laity they provided much thinner fare.[26] The only reasonable explanation for this is that word stress was becoming steadily weaker in spoken French and phrasal stress proportionately more salient.

Syllabic Regularity in Old French

An alternative mode of versifying in French seems to date from only forty years later than the two poems in Clermont. Composers of *octosyllabes* and their audiences doubtless learned to count syllables up to eight rapidly and intuitively so that the prop of accentual regularity was no longer necessary. But the earliest surviving *octosyllabes* that dispense with patterns in word stress are slightly later than the poems that illustrate the next stage in the history of French verse design. French metrists are adamant that eight syllables is the maximum length of an undivided line but longer lines are attractive because they can hold so much more meaning.

The first French solution to composing a regular line of more than eight syllables appears in two poems dated to c. 1020, the French *Vie de Saint Alexis* and the Occitan *Boecis*.[27] The Occitan poem is in the same meter as the French except that it has masculine rhyme instead of assonance. The *Vie de Saint Alexis* was clearly composed in the Île de France, but the scribe who transmitted it introduced some Anglo-Norman dialect features into his text. While the Latin origins of the *octosyllabe* are obvious, the origin of the French *vers de dix* is controversial.

Michel Burger argues that the *vers de dix* or *décasyllabe* derives from the Medieval Latin *senarius* with twelve syllables to its final stress (which was usually

[26] Note that the early medieval texts in Romance that have survived are far fewer than contemporary Latin texts, and their authors were probably unaware of one another. These Romance texts have been likened to 'islands floating in a sea of Latinity'; see Whinnom, 1994:97.

[27] For the text of the *Vie de Saint Alexis*, see Meunier, 1933; for that of *Boecis*, see Lavaud and Machicot, 1950.

secondary), but only ten to the primary stress of the same word.[28] D'Arco Silvio Avalle, however, argues that the French meter evolved from Latin songs (*tropes*) inserted into the service of the mass.[29] These, he points out, were given an oxytonic pronunciation in France making their final syllable a stress peak. The first Latin *vers de dix* support Avalle's argument; they mourned the death of the English King William the Conqueror and date from about fifty years after the *Vie de Saint Alexis.*[30] The following lines from the *Vie de Saint Alexis* reveal the verse design of the earliest *vers de dix;* here I place syllables that do not contribute to the syllable count in brackets and underline the ordinal numbers of syllables bearing phrasal stress:

(13)	Bons fut li **sec**[les]	al tens anc**ïenur**	[1er $\underline{4}^{e}$ 6^{e} $\underline{10}^{e}$]	(1)
(14)	Al tens Nö**é**	et al tens Abra**ham**	[2^{e} $\underline{4}^{e}$ 7^{e} $\underline{10}^{e}$]	(6)
(15)	Dunc prist mui**ler**	vai**lant**^{e} et ho**nure**[de]	[2^{e} $\underline{4}^{e}$ 6e 8^{e} $\underline{10}^{e}$]	(19)
(16)	Oz mei, pul**ce**[le]!	Ce**lui** tien ad es**pus**	[1er $\underline{4}^{e}$ 6e 7^{e} $\underline{10}^{e}$]	(36)
(17)	Ki nus ra**ens**[t]	de sun sanc pre**cïus**	[2^{e} $\underline{4}^{e}$ 7^{e} $\underline{10}^{e}$]	(37)
(18)	Dunc en eis**sit**	de la **cam**bre sum **pe**[dre]	[$\underline{4}^{e}$ 7^{e} $\underline{10}^{e}$]	(44)

("The world was good in ancient times;" "at the time of Noah and of Abraham;" "then he took a wife, worthy and honored;" "Listen to me, maiden, take him for a husband;" "who redeemed us with his precious blood;" "then he left his father's bedroom.")

The only regular features of these lines are the phrasal stresses in $\underline{4}^{e}$ and $\underline{10}^{e}$, and the number and position of strong syllables vary from line to line. Note that the poem is in assonating strophes of five lines, and some of its assonances are feminine (as in (15) and (18) above). Note also that assonance sometimes slips into full rhyme (as in (16) and (17) above), and that first hemistichs may also be feminine: an extrametrical syllable (given here in brackets) may appear after syllables four and/or ten, so that a line may contain as many as twelve actual syllables. This is a very different way of counting syllables from the normal Medieval Latin mode.

Elision in this poem applied within hemistichs (as in example (15)), but not between them, making this early *vers de dix* a strongly divided line, a 4 + 6 rather than a unified 10. This sharp division allowed the poet to place feminine words at the caesura, even when elision was not possible (as in (16) above). Such a caesura was termed *césure épique* because it typified the heroic narratives (called *chansons de geste*) that were popular favorites, and which French monasteries produced in large numbers over the next two centuries. In subsequent scansions I shall show

[28] See Burger, 1957: 107–26.

[29] See Avalle, 1963: 33–39.

[30] For the text of *Chant sur la mort de Guillaume le Conquérant*, see Du Méril, 1843: 294–96.

caesura by double slashes and epic caesura by bracketing the mid-line extrametrical syllable.

Medieval French poets also found other ways of producing lines of ten syllables, but the earliest surviving witnesses are a century later than the *Vie de Saint Alexis*. A formula of 6 + 4 fulfills the same counting function, breaking the line down into sub-units of less than eight syllables. A *chanson de geste* called *Girart de Roussillon* is an early example of the *vers de dix* of 6 + 4: it was composed at some time between 1136 and 1180 in a language that is intermediate between French and Occitan. The following lines from Hackett's edition of *Girart* demonstrate the three possible line lengths in this meter:[31]

(19) per quant sunt espan**dut** // de sanc mil mui [2^{e} $\underline{6^{e}}$ 8^{e} $\underline{10^{e}}$] (15)

(20) El n'ai les claus des **can**[bres] // o lei con**du**[che] [2^{e} 4^{e} $\underline{6^{e}}$ $\underline{10^{e}}$] (3)

(21) S'esta**veit** desos **l'on**[bre] // d'un auli**ver** [3^{e} $\underline{6^{e}}$ $\underline{10^{e}}$] (25)

("In this way their number was increased by 5,000;" "She had no keys for the rooms where she led him;" "stretched out under an olive tree.")

Once again, the position of the phrasal stresses in this poem is fixed, and that of the strong syllables is not: this is a stress-syllabic meter that regulates only phrasal stress, and its syllable count is a strongly divided 6 + 4.

There is also a third way of crafting lines of ten syllables, and that is by dividing the line into 5 + 5, making it a *décasyllabe a césure médiane*. The earliest surviving *vers de dix* of this type are found in carols and folk verse dating from the twelfth century. Paul Verrier collected a number of these poems in his study of Old French versifying, and three of the lines he quotes are given below:[32]

(22) Si ait endur**é** // bien et loyau**ment** [2^{e} $\underline{5^{e}}$ 6^{e} $\underline{10^{e}}$]

(23) Ma**lois** soit de Deu // ki me fist non**ne**[te] [2^{e} $\underline{5^{e}}$ 8^{e} $\underline{10^{e}}$]

(24) **Dame bon**^{e} et **sai**[ge] // av**rai** je se**cours** [1er 3^{e} $\underline{5^{e}}$ 7^{e} $\underline{10^{e}}$]

("If he had endured well and loyally;" "May he be cursed of God who made me a nun!;" "O Lady, kind and wise, I would be safe.")

Once again, the positions of strong syllables and phrasal stresses show that this is a syllabic meter of 5 + 5.

Examples (13) to (24) demonstrate that, although three different templates were employed in medieval France for the *vers de dix* (4 + 6, 6 + 4, 5 + 5), a single set of correspondence rules prevailed. It applied equally to each hemistich, and in terms of PT the last three parameters were position size: one syllable (plus a

---

[31] For the text of *Girart de Rousillon*, see Hackett, 1953–55.

[32] See Verrier, 1932: 159–60.

post-tonic syllable in the final position); prominence type: phrasal stress; and prominence site: the final position, where such stress was mandatory.

At the end of the twelfth century a new template appeared that soon surpassed the others in popularity for epic and narrative verse. This was a longer line, a *dodécasyllabe* of 6 + 6, which had first appeared earlier in the century but was popularized by a work composed in 1180.[33] The story of the *Roman d'Alexandre* had been told before, first in *octosyllabes*, then in *décasyllabes*, but Alexandre de Bernay (or de Paris) produced a dodecasyllabic version that gave the meter its modern name, the *alexandrin*. This poem opens:

(25) L'es**to**re d'Ali**xan**[dre]   vus <u>voel</u> ci commen**cier**   [2e <u>6e</u> 8e <u>12e</u>]
(26) En rou**mans**, c'a gent **lai**[e]   doit **au**que profiteer   [3^{e} <u>6^{e}</u> 8^{e} <u>12^{e}</u>]

("You will find the story of Alexander here in French, so that the laity may profit by it.")

The poet's verse template (6 + 6) may differ from those of the early types of *vers de dix*, but the correspondence rules are the same: the final syllable of each hemistich bears the only mandatory stress, which may be followed by a post-tonic syllable that is not included in the count.

This two-part *alexandrin* with epic caesura dominated French long-line versifying until the fourteenth century, when a more unified *vers de dix* came back into fashion. After that French audiences had to wait until the sixteenth century for a unified *alexandrin* to become the canonical French long line. It was employed for everything from epic to drama, and the reason most often given for its popularity is that its length makes it closest to prose.[34] The *alexandrin* also has metrical advantages: an unbroken series of sixes is easier for poets to produce and for audiences to recognize; and the greater distance between rhymes makes them less obtrusive. Nor is the contrast between the unrhymed first hemistich and the rhymed second of the *alexandrin* without aesthetic appeal.

While the *vers de dix* and *alexandrin* took turns in dominating medieval French long-line verse, the *octosyllabe* remained the favorite short-line meter. It was a line of eight syllables in which the same principle, that of regulating only phrasal stress, prevailed. I shall illustrate its verse design by lines from *Le Roman de la Rose*, which is the work of two poets: Guillaume de Lorris composed the first part c. 1136, leaving the poem unfinished; Jean de Meung added the much longer second c. 1180.[35] The first part is an allegory of romantic love, the second is an examination of life. Moving between the two parts is rather like stepping from *Troilus and Criseyde* into *The Canterbury Tales*. The whole, which was

[33] For the text of the *Roman d'Alexandre*, see Armstrong et al., 1937.

[34] See Kastner, 1903: 144–46.

[35] For a full text of *Le Roman de la rose* see Langlois, 1914.

probably the best-known poem of the entire European Middle Ages, contains many thousands of rhymed octosyllabic couplets. After the initial vogue for assonating *laisses* of *vers de dix* in *chansons de geste* this form became the most popular for narrative verse in medieval France. The following lines are from Lorris's part of *Le Roman de la Rose*:[36]

(27)	Vers une riviere m'**adrec**[e]	[5^{e} 8^{e}]	(2)
(28)	**Cler**^{e} es**toit** l'eau^{e} et aus**si** froid	[1e 3e 4e 7e 8e]	(8)
(29)	A regar**der** le lieu plai**sant**	[4e 6e 8e]	(15)
(30)	Les **ima**ges et les pein**tur**[es]	[3e 8e]	(32)
(31)	**Tou**te sa **test**^{e} es**toit** che**nu**[e]	[1e 4e 6e 8e]	(44)
(32)	Car touz ses cors es**toit** se**chiés**	[2e 4e 6e 8e]	(48)

("I made my way to a river bank;" "The water was clear and pretty cold;" "To look at the pleasant place;" "The images and pictures;" "All her head was hoary;" "For all her body was dried up.")

This *octosyllabe* is a line of eight syllables, strictly counted and meticulously rhymed: word-final *-e* is elided before a following vowel or diphthong; within words the adjacent vowels -ai-, -au-, -ei-, -ie-, -oi, and -ou- usually become diphthongs. The ordinal numerals in brackets show that the strong syllables of polysyllabic words and stressed monosyllables may appear in any position in the line. Thus examples (29), (31), and (32) could have been generated by the verse design of the *Vie de St Léger*, but (27), (28), and (30) could not. Lines like these, with strong syllables in positions 3 and/or 5, appear at random and in large numbers in Guillaume de Lorris's poem. Note also that the poet seems to have had no compunction about placing syllables that once carried word stress next to one another, as in positions 3–4 and positions 7–8 of example (28).

Traditionally French metrists have described the *octosyllabe* as a line of eight syllables to the final stress, giving it a template of [$x^1 x^2 x^3 x^4 x^5 x^6 x^7$ PS], where x represents any position without phrasal stress (PS). The only contrast in this template is that between seven syllables without phrasal stress and one syllable with it. Its description according to PT would thus be as in Figure 1 below.

Position Number:	eight
Orientation:	right-strong (with the above template)
Position Size:	1 syllable (plus an optional post-tonic syllable in position 8).
Prominence Type:	Phrasal Stress
Prominence Site:	Line-Final Syllable

Fig. 1: Parameters of the French *Octosyllabe*

[36] The line numbers in parentheses refer to the extract given in Woledge, 1961: 144–50.

The correspondence rules of the meter clearly changed between 990 and 1136: any constraints on weak positions were abandoned as word stress weakened.[37]

The Subsequent History of Three French Meters

The *octosyllabe* has never lost its popularity, but the vogue for the *alexandrin* reached its peak in the late thirteenth century. In the fourteenth its use declined rapidly and by Chaucer's time the line of 6 + 6 had been virtually abandoned. The reasons for this include the meter having been too closely associated with Saints' Lives and tales of Christian heroism. Throughout Western Europe rising literacy among the laity gradually moved the center of poetic production from cloister to court, and the *alexandrin* had been one of the distinguishing features of priestly poetry.[38] When the *alexandrin* was revived in the sixteenth century it was a different meter: epic caesura was no longer tolerated and feminine words could only be used at the caesura if they ended in a schwa that could be elided.

When the *vers de dix* returned to favor in early fourteenth-century France, it was also a very different *vers de dix* from those composed in the eleventh and twelfth. First, the line of 6 + 4 did not return, because the *alexandrin*'s 6 + 6 had made it redundant: any poet who set up a rhythm of sixes found it easier to continue with it than to switch to alternating sixes and fours. Moreover, the 6 + 4's structure had always contravened Behaghel's fourth law: in terms of linguistic bulk the 6 + 4 ended with a whimper while the 4 + 6 ended with a bang.[39] Secondly, the line of 5 + 5 had always had a peasant aura, and doubtless peasant poets continued to employ it into the fourteenth century.[40]

The elimination of both rival templates left the 4 + 6 supreme in the fourteenth century, but it had undergone many changes. The most important was the result of the 4 + 6 line's having proved useful for other genres than *chansons de geste*. Many medieval French (and Occitan) poets included *vers de dix* in lyric poetry for aesthetic reasons: a longer line could not only bear a larger semantic burden; it offered the chance of a more intricate melody. However, the strongly divided line of poems like *La Vie de Saint Alexis* or *Boecis* presented them with a

---

[37] For the loss of French word stress, see Ewert, 1943: 104–07

[38] See Duffell, 2007: 85–96.

[39] The "Law of Increasing Constituents" was first identified by Otto Behaghel in the last volume of his four-volume work *Deutsche Syntax* (1923–24): it states that the shorter of two phrases normally precedes the longer. This law can be observed in conventional forms of address, such as "Lords, Ladies, and Gentlemen" and "Friends, Romans, and Countrymen"; see Best, 2007: 110–42.

[40] When Bonaventure des Périers (d. 1544) tried to revive the 5 + 5 in the sixteenth century, he was largely scorned and his meter was dubbed the *taratantara*; see Des Périers, on the website given in 'Works Cited.'

problem: any line with a feminine word at the caesura had eleven syllables, not ten, and so wouldn't fit the same music. These lyrics, however, were mostly addressed to women, and so their composers often wanted to place a feminine noun or adjective at the caesura.[41] They therefore placed such words so that their post-tonic syllable was in position 4 of the line (coinciding with the musical beat). This doubtless led performers (*jongleurs*) to give that post-tonic syllable a great deal more emphasis than it would receive in normal speech.

This device naturally became known as *césure lyrique*, and the weakness of word stress in the language must have helped the acceptance of something that was comparable to the Move X rule in English. In English speech clashing stresses force such a strength shift; in sung French verse the musical beat compelled it. We cannot be sure what happened to lyric caesura in unaccompanied recitation, but it is unlikely that speakers who begrudged the first syllable of the word *dame* a stress peak would make one of the second.[42] More probably a short pause after the word enabled the audience to pick up the syllabic rhythm of 4 + 6 that ran through all the lines, but the strong phrasal stresses in position 4 that characterize the lines of *La Vie de Saint Alexis* would certainly not have been part of the performance.

The substitution of lyric for epic caesura was not the only way in which the new *vers de dix* was less strongly divided than the earliest verse based on this template. The elision of a final schwa at the caesura was also a common device enabling feminine words to be employed mid-line, as the following examples taken from three different *ballades* by Guillaume de Machaut (b. c. 1300–d. 1377) show:[43]

(33) Ha! For**tu**ne, // qui es **gou**ffres et <u>puis</u> [$\underline{3}^{\underline{e}}$ 7^{e} $\underline{10}^{\underline{e}}$] (1, 9)
(34) Et les **gou**tes // de **plui**^{e} et de la <u>mer</u> [$\underline{3}^{\underline{e}}$ 6^{e} $\underline{10}^{\underline{e}}$] (2, 3)
(35) Quant à vous **pens**^{e} // et je sui **en**tre <u>gent</u> [$\underline{4}^{\underline{e}}$ 8^{e} $\underline{10}^{\underline{e}}$] (2, 11)
(36) **U**ne pen**se**^{e}, // un de**sir**, un vou**loir** [1er $\underline{4}^{\underline{e}}$ 7^{e} $\underline{10}^{\underline{e}}$] (5, 12)

("Ha! Fortune, who art a gulf and a pit;" "And the drops of rain and of the sea;" "When I think of you and I'm in company;" "One thought, one desire, one will.")

Examples (33) and (34) contain lyric caesuras, which I have already discussed, but the other features work even more effectively to unify the line. Examples (35) and (36) have elision at the caesura. Since some other lines have the mid-line

[41] The word *dame* (*dompna* in Occitan) was a particular favorite for positions 3–4 in lyric *vers de dix*; see, for example, the *chansons* of Conon de Béthune (b. c. 1150–d. c. 1219) in Woledge, 1961: 104–11.

[42] For a discussion of how French sung verse allows unstressed syllables to be matched to downbeats and the performance implications, see Dell and Halle, 2005.

[43] The numbers in parentheses refer to the poems and lines of ballades in Woledge, 1961: 220–26. For the complete works of Machaut, see Hoepffner, 1908.

equivalent of *enjambement*, the division into 4 + 6 in this meter is blurred in a variety of ways. A strongly divided *vers de dix* has by the fourteenth century become a unified *décasyllabe*.

French Poetic Rhythm

Poets produce a variety of rhythms in their verse by repeating different types of event in different ways. Some of these events are repeated within lines and some between them, and French verse is particularly rich in the second type. The first of these *inter-linear* events is the strophe: a series of strophes provides a simple primary rhythm, but its events are complex and intricate. French lines are also events: a series of eights provides a complex primary rhythm, and a series of alternating fours and sixes provides a complex secondary one; and the inclusion of lines of different lengths in a poem makes for an even more complex rhythm. Stress in French verse also creates an inter-linear rhythm: the mandatory line-final stress setting up a pulse with those in other lines. Rhymes too produce inter-linear rhythms, simple ones in the case of couplets, and complex ones in longer strophes. Finally, French poets can derive a complex rhythm from their lines' cadences: from the interplay of masculine and feminine lines.[44]

In comparison, French verse is poor in *intra-linear* events: hemistichs provide one type: thus a four contrasting with a six produces a complex secondary rhythm; but only longer lines are regularly divided in this way. Rhyme may also occur within the line (*leonine* rhyme), but it is the exception rather than the rule. So, this leaves only the syllables themselves, a single type of event that occurs a given number of times in each line, creating what would be a complex primary rhythm, except for the fact that the final syllable in each line or hemistich bears phrasal stress. As noted, the only rhythmic contrast within French lines is between a series of unstressed syllables and a single stressed one. To the ears of some English speakers French lines lack rhythm.[45]

A number of modern writers have tried to fill this void: their names, Volkoff, Dragonetti, and Pensom, indicate that this is not a native French undertaking.[46] Their methodology has been to survey the missing word stresses in the line and to calculate the chances that their position is random. Their results have been consistent: they show that constructing feet based on these phantom stresses produces variety rather than regularity—few lines, and even fewer passages of verse, contain a dominant type of foot. There is strong evidence that the author

[44] For the so-called *règle d'alternance des rimes*, see Kastner, 1903: 63–64.

[45] See, for example, Lewis, 1938: 31.

[46] See Dragonetti, 1960, Volkoff, 1978, and Pensom, 1982. Note that many writers attribute the lack of blank verse in French to the weakness of word stress; see, for example, Scott, 1980: 77.

of the *Chanson de Roland* avoided clashing stresses, but word stress was much stronger at that time.[47] The evidence that modern poets avoid such clashes is less clear. Most French academics feel flattered to have foreign scholars digging so deep into their language and literature, but few are convinced that a bonanza will be found.

There is one French scholar who has taken the opposite path, and I find his arguments more convincing. Benoît de Cornulier bases his theory of French verse rhythm on the emptiness of French lines, relegating the unstressed syllables in the line from events to intervals.[48] He points out that only two languages have what he terms *un métrique de syllabes indifférenciées*: Japanese and French. The moraic meters of Japanese depend heavily on the fact that the language's poets and audiences learn to recognize the length of time occupied by five or seven light syllables; in this sense Japanese meters are quantitative. Cornulier argues that the tendency to syllable-timing in French has made it possible for poets to create similar quantitative rhythms by placing phrasal stresses at equal time intervals in their verse.

The practice in French drama of timing lines so as to allow for unelided, but unpronounced, schwas makes this hypothesis more credible. This skill in timing became an art at the end of the nineteenth century in the performances of the famous actress Sarah Bernhardt.[49] To amuse her fans after the show, she used to recite a passage of *alexandrins* adding or subtracting two syllables from one of its lines, and she used to challenge her audience to identify which line she had mutilated. So skilled was the diva in compensating for the syllabic irregularity that listeners were forced to guess, and most guessed wrong. Clearly, Bernhardt could time her phrasal stresses to perfection, but her audiences, too, were showing the ability that Cornulier posits: they were recognizing equal time intervals.

Note that, in terms of Attridge's theory, this makes the French *octosyllabe* a line with a single beat, provided by a phrasal stress reinforced with rhyme that occurs at regular intervals. The *vers de dix* is, similarly, a two-beat line with a shorter interval followed by a longer. Clearly, recognition of this rhythm depends upon the French language having a tendency to syllable-timing and no word stress to compete for attention with the phrasal stresses. The poets of many languages have attempted to imitate the regularities of French verse, but in doing so they have encountered the problem that French verse is a stylization of the French language.[50] Hanson and Kiparsky's principle of fit argues that meters evolve so as to accommodate the lexicon of the language; but this principle is

[47] For the argument that earlier French poets avoided such clashing stresses see Pensom, 1982: 27–28.

[48] See Cornulier, 1995: 111–15.

[49] For the actress's own version of the many legends about her, see Bernhardt, 1907.

[50] For the problems facing imitators of French syllabic verse in other languages, see Duffell, 2008a: 45–46.

equally applicable to its phonology, and I have given many examples, from Ancient Greek to Japanese, of modes of versifying that are a perfect fit for their languages' phonology. This is nowhere truer than in the case of France: French versification is a perfect fit for a syllable-timed language with only phrasal stresses.

In the chapters that follow I shall show how Medieval English poets attempted to overcome the problems caused by this perfect fit between the meters they wanted to imitate and the language from which they had to be divorced. I shall document the limits of their achievement, and then I shall examine how Italian poets were rather more successful in tackling the same problem. Finally, I shall show how Chaucer, with a little help from the Italians, overcame the problem for the English language and helped found an enduring tradition of versifying in English.

5
Versifying in England

Versifying in English probably antedates versifying in French, but it was a very different English from any spoken today. The closely related varieties of West Germanic that arrived in England more than a millennium and a half ago, usually known as Old English (OE), have coalesced and changed in many ways.[1] This language of England, and later the USA and much of the world, has been converted from a synthetic language with many inflections, like Sanskrit, to an analytic language of linked monosyllables, more like Chinese. The sounds of English vowels and diphthongs have changed almost beyond recognition, and the lexicon has become swollen with foreign words, most of them of Romance origin. Yet, some of the language's Germanic features have been retained, the most important for versifiers being strong word stress with an underlying rhythm of moraic trochees. Such changes as there have been in English stress have left the basic rhythmic structure unaffected.[2]

OE poetry has been preserved in just four witnesses dating from the tenth and eleventh centuries, but it is clear that some of the poems concerned date back to pre-Christian times, and a long period of oral transmission preceded their committal to the written language.[3] Indeed, a contemporary chronicle even gives the name of the seventh century's most famous poet, Caedmon, and one of his poems, a hymn, has survived.[4] OE may have been recorded in Germanic runes before the kingdoms of England converted to the faith of Rome but, once kings were converted, priests endeavored to bring the Gospel to the people in their own language; and for this they simply borrowed the Latin alphabet, adding a few new characters.[5] Thus English had a phonetic script before French, and this is why English scholars, such as Alcuin, were not affected by a logographic convention when they pronounced Latin. This English Latin (which may have

---

[1] For the dialects of Old English, see Crystal, 2004: 34–56; for the chronology of subsequent changes in the English language, see Barber, 1993: 127–98.

[2] For the changes in Old and Middle English stress, see Hayes, 1995: 117–18 and 148.

[3] For the origins of OE poetry in Germanic songs and chants, see Hamer, 1970: 13–14.

[4] For Bede's account of the poet Cædmon, see Mitchell and Robinson, 1982: 204–09.

[5] See Mitchell & Robinson, 1982: 13–16.

sounded very different from Cicero's) offered Charlemagne a basis for unifying the liturgy of a polyglot Christian empire.[6]

Writers' confidence in the English language grew as its kings defeated, treated with, or submitted to rivals from Denmark, speakers of a mutually intelligible language (Old Norse). In the early eighth century the Northumbrian Bede had written his history of the English people in Latin, but in the ninth century it was translated into OE, and by AD 900 the monks of Winchester were recording each year's events in the local variant of English.[7] Thus in 1066 English was a language with a considerable literature, and English culture was in many ways more advanced than that of the Norman conquerors. The Normans, however, had not only cavalry and castles, but also the vast cultural resources of France to draw upon.[8]

Barely a dozen verse texts in OE have survived from the period after 1066, and in 1154 the monks of Winchester ceased to update the Anglo-Saxon Chronicle. We do not know why this recording of events in OE stopped abruptly, but it seems likely that hopes of English liberation died with the undisputed accession of the vigorous (and fertile) Henry Plantagenet. The first period in the history of versifying in England is thereby neatly demarcated. By the thirteenth century, the literate minority (no more than 10 percent of the population) were bilingual, and the majority were using a large number of French loan words: thus *color* and *beauty* could not have displaced *hue* and *fairness* unless L1 English speakers knew what the French words meant.[9] A new English was evolving that would interweave the two streams of vocabulary while clinging to the wreck of the old Germanic grammar, and its phonology would be storm-tossed for centuries, partly as a result of this commingling.[10] All these changes posed a challenge to the way that poets had versified in the old language.

Versifying in Old English

Anglo-Saxon poets inherited a Germanic mode of versifying with a long oral history, and all the surviving OE poems are in the same meter, known as OE *alliterative meter*. The majority of lines have four strong stresses reinforced by an alliterative pattern, as in the following examples taken from four different poems:[11]

---

[6] For OE pronunciation, see Barber, 1993: 107–13; for Alcuin's reforms, see Wright, 1994: 118; for a brief historical survey of Latin pronunciation, see Kelly, 1986–87.

[7] For *The Anglo-Saxon Chronicles*, see Savage, 1983; for the OE translation of Bede (b. 673–d. 735), see Rowley, 2011.

[8] For a modern assessment of the Norman Conquest, see Davies, 1999: 253–54.

[9] See Davies, 1999: 237–38.

[10] See Barber, 1993: 144–74.

[11] See Hamer, 1970: 54, 100, 156, and 186.

(1)	Fōtum ic fēre, // foldan slīte	(*Riddles*, 12, 1)
(2)	Bitre brēostceare // gebiden hæbbe	(*The Seafarer*, 4)
(3)	And swegles drēamas // þurh his sylfes miltse	(*Judith*, 350)
(4)	Lidmen to lande // linde bæron	(*Battle of Maldon*, 99)

("I go on foot and beat the ground;" "I have experienced bitter anxiety;" "And heavenly joys through his own mercy;" "Seafarers bearing to land the linden.")

Here I have used a double slash to separate the first half of each line (the *a-verse*) from the second (the *b-verse*), and I have marked strong stresses by placing the syllable onset in bold typeface. I have also marked alliteration by underlining and its absence by placing the onsets in bold typeface without underlining.

These lines, which are among the least complex, demonstrate the key metrical features. Most lines contain four strong stresses, and these are reinforced by alliterative patterns: the onset of the first stressed syllable is repeated in the second and / or third but not in the fourth. Secondly, unstressed syllables are less strictly regulated: they are variable in number and also in their location relative to the stresses. It should be noted that some lines carry extra syllables that lead scholars to argue that they are either hypermetric or are expansions of the basic pattern.

The crafting OE lines seems to have been a complex and subtle process, and it is clear that OE poets favored certain configurations of stress in their lines and avoided others, and the most enduring analysis of these preferences is known as *reference theory*. In 1885, the German scholar Eduard Sievers first noted that just five basic accentual configurations account for 80 percent of the verses in *Beowulf*.[12] Those configurations are illustrated in Figure 1, and my notation uses upper-case *S* for primary stress and lower-case *s* for secondary, and I place feet in brackets: as well as syllabic trochees and iambs, there are monosyllabic feet, which I mark [S !]; they could be regarded as moraic trochees, while [S w w], [S w s], and [S s w] could be regarded either as different types of dactyl or as trochees followed by an extrametrical syllable. Note that I have divided Sievers Type D in order to show the differences between these trisyllabic stress configurations:[13]

[12] See Sievers, 1885.

[13] References to *Beowulf* are to the text of Wrenn and Bolton, 1988, and the source of this table is Stockwell and Minkova, 1997: 69.

Sievers Type	*OE Example*	*Beowulf (line no)*	*My Scansion*
A	Lāðan līges	(11a)	[S w] [S w]
B	Nē lēof nē lāð	(511a)	[w S] [w S]
C	Mid scip-herge	(243a)	[w S] [S w]
D1	Flōd fæðmian	(3133a)	[S !] [S w w]
D2	Eall ēðelwyn	(2885a)	[S !] [S w s]
E	Fēasceāftum men	(2285a)	[S s w] [S !]

("Fierce fires;" "Neither friend nor foe;" "With sea-borne warriors;" "Flood to embrace;" "All to their happy homes;" "For needy men.")

Fig. 1: Sievers Types Analyzed in Terms of Feet

A number of other configurations make up the remaining 20 percent of verses. They include half-lines with an extra stress, with a grammatical monosyllable in place of a stress, and with extrametrical material. Some configurations, however, are not attested, and OE poets seem to have observed exclusions as well as preferences.[14]

Other theories of OE meter have been proposed as alternatives to reference theory, among them that of Geoffrey Russom, which set out a linguistic theory to account for 100 percent of *Beowulf*'s lines. He argued that they were based on nine types of foot, which were identical to the stress profiles of OE words: they were *word-feet*.[15] Figure 2 below shows the nine types in Russom's notation, in which my [S !] is reduced to S. I have rearranged the nine types under three headings, trochaic feet, dactylic feet, and light/long feet.

Trochaic	*Dactylic*	*Light/Long*
S	S x x	x
S x	S s x	x x
S s	S x s	S x x s

Fig. 2: Russom's Inventory of Foot Patterns

[14] Cable, 1974, put forward an explanation of why OE poets may have avoided some configurations of stress. He argued that OE poets avoided the stress pattern w s^w s^w, although it was common in OE prose, because it presented too many stress contrasts. It also produced two consecutive increases in stress, which would have badly disrupted the meter's prevailing (falling) rhythm.

[15] See Russom, 1987.

This inventory ignores anacrusis, but its light/long category enabled Russom to account for far more than the 80 percent of lines categorized by Sievers.[16] Russom argued that OE verse design allowed 25 of the 45 possible combinations of these foot types to form half-verses. He examined the relative frequency with which each of these combinations occurred and ordered them in terms of metrical complexity. And he showed that the half-verses containing a third foot would be better described as having *overlapping feet.*[17] Russom derived from his analysis a set of rules and exceptions that have attracted subsequent criticism, but which provided many new insights into the meter.

Chris McCully and Sharon Hilles provided further linguistic analysis of the OE alliterative line in a pedagogic work on the language that combined reference theory with optimality theory.[18] They demonstrated that a series of ranked constraints are capable of generating the lines of this meter, and those constraints (C1-C4) are listed below.[19]

> (C1) The long lines must consist of two *verses*, each containing four positions, two *lifts* (L) and two *dips* (x) filled with linguistic material.
> (C2) The endings of verses are strictly regulated: verses must close in either a stressed syllable or a single unstressed syllable.[20]
> (C3) The structure of the line is hierarchical and left-strong as in Figure 4:[21]

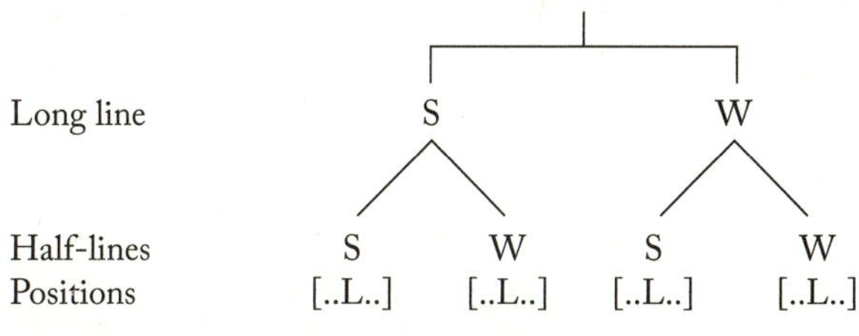

Fig 3: Relative Strength of Elements within OE Line

---

[16] The inclusion of the long foot S x x s in Russom's list suggests that OE alliterative might fall within the category that Russian metrists term the *taktovik*; see Tarlinskaja, 1993: 13.

[17] Russom, 1987: 61 employs the term *overlapping feet* for lines with more than four beats; other writers refer to them as *extended* or *expanded* lines.

[18] See McCully and Hilles, 2005.

[19] Pairs of positions in Figure 4 are notated .‘. .L. . .’ in order to show that they may be expanded and may either precede or follow lifts.

[20] McCully and Hilles, 2005: 170.

[21] McCully and Hilles, 2005: 182.

> (C4) There are two constraints on alliteration within this structure: (a) a weak position within a weak position can never alliterate, and (b) alliteration migrates to the strongest positions within each line.

Note that lifts must be realized by a stressed heavy syllable (like *break* in Modern English) or by two light syllables the first of which is stressed (like *pretty* in Modern English); metrists term the latter *resolution*.[22] Dips must be realized by a single unstressed syllable or by between two and four unstressed syllables termed *expanded dips*. Only one of the two dips in any half-line may be expanded in this way.[23] These constraints are capable of generating five types of line analogous to the Sievers types, and they can account for the half-line patterns that never occur.[24] McCully and Hilles round off their analysis by observing:[25]

> However tricky or controversial [our account of OE metrics may be], it's a salutary thought to remember that an unlettered animal husbandman from Whitby, living towards the end of the 7th century, mastered the principles and constraints of OE verse in a single night.

In summary, there are five important points to be taken from the above examination of OE meter that have a bearing on the main focus of this volume. They are: (1) OE poets counted not syllables but beats and offbeats (lifts and dips); (2) they employed a four-beat structure that has clear parallels with some Modern English meters; (3) they embellished some of those beats with an alliterative pattern; (4) they gave their lines rhythmic variety by varying the size of dips; (5) they based their versifying upon the rhythms of the language itself.

Middle English Alliterative meter

William of Normandy seized the English Crown in 1066; the Normans were Vikings who had adopted the language and culture of France. For William that culture was cavalry, castles and Catholicism, and with those three he maintained his rule. Thus it was that from 1066 to 1362 French was the language of the English State, Latin the language of the Church, and English the language that the common people spoke at home. Large numbers of the Anglo-Danish population perished when they resisted William's rule, and many of its former rulers and landowners were dispossessed.[26] William eventually replaced almost the entire

---

[22] McCully and Hilles, 2005: 166–68.

[23] McCully and Hilles, 2005: 173.

[24] McCully and Hilles, 2005: 174–75.

[25] McCully and Hilles, 2005: 183. This refers to the story of Caedmon's inspiration told by Bede and related on pp. 8–10 of the volume.

[26] For the impact of the Norman Conquest, see Davies, 1999: 237–38.

upper stratum of English society by French immigrants, and with these new lords came thousands of French retainers and tradesmen, men like Geoffrey Chaucer's ancestor, whose family name (*Chausseur*) reflected its origin in cobbling.[27]

It clearly benefited both the rulers and the ruled to become bilingual to some extent. Even at the lowest level in society the thousands of English slaves who labored to build castles and cathedrals needed to understand the instructions of French architects and masons. Their masters, like the British of the Indian Raj, could only gain from knowing something of the language in which the next uprising was being planned. For the English language to have gained so many French words, L1 French speakers must have spoken to L1 English speakers, and the listeners must have known what the words meant.

During the period of French ascendancy OE became Middle English (ME): the most obvious differences between the two were the loss of inflections (most of which were reduced to schwa as in French) and the absorption of large numbers of French words.[28] What ME retained was a basically Germanic grammar, a readiness to form new compounds, and its strong word stress. In the thirteenth century a number of written texts in this new language appeared, some of which have survived, and in the fourteenth English was given new impetus by a disaster. The Black Death arrived in England in 1348 and wiped out a large proportion of the population.[29] As a result, vast number of posts formerly held by L1 French speakers became available, posts for which there were no French candidates, because the Black Death had created even more vacancies in France. L1 English speakers stepped into the breach, and they prospered, which led to the recognition of English as a second official language in 1362.[30]

Works in OE continued to be copied in England until late in the twelfth century; the most important of the surviving texts are the sermons of Ælfric (b. c. 955–d. c. 1010), and the long poem *Brut* by Laȝamon ("Lawman"), who employed a deliberately archaic diction in the poem, which dates from just before or soon after 1216.[31] By the time that Laȝamon wrote, however, the first poems had appeared in ME that reflected contemporary speech. These all departed from the alliterative tradition and reflected a great deal of French influence, and I shall examine the most important from a metrical point of view later in this

[27] Most of the immigrants came from Normandy in the eleventh and early twelfth centuries, and from Anjou in the late twelfth; when the Plantagenets lost almost all their French lands in the early thirteenth, many of their supporters made their way to England. See Davies, 1999: 304–05.

[28] See Barber, 1993: 134–35.

[29] See Davies, 1999: 356–57.

[30] See Davies, 1999: 361–63.

[31] For Aelfric's *Lives of the Saints*, see Skeat, 1881, and the website with Aelfric's text; for Laȝamon's *Brut,* see Allen, 1992; for Laȝamon's skill in the use of both rhyme and alliteration, see Allen, 2002.

chapter. In continuation of the story of alliterative verse, it enjoyed a remarkable revival in the fourteenth century, when some poets in areas distant from London began versifying in something like the OE manner.[32] They may have been influenced by the survival of alliterative verse based on beats in popular drama.[33]

Most of the poets employing this new alliterative meter wrote in the dialects of the North and West of England, but one Southern poet, whose name was probably William Langland, employed it in a more Southerly variety of English. Langland, a poor minor cleric who was a contemporary of Chaucer, seems to have been a native of somewhere West of Oxford. He wrote (and rewrote) his poem *Piers the Plowman* as a long religious allegory. Its design's resemblance to that of OE alliterative verse is clear from its opening lines:[34]

(5) In a somer seson • whan soft was the sonne,
(6) I shope me in shroudes • as I a shepe were,

("On a summer day when the sun was warm I draped myself in cloths like a sheep.")

This meter differs from that of *Beowulf* in a number of ways; first there is a less disciplined use of alliteration. Many lines are like (5) in having their fourth primary stress alliterate; many lines have an extra alliteration; more intricate patterns of alliteration are often woven between lines; and intervals between stress peaks often contain four syllables.[35]

The author of these lines did not especially favor the six most common rhythmic patterns that reference theory identifies as dominating the older form, but he does seem to have done something else that is equally interesting. He favored lines ending in the accentual pattern: s w w s (+ w in most lines, if we assume that any final schwa is pronounced). The whole poem shows a preference for this close, and I shall term this feature the *favored cadence*, because it is also a feature of other ME alliterative poems.[36] Its role in shorter lines will be discussed

[32] For the fourteenth century alliterative revival, see Turville-Petre, 1977. The question of whether there was continuity between OE and ME alliterative versifying polarizes opinion among modern scholars, but it seems likely that more OE texts were available in the twelfth and thirteenth centuries than have survived until today; see Minkova, 2009: 210.

[33] Between the thirteenth and sixteenth centuries the tradesmen of towns in the North and Midlands staged mystery plays at the time of Corpus Christi, and the texts of some of these plays (from four towns) have survived; see Beadle and King, 1984.

[34] For the text of *Piers the Plowman*, see Skeat, 1869.

[35] For the size and accentual configuration of intervals in the ME meter, see Andrew and Waldron, 1987: 47.

[36] See Duggan, 1986.

in the next section, but another alliterative long-line poem will show that this is not just one poet's stylistic preference.

This favored cadence appears even more strongly at the opening of *Sir Gawain and the Green Knight*, a long poem found in a single late-fourteenth-century witness from the North-West of England. The language is the dialect of that region, and contrasts with the language of Langland's poem, which is a curious mixture of Southern and Midland dialects. *Sir Gawain* begins:[37]

(7) Siþen þe sege and þe assaut • watz sesed at Troye
(8) Þe borȝ brittened and brent • to brondez and askez,
(9) Þe tulk þat þe trammes • of tresoun þer wroȝt
(10) Watz tried for his tricherie, • þe trewest on erthe.

("After the siege and assault on Troy, the town was destroyed and burnt to charcoal and ashes; the man who plotted the treason that took place there was tried for his treachery, the truest on earth.")

The favored cadence is, of course, the one that closes Latin dactylic hexameters, and this is probably a coincidence; I have chosen a passage with this cadence throughout, but it occurs in only about half the total lines in the poem, as I shall show later in this section. Note that the a-verses of (7) and (8) have a third beat and alliteration.

The poet who wrote *Sir Gawain*, like many of his contemporaries, employed this meter in long strophes that closed with shorter, rhyming lines. These formed what is known as a *bob and wheel*, and the first strophe of *Sir Gawain* closes as follows (lines 14–19):[38]

(11) On mony bonkkes ful brode • Bretayn he settez
(12) With wynne
(13) Where werre and wrake and wonder
(14) Bi syþes hatz wont þerinne
(15) And oft boþe blysse and blunder
(16) Ful skete hatz skyfted synne.

("He settled with joy on the broad shores of Britain, where war and destruction and mishap have often since found a home, and where both happiness and folly have quickly led to sin.")

The *bob* (12) is a line with a single beat (rhymed a), and the *wheel* (13–16) a quatrain of three-beat lines (rhymed baba). Note that, while the rhymes are usually

[37] See Andrew and Waldron, 1987: 207–300. The most recent edition of the poems of the *Gawain* poet is that of Putter and Stokes, 2014.

[38] For *bob and wheel*, see Schipper, 1910: 191 and 281.

precise, some of the alliterations (such as *s-* with *sk-*) do not meet the strict standards of OE meter.

Donka Minkova offers an optimality-theory-based analysis of the ME alliterative long line that adds logical rigor to the idea of a favored cadence.[39] First, she proposes the hierarchical structure shown in Figure 4 below for the verse design:

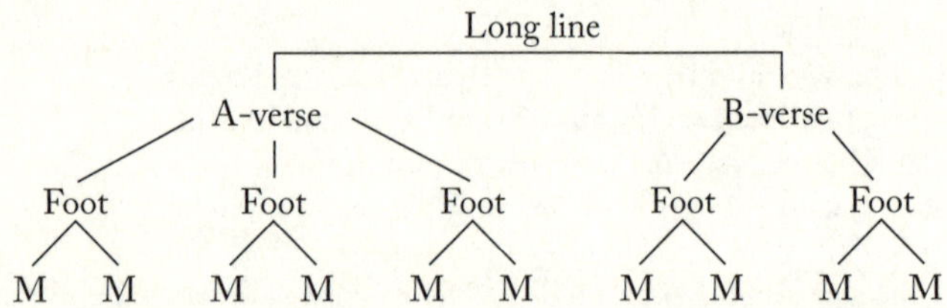

Fig. 4: Hierarchical Structure of ME Alliterative Long Line

In this structure lines and half-lines are left-strong but feet are right-strong; note that the third foot in the a-verse is optional and no b-verses are extended in this way.

The constituents of feet ('M' in Minkova's notation) are rises and dips: a rise must be a single stressed syllable (S), while dips may consist of a single unstressed syllable (notated w), or of two or three unstressed syllables (notated W); a line may also end in an optional unstressed syllable (notated ‹ ›). Only the b-verse is strictly regulated: it must contain two S constituents, and must not contain two w or two W constituents. This means that only four types of line are found; I list them in Figure 5 below, together with an example from *Sir Gawain* and the range of percentages (rounded) found by different editors in different poems.

Type	*Sir Gawain*	*(line)*	*range*
(a) w S W S	þat godly hym gret	(842)	46–59%
(b) S W S ‹ ›	gered in grene	(179)	7–19%
(c) W S w S ‹ ›	of þy grete words	(325)	5–17%
(d) W S S ‹ ›	with a brod egge	(212)	6–21%

Fig. 5: Types of B-verse

Optimality theory accounts for these types by hypothesizing a series of ranked constraints. The highest ranking of these disallows anything other than a single stressed syllable from occupying S positions, and every type of line observes this. In contrast, the constraint on anything other than a single syllable occupying weak positions is low ranking because it is violated in all four types. Other

[39] See Minkova, 2009.

constraints disallow w + w, or W + W, in the b-verse, or two adjacent S positions (violated only in (d)), or unfilled positions (violated in (b) and (d)).

The most recent analysis of ME alliterative meter is that of Ad Putter and Myra Stokes in their edition of the *Gawain* poet's works.[40] Although they do not describe the meter in terms of optimality theory, they reach the same conclusions as Minkova. They also note that when the a-verse contains only two lifts both dips must be extended beyond a single syllable.[41] This ensures that ME alliterative lines, like those of Latin elegiac couplets and English common measure, have a longer, more variable element, followed by a shorter, more strictly regulated, one. There can be no doubt that presenting a cogent argument or a gripping narrative in the ME meter called for skillful crafting.

The subtleties of this verse design, often hidden by copying errors, were lost in the steady advance of meters based on other principles, but Northern English and Scottish poets continued to compose this type of strophic verse, with lines of different lengths and both rhyme and alliteration, until the beginning of the sixteenth century.[42] The most popular design excluded the bob and divided the strophe into an eight-line *stanza* and a five- (occasionally six-) line *cauda*.[43] Chaucer clearly knew of this type of verse, because he refers to it, somewhat disparagingly, in *PP* (40–44), where the parson says:

(17) I wol ful fayn, at Cristes reverence,
(18) Do yow plesaunce leefful, as I kan.
(19) But trusteth wel, I am a Southren man,
(20) I kan nat geeste 'rum, ram, ruf,' by lettre,
(21) Ne, God woot, rym holde I but litel bettre;

("I will gladly, out of respect for Christ, amuse you as honestly as I can. But please accept that I am a Southerner, so cannot craft alliterative verse; and, God knows, I hold rhyme but little better.")

Chaucer here employs the derogatory Southern term *rum, ram, ruf* for Northern verse, but the parson is equally dismissive of rhymed verse, because he regards poetry itself as a trivial diversion from the grim business of life and death. The word *geeste* in example (20), however, implies that composing in the Northern manner required skill. Its many complex features, a powerful rhythm, alliteration, rhyme, varying line lengths, and accentual cadences, make this mode of versifying well worthy of our respect.

---

[40] See Putter and Stokes, 2014: xxi–xxviii.

[41] See Putter and Stokes, 2014: xxvii.

[42] For the later use of these verse and strophe designs, see Amours, 1897.

[43] For analyses of strophe design in medieval alliterative verse, see Fein, 2000 and Kennedy, 2000b.

By the sixteenth century this type of verse had evolved into a more regular form known as *tumbling verse.*[44] Over the intervening period the alliterations became fewer, the rhymes more salient, and the intervals between the four beats mostly contained two syllables. This gave the lines a prevailing triple-time rhythm that was far from the natural rhythm of English speech (which contains more duple time). The rhythm of tumbling verse is perhaps too distinctive and mechanical, and in large doses it can distract the reader from the lines' content. Nevertheless, Spenser employed it in his *Shepheardes Calender* to demonstrate his versatility, and James Hogg used it in several poems to flaunt his Scottish credentials.[45]

Versifying in Anglo-Norman

The alternative to 'rum, ram, ruf' for the poets of medieval England was verse that replaced alliteration with rhyme and attempted to count syllables in the French manner. A great deal of French verse composed in England in the 300 years following the Norman Conquest has survived. Most of these verse texts are in the variety of French that is known as *Anglo-Norman* (AN) or *Insular French.*[46] AN developed from the dialect of Normandy, which is still spoken today in the Channel Islands. The difference between AN, the French of Stratford-atte-Bowe, and Francien, the French of Paris, was as great as that between any two dialects of ME. Francien became the language of the English court on the accession of Henry II in 1154, and as a royal servant Chaucer spoke Francien; his friend Gower as an English landowner spoke AN.

Many AN poems were composed and copied in the religious houses: Chaucer's reference to Stratford-atte-Bowe is to St Leonard's nunnery, which was a daughter house of the great Abbey of nearby Barking, an institution noted for the many manuscripts it produced and for having among its abbesses two English queens and the sister of a saint.[47] The genres in which the religious houses specialized were Saints' Lives and heroic Christian narratives, but by the thirteenth century political songs and satires were also in circulation.[48] AN poets naturally

[44] For tumbling verse, see Schipper, 1910: 117–19, and Ker, 1898.

[45] Spenser employed tumbling verse for 'February,' 'May,' and 'September,' in *The Shepheardes Calender*; see McCabe, 1999: 40–127. James Hogg employed a similar meter in a number of minor poems; see Mack, 1970.

[46] For analyses of AN versification, see Vising, 1884 and Duffell, 2005.

[47] The Queens who governed Barking Abbey were both named Maud, and the Saint whose sister was abbess there was Thomas de Becket. St Leonard, whose shrine was at Stratford-atte-Bowe was the patron saint of the incarcerated; see the *House of Fame*, I, 117, and John Fyler's note in Benson, 1988: 979.

[48] See Aspin, 1953: 79–88 and 90–114.

followed the French practice of systematic rhyme and employed alliteration only as an occasional embellishment.

Since many people, both religious and lay, traveled between England and France in this period, and some manuscripts also moved between the two countries, we might expect other similarities between versification on the two sides of the Channel besides rhyme. Indeed, in some verse texts there are similarities, probably because their authors were in close contact with poets in France or had a much deeper knowledge of poems composed in that country.[49] Many AN texts, however, have three features that are found nowhere else in French poetry. These three features were the poet's choice of meter, the treatment of feminine lines, and the inaccuracy of syllable count. I shall examine each in turn.

AN poets largely ignored the fashions for the *vers de dix* and *alexandrin* that prevailed in France during this period and the many strophe designs that French poets devised. They almost always employed the same meter, regardless of genre: rhymed octosyllabic couplets.[50] Although the octosyllabic poems of the Norman poets Wace and Benoît de Saint Maure were very popular in England, this cannot explain the English concentration on one meter, because the earliest AN *octosyllabes* antedate both Norman poets. A much more likely explanation for the monopoly is that the *octosyllabe* had a clear affinity with the OE alliterative meter: its structure is open to interpretation as four beats and four offbeats. This is the simplest form of verse and is found everywhere from traditional children's rhymes to the lyrics of modern rap music.[51]

The second difference between Insular French versifying and that of France itself is that many AN poets seem to have been unable to count syllables by ear. They give their feminine lines seven syllables instead of eight as if they were counting Latin syllables on the page.[52] This anti-rhythmic mode of counting was also a feature of some medieval Portuguese verse (and of course of modern syllabic verse, such as that of Marianne Moore), and it suggests that these AN poets were counting by eye and not by ear.[53] Since English verse had traditionally ignored syllable count and its folk verse was based on beats, it would not be surprising if some bilingual poets whose L1 was English were confused by the French practice.

---

[49] One such poet (who was among the most scrupulous in counting syllables) wrote, 'Un faus françeis sai d'Angleterre'; see Legge, 1963: 63.

[50] See Legge, 1963: 15.

[51] See Burling, 1966: passim and Attridge, 1982: 94–96.

[52] Syllables are counted anti-rhythmically in almost half of the poems in Aspin's selection of AN political songs; see Duffell, 2008a: 77.

[53] Note that anti-rhythmic counting, which includes line-final post-tonic syllables in the count, is not the same as *orthographic counting*, which would treat the word *Leicester* as three syllables. So prevalent are lapses into anti-rhythmic counting in early Hispanic verse texts that Spanish metrists have hypothesised what they term the *ley de Mussafia* to account for it; see Duffell, 2007: 37.

The third unique feature of verse texts in AN is that in many poems a high proportion of lines do not contain eight syllables by any method of counting: in these poems line length varies from six syllables to nine according to the French definition. Since, as noted in Chapter 4, a regular syllable count is an essential ingredient of French poetic rhythm, this presents metrists with a problem. In 1884, Johan Vising studied the chronology of this irregularity and concluded that it varied significantly by century: it is present in 42 percent of AN poems composed in the twelfth century, 93 percent of those composed in the thirteenth, and 100 percent of those composed in the fourteenth.[54] This could be the result of a rising proportion of manuscript copyists having English as their mother tongue, but it certainly shows that by 1300 syllabic irregularity was widely accepted.

The syllabic irregularity is illustrated below by three lines from the *Lament for King Edward II*, which dates from soon after 1327; the line numbers are given in parentheses.[55]

(22) En temps d'yver moy **survygnt** damage (1)
(23) **Terrien amur** tost **esteint** (11)
(24) **Mainte**nant santz **delay** (65)

("In the winter time harm befell me;" "Worldly love lasts so long;" "Now without delay.")

Example (22) has nine syllables, (23) has seven, and (24) has six. Duffell, 2005 shows that approximately 43 percent of the largely octosyllabic lines in three AN political poems have other than eight syllables.[56] Vising dismissed the possibility that scribal error was responsible for the irregularity of AN octosyllabics after a careful comparison of copying errors in works composed on both sides of the Channel.[57] Instead he argued that the irregularity of AN verse texts, like the grammatical and phonological infelicities of the language, resulted from the ignorance and carelessness of AN versifiers.[58] But the tolerance of alternative grammatical forms and phonological variants in a language is something very

---

[54] See Vising, 1884: 68–91.

[55] The sample of 300 lines consisted of the *Lament* plus two other political ballads: *Thomas Turberville*, which can be dated to around 1296, and the *Elegy on King Edward I*, which dates from soon after 1307. Some 43 percent of the sample's lines had other than eight syllables.

[56] See Duffell, 2005: 113–17.

[57] See Vising, 1884: 28 and 145; for copying errors in French scriptoria, see Duffell, 2003: 113–114.

[58] See Vising, 1884: 53.

different from ignoring rhythm or being unable to count. The AN political songs do not lack wit, nor the AN religious poems knowledge of writ or doctrine.[59]

If scribal error and authorial negligence are not responsible for the syllabic irregularity of AN verse texts, then there is a third, and far more credible, explanation for them. AN poets may have been counting beats, just as contemporary ME poets counted beats in their alliterative verse.[60] In examples (25) to (27) above I have used bold typeface and underlining to show that each of these lines contains four beats according to the ME way of counting. This regularity is found in all 300 lines of my AN sample, making them not failed *octosyllabes*, but successful four-beat dolniks. Fitzroy Pyle had first noted the accentual regularity of AN octosyllabics more than seventy years ago, noting ironically that this typically English meter was first pioneered in French.[61] But counting beats in this way is only possible if AN, unlike continental varieties of French, had strong word stress, and this has a bearing on the relationship between Gower's AN and Chaucer's ME versifying.

Rhymed Verse in Middle English

Two of the earliest surviving ME verse texts are the anonymous *Poema Morale*, which dates from c. 1170, and the *Ormulum* (named after its author Orm), which dates from c. 1190.[62] The language of the 400-line *Poema Morale* shows that it was composed in the South of England, while that of the 19,000-line *Ormulum* reveals its North-East Midlands provenance. Parts of the *Poema Morale* have survived in different manuscripts, while the *Ormulum* is preserved in a single, and singularly ugly, witness. The *Poema Morale* may be classed as a series of homilies suitable for inclusion in sermons, and the *Ormulum* as a series of sermons ready for delivery. The verse design they share is borrowed from medieval Latin: they are products of the generation immediately following that of Walter of Chatillon,

[59] Another of the AN political songs in Aspin's collection, *Against the King's Taxes*, shows the sophistication of the poet. This poem is in an adaptation of the Latin Goliardic meter: its first hemistichs are in AN, and its second in Latin, and to both the poet seems to have applied the English convention of anacrusis. As a result this cleverly adaptive, macaronic satire is one of the most syllabically irregular of all the AN poems. The use of anacrusis in *Against the King's Taxes* also suggests that AN poets may have been counting something other than syllables. See Vising, 1884: 53.

[60] This case is made in detail in Duffell, 2005: 113–17.

[61] See Pyle, 1935: 41–42.

[62] For the text of *Ormulum*, see Holt, 1878; for the *Poema Morale*, see the website noted in 'Works Cited.'

when Latin verse with prevailing accentual rhythms was being composed and read in most of the religious houses in Western Europe.[63]

The meter of the two poems, the *iambic septenarius*, which in the Classical period served mainly for dialogue in comedies, has fifteen syllables with a caesura after the eighth.[64] It is a strongly divided line, the first hemistich being an iambic tetrameter and the second an iambic trimeter (often with a feminine rhyme); some modern editors lay out the septenarius as one line with a caesura, some as a couplet. PT would describe its verse template as eight plus seven right-strong positions, therefore w^s w^s w^s w^s : w^s w^s w^s(w). The chief difference between the two ME poems is that the lines of the *Poema Morale* are in rhymed couplets, while *Ormulum* is unrhymed. Both poems show sporadic alliteration, which is rather more skillfully employed in the first.

The following examples (*Poema Morale*, 3–4, and *Ormulum*, 3,494–95) show the similarities between the two poets' versifying:

(25) Wel **long**[e] ich **hab**be child **ibon**   a **wor**de & a **de**de
(26) [ ] thah ich bo a **win**tre ald   to ʒung ich em on **re**de.
(27) He chǣs himm **so**ne **kin**nessmenn   all **swill**ke summ he **woll**de
(28) & whǣr he **woll**de **bo**renn ben   he chǣs all att hiss wille

("Too long I have been a child in both word and deed; although I am old in age, I am young in judgement.' 'He chose his own kinsmen, the exact family that he wanted, and a place of birth to suit himself.")

Both poets clearly used not only syllables with primary and secondary stress to represent beats, but also monosyllables of any type (for example, '&' in (25) and 'att' in (28)). The verse design of these poems is undoubtedly iambic, but headless lines like example (26) are not uncommon. Clearly, the authors of these two poems realized that ME had an affinity with medieval Latin that most varieties of French lacked: it was possible to create an accentual rhythm within lines by alternating peaks and troughs of stress. The frequency with which articles and other unstressed monosyllables occur before lexical words in English was probably what led them to make most of their lines iambic, and the result was something very close to stress-syllabic verse. By my calculation headless lines represent 19 percent of total in *Ormulum*, giving it a broadly similar level of rhythmic variety to poems in the Latin Goliardic meter, where 15 percent of lines are not trochaic.

The meter of these two early ME poems is still in use and it is termed *common measure*. Although it is convenient to attribute their meter to the influence of Medieval Latin versifying, it is difficult to understand how it could migrate from sermons to English folk verse. It seems much more credible that the migration

[63] For Goliardic meter, see Greene and Cushman, 2012: 574.

[64] See Gildersleeve and Lodge, 1953: 464–65.

was in the opposite direction, and that these two monks had oral, native folk measures as well as learned foreign ones as models. The problem with this hypothesis is that oral verse often goes unrecorded for centuries (in Homer's case at least four). Folk meters with the *Poema Morale*'s and *Ormulum*'s 4 + 3-beat structure are first witnessed in texts dating from the sixteenth century, but my guess is that they were a feature of oral verse for centuries before that. The content of the poem *Sir Patrick Spens* quoted in Chapter 2 certainly suggests that it dates from the thirteenth century. And the anonymous ballad entitled *The Death of Robin Hood* has only sixteenth-century witnesses, but its action takes place centuries earlier.[65]

I shall postpone discussion of three of the finest surviving ME (or Scots) rhymed poems until the next chapter, because I want to make a detailed comparison between their versification and that of Chaucer's shorter line. Nichole of Guildford's *The Owl and the Nightingale* (*O & N*) dates from around c. 1200, while the other two poems, the Gawain poet's *Pearl* and John Barbour's *Brus*, were composed in the late fourteenth century. In the course of that comparison I hope to establish how much iambic regularity was present in ME verse designs before Chaucer, and to what extent he was a metrical innovator in the shorter line of his earliest verse.

I shall therefore close this chapter by looking briefly at a poetic genre that Tarlinskaja used to help justify her case that most surviving ME rhymed verse is syllabically irregular.[66]

Middle English Metrical Romances

About eighty *metrical romances* have also survived from this period, tales of adventure told in strophes of the type Chaucer lampoons in *ST*, many of which contained tail-rhyme.[67] Their verse design, like that of the AN and ME political songs, is also less iambic than *Ormulum*'s, as can be seen in the poem *Guy of Warwick*, which dates from c. 1300.[68]

Guy of Warwick was based on an original in AN, and the longest version of the poem contains some 12,000 lines, in 12-line strophes rhymed aab ccb ddb eeb. The correct treatment of word-final schwa in this poem is, in fact, problematic, since many of its lines have eight syllables only if such a schwa is pronounced; for example:

---

65 For *The Death of Robin Hood*, see Graves, 1957: 118–25.

66 See Tarlinskaja, 1976: 255–57.

67 For tail rhyme, see Schipper, 1910: 277 and Gray, 1986: 149–50.

68 For the *Stanzaic Guy of Warwick*, see Wiggins, 2004; her text is also available on the website given in 'Works Cited.'

(29) To **Walling**forth **to**ke the way (26)
(30) He tok **alle** his **fa**ders lond (34)

("He made his way to Wallingford;" "He inherited all his father's land.")

Moreover, many of *Guy of Warwick*'s lines without such schwas are irregular in syllable count. For example, we find:

(31) As man [ ] most of might (9)
(32) [ ] **Bal**der bern was non in bi (10)
(33) He slough a dra**goun** in Nor**thhum**berlond (23)

("A man of enormous strength; none could match his bravery." "He slew a dragon in Northumberland.")

The first two of these lines have seven syllables and the third has ten, and the most reasonable assumption to make from this irregularity is that the poet was counting beats, not syllables, and that he set the size of offbeats at between zero and two syllables.

My analysis of *Guy of Warwick* supports Tarlinskaja's conclusion that ME metrical romances had a dolnik verse design, like that of the traditional English and Scottish ballads. Certainly, such a design would have had two advantages for versifiers in ME: the first was that counting only beats and leaving offbeats variable solved the problem created by some readers pronouncing word-final schwas and others deleting them. The second advantage was that ME speech had another ambivalent feature: readers might accentuate loan words like *beauty* and *honour* on either syllable, and dolnik meters could accommodate both. Thus in example (36) the first syllable of the word *dragoun* can be stressed providing the reader syncopates the next syllable, or manages a triple offbeat. The variability in the size of offbeats, which matched these variables in pronunciation, made the dolnik a perfect fit for the Middle English language.

Conclusion

As OE evolved into ME, and AN became divorced from Continental varieties of French, the poets of England adopted new modes of versifying, but they retained a traditional English preference for lines with four beats. In the fourteenth century, there was even a revival in the North West of England of the use of long lines with systematic alliteration. Yet, for the most part, the poets of England embraced rhyme and reduced the size of the intervals between the four beats so as to produce shorter lines. An overwhelming majority of these intervals contained a single syllable, giving most lines a duple-time rhythm. Such syllabic regularity as can be found in ME and AN came not from the timing of phrasal stresses, as in France, but by alternating syllables with and without word stress.

The syllabic and rhythmic irregularity of ME rhymed verse is only partly the result of copying errors. Poems contain systematic irregularity, too: the poets of England clung to the anacrusic principle; that is, opening offbeats are optional. Most lines have an offbeat before the first beat, but some lines do not, and those that do not have a trochaic rather than an iambic rhythm. A less frequent source of irregularity was allowing a line an initial or medial double offbeat. Nineteenth-century critics divided ME verse designs into *native English meters* and *foreign meters*, but modern critics see the similarities as well as the differences between them.[69]

What the majority of ME lines shared was four rhythmic beats; some ME poets used systematic alliteration and favored extended dips between those beats, some preferred rhyme and favored intervals of one syllable. Modern research has shown that the designs of both the longer alliterative line and the shorter rhymed one are more intricate and sophisticated than they at first appear. In this chapter, I have presented some of the modern research into the OE and ME long alliterative lines and into the approximately octosyllabic AN line, and in the next I shall look in more detail at the ME shorter rhymed line. This was the meter in which Chaucer chose to compose his earliest English verse, and I shall attempt to identify his contribution to its development.

---

[69] For use of the category *native meters*, see Schipper, 1910: 15–125; for "meters of the foreigner," see Lewis, 1898: passim.

6
Chaucer's Tetrameters

Marina Tarlinskaja introduced the term *four-ictic dolnik* from Russian metrics to describe the verse design of the shorter ME line of approximately eight syllables, and she included the first two poems analyzed in this chapter in that category. By her calculation only 70 percent of lines in *The Owl and the Nightingale* (*O & N*) and only 55 percent of the lines in *Pearl* have eight syllables to the final stress.[1] Tarlinskaya's scansion of these texts, however, discounted only those word-final schwas that immediately preceded a vowel, and subsequent research has confirmed that ME speakers deleted far more schwas than that, even at the date when the earlier of these two poems was composed (c. 1200).[2]

More recent writers such as Hoyt Duggan and Ruth Kennedy have challenged Tarlinskaja's conclusions and they argue that *O & N* and *Pearl* were far more regular than at first appears.[3] Duggan showed that copyists of ME verse texts were often prolific in their errors, and he argued that many of those errors made the lines more irregular.[4] Duggan's method was to take two witnesses of the same text and divide its lines into those that were the same in both manuscripts, and those that differed; he called the former 'authorial' lines and the latter 'scribal' lines.[5] Obviously, one, if not both, of the lines classified as 'scribal' must have contained a copying error, either in its text or its exemplar. When Duggan analyzed alliterative long lines in a poem with two witnesses, he found that in 99 percent of the 'authorial' lines the b-verse closed in one of the rhythmic patterns I listed in Chapter 5, whereas few 'scribal' lines did so. This he took to be strong evidence that the poet's design contained elements of which the scribes concerned were unaware.

More controversially, both Duggan and Kennedy extended this argument and applied it to one of the poems I have selected for analysis.[6] This is the poem

---

[1] See Tarlinskaja, 1976: 256.

[2] For schwa deletion before consonants in ME, see See Minkova, 1991 and Barber and Barber, 1991.

[3] See Duggan, 1986 and Kennedy, 1999.

[4] See Duggan, 1996: passim.

[5] For authorial and scribal lines, see Duggan and Turville Petre, 1989.

[6] See Kennedy, 1999.

Pearl, for which there can be no division into 'authorial' and 'scribal' lines because it has only one witness.[7] It is also difficult to apply this argument to another of my selected poems, *O & N*, since most of its irregularities appear in both surviving manuscripts.[8] The hypothesis that scribes produced most of the text's metrical irregularities is very reasonable in the case of the longer alliterative line, which most poets had abandoned by the fifteenth century, but by then the shorter line had become the iambic tetrameter, and errors in favor of regularization would surely have been more likely. Both *O & N* and *Pearl* are long poems, and making them regular would involve emending hundreds of lines in both poems, unaided by manuscript evidence. Editorial intervention on this scale is controversial because, to use Duggan's own metaphor, licensing two libertines doesn't necessarily restore virginity.

In this chapter I shall examine just how irregular these two poems are and what can be the causes of this apparent regularity. I shall then move on to discussing whether Chaucer or his Scottish contemporary John Barbour advanced the cause of iambic regularity in their shorter lines. The first of the four medieval verse texts analyzed in this chapter is *O & N*, the earliest surviving complete poem in ME: it was composed fairly early in the thirteenth century; the second is the anonymous *Pearl*, which has been dated as c. 1375; the third is John Barbour's *The Brus*, which was completed in 1376;[9] and the fourth is Chaucer's *The Book of the Duchess* (*BD*), which was composed in 1369 or shortly after. My sample of each work will be its first 300 lines.The metrical features examined will be: (1) the use of rhyme and alliteration, (2) the number and nature of the beats in the lines, (3) the size of the intervals between them, and (4) the total number syllables in the line. I shall quote individual lines from each work to illustrate key metrical features, and quantify my observations from samples. (Since the Cotton manuscript in the British Library is in two hands, I have taken a control sample of *O & N*'s last 300 lines to check whether they match the first 300 metrically or whether there is evidence for two different verse designs.)

The Owl and the Nightingale

J. A. W. Bennett noted that this poem had been described as "miraculous," and he argued that the poet "showed a delicate humour, a rich humanity, and a sensitivity to nature that amounted to genius."[10] *O & N* is an *altercatio* or debate that proceeds for almost 1800 lines and its author is generally thought to be the

7 For the text of *Pearl*, see Andrew and Waldron, 1988.

8 For the text of *The Owl and the Nightingale*, see Stanley, 1972.

9 For the text of Barbour's *Brus*, see Gray, 1935.

10 See Gray, 1986: 1.

Nichole of Guildford who adjudicates the debate.[11] The poet seems to have been resident in Dorset at the time of composition and the poem's dialect reflects its Southern English provenance.

O & N's strophe design is the rhymed couplet, and the majority of its line-end repetitions are *rimes simples* (the repetition of a syllable's nucleus plus any coda), but some are *rimes riches* (where the onset is also repeated).[12] This full repetition was greatly esteemed in France, but is too rich for modern English tastes; examples of it in *O & N* include 'lete / forlete' (lines 35–36), and 'bispel / spel' (127–28). Repetition of the same word but with a different meaning was also acceptable to some ME poets (for example, in Chaucer's 'seke' meaning *seek* and 'seke' meaning *sick* in *GP, 11–12*), but the nearest thing to it in my *O & N* sample is the curious rhyme of the same word with different scansions: 'war^{e}uore' with 'wareuore' (267–68).

O & N's rhymes are precise: their nuclei (plus any codas) are more than approximate, and 82 percent of them are of words ending in schwa, like *tale* and *nightingale* (3–4); masculine rhymes like 'smal / al' (73–74) account for 15 percent of total, and feminine rhymes for only 3 percent; only one of the feminine rhymes,'broþer / oþer' (117–18), does not involve verbal inflections. There is no rhyme of forms ending in schwa with schwa-less forms in my sample and this, together with the high proportion of rhymes in schwa, suggests that syllabification of word-final schwa was the poet's norm.

Apart from rhyme, the only metrical feature shared by 100 percent of *O & N*'s lines is four syllables that realize *beats* according to Attridge's rhythmic theory; these are mostly stressed syllables, but up to two beats in any line may be realized by unstressed monosyllables.[13] If we assume, with Tarlinskaja, that *O & N*'s author syllabified word-final schwas except before a vowel or diphthong (where they were elided, as in French verse), only 73 percent of lines in my sample contain exactly eight syllables.[14] This compares with Tarlinkskaja's figure of 70 percent in her 500-line sample, showing a difference that is not statistically significant.[15] But schwa deletion in ME was well under way in 1200 and Tarlinskaja's assumption is almost certainly incorrect.

There are two types of line in *O & N* that seem to have been systematically irregular, one with seven syllables and one with nine. The first is the *headless* line, which observes the anacrusic principle: that is, the line lacks an opening

[11] See Gray, 1986: 4.

[12] *Rime riche* (as in *main / demain*) is very common in modern French poetry but was the exception in medieval verse; see Kastner, 1903: 48–54.

[13] See Attridge, 1982: 164–68.

[14] This assumption is supported by the poet's use of rhyme, borrowed from France, and by the greater syllabic and accentual regularity that results from applying it in *O & N*. It is also the basic assumption for Chaucer's verse in Barber and Barber, 1990–1991.

[15] See Tarlinskaja, 1976: 256–57.

offbeat.[16] This not only produces seven syllables but also a trochaic rhythm, as can be seen from the following example:

(1) [ ] Þu art **lod**lich & un**cle**ne (91)

("You are loathsome and unclean.")

The second type of systematic irregularity is usually described as *epic caesura*, because of its similarity to the presence of an extrametrical syllable in early French *vers de dix*.[17] Rhythmically, the poet treats each half line as if it were a line, and this emphasizes that the ME line is not just a line of four beats, but one of 2 + 2 beats. Such lines have not so much a mixed rhythm as a rhythm of paired iambic dimeters. The following lines are possible examples of epic caesura in *O & N*:

(2) Riȝt swo ho **we**[ren] // i**peint** mid **wo**de (*O & N*, 76)
(3) Þe **niȝ**tingal[e] // bi**gon** þe **spe**che (13)

("Just as if he were painted with charcoal;" "The nightingale spoke first.")

I say 'possible examples' because they involve words that may have other scansions: *weren* has a doublet *were*, the schwa of which was usually deleted, and it could also be reduced to *wer'n* by syncope. And the final schwa of *niȝtingale* sometimes requires deletion to produce eight syllables in *O & N* (as in line 1711), and sometimes requires syllabification (as in line 1781).

This brings me to a major obstacle to correcting Tarlinskaja's 70 percent: *para-phonology* (alternative pronunciations of the same word) was very extensive in ME. In Modern English, alternative syllabifications are mostly of a few words with optional syncope, like *medicine*, and *feverish*, and *liquorish*, all of which are sometimes pronounced as two syllables and sometimes as three. ME, on the other hand, was a language in the process of far more changes, lexical, morphological, and phonological, and so a large number of ME words had *para-phones*. (I may be coining a new term here, but Duggan's term *monosyllabic doublets* describes only one common type of ME para-phonology, and a more inclusive term is required).[18]

[16] Headless lines are among the reasons for apparent irregularity in ME verse argued by Duggan, 1996: 228. In my scansions the symbol *[ ]* indicates a void position or implied offbeat and the subscript symbol $_{H}$ indicates hiatus between a final and an initial vowel. The symbols *[ ] //* indicate that a post-tonic syllable mid-line is not included in the count (epic caesura); for brevity I shall describe such lines as *divided lines*, because their mid-line post-tonic syllables are extrametrical (like those at line ends).

[17] For epic caesura, see Schipper, 1910: 145, and Duggan, 1996: 229–30.

[18] See Duggan, 1996: 225. The reader may be forgiven for guessing that a *monosyllabic doublet* was a medieval one-piece costume.

Accepting that some common words in ME could be pronounced either as disyllables or monosyllables would increase the number of lines in *O & N* that have eight syllables; for example, pronouncing *never* (287) and *oþer* (286 and 299) as *ne'er* and *o'er* gives these lines only eight syllables, even though these words must be counted as disyllables to make some other lines octosyllabic. A very common example of ME para-phonology is involved in other lines that do not at first sight seem to contain exactly eight syllables. There are ten lines in my sample from *O & N* that would become octosyllabic if their second- or third-person singular inflections (*-est* and *-eþ*) suffered syncope, as in the following examples:

(4) Þu fed^{e}st on hom a wel ful **fo**de (94)
(5) Of **li**ȝte nabb^{e}þ hi **non**^{e} **imunde** (252)

("You're bringing them up with foul habits;" "they don't like the light.")

In some lines, however, such an inflection requires syllabification to produce eight syllables. It would therefore appear that the poet sometimes counted such words as one syllable, for example, 'cuþ^{e}st' in 90, and sometimes as two, for example, '**þ**retest' in 83. Sometimes the orthography of the manuscript is a guide to whether such inflections should not be syllabified (by omitting the vowel), but more often this vowel is present.

Other examples of para-phonology in ME include the deletion of final schwas in very common disyllables even before a consonant. Thus in *O & N* deleting the final schwas of *hir*^{e} (70) and *on*^{e} (85 and 146) produces eight-syllable lines. Syncope also offers the opportunity to reduce many lines' count to eight syllables, for example, *sum*^{e}*re* (1), *o*þ^{e}*res* (9 and 11), *spet*^{en}, (39), and *e*ȝ^{e}*ne* (75). Moreover, the name *Alured* could be two syllables (235) or three (294), and the words *svik*^{e}*ldom* (163) / *svik*^{e}*dom* (167) and *sped*^{e}*stu* (169) seem to be disyallbic. A good case could be made for each of these scansions, and accepting them all would leave just three lines with redundant word-final schwas in my sample (62, 160, and 198), and reduce the number with nine syllables to just one (231).

Although some of the revised scansions I have proposed may be incorrect, it is clear that *O & N* is much more regular than is at first apparent. On closer inspection, therefore, the proportion of lines in my sample can be classified as in Figure 1 below. Here lines with epic caesura are labeled *8e*, headless lines are labeled *7h*, and the remaining lines are labeled ~8.

	Syllables			
	7h	*8*	*8e*	*~8*
% of lines	5	86	3	6

Fig. 1: Syllable Count in *O & N*

Included in the 6 percent of lines under the heading *~8* are lines where there appears to be an implied offbeat mid-line (for example, lines 100 and 136), and lines where eliding a word-final schwa would reduce the number of syllables to seven (for example, lines 17 and 92). The first shortfall may be due to scribal error, and the second to authorial forgetfulness.

The above statistics show that *O & N* is not as regular in syllable count as the French verse that English poets were imitating, but the poem has a property that French verse lacks, accentual regularity: both the 73 percent of lines that are superficially octosyllabic and the 86 percent that my analysis has offered as an alternative have an overwhelmingly duple-time rhythm. Therefore, only 3 percent of lines in my sample (other than headless lines) contain the strong syllable of a polysyllabic word in an odd-numbered position, including the following lines:

(6) Þar þo [vle] song **hire** **ti**de (26)
(7) [**Gret**ter^{e}] is þin heu^{e}d þan þu al (74)
(8) Ac þu [**þre**test] to **mi**ne fleshe (83)

("Where the owl kept her singing her hours;" "your head is bigger than the rest of you;' 'You threaten to do me bodily harm.")

Here I have bracketed the word in which this occurs to show that PT would explain (7) by the closure principle and (6) and (8) by the bracketing condition. There are alternative scansions to these three lines: deleting the final schwa of *hir^{e}* would restore regularity to (6), and applying syncope to **Grett**^{e}r^{e} in (7) and **þret**^{e}st in (8) would produce headless lines, if slightly clumsy ones.

Overall, my analysis supports Dutton's argument, at least for this poem: *O & N* is much more regular in syllable count than Tarlinskaja's statistics suggest. Close to 90 percent of *O & N*'s lines have eight syllables and an iambic rhythm. Most of the remainder are headless lines with a trochaic rhythm. The lines in my control sample (1497–1796) are within a few percentage points of these figures; the differences are not statistically significant, indicating a single author and a single verse design for the whole poem.

It is reasonable to conclude that Nichole of Guildford exploited the extensive para-phonology of ME in order to achieve a line with four beats at intervals of one syllable. The vast majority of *O & N*'s lines can be scanned as eight syllables with an iambic rhythm, while most of the remainder lack an initial offbeat and thus provide a trochaic rhythm as a source of variety. An even smaller number add to that variety by treating the four beats as two pairs of beats (epic caesura). The resulting verse design is best described as an 'iambic tetrameter with some traditional features.' My analysis of *O & N* shows that the poet's metrical intention was a prevailing duple-time rhythm rather than an invariable eight syllables, and that he achieved such a rhythm skilfully and efficiently. When its versification is taken into account, the poem shines even more clearly as a beacon to guide subsequent English poets.

Pearl

In Bennett's ranking of medieval poems, the 1212-line *Pearl* stood above the *Canterbury Tales* and below only Dante's *Commedia*; but then, one of Bennett's criteria was spiritual vision.[19] *Pearl*, which takes the same dream form as *Le Roman de la Rose* and many other medieval poems, tells how its narrator survives grief over a dead child (a lost pearl) and finds comfort in the prospect of heaven (a pearl of even greater price). It dates from a quarter of a century after the arrival of the Black Death in England (1347), and its subject was a pressing one to generations that had watched their children die.[20] *Pearl* is a work of great learning and artistic sophistication: besides its spiritual qualities, Bennett lauds the poem's "brilliance of surface, tightness of texture, complexity of construction, range of language, and freshness of metaphor,"[21] but he makes little comment on its meter.

Pearl contains 101 strophes, each consisting of 12 lines rhymed abab abab bcbc, an exacting strophe design that forced the poet to find six rhymes for many words and four rhymes for many others. The anonymous poet achieves this with the same skill that he turns phrases from the Vulgate into vivid Middle English, and brings together Holy Writ and everyday life. *Pearl*'s verse design, however, on first sight seems much less sophisticated, and since it is found in a unique manuscript the poem cannot be divided into what Hoyt Duggan terms 'authorial' and 'scribal' lines.[22] The scale of the syllabic irregularity in *Pearl*, however, is much greater than that found in *O & N*.

Although Richard Osberg based his analysis of the poem on syllabifying and eliding word-final schwa, Duggan argues against it on the on the evidence of *Pearl*'s rhymes.[23] The poet's rhymes, unlike Chaucer's and Gower's, sometimes ignore final schwa: 'not' (34) rhymes with 'spotte' (36), 'fonte' (170) with 'blunt' (176), 'prys' (193) with 'devyse' (199), and 'byseme' (310) with 'dem' (312). The language of *Pearl* is the North West Midlands dialect of ME, and it is possible that by 1375 some of its speakers deleted most, if not all, word-final schwas. We know that while many such schwas were still pronounced in the East Midland dialect, word-final schwa had all but disappeared from the speech of Scotland.[24] This points to an alternative way of counting *Pearl*'s syllables, one in which all word-final schwa are deleted. In my sample of 300 lines, 47 percent

[19] See Gray, 1986: 236.

[20] See Davies, 1999: 409–13.

[21] See Gray, 1986: 239.

[22] For a defense of the hypothesis that ME English texts contain "authorial lines" and "scribal lines," see Kennedy, 1999: 234–35.

[23] See Osberg, 1996: 150–74; for the counter argument see Duggan, 1996: 226.

[24] For an account of ME dialects and a linguistic map, see Barber, 1993: 137–40; for the overall progress of schwa deletion, see Minkova, 1987.

are octosyllabic on first sight if word-final schwa is deleted, but only 36 percent are this regular if such schwas are syllabified. I am not suggesting that either extreme was the poet's intention, but it indicates a balance between deletion and syllabification that I shall bear in mind in my analysis.

The 47 percent regularity is boosted to 61 percent when headless lines and lines with epic caesura are included as permissible variants of the regular line. Thus 7 percent of *Pearl*'s lines qualify as headless by virtue of having seven syllables and all their strong syllables in odd-numbered positions. They include the following lines:

(9) [ ] **Blo**mez blayke and blwe and rede (27)
(10) [ ] Py3t in perle, þat **pre**cios pyse (229)

("Flowers black and blue and red;" "decorated in pearl, that precious piece.")

And a further 7 percent can be classified as having epic caesura, including the following lines:

(11) Þe **gle**mande **glo**[ry] // þat of hem glent (70)
(12) I hoped þat **gost**[ly] // watz þat por**pose** (185)

("The gleaming glory that from them glinted;" "I hoped that the motive wasn't base.")

This figure of 61 percent regularity can be increased significantly only by assuming that the author is exploiting para-phonology on a far grander scale than *O & N*'s.

Most readers of English poetry are aware that some words are sometimes treated as two syllables and sometimes as one. The words concerned are mostly very common words, such as *prayer* and *heaven*, and their syllabification varies far more from poet to poet than it does within poems.[25] In order to maximize the number of octosyllables in *Pearl*, however, we have to assume both inconsistency and syllabic ambivalence in a very large number of words. This includes inflec-

[25] Thus George Herbert treats both these words as having two syllables in his poem *Prayer* (lines 1 and 11), while Ralph Hodgson treats '**hea**ven' as two syllables but 'prayer' as one in his poem *T'would Ring the Bells* (lines 1 and 6). In contrast, Milton treats *heaven* as one syllable throughout *Paradise Lost*, usually spelling it 'heav'n'; and, similarly, he spells *given* as 'giv'n.' But normally each poet makes a decision on the syllabification of these words and sticks to it in the crafting of any one poem. For Herbert's poem, see Gardner, 1972: 255–56, and for Hodgson's poem, see Gardner, 1972: 838. For Milton's varying treatment of 'heav'n' / 'heaven,' see *Paradise Regained*, I, 20, 78, and 81 (Leonard, 1998: 407–9).

tions in the declension of nouns, where final *-ez* and *-es* need sometimes to be syllabified and sometimes not; and in the conjugation of verbs final *-est*, *-eth*, *-ed*, and *-en* need to be ambivalent. Accepting such flexibility on these suffixes would bring the proportion of lines with eight syllables to a new total of 73 percent.

Counting word-final schwas whenever such a treatment would help regularize the line's count (but not otherwise) would increase the number of octosyllabic lines to 78 percent. Finally, applying syncope whenever it helped regularize would increase the number of octosyllabic lines in *Pearl* to 88 percent, comparable with the 86 percent given for *O & N* in Figure 2. But syncope would have to be applied to a much longer list of words in *Pearl*: a list that contains words of many different categories including *color, water, juel, lyttel, after, reken, dewyne, heven, spyryt, marvayl, emerad, sapher, mayden, lenger, heþen, coroun, paradys, byȝonde, eȝen, open, ryal,* and *another.*[26]

The foregoing analysis shows that massaging the lines of *Pearl* to produce eight syllables is a far bigger undertaking, and a less defensible procedure, than that of regularizing *O & N*. The scale on which para-phonology must be assumed is daunting, and it would have made performing *Pearl* aloud to an audience a nightmare experience. In order to give lines so packed with para-phones a regular rhythmic delivery, performers would need to rehearse them carefully, because they would not know how to pronounce the words at the beginning of each line until they had reached its end. Additionally, the proportion of lines requiring this effort is at least 27 percent because many of the headless lines and lines with epic caesura are equally unpredictable.

In their recent edition Putter and Stokes describe the meter of *Pearl* as an iambic tetrameter, thereby supporting Duggan and Kennedy.[27] Putter and Stokes base their conclusion on the factors I have discussed above: extensive para-phonology, many syncopes, and a number of headless lines and epic caesuras. They do however add one rider: "Since English is stress-timed . . . the pulse is not affected by the inclusion of more than one unstressed syllable in the 'dips' between the stresses. This in fact happens less often than might appear." Clearly this rider invites Occam's razor: if the pulse of the lines isn't affected by double offbeats then all the syncopes and other devices I have examined are unnecessary.

In addition, if the double offbeats in *Pearl* are many, then the meter is better described as Tarlinskaja's four-ictic dolnik with a constraint against stress clash. *Pearl*, however, has another feature that distinguishes it from *O & N*: its beats are marked by (unsystematic) alliteration. It runs through almost all the examples I have given, and some measure of its extent can be given by comparing the average number of alliterating beats per line in four English poems. This comparison appears in Figure 2 below:

[26] Some of these examples of syncope are more credible than others; see Minkova, 2009.

[27] See Putter and Stokes, 2014: 7.

Beowulf: 2.34	*O & N:* 0.47
Guy of Warwick: 0.65	*Pearl:* 2.18

Fig. 2: Alliteration Rate of Four Poems

Pearl and *Sir Gawain and the Green Knight* can thus be seen as part of the same movement to revive traditional modes of versifying; and if, as we believe, the same poet composed both poems, then he had considerable experience in managing double offbeats to produce a complex and attractive rhythm.

On balance, I prefer Tarlinskaja's description of *Pearl*'s verse design, although her scansion of ME texts overestimates the number of word-final schwas that should be syllabified. She divides English verse into three categories: *iambic* (95 percent of intervals contain exactly one syllable), *transitional* (80–95 percent), and *dolnik* (fewer than 80 percent).[28] My analysis shows that too much should not be read into her term *transitional*: the early dates of *Ormulum*, the *Poema Morale*, and *O & N* prove that it has little chronological justification. From the beginning of ME versifying some poets composed four-beat lines with regular duple-time rhythms and some did not.

Barbour's *Brus*

John Barbour (b. c. 1320–d. 1395) was a Scottish prelate who probably studied at both Paris and Oxford Universities and became archdeacon of Aberdeen's cathedral. He was a trusted royal adviser and composed the great patriotic poem *The Brus*, which tells the story of the First War of Scottish Independence.[29] Its centerpiece is the Battle of Bannockburn, where Robert the Bruce defeated the forces of the English King Edward in 1314. The poem's 13,000+ lines go on to cover the early years of the Stewart dynasty that produced Barbour's patron Robert II. *The Brus* dates from 1376 but has survived in only two manuscripts, copied by the same scribe a century later. A second poem that has survived in a manuscript of roughly the same date, *The Buik of Alexander*, has also been attributed to Barbour, but its iambic pentameters show clearly that it is a fifteenth century composition (see Chapter 10).[30] While there may have been some scribal interference with the text of *The Brus*, the poem's language and meter suggest that it was minimal. The strophe design of *The Brus* is the rhymed couplet, and most of its rhymes are precise. Barbour's verse design gives almost all the poem's lines eight schwa-deleted syllables, and most lines have a potential for an iambic deliv-

28 See Tarlinskaja, 1976: 257.

29 For the Anglo-Scottish Wars, see Davies, 1999: 318–23; for Robert II of Scotland, see Davies, 1999: 374–75.

30 For *The Buik Of Alexander*, see Mitchie, 1925.

ery, because their strong syllables usually fall in even-numbered positions. Once readers have become used to the spelling, *The Brus* strikes them as remarkably modern in outlook: the most famous passage of the poem (1, 225–40) prefigures the sentiments of John Quincy Adams or Martin Luther King centuries later, and it makes citizens of the USA want to run up a flag and salute.[31]

Barbour's language is simple, direct, and highly monosyllabic. It also eschews the artifice of alliteration; on average only 18 beats per 100 lines share an onset with another beat in the same line, a level I have found in random samples of Modern English prose (where units of approximately eight syllables can be measured as a control). Barbour also uses rather more enjambment between couplets than many medieval French poets, and this makes his language sound more like normal speech. His syntax flows as freely as his emotions.

Barbour's poem is syllabically very regular, the chief exception being that 7 percent of the lines are headless, like the following:

(13) [V] For that tyme wes pes and rest (80)
(14) [V] **'Schyr,'** said he, 'sa God me save (157)

("for that was a time of peace and ease;" "'Sir,' he said, 'as God may save me.'")

The 1 percent of lines in *The Brus* that lack a syllable elsewhere in the line are probably the result of copying errors, and they cry out for editorial emendation; for example:[32]

(15) Tret it and bryng {it?} till en**dyng** (35)
(16) Off **alkyn tym**^{e} {all} the mo**vence** (134)

("Deal with it and bring it to a close;" "'the events of every era.")

The 2 percent of lines with an extra syllable, on the other hand, are not so easy to regularize. For regularity 'never' and 'quhether' must be monosyllables and synizesis must be assumed between words like 'ony of.'

The same metrical ambivalence seems to apply to plurals and past participles in *The Brus* as is found in *Pearl*; for example, either 'landis' must be a monosyllable or 'renownyt' a disyllable in line 32, but not both. The syllabification of such suffixes varies from line to line; thus 'hangyt' seems to be one syllable in line 278,

[31] For the views on freedom (1840) of the USA's sixth president, see the website listed under Adams in 'Works Cited'; for Martin Luther King's 'I Have a Dream' speech (1963), see the website listed under King.

[32] Curly brackets { } in my scansions indicate a suggested editorial emendation of the text.

but 'makyt' two in line 284. Some lines in *The Brus*, however, are more difficult to regularize; for example, the following:

(17) Throu slycht that he ne mycht throu mais**tri** (112)
(18) To do the thing that he wes on set (300)

("Through deceit what he could not by skill;" "to do the thing that he was set on.")

Nevertheless, 90 percent of Barbour's lines have eight syllables, 7 percent are headless, and only 3 percent have a syllable too many or too few. Those figures suggest that his verse design was very similar to that of *O & N* and that the 3 percent of lines lacking eight syllables (other than those that are headless) may be copying errors.

Almost all Barbour's lines have masculine rhymes, if only because he rhymes 'fel**lone**' with 'na**tion**' (193–94), 'fo**ly**' with 'to be' (220–21), and 'thing' with 'lik**ing**' (225–26). It is difficult to speak with certainty of the rhythm of Barbour's lines: my observation, above, that it is iambic is based on the position in the line of clitic groups like 'to do' and 'the thing' in example (18): they almost invariably occupy odd-even positions, suggesting a w^s bracketing in the template. Many polysyllables, in contrast, seem to be accentually ambivalent, including '**Ro**bert' / 'Ro**bert**' and '**Scot**land' / 'Scot**land**.' The first of these words is a French borrowing and the second a compound, and Barbour, we must remember, was a graduate of the University of Paris. To Barbour, whose poem is very much in the mold of a French epic, its lines' eight syllables were probably more important than the stress pattern.

Despite these reservations, it is possible to detect what we may be termed inversions in *The Brus*: the following are examples of first-, second- and third-foot inversion respectively:

(19) **Stor**ys to rede are dela**ti**bill (1)
(20) And thar **doch**trys dis**pi**tusly (200)
(21) Lay **deso**lat **ef**tyr hys day (40)

("Stories are delightful to read;" "and their daughters disgracefully;" "lay desolate after his day.")

Clear examples of initial inversion in *The Brus*, such as (19), are very few, probably because headless lines offered Barbour a more striking change of rhythm. Many more inversions may lie hidden in the poem by the possibility of stress shift, which seems to have been much more acceptable in Middle Scots than in Modern English, where the Move X rule is of limited application.[33]

[33] For the limits of stress-shift in Modern English, see Hayes, 1995: 382–91

In conclusion, Barbour's poem is further evidence of how fourteenth-century poets in both England and Scotland crafted iambic tetrameters that retained some traditional features, which in Barbour's case are mostly headless lines. For what happened to those traditional features I need to look further South, to London. It is at this point that I can turn to the work of Barbour's English contemporaries, John Gower (b. 1330–d. 1408) and Geoffrey Chaucer (b. ?1340–d. 1400), and examine their contributions to the history of the iambic tetrameter.

Chaucer's *The Book of the Duchess*

Chaucer began versifying in English several years before the most likely date of composition of *Pearl* and *The Brus*, and I close this chapter with a metrical analysis of one of his earliest surviving poems in English, *BD*. This poem may, or may not, have been composed before Chaucer translated *Le Roman de la Rose* into English, but *BD* is a safer place for me to begin because there is some doubt as to whether the surviving *Romaunt of the Rose* is the one that Chaucer worked on. The duchess in *BD* was Blanche, John of Gaunt's first wife, who died in 1369. Since by 1372 there was a new duchess, to whom Chaucer's wife was very close, *BD*'s composition would have been most opportune between those dates. *BD* is certainly a product of Chaucer's youth, and Pearsall argues that this shows in the way that the author naively parades his learning.[34]

The strophe design of *BD* is the unpretentious rhymed couplet, very different from the elaborate twelve-line stanzas of *Pearl*. If, as Pearsall argues, Chaucer composed his decasyllabic poem *ABC* only after his visits to Italy, then all Chaucer's early poetry employs the strophe and verse designs that dominated versifying in England for 300 years after the Norman Conquest: rhymed couplets and approximate octosyllables.[35] At first sight, therefore, the young poet was metrically conservative and content to show what he could do on the same ground as many English poets (whether composing in AN or ME) had chosen before him. He was also following the example of French poets, who first turned to octosyllabic rhymed couplets for their narratives in the twelfth century, when they tired of the *vers de dix*, and when audiences began to prefer Occitan rhyme to French assonance.

Chaucer employed the couplet in his early short-line poems (*BD*, his contribution to *The Romaunt of the Rose*, and the *House of Fame*), and he returned to it in his later long-line works (*The Legend of Good Women* and *The Canterbury*

[34] For weaknesses in *BD* that Chaucer remedied in his later work, see Pearsall, 1992: 92.

[35] For the dating of the *ABC*, see Pearsall, 1992: 83–84. Laila Z. Gross, the editor of this poem in Benson, 1988, supports an earlier date on the grounds that Chaucer may have derived *ABC*'s decasyllables from Machaut's, but the radical difference between French and English decasyllables is demonstrated in Chapter 9 of the present volume.

Tales). His choice of short-line couplets for his translation of *Le Roman de la Rose*, which employs the same metrical features, was predictable; he probably continued to use the same strophe and verse design because both were in vogue, and because couplets were easy. The English language, with its left-strong nouns and adjectives, has fewer rhymes than right-strong French, as Chaucer bewailed in his *Complaint to Venus*;[36] but couplets are also easier on an audience whose members have to listen to hundreds of lines, and whose attention spans may well have slipped to two lines by the end of the performance.

Couplets at their simplest are *closed*, like the Latin elegiac couplet, and enjambment between couplets was rare in medieval French verse, so there were many models for narrative rhyming couplets, but not for open ones.[37] Chaucer, however, even from the first, was prepared to break with this end-stopped tradition. The following enjambments from *BD* (lines 902–5) are typical:[38]

(22) I have no wit that kan suffise >>
(23) To comprehende hir beaute.
(24) But thus moche dar I sayn, that she >>>>
(25) Was whit, rody, fressh, and lyvely hewed.

This passage suggests that Chaucer's verse design was neither perfectly iambic nor fully octosyllabic: in example (23) the final schwa of 'comprehende' needs to be syllabified before *h* if the line is to have eight syllables, and in (24) 'moche' requires schwa deletion before a consonant to the same end, while (25) has not only nine syllables but also five beats.

Another important point that emerges clearly from these lines is that Chaucer has rejected alliteration (perhaps as a grim fact of Northern life). Pearsall notes that Chaucer reserves alliteration for special occasions such as battle scenes (where I suspect a bit of verbal violence created valuable vibrations among an audience of largely Germanic extraction).[39] In *BD* there are many alliterative pairs, such 'leef nor looth' (8) and 'wel ye woot' (16), but no *tours de force* of onset repetition and the poem's alliteration rate is no higher than that in *The Brus*. Chaucer's tastes in this respect, like Barbour's, were more French than English.

---

[36] See *The Complaint of Venus*, lines 79–80: 'And eke to me it ys a gret penaunce / syth rym in Englissh hath such skarsete' (Benson, 1988: 649).

[37] For rare examples of enjambment between French couplets, see Woledge, 1961: 26 (from *Le Roman de Brut* by the Norman poet Wace), and 1961: 40 (from *Le Roman de Troie*, by Benôit de Sainte-Maure).

[38] I shall give no further translation of Chaucer's or Gower's lines in the East Midlands dialect of ME: as examples (22)–(25) in Chapter 6 demonstrate, this dialect gave birth to Modern English, and Benson, 1988 glosses words in it that have been lost or have radically changed in meaning.

[39] See Pearsall, 1992: 45.

A further aspect of French fashion in *BD*'s versification merits only brief comment. In *BD* Chaucer followed neither *O & N*'s poet, who favored feminine lines, nor John Barbour, who favored masculine ones. The ratios of masculine to feminine lines in my three samples (if line-final schwa is pronounced) is *O & N*: 15:85, *Brus*: 96:4, and *BD* 57:43. While the French vogue for alternating the two types of line had not yet developed, late-fourteenth-century French poets usually achieved the sort of balance between masculine and feminine lines found in *BD*. So, once again, Chaucer seems to have followed French models.

As in the case of *O & N*, employing the French convention for dealing with word-final schwas makes the largest number of *BD*'s lines octosyllabic. Since this is consistent with the results of Barber and Barber's research on the *Canterbury Tales*, it seems probable that Chaucer intended most of such schwas in *BD* to be syllabified before a consonant and elided before a vowel, diphthong, or *h*. Chaucer's versifying practice was thus somewhat behind the norm for schwa deletion in the East-Midlands speech of 1368. Since schwa deletion seems to be almost complete in *Pearl* and *The Brus*, the most appropriate comparison for *BD*'s syllable count is that of *O & N*.

The same conventional ME sources of syllabic irregularity can be found in *BD* as in *O & N*. Most of the lines in *BD* with seven syllables are headless lines, including the following:

(26) [ ] Such a **tem**pest gan to **rise** (70)
(27) [ ] That she had, this **no**ble wif (86)
(28) [ ] **Ju**no bad thow **shul**dest goon (187)

Most of those that are not headless (because their strong syllables fall in even-numbered positions) contain a word-final schwa that, if elided, would rob the of line eight syllables.

(29) I **hol**de$_{\text{H}}$ hit be a sick**nes**se (36)
(30) That **ma**de$_{\text{H}}$ hir to **sle**pe **so**ne (130)

Like example (23), this shows that the aspiration of *h* in native words precluded elision in the French manner.[40] The only seven-syllable line in my sample that is not headless is:

(31) No tre, ne noght [V] that ought was (158)

As a rare exception, this line may simply contain a scribal error: the word *elles* occurs two lines later and it is editorially tempting to insert the same word in this line.

[40] For the variation of aspiration in English according to social class, see Crystal, 2004: 411–12.

Many of *BD*'s lines that appear to have nine syllables can be attributed to the ME convention of epic caesura, including the following:

(32) And **shew**^{e} hir **short**[ly], // hit ys no nay (147)
(33) That ys hys **god**[desse] // I shal soo do (268)
(34) **Anon** her **her**[te] // be**gan** to **er**me (80)
(35) Hym thar not **ne**[de] // to **turn**en **of**te (256)

In (34) and (35) schwa deletion giving hert^{e} and ned^{e} are credible alternatives to epic caesura, and most of the remaining lines that appear to have nine syllables can be reduced in this way. Thus counting *ever*, *never*, and *even* as two syllables gives 2 percent of total lines a ninth syllable and pronouncing them 'ne'er,' 'e'er,' and 'ev'n' reduces the number of syllables to eight

Chaucer probably also pronounced the word *sorwe* as a monosyllable, since it occurs often in my sample and would always give the line nine syllables if disyllabic. As noted above, the suffix *-eth* should also be discounted, and *certes*, *whiles*, and *evil* seem as likely to be monosyllables as disyllables. These adjustments would leave just one hypermetric line in *BD*:

(36) For him, alas, she **lo**ved alder**best** (87)

Again, this may be a scribal error, and it is editorially tempting to substitute *best*^{e} for 'alderbest.' As it stands, the syllabification of the verbal suffix *-ed* would make this line an iambic pentameter; so perhaps the scribe had been copying too many of them.

There are some lines in my sample where the existence of an unelided schwa that disturbs the regularity of the syllable count cannot be accounted for by epic caesura. In the second part of their study Barber and Barber argued that many common words had final schwas that were often written, but never pronounced in the late-fourteenth-century East Midlands dialect, and that Chaucer's practice recognized this.[41] The number of lines with eight syllables in my *BD* sample would increase by 3 percent of total if *suche*, *sothe*, *beste*, *ofte*, *amydde*, *somme*, *there*, and *moche* were monosyllabic. An even bigger increase would result from a number of fairly common verbs having become irreversibly monosyllabic in the East-Midlands dialect by Chaucer's time. Some 6 percent of *BD*'s lines contain an extra schwa from the verbs *nede*, *love*, *made*, *wepte*, *wille*, *yeve*, *speke*, *dide*, *myghte*,

---

[41] For a detailed analysis of words where Chaucer seems never to have syllabified word-final schwa, see Barber and Barber, 1991. Word-final schwa deletion has turned most word-final *-es* into orthographic conventions. By Chaucer's time many word-final *-es* must have achieved this status, and Chaucer trusted his readers to identify them. Some writers use the terms *organic* and *inorganic -es* rather than *syllabic* and *orthographic*, but I have refrained from doing so because the word *organic* has acquired too many other meanings in twenty-first-century English.

make, and *mette*. Finally, a further 1 percent of total lines in my *BD* sample would have eight syllables if three apparently trisyllabic words were stressed on their first syllable and made disyllabic: *nature*, *renynge*, and *slepynge*.

Chaucer, unlike *Pearl*'s poet, is consistent in his syllabification of individual words, with only one exception in my *BD* sample, which occurs in the following lines.

(37) I may nat **sle**pe wel nygh noght (3)
(38) To slepe that ryght **upon** my book (274)

Apart from this exception, treating this list of common verbs as monosyllables leaves only one redundant word-final schwa in my sample, that in the following line:

(39) Til he com to the **der**ke va**le**ye (155)

The elision of the schwa of 'derke' would be very irregular, because such adjectival inflections were the last word-final schwas to disappear from English speech and the rhyme requires the scansion I have given for 'valeye.'[42]

The explanation of apparent irregularities given above means that *BD* compares with *O & N* in syllable count as in Figure 3 below:

	Syllables			
% of lines	*7h*	*8*	*8e*	*~8*
O&N	5	86	3	6
BD	8	86	4	2

Fig. 3: Syllable Count in *O & N* and *BD*

From these figures I would argue that the verse designs of *O & N* and *BD* were very similar: they were iambic tetrameters that retained some traditional features of English versifying. The great majority of lines are iambic but their designs allow headless and divided lines. Both these features offered valuable rhythmic contrasts: headless lines a strong one, and divided lines, with their epic caesura, a gentler one.

Because *BD* contains these features borrowed from folk verse, inversion plays only a very small part in adding rhythmic variety to its lines: by my calculation 2 percent of *BD*'s lines have initial inversion, 4 percent have inversion in the second foot, and 1 percent have inversion in the third. Examples of each are:

(40) **Whe**ther my lord be quyk or ded (121)
(41) Then **play**^{e} **ei**ther at ches or **ta**bles (51)

---

[42] See Minkova, 1990: passim.

(42) He **tak**[e] up <u>Seys</u> **bo**dy the <u>king</u> (142)

All three of these percentages for polysyllabic inversion are very low, as they are for the same feature in *O & N*, probably because the alternative sources of rhythmic variety in the ME four-beat line reduced the attraction of trochaic inversion, which is common line-initially in the iambic verse of Modern English poets.

Conclusion

My analysis of four ME poems' versification shows that three of the poets composed iambic tetrameters that retained some traditional features. The fourth, the *Pearl* poet, seems consciously to have cultivated a rhythmically less regular type of line with strong alliterative beats. Many of his lines are easy to perform as dolniks and difficult to perform as anything else. Nichole of Guildford, Barbour, and Chaucer, on the other hand, composed lines that were mostly octosyllabic and also iambic. But there is little evidence from *BD*'s versification that Chaucer was a radical innovator (other than in his freer use of enjambment); he may have been a little more careful in incorporating French-derived elements (such as rhyme and elision) into his practice, but he also observed the English convention of allowing both headless and divided lines. Barbour rejected the divided line, but found the headless line more difficult to renounce; in the next chapter I shall demonstrate how the headless line was eventually discarded, and also how the loss of such lines created a new problem for the English iambic tetrameter: the risk of rhythmic monotony.

7
Gower's Tetrameters

In the 1370s two poets began to experiment with new modes of versifying in England and in doing so they altered the history of English meter. This chapter will explore the links between the two men and compare their short-line verse.

Chaucer and Gower

English poets are rather like London buses: you wait ages for one and then two come along. The ivory stage of English poetry has featured a large number of double acts: Chaucer and Gower, Wyatt and Surrey, Sidney and Spenser, Shakespeare and Jonson, Milton and Marvell, Wordsworth and Coleridge, Keats and Shelley, Tennyson and Browning, Pound and Eliot. In some cases these pairs of poets were no more than rivals or admirers of one another's work, but in many there was real collaboration involved. Wyatt and Surrey traveled to France together in 1532 to seek out the sonnet; Sidney and Spenser worked together to establish the principles of stress-syllabic verse just before 1580; Wordsworth and Coleridge devised a joint program for poetry around 1798; and in 1922 Pound guided Eliot through his revision of *The Waste Land* and into free verse.[1] Much of the energy and innovation in English poetry seems to have derived from partnerships, but Pound and Eliot (both exiles) are notable exceptions to the individualism of American poetic genius. Poe and Longfellow were born within two years of one another; Whitman and Dickinson died within six years of one another; but we can only dream of what collaboration between either of these two pairs of poets might have produced.

In discussing the extent to which Chaucer's and Gower's versifying was interconnected, I shall have to make many references to their lives. For details and documents I shall rely upon the excellent biographies by Derek Pearsall and John Fisher, but I shall base my chronology on the former.[2] Some of my observations will be much less scientific than the work of these two authors: as professional literary biographers they must examine the evidence with care and be guarded in

[1] See Duffell, 2008a: 118–31, 164–67, and 195–201.

[2] Pearsall, 1992 and Fisher, 1964.

their judgments; but I shall sometimes point out coincidences between historical events and metrical features, and I shall leave the reader to judge whether the two add up to something more. Overall, I believe that there is a strong case that Chaucer influenced Gower's metrics and a much weaker one that that Gower influenced Chaucer's, but I also see signs that both these men's (very different) personalities were at work in the revolution that took place in English versifying during the closing years of the fourteenth century.

The two poets were undoubtedly close friends between 1377 and 1390, and probably for longer. When Chaucer traveled to Italy in 1378 he appointed Gower to be one of his executors, and each man dedicated his first major English poem to the other. From 1377, Gower's home in Southwark was a short ride from Chaucer's in Aldgate (a very short one for a diplomat who was prepared to ride to Italy on his master's business), and it would have been easy for the two men to make frequent contact. Professional collaboration between the two poets was clearly more than possible: it is difficult to imagine that they shielded what they were working on from one another's eyes. Collaboration must be suspected because the directions in which each was taking versifying were remarkably similar: they regularized both AN and ME octosyllabics, and they both experimented with deviant decasyllables, lines such as no French nor English poet had ever composed, and lines that deviated from the existing norms in parallel ways. Their reforms of AN and ME versifying were so similar as to suggest a program, rather like the one that Wordsworth and Coleridge followed more than 400 years later.[3] In this chapter, and again in Chapters 9 and 10, I shall give a detailed account of Chaucer's and Gower's crafting of lines to support this comparison.

First, however, I should like to discuss two things that I believe are related: the language in which each poet chose to compose, and the poet's personality. The mother tongue, or *L1*, of both poets was English, the new English (ME) that was packed with French words, but they also shared a first reading language, or *R1*, of French. There is more evidence in Chaucer's work than in Gower's that the poet had also read many English works, but their English reading would have been relegated to second place by the fact that English literature was at that time so meager, and French literature so much wider and deeper. Knowledge of that wealth of French literature is manifest in both poets' work, and it would be naive to assume that Chaucer wrote in English because his French wasn't good enough; when he became a page at a French-speaking court his career must have depended upon mastering that language.

We cannot be certain whether Chaucer began his poetic career by composing in French; given his position at court, the chances are high that as a young man he would have tried his hand at set French forms, such as the *ballade*. The poems of 'Ch' in the manuscript now in Pennsylvania may not be his, but he

[3] See the *Preface to Lyrical Ballads* (1802) in Gill, 1984: 594–615.

could well have composed poems like them.[4] Pearsall argues that Chaucer probably abandoned his only attempt at composing *terza rima* because he saw how much better Dante did it; the author of poems like those identified as by 'Ch' might equally have abandoned both courtly lyrics and versifying in French because he saw how much better Machaut did it.[5] By the time that he began *Troilus and Criseyde* Chaucer had seen his niche in literature: stories that imitated life; stories containing realistic characters; stories that invited comment both deep and comic. The mature Chaucer left declarations of love to his characters, where he could depict both pathos and bathos.

Nothing shows the new objectivity that Chaucer brought to medieval poetry more clearly than his treatment of the invocation that precedes Troilus's story. In the *Filostrato*, which was Chaucer's model, Boccaccio calls upon his *bella donna* to be his muse, and he addresses her with all the hyperbole customary in the courtly lyric; for example, the light that shines from her eyes will guide the poet like a star, and she will govern his mind and guide his hand in the enterprise of telling the story. Chaucer, however, although he translated much of the *Filostrato* word for word, invoked the fury Tisiphone (literally, 'the voice of fate') instead.[6] This is a far more appropriate choice of muse, given 'the double sorwe of Troilus,' but Chaucer went on to replace the romantic effusions of Boccaccio with the laconic statement:

(1) Ffor I, that God of Loues seruantz serue, (*TC*, 15–16)
(2) Ne dar to Love, for myn vnliklynesse.

These words, from a middle-aged man embroiled in a rape case, have a brutal sincerity that is almost entirely absent from the poetry of his time.

Paradoxically, 'moral' Gower never outgrew his taste for romantic hyperbole: he continued to compose courtly ballads until the end of the century, when he presented a volume of old ones (the *Cinkante balades*) to his royal master, and composed new ones (the *Traité*) for the bride of his old age.[7] Gower's 'morality,' his obsession with obedience to God and ordering the affairs of men, distances him from the modern reader. But, from the *Mirour de l'Omme* (begun c. 1375) to the *Confessio Amantis* (still being revised in the 1390s), Gower was fixated on the hierarchy and genealogy of sin, the classification of its cures, and the gulf between the way humans behaved and the way they should behave.[8] The obsessive

[4] Wimsatt, 1982.

[5] See Pearsall, 1992: 112

[6] Chaucer's 'goddesse of torment' was Tisiphone, daughter of Night and Acheron; see Wright, 1984: 688.

[7] For Gower's French and Latin works, see Macaulay, 1899 and 1901.

[8] All references to Gower's *Confesssio Amantis* in the present volume are to Peck, 1980.

personality that seems to underpin his work made him the ideal candidate to regularize AN and ME verse; what is more difficult to explain is why Chaucer, with his more tolerant temper, should have joined in that task. However, Chaucer had more models of regularity to inspire him—those of Italy as well as those of France.

Both Chaucer and Gower sought fame: the virtual immortality that poets enjoy as long as their work is read, and the expansion of ego they experience as their names and influence spread. Chaucer devoted his last major short-line poem to the subject of fame, and Gower clearly wanted the widest possible audience for his vital message. Gower's chosen route to poetic fame must have seemed the safe one at the time: writing in French, which was the language of several royal courts and had survived for 500 years, or in Latin, which was the language of the Western Church and had survived for two thousand. Chaucer took a riskier route: English had many more speakers and a larger literature than Cornish (for example), but both had been languages of an underclass until relatively recently.[9] Had the Plantagenets been able to consolidate their victories in the Hundred Years War and establish a giant Western European super-state, their official language would almost certainly have been French. Thus it was that only after the resounding success of Chaucer's *Troilus and Criseyde* did Gower decide to compose in the upstart language, English

Chaucer took greater risks in life as well as in language: traveling the continent in wartime and on at least one occasion getting involved in the action, was a much more hazardous lifestyle than property dealing and renovating a priory in England. The riskiest thing that Gower seems to have done in his whole life was to get married when he went blind, but his wife's story remains unwritten. Chaucer took greater risks with his subject matter, too: he showed powerful people at their worst (but without comment), and he could be as bawdy as Boccaccio in the *Decameron*, or Juan Ruiz in the Spanish *Libro de Buen Amor.*[10] Gower, in contrast, was ever mindful of his soul when he wrote on subjects like incest (which he found particularly fascinating). From their lives, their subject matter, and their choice of language a picture emerges of 'chancy Chaucer' and 'cautious Gower.'[11] To metrists this appears to have been a most productive combination.

---

[9] The Cornish language was declared "not officially extinct" by UNESCO in 2010, and the number of Cornish speakers is now growing; for a brief introduction to the language, see Smith and Hooper, 1972.

[10] For the *Libro de Buen Amor*, see Gybbon-Monypenny, 1988; for the *Decameron* see Wallace, 1991.

[11] Ironically, Chaucer's journey in 1366 to what is now Spain went unnoticed for centuries because a scribe made his name look like 'Chancer' in the records of the Kingdom of Navarre; see Pearsall, 1992: 51–53.

Chaucer's *House of Fame*

There was an interval of more than five years between Chaucer's composition of *BD* and *The House of Fame* (*HF*). In that interval Chaucer made his first journey to Italy, and also developed a close friendship with John Gower; certainly by 1378, when both *HF* and Gower's *Mirour de l'Omme* (*MO*) were completed, the two men were living across the river from one another in Aldgate and Southwark. Chaucer had begun work on *HF* c. 1375 and it shows the influence of his first Italian journey: the poem has even been described as an "imitation of Dante's Divine Comedy." This is unfair on both poets: Chaucer's unfinished 2,158 line poem is much lighter in weight, but has a comic genius and humanity that make a refreshing contrast to Dante's idealism and intensity. John Fyler's comments, however, that the two poems "have several interests in common," and that *HF* "is Chaucer's fullest exploration of the poet's position" are both very apposite.[12]

Once again Chaucer chose the rhymed couplet as *HF*'s strophe design and the poem was to be his last major work in the English shorter line. Chaucer must have long been aware that Francien verse was more polished and regular than any composed in ME or AN, but by 1375 he must also have known that the best Italian verse had harnessed syllabic regularity to a language with strong word stress and had ridden both to a triumphant conclusion. Just as Dante employed Virgil as a guide in his quest for fame, so Chaucer used both poets in *HF* to help him decide whether he wanted to be a poet, rather than just a courtier. It is even possible that Chaucer left *HF* unfinished because, although his choice was the poet's role, he had discovered a better meter.

I shall begin by comparing the verse design of *HF* with that of *BD*. If I employ the same methods of counting that produced the statistics given for *BD* in Chapter 6, then 84 percent of *HF*'s lines contain eight syllables, and a further 13 percent contain seven with a trochaic rhythm that contrasts neatly with the iambs that prevail in the eight-syllable lines. On this basis 97 percent of *HF*'s lines can be classed as iambic tetrameters with some traditional features, compared to the revised figure for *BD* of 94 percent. Although the difference between 97 percent and 94 is barely significant on this size of sample (300), the number of apparently irregular lines in *HF* is far lower than in *BD* (16 percent versus 28 percent). Since I applied the same methods of reducing the apparent irregularity of the text to both poems, Chaucer may not have made his lines more regular, but he certainly made their regularity easier to recognize. This would surely have impressed readers, gratified performers, and delighted John Gower.

In *HF* Chaucer shunned the double offbeat but embraced the headless line; the latter can appear in any of three rhythmic contexts; the first is when the

[12] See John M. Fyler's introduction to *The House of Fame*, in Benson, 1988: 348.

headless line offers a rhythmic contrast with the previous line, trochees balancing iambs, as in:

(3) That hyt was **pitee** for to **here** (189)
(4) [ ] When hir **spirit** gan appere (190)
(5) Hys **fader ek**^{e}, and his mey**nee** (194)
(6) [ ] With hys **shippes** gan to **saylle** (195)

The second context is when consecutive headless lines have a cumulative effect, breaking up a long iambic passage, as in:

(7) [ ] And moo **ryche** taber**nacles** (123)
(8) [ ] And with **perre** moo **pynacles** (124)

The third context is when an isolated headless line rounds off a very long iambic passage, as in:

(9) "[ ] Hyt is not al gold that **glareth**" (272)

The difference between the 13 percent of headless lines in my *HF* sample and the 8 percent in my *BD* sample is highly significant statistically (to three standard errors), and there is no doubt that in the later poem such lines represent an important technical resource.

A possible explanation for this dramatic increase in the proportion of headless lines is that Chaucer was actively seeking more rhythmic variety in his shorter line. The trochaic headless lines offer the strongest possible counterpoint to the dominant iambic rhythm of the meter, and Chaucer seemed to want more of it as time went on.

In contrast, there is scant evidence in *HF* of divided lines: there are two lines in my sample with an extra syllable immediately following the second beat:

(10) Why this a **fan**[tome], // why **thes**^{e} oracles (11)
(11) I not; but **who**[so] // of **thes**^{e} miracles (12)

I have scanned these as divided lines, but both have alternative explanations: 'fantome' in (10) could become a monosyllable by syncope, and the syllables at the caesura in (11) could simply be merged by synizesis. On balance I prefer the epic caesura explanation: its use was so common in ME verse, including Chaucer's *BD.*, and 'fantome' makes a very ugly monosyllable. The two remaining candidates for epic caesura in my sample both involve the final schwa of a common word:

(12) But as I **slep**[te], // me **mett**^{e} I was (119)
(13) **Withoute dre**[de], // this ys no lye (292)

Both the words concerned could have become irreversibly monosyllabic by 1375, but I have counted them as having epic caesuras in my statistics.

One of the reasons why lines with redundant word-final schwas are few is that the frequency of elision has risen: in *BD* there are 24 elisions per 100 lines and in *HF* there are 30; the difference is just statistically significant (to two standard errors). From this we may conclude that Chaucer became more concerned to avoid syllabic ambiguity and the inconsistent performances it might produce. There are a few other lines in *HF* where word-final schwa needs to be deleted before a consonant in order to produce eight syllables, but they are almost all involve common words that Chaucer's readers might have recognized immediately as monosyllables despite their spelling, words like *moche*, *have*, *these*, and *oure*. The words 'dreme' (line 83), and 'sone' (160) are also likely to have been monosyllabic, and 'towardes' (196) can obviously be disyllabic.

Other than the candidates for epic caesura (examples (10) and (11 above), there are only three lines in my sample that could be credited with nine syllables. Two contain the third-person inflexion -eth; 'cometh' (line 71) and 'clepeth' (73) need to be monosyllabic to give the line eight syllables. Although 'longeth' (244) and 'knoweth' (290) need to be disyllabic to the same end, the analysis of four poems in Chapter 6 confirms Duggan's argument that such verb forms could be either one syllable or two. Only a very clumsy syncope, however, could reduce the following line to eight syllables:

(14) For to gret **fe**[ble]ness^{e} of her brayn (24)

It is possible that Chaucer deliberately crafted a metrically feeble line in imitation of the meaning, but 'feblenesse' is probably a scribal error for *feblesse*, which would give eight syllables.[13]

There are also two lines in my *HF* sample where a word-final schwa requires syllabification before *h* to give a total of eight syllables, which compares with fourteen similar examples in *O & N*. The two lines are:

(15) To **un**derstonde hyt a**ryght** (50)
(16) And ther he **shul**de his folk **fyn**de (237)

Again Chaucer seems to have been taking more care in employing the French elision convention than *O & N*'s poet, and both the examples in *HF* involve a Germanic word that would be aspirated by most people in 1375.

Most of the octosyllabic lines in *HF* have a clearly iambic rhythm: by my calculation only 1 percent of first feet contain polysyllabic inversions, as do 4

[13] Chaucer used the word 'feblesse' (from French) in *Troilus and Criseyde*, 2:863; see Davis, et al. 1979: 54; there is no entry for this word in the glossary of Benson, 1988.

percent of second feet, and 1 percent of third feet. Examples of inversion in each position are:

(17)	Eyther on **morwes** <u>or</u> on evenes	[1st-foot]	(4)
(18)	As yf **folkys** com**plexi**<u>ons</u>	[2nd-foot]	(21)
(19)	Ther <u>saugh</u> I <u>such</u> **tem**pest^e aryse	[3rd-foot]	(209)

The dearth of initial inversions probably results from the fact that headless lines offered Chaucer a more emphatic and more prolonged change of rhythm. In total, inversion is as common in *HF* as in *BD*, which is further evidence that Chaucer was not seeking to make his lines more iambic in this period.

In summary, the most important developments in Chaucer's later line are his greater use of headless lines and his severe reduction in divided ones. As a result *HF* has a more pronounced duple-time rhythm than any of the poems analyzed in Chapter 6, and the fact that one line in seven is headless ensures that the poem is not strictly iambic. Chaucer does seem to have gained greater mastery of his meter in the years between *BD* and *HF*: his handling of word-final schwa is more consistent and he takes more care to avoid double offbeats. But, like Barbour, Chaucer favored the abrupt change in rhythm that the headless line offered. Just across the river from Chaucer, however, John Gower was making his own attack on syllabic and rhythmic irregularity, and, remarkably, he was doing it in French.

Gower's *Mirour de l'Omme*

In order to quantify Gower's metrical experiments I shall use as control the *Roman de la Rose* (*RR*), the most famous medieval poem in *octosyllabes*, and as usual the first 300 lines will form my sample.[14] I examined this poem briefly in Chapter 4 and showed it to have no other accentual regulation than the final phrasal stress in position 8 of each line.[15] In summary, the rhythm of the French *octosyllabe*, is a series of stressed eighth syllables: today strong syllables within the line are not stressed, and in the thirteenth and fourteenth centuries the stress of such syllables was probably so weak in the French of France that it could easily be ignored by versifiers and their audiences. John Gower, however, composed in AN, which had stronger word stress, probably as a result of its contact with English; and so whether there are potential iambic rhythms in his lines remains to be shown.

[14] They are the work of the first of the poem's two authors, Guillaume de Lorris (fl. c. 1240).

[15] Chaucer translated these lines, probably in the late 1360s, in the text of the English *Romaunt of the Rose*. See the editor's comments in Benson, 1988: 686.

MO is a 32,000 line poem in French; its language is basically AN, but it contains many continental forms, doubtless influenced by the author's wide reading.[16] Gower chose French, not because it was his mother tongue, but because the language had status and, above all, was safe. French had endured for 500 years (and has now lasted a further 600): an author seeking lasting fame (and hoping to save future generations of souls) could do worse than write in French. In 1375, however, English must have seemed precarious, because for 300 years French words had been replacing English ones. French words like *color* had eclipsed English ones like *hue*; and the long word *beautiful* was about to consign the wonderful word *wlonk* to oblivion. Nor was it clear that English syntax and phonology would escape this transformation: adjectives were creeping behind nouns, educated people dropped their aitches, and the royal family were not the only people using the word *one* in imitation of the French *on* (from *om*, in imitation of the Old Germanic *mann*).[17]

In 1375 the tide of English (legal since 1362) was definitely coming in, but French was a safe haven, and Gower was a timorous soul; and in *MO* he detailed the many reasons why Christians should be afraid for their souls. In his next major work the *Vox clamantis* (written in Latin in case the last survivor should be the Pope) Gower's tone became apocalyptic, as he mistook civil unrest for the breakdown of civilization. Paradoxically, Gower's love of order probably led him to become a metrical innovator: I suspect that the untidiness of AN and ME versification was almost unbearable to a man who may have rebuilt a priory in order to be able to copy-edit the output of its scriptorium. The picture I have drawn of Gower as an obsessive is heavily dependent on my analysis of his versification, but the few details of his life that we know seem to point in the same direction. In this section I shall examine the first piece of metrical evidence.

Gower's strophe design for *MO* reveals an appetite for hard work: the poem is composed in 12-line stanzas rhymed aab aab bba bba. This meant that he had to find five other rhymes for every word he used line-finally, and so to construct nearly 3,000 strophes with this structure was in itself no mean feat. Gower was certainly up to the task, but it is what he did with the verse design of the *octosyllabe* in *MO* that is most remarkable: barely 6 percent of its lines contain a strong syllable in either position 3 or 5. Among those lines are found the following:[18]

---

[16] For a recent analysis of Gower's language, see Merrilees on the website given in 'Works Cited.'

[17] For the invasion of French vocabulary and other changes in ME, see Crystal, 2004: 145–62 and 222–48; for the French derivation and use of *on*, see Davau, Cohen, and Lallemand, 1972, 848. This use of *one* was permitted English commoners until the mid-twentieth century, but is now regarded as ungrammatical and a royal privilege; see Pearsall, 1998: 1295.

[18] Since the word *pecché* appears in *O & N* (line 841) with stress on the first syllable, it is possible that the apparent inversion in example (20) is an Anglicism.

(20) Le noun du pec**ché** soule**ment** [5 8e] (59)
(21) Des tous **an**gres espiri**tieux** [3 8e] (62)

("The name of sin alone;" "of all the spiritual angels.")

The remaining 94 percent of lines in my sample have either a strong syllable or a lexical monosyllable in position 4. Lines like the following, with a grammatical monosyllable in that position, are rare:

(22) En plour et en ghemissement [8^{e}] (180)

("In weeping and in groaning.")

The other peculiarity of Gower's versification is that, although his lines are otherwise meticulous in syllable count, the word *come* (Modern French *comme*) is always a monosyllable, indicating that its schwa had been so long deleted in AN that no reader would think of pronouncing it. The following examples (the first of which is an exception to Gower's norm of a strong syllable in position 4) demonstrate this peculiarity:

(23) Com[e] je vous seray devi**sant** [5^{e} 8^{e}] (238)
(24) Ensi com[*me*] je le vous ay dit [2^{e} 8^{e}] (265)

("As I shall be explaining;" "then, as have already told you.")

Note that in (24) Macaulay added the '*–me*' that I have bracketed. It seems reasonable to conclude from this, and from the evidence I discussed in Chapter 5, that by 1375 AN shared a number of features with ME, including selective schwa deletion and perceptible word stress.[19]

In summary, Gower's *octosyllabes* are stress-syllabic: they are iambic tetrameters like those found in ME rhymed verse, but without the English traditional features that divide the ME meter from the modern one. Because Gower was writing in French, with its own centuries-old tradition of strictly counted *octosyllabes*, both headless lines and epic caesuras were unthinkable. We cannot tell whether Chaucer and Gower ever discussed versifying at any of the meetings that led to the older poet becoming the younger poet's executor. But, if they did, it had no effect on the way the two poets versified—at least, not until Chaucer's second visit to Italy.

[19] See Duffell, 2005: 122.

Gower's *Confessio Amantis*

While Chaucer was translating the *Filostrato* into English Gower began berating in Latin the broken society of Ricardian England. The Peasants' Revolt didn't bring about the end of the world; it performed the more useful task of scaring John of Gaunt, so that he dropped both a poll tax and a statute of laborers that would have reduced England's peasants to Russian serfs.[20] In the period that followed, Chaucer's *Troilus and Criseyde* gained a wide audience and critical acclaim. Meanwhile English was gaining respectability, and by the end of the century an English king was prepared to address parliament in that language. John Gower welcomed his new king with a poem in the newly prestigious tongue, but he had first decided to take a chance on the neophyte ten years earlier. By then Chaucer was working on his masterpiece, a scandalous collection of stories about earthly life and love. Gower decided to match it with his own tale in which he could indulge in similar descriptions of sex and violence while giving them a moral twist.

CA occupied Gower from 1386 to 1393, as he wrote and rewrote it like a true obsessive. The first version was dedicated to King Richard II and Chaucer, the last to Richard's murderer, Henry IV. Some critics have read a rift between the two poets into the loss of Chaucer's name between dedications, but a much likelier cause is that Chaucer was not one of Henry's favorites. Although Henry's father, John of Gaunt, had been Chaucer's paymaster, the poet was probably too intimately connected with Richard's branch of the family to gain the favor of the usurper.[21] In *CA* Gower proved that he had a considerable narrative gift, a sure touch with the English language, and an appetite for scandal, particularly if it involved incest. He also showed that almost anything he could do by way of versification in French he could do even better in his mother tongue.

The exception was strophe design: Gower must have concluded that finding six rhymes for every word was near to impossible in English and, since he couldn't beat Chaucer, he joined him in the rhymed couplet. But Chaucer's longer line seems initially to have been a step too far for Gower; he paid tribute to it in a short *Complaint* in Book VIII, but the remainder of *CA* is in the shorter line that both men had employed before, most notably in *HF* and *MO*.[22] The octosyllable of *CA*, however, is a new and remarkable thing, as I shall demonstrate by a quantified analysis of the first 300 lines of Gower's *Prologus*.

The prologue to *CA* begins with a short plea in Latin for the poet to be forgiven for not writing in a higher-status language, but then Gower continues

[20] For the Peasants' Revolt of 1381, see Davies, 1999: 361; for the alternative fate of the Russian peasantry, see Davies, 1996: 587–88.

[21] For Chaucer's connection to John of Gaunt, see Pearsall, 1992: 82–93; for the seizure of the English throne by his son, see Davies, 1999: 368–69.

[22] The complaint was Chaucer's preferred short form; Gower's complaint in *CA* (VIII, 2217–2300) also employs Chaucer longer line and favorite strophe design, 'rhyme royal.'

confidently in English. He first depicts authorship as a sort of duty to pass wisdom on to posterity, but then notes that a surfeit of wisdom dulls the wit. He describes his own artistic intention in lines 17–20 as a combination of instruction and amusement:

(25) I **wolde** go the **middel weie**
(26) And **wryt**e a bok **betwen** the **tweie**
(27) Som**what** of lust, some**what** of **lore**,
(28) That of the **lass**e or of the **more**.

When word-final schwas are treated consistently these lines are regular in both syllable count and rhythm; and Gower was remarkably consistent. Such regular passages occur in other poets' work, in Chaucer's, and Barbour's, and even in *Pearl*, but what distinguishes *CA* from its predecessors is that its regularity is sustained for more than 30,000 lines.

Some 99 percent of the lines in my *CA* sample are octosyllabic, at least if reasonable assumptions are made about syllabification of certain words: *here* (lines 51 and 257) and *heved* (152), which must be monosyllables despite their second schwas; *hevene* (141) and *povere* (226), which must be disyllables; and *unevene* (170) which must be trisyllabic. When Gower does not wish to count the final syllable of the second person singular inflection in *CA*, he indicates this in the spelling (thus *takth* in line 205). Unusually, the word *oure* must be two syllables in line 5 unless this line is a syllable short, like line 83. And two other lines, (184) and (222), require hiatus before an *h* to make them octosyllabic.

Similarly, between 94 and 98 percent of lines in my *CA* sample are regularly iambic in rhythm. It contains four indisputable examples of initial inversion, all involving prepositions: *after* (lines 54, 138, and 174) and *under* (108), and it may be that Gower did not regard the weak stress of these words as important. The name *Simon* (241) is a slightly less solid example of initial inversion because medieval writers took liberties with the pronunciation of foreign names (for example, rhythmic regularity in *HF* requires both *Juno* and *Juno*). The four remaining candidates for initial inversion, *wrytinge* (38), *purpose* (53), *justice* (102), and *worshiped* (105), are less clear. All these words count as three syllables and an AN pronunciation with stress on the second syllable is not out of the question. If all these were examples of initial inversion it would represent 3 percent of total lines in the sample, but I am not convinced that Gower employed this form of tension deliberately for rhythmic variety, as later English poets did. More importantly, he eschewed the traditional headless line, and seems to have been more tolerant of rhythmic monotony than most poets.

There are also nine possible inversions within the lines of my sample: two of them (118) and (142) again involve the word *under*. Another possible inversion concerns the word *wisdom*, which appears to be accentually ambivalent from the following lines:

(30) That <u>it</u> to **wis**dom <u>al</u> be**lon**geth (67)
(31) Which[e] <u>of</u> wis**dom** the **ver**tu **sough**ten (197)

The remaining possible inversions are all in the second foot, and all the words concerned end in elided schwas: *seknesse* (line 61), *knighthode* (89 and 99), *justice* (131), *cursinge* (274), and *clergie* (281). Once again, an AN accentuation of their second syllable is a possible explanation for the apparent irregularity.

From this analysis of syllable count and accentuation, *CA* qualifies as the first poem in *strict iambic tetrameters* in the English language. Gower's poem is not only the first example of this meter, it is one of the most regular: lines of other than eight syllables to the final stress are so rare that they should probably be regarded as scribal errors, and most of the very few candidates for inversion have alternative explanations. In *CA* the English iambic tetrameter at last lost its traditional irregularities: future poets would refine specific features, but Gower's verse design would be recognizable in English poetry for the next 600 years.

I have ascribed Gower's pursuit of regularity to an obsessive personality: he seems to have liked everything neat and tidy, from the genealogy of sin to the social order, from emotional life to lines of verse. In Gower's world, when a man went blind he got married in order to preserve his daily routine; and when he got married he presented to his wife a polished set of French *ballades*. Gower's readers should be grateful that he lived a long and well-ordered life, but his versification sometimes suffers from being too regular. It is Gower's narrative gift, rather than his relentless four iambs, that leads the reader to the end of each story, and when the poet stops to moralize the *CA*'s short lines sometimes seem unsuited to the task.

I shall not include the story of Gower's iambic tetrameter over the centuries that followed in the Epilogue to this volume, because its form changed little and its popularity never waned. Although later poets employed more inversion in this meter, it could not rival Chaucer's longer line for long poems on elevated subjects.

Gower's Influence on Chaucer's Shorter Line

If Gower's example in *MO* helped Chaucer realize that syllabic and accentual regularity are not incompatible, this would have contributed to *HF*'s being more regular than *BD*. It is more difficult to detect whether *CA*'s versifying had any influence on Chaucer's because by 1390 Chaucer was committed to a longer line. The twelve shorter lines included in *Anelida and Arcite*, which were composed several years before *CA* was begun, contain two lines (258) and (266) that are irregular by Gower's standards. One other poem accepted as Chaucer's, the *Proverbe*, also employs the shorter line in its two quatrains (rhymed abab cdcd), but it is of uncertain date. Since three of its eight lines are headless, its versification shows none of Gower's regularizing influence. Many critics have argued that this poem cannot be Chaucer's because of the bad rhyme 'compass'/ 'embrace,' but this is the least of the poem's metrical irregularities.[23] It is quite possible that some other versifier, less competent at rhyme and less scrupulous about elision, has sought immortality for his own mediocre composition by including it, thus labeled, in an early manuscript containing Chaucer's work.

The only shorter lines by Chaucer that almost certainly post-date Gower's *CA* are to be found in the Tale of Sir Thopas (*ST*), a work that is in many ways deliberately awful, but which also confirms Chaucer's skill as a versifier. Alan Gaylord, in a witty and perceptive essay, described the prosody of this tale as both "dainty doggerel" and "elvyssh," and my own analysis of its 203 lines confirms that this parody of the ME metrical romance is lightly and skilfully crafted.[24] Since I shall analyze the strophe design of *ST* in a later chapter, I shall note here only the peculiarities of its three verse designs.

The first design has four-beats, and generates 132 verse instances; the second has three beats, and generates sixty-six instances; and the third has a single beat (a *bob*), generating just five instances. I have deliberately employed a mixture of rhythmic and generative theory to describe the 203 lines because in *ST* Chaucer converted the dolniks of *Guy of Warwick* into something close to stress-syllabic meters.

The poem's bobs are all perfect iambs (if their post-tonic syllable is ignored): 'In towne' (line 793), 'So wilde' (803), 'With mace' (813), 'Thy mawe' (823), and 'In londe' (887). And of the sixty-six three-beat lines in *ST* sixty-four are iambic (the exceptions are the headless lines 806 and 816). The four-beat lines of *ST*, however, show vestiges of the rhythmic variety found in *BD* and *HF*. This can be seen from a statistical analysis, because *ST*'s 132 four-beat instances make a sufficient sample for quantified comparison with the lines of *BD*, *HF*, and *CA*. This is given in Figure 1 below.

Percentage of 4-beat Lines	*BD*	*HF*	*CA*	*ST*
8 Syllables	86	84	98	91
Headless Lines	8	13	0	4
7 Syllables (Other)	1	1	0	2
Epic Caesurae	4	1	0	2
9 Syllables (Other)	0	1	0	1
Deviant *-es*	1	0	1	0
TOTAL (length)	100	100	100	100
Inversions	7	7	5	2

Fig. 1: Metrical Comparison of Four Poems

[23] Gross notes the previous editors who have doubted or believed that this poem is Chaucer's; see Benson, 1988: 636.

[24] Gaylord, 1979.

These statistics do no more than suggest that *ST*'s four-beat lines are more regular than those of Chaucer's other poems, because most of the differences are not significant. But there are at least some grounds for suspicion that Gower's influence was pulling Chaucer towards greater regularity.

Perhaps the most notable feature of *ST*'s lines is that the rhythm of its four-beat lines is almost entirely duple-time. This makes the polysyllabic inversions in the very first line of the tale very striking: they give the tale a strongly trochaic opening:

(32) **Lis**teth, **lor**des, in good in**tent** (1)

Reducing 'lordes' to a monosyllable would make this a headless line, but Chaucer reserves alliteration for special occasions, as noted above, and the unusual opening of this line seems designed to make the audience sit up. It is just possible that Gower's example influenced Chaucer to make more sparing use of headless lines in *ST* and to be more tolerant of a regular iambic rhythm. Certainly, with these few exceptions, Chaucer's *ST* is as iambic as Gower's *CA*. In these two poems we see the advent in ME verse of a new level of rhythmic regularity.[25]

The clearly dominant iambic rhythm of *ST* raises the question of what Chaucer meant by 'doggerel' when he put that word in the Host's mouth (line 925). This is the word's first recorded occurrence, but Chaucer must have thought that it conveyed something to his audience. The modern definition of *doggerel*, at least as given in A. J. Cuddon's *Dictionary of Literary Terms*, is "rough, badly made verse, monotonous in rhythm and clumsy in rhyme."[26] Chaucer's rhymes in *ST* are good in the technical sense of a precise repetition of nucleus and coda, but his use of words for their rhyme rather than their meaning leaves him open to the last of these charges. Whether Chaucer's rhythm in this tale justifies 'monotonous' is more debatable: if we include headless lines, the number of *ST*'s lines with inversion match Gower's, but a line with four trochees provides much greater variety than a simple inversion. Writing more than a century ago, George Saintsbury used the term *doggerel* to describe the opposite to rhythmic monotony; it was his word for any verse that lacked iambic regularity; for example, the entire *oeuvre* of Lydgate.[27] On the basis that rhythmic regularity is a vogue and is forever changing, I would absolve *ST* of *doggerel* but support Gaylord's term *dainty*.

[25] For a comparison of the earliest European poems to qualify for Tarlinskaja's category 'iambic,' see Zonneveld, 2000. The Dutch *Life of St Lutgart* (composed c. 1270), unlike the English poem, is rhymed; Zonneveld concludes that both derived their meter from the Latin *septenarius*.

[26] See Cuddon, 1977: 199.

[27] See Saintsbury, 1906: I, 223 and passim.

Conclusions

This chapter has traced the development of the iambic tetrameter in the period between 1375 and 1400. It shows that it was Gower who took the first step towards making this meter strictly stress-syllabic in French: he favored French versifying traditions rather than English ones, and jettisoned both the headless line and the epic caesura. Chaucer, on the other hand, neglected the epic caesura but cultivated the headless line as a source of rhythmic variety. In *MO* Gower found a source of rhythmic variety in the small proportion of lines that allowed strong syllables in weak positions, in the traditional French manner.

When Gower decided at last to compose in English he eschewed both the traditional sources of variety, French and English: the result was a meter almost indistinguishable from the modern iambic tetrameter. But in *CA* Gower made very little use of inversion, and so his iambic tetrameters risk rhythmic monotony. He relieved this by continually changing the subject matter, but reading his long poem is still a more forbidding task than reading Chaucer's *Canterbury Tales*.

Gower's example did not inspire Chaucer to abandon the headless line, although in his final sortie into that meter, *ST*, Chaucer employed fewer such lines and produced a smoother iambic regularity. However, by then Chaucer's preferred meter was a longer line, one that Gower eventually joined him in celebrating. It is now time to pursue that longer line's origins.

Chaucer deserted the shorter line, at least for serious purposes, when he left *HF* unfinished, probably early in 1378. This was the year of his second visit to Italy, and thereafter Chaucer employed a longer line. He had for many years known French *vers de dix* without being tempted to mimic them in English. His friend Gower had also preferred the *octosyllabe* to the *vers de dix* for *MO*. Chaucer's visit to Italy changed his choice of line length in English, and Larry Benson explains his motivation in a way that is wholly credible:[28]

> Chaucer was deeply affected by the pseudo-classical style that allowed Dante and Boccaccio to raise their vernacular to epic heights. He drew heavily on that style in the invocations in *The House of Fame*, but the four-beat couplet, which he was then still using, seems more suited to parodying than reproducing the classics ("I wol now synge yif I kan / The armes and also the man," *HF*, 143–44). Chaucer apparently found the longer line and less obtrusive rhyme scheme of his new stanza better suited to achieving in English some of the elegant effects he admired in Boccaccio.

In order to understand Chaucer's verse art we need to examine the precise nature of those elegant effects in the verse of Dante, Boccaccio, and Petrarch (the last of whom Benson doesn't cite). The production of those effects had been "a craft

[28] See the editor's introduction to *The Parliament of Fowls* in Benson, 1988: 384.

so long to lerne" for the Italian poets, just as it had been for Chaucer. In the next chapter I shall cross the Channel and the Alps, as Chaucer did in 1372 and 1378, in order to examine how Italian poets developed and perfected their longer line.

8
Versifying in Italy

Being the son of a rich vintner gave Chaucer an opportunity denied most Englishmen of his generation. Since England was almost constantly at war with France the London wine trade was in the hands of Italians, and so Chaucer had Italian friends and learned some Italian. We do not know how much, but it was enough to give him a head start when he was sent to Italy on his royal masters' business in 1372, and again in 1378. Whatever its professional uses, Chaucer's Italian enabled him to read, enjoy, and admire the works of the greatest Italian poets of his day, Francesco Petrarca (b. 1304–d. 1374) and Giovanni Boccaccio (b. 1313–d. 1374), and of their fellow Florentine Dante Alighieri (b. 1265–d. 1321). Since Italian poets versified in a very different way from the poets of France or England, this chapter will be devoted to an examination of medieval Italian verse craft and of the types of verse design Chaucer encountered in his reading.[1]

Many of the differences between Italian and French verse designs are the result of differences between the two languages, and so I shall preface this examination with a brief note on the features of Italian that are most important to versifying in that language, and to the subject of this volume.

The Italian Language

The same forces that produced Gallo-Romance on one side of the Alps produced Italo-Romance on the other: the influence of foreign tongues spoken by invaders and settlers combined with some tendencies already present in Latin. But the foreign tongues in what is now Italy were much more diverse and more unevenly distributed: at different times, Gothic, Langobard, and French kings ruled over most of the North, Greeks from Byzantium ruled over much of the East and center of the Peninsula, and Arabs and Normans ruled Sicily.[2] Moreover, none of these powers lasted for very long, at least not compared with the Frankish dynas-

---

[1] See Pearsall, 1992: 102–9.

[2] See Migliorini, 1966: 35–40.

ties of France, and none established a single variety of Italo-Romance that could rival the French of Paris in authority. The people of medieval France spoke many different dialects, but it benefited every subject to be able to communicate with the king's agents, and every writer to have an audience across the royal domains. In contrast, disunity and discontinuity encouraged at least fourteen different dialects of Italo-Romance to flourish locally.[3]

These varieties of Romance did not enjoy complete isolation, however, because there were a number of factors that encouraged the people of what became Italy to learn something of one another's dialects. The first was the Church: although each region could supply its own priests the various orders evangelized across regional borders. Catholic priests must always look over their shoulder to Rome, and for that Latin was more than adequate, but some acquaintance with Genoese was more useful for making new converts in Genoa. The second was commerce: the language that clinches the sale is always the buyer's, and in order to buy things every region's merchants had to sell something. A number of references in Latin to the Italo-Romance vernaculars (*vulgaria*, plural) have survived from the eleventh and twelfth centuries, but the only vulgar texts to survive are fragmentary: appendices to legal documents, formulae for confession, and brief additions to Latin poems.[4]

From these fragments emerge a picture of dialects that shared many of the characteristics of the modern language. The changes in Latin that produced Italo-Romance were rather different from those that produced Gallo-Romance. First the values of the Latin vowels were generally unchanged, and secondly final vowels were retained, ensuring that the language did not become oxytonic like French. But final consonants and initial vowels disappeared to give Italian words their distinctive shape: most begin with a consonant, end with a vowel, and are stressed on their penultimate or antepenultimate syllables. Words with final stress and lexical monosyllables are very few. Some of the changes to Latin were similar to those the other side of the Alps: for example, the palatization of *c* and *g* and the loss of unstressed syllables within long words; others were not: for example, the doubling of many consonants and change of pretonic *e* to *i*.[5]

The most important change affecting versification was that accent developed in the same way as in France; whether or not Classical Latin had all the features needed to qualify (volume, duration, and pitch change), Italo-Romance was spoken with the strong dynamic accent typical of the Germanic languages.[6] Unlike that of French, Italian word stress has never weakened, perhaps because its position in the word was not predictable, and therefore significant. Italian accent differs from Germanic mainly in that secondary stress (*nebenton*) is so weak

[3] See Elcock, 1960: 469–70.

[4] See Elcock, 1960: 460–64 and Migliorini, 1966: 60–69.

[5] See Migliorini, 1966: 45–46 and Elcock, 1960: 475–81.

[6] See Migliorini, 1966: 21.

that many linguists deny its existence.[7] This too has implications for versifying: it makes beats harder to find and the intervals between them longer and more irregular.

The Earliest Italian Poetry

Italian literature begins at the turn of the thirteenth century; it offers almost no parallel to the many Saints' Lives, *chansons de geste*, and courtly lyrics that were composed in France in the eleventh and twelfth. Very little poetry was composed in Italy during this period. The literate classes seem to have been too busy just surviving, and preserving the literary relics of the past, to produce new markings that might find a place in history. Of course the speakers of the various dialects must have passed on proverbs and nursery rhymes, and invented derisive and bawdy chants, but such folk verse tends only to be recorded when it has become a curiosity, if at all. So the evidence of how the earliest Italian poets versified is very thin and somewhat confusing.

The earliest surviving Italian poems date from 1220 or soon after, when the vogue for the *alexandrin* with epic caesura, set in monorhyme quatrains, was at its height in France. These poems include a poem on the torments of hell by Giacomino da Verona, *Il libro delle tre Scritture* by Bonvesin de la Riva, and an anonymous poem known as the *Proverbi de femene*.[8] Note that Italian poets and critics call the *alexandrin* a *settenario doppio* because they expect hemistichs to end in a post-tonic vowel and include them in their count.[9] Some of the lines in these texts have the wrong number of syllables but there is no doubt that these poets were endeavoring to count syllables in the French manner.

Another early poem that is far from syllabically regular is the *Ritmo cassinese*: its strophes begin with a series of lines of 7F syllables and end in lines of 10F and, while the shorter lines are counted accurately, many of the longer ones contain the wrong number of syllables.[10] In some other early verse texts we can also

---

[7] See Bertinetto, 1981: 99.

[8] For the *Proverbi de femene*, see Migliorini, 1966: 74; for *Il libro delle tre Scritture*, see Fiorentino, 1964: 76–78.

[9] French syllable counting assumes that masculine lines are the norm, although they account for little more than 50 percent overall in French poetry. Italian counting assumes that feminine lines (*piani*) are the norm, as they are in Italian, where *bruschi* (masculine lines) and *sdruccioli* (proparoxytonic lines) are rare. A line of 10 syllables to the final stress is thus a *décasyllabe* in French but an *endecasillabo* in Italian; to avoid confusion I shall refer to such a line as having 10F (*piano*) or 10M (*brusco*) syllables.

[10] For a text of the *Ritmo cassinese*, see Bonghi on the website given in 'Works Cited'; Bonghi's text follows Contini, 1960. The irregularity of the lines in this poem leads Elcock to describe its versification as 'homespun' (1960: 467).

detect quite different rhythms from those produced by counting syllables and regularizing phrasal stresses. These are the *Laude*, or praise poems, which are known by the names of the cities where they were composed, and some of them are far from regular in their syllable count: lines of 7F syllables are mixed with lines of 6F and even 8F, but not quite at random, because consecutive lines are often of the same length.[11] Many medieval poems in Hispano-Romance show the same variability, and Spanish metrists describe such verse as *verso fluctuante*; it is probably best explained as the result of versifiers' judging the lines to be equivalent because they have either the same number of syllables, or of peaks of stress, or of both.[12] Some scholars thus argue that syllabically irregular verse preceded regular in all the European languages.[13]

There are signs of accentual regularity in some of the earliest Italian verse, and Pasquale Leonetti noted that a number of poems show consistent triple-time rhythms.[14] They are from the *Laude cortonese* , the *Laude urbinate,* and the *Rime antiche senesi*. Many lines in these poems have the same accentual rhythm [(w) S w w S w] as English tumbling verse, even to the detail of allowing zero anacrusis (which produces the hemistichs with 4F syllables). Another early Italian poem that shows the same dominance of triple time and use of the anacrusic principle is *De la diversità de contemplazione de croce* by Jacopone da Todi (b. 1236–d. 1307). This meter harks back to the couplets of the *laude* quoted above, and it is virtually identical to the verse design of Castilian *verso de arte mayor* or English tumbling verse.[15] The accentual tendency in early Italian verse was quickly challenged by foreign syllabic meters; thus another of Iacopone's poems, *Del iubilo del core che esce in voce*, is in strictly counted alexandrines.[16]

Anthologies of Italian poetry generally begin with a work dating to 1225, the *Cantico delle creature* of Saint Francis of Assisi (b. 1186–d. 1226).[17] This poem is very irregular in several ways: its eleven strophes vary from two to five lines in length; their lines may rhyme, assonate, or be unrhymed; and the lines vary considerably in syllable count. The meter of this poem can be classified only as free verse, and of a type that many metrists regard as the freest: it has *interior rhythms*: its most important repeated events are semantic, syntactic, and lexical items.[18] Francis begins most strophes with the rhythmic formula "Laudate si' mi

---

[11] For the texts of a number of *Laude*, see the website given under *Laude* in 'Works Cited.'

[12] For *fluctuación sillábica*, see Navarro (Tomás) 1974: 75–76.

[13] See Baehr, 1970: 177 and Contini, 1972: 247.

[14] See Leonetti, 1934: II.1: 18–19.

[15] See Ker, 1898: passim; for a detailed analysis of the Spanish meter, see Clarke, 1964: 51–211.

[16] See Fiorentino, 1964: 81–82.

[17] See, for example, Kay, 1958: 1–2.

[18] See Utrera, 2010: 145–72.

Signore," and repeats the word *frate* or *sora* in almost every strophe. This powerful poem is crafted in a mode that is without parallel in Europe until the twentieth century.

Versifying in Occitan

Although Italian poetry begins only in the thirteenth century, educated Italian poets were already active in the eleventh and twelfth—but they composed in Occitan.[19] This was the *langue d'oc*, the variety of Gallo-Romance that developed in the Southern half of France, far from the authority of the French king and the influence of his court language (the *langue d'oïl*). The nobles of the South were nominally vassals of the King of France but they enjoyed considerable political independence: the two greatest lords ruled Aquitaine and Toulouse. When Eleanor of Aquitaine married two kings in rapid succession Aquitaine became engulfed in international politics, and Toulouse became the center of an Occitan sphere of influence that stretched from Valencia on one peninsula to Sicily at the foot of another.[20] Thus it was that the educated poets of Italy (until the thirteenth century) and Catalonia (until the fifteenth) preferred to compose in Occitan rather than their own mother tongue.[21]

The best known Italian troubadour composing in Occitan was Sordello (b. c. 1210–d. 1269), and his versifying follows faithfully that of his Occitan predecessors.[22] Occitan poets are noted for their remarkable felicity in the use of rhyme, which seems to have been employed in Occitan before it was in French.[23] They used lines of every length in ingeniously wrought strophes, but for one type of poetry, the political songs known as *sirventes*, they usually employed *vers de dix* with lyric caesura. And one Occitan poet in particular, Peire Vidal (fl. 1180–1204), composed more flexible *vers de dix* in which some lines divided 6 + 4 syllables and others had a revolutionary new way of accommodating feminine

[19] See Elcock, 1960: 401; for an account of the relationship between politics and poetry in Occitania, see Harvey, 1999.

[20] The Occitan language shared some of the features of Italian and some of French: thus its vowels largely retained their Latin values, while its consonants resembled their French equivalents. Occitan retained word-final-*a*, both long and short, and its post-tonic syllables were less vulnerable to weakening and loss than those of French. Occitan nevertheless had many more stressed monosyllables than Italian, and many lines of Occitan poetry are entirely monosyllabic. See Hamlin, Ricketts, and Hathaway, 1967: 13–37.

[21] For Italian troubadours, see Cabré, 1999; for details of all the surviving Occitan manuscripts and poems, see Ricketts, 2001.

[22] For Sordello's poems, see Boni, 1954.

[23] For the case that French poets derived full rhyme from Occitan, see Elcock, 1960: 391.

words mid-line.[24] This was to balance an extra syllable before the caesura by one fewer following it, giving the line a formula 4F + 5M/F syllables.

Between the time of Vidal and that of Sordello a disaster struck Occitan culture. The nobles of Southern France had scorned Pope as well as King and shown a remarkable tolerance of new ideas, tastes, and religions. For years the Roman Church looked on in horror, but in 1208 Pope Innocent III proclaimed a Crusade against the Occitanian heretics.[25] Since Crusaders had their sins absolved in advance, the barons of Northern France and England poured south to murder, rape, and pillage with papal blessing. The people of the stricken land fought stubbornly and bravely for years, but by the middle of the thirteenth century their culture had been extinguished and their land confiscated. The atheist Emperor Frederick II, however, gave asylum to Occitanian refugees in his court at Palermo, troubadours as well as their audiences, and the poets of Palermo soon learned from them.[26]

The *Endecasillabo* and the *Sonetto*

While Sordello was living in the past (and Aragon) and composing Occitan lyrics, educated poets in Sicily began to compose in their own language.[27] Their models were Occitan and they derived most of their tastes and forms from the troubadours. In particular, the poets at Frederick's court showed great enthusiasm for the Occitan *vers de dix.*[28] Since, on average, Italian words are longer than their French or Occitan equivalents, Sicilian poets required a longer line in order to carry as much semantic content as a shorter Occitan line. They also had a problem with the fixed caesura of the 4+ 6 *vers de dix*. Italian has very few oxytonic words or stressed monosyllables and a plethora of paroxytonic words that somehow had to be fitted into the middle (as well as other parts) of the line. The Occitan poets had solved the problem of feminine words mid-line by employing lyric caesuras in 14 percent of their lines, and clearly the Sicilians could have in-

[24] For Vidal's poems, see Avalle, 1963.

[25] For the Albigensian Crusade, see Davies, 1997: 361–62.

[26] See Migliorini, 1966: 84.

[27] Though it had many features of the Sicilian dialect, the language in which they composed was a sort of common denominator of many dialects. In his *De vulgari eloquentia* (1303) Dante pondered which of the Italo-Romance dialects was fit to become a literary language, and he concluded that none was (see Ferrers Howell, 1973). Yet somehow good poets had composed poems in what Dante called *sermo illustre* ('elevated speech'). The speech of educated people all over Italy became steadily more Tuscan as the prestige of the Florentine poets Dante, Petrarch, and Boccaccio won wide admiration. The Italian language thus represents the victory of literature over politics.

[28] For Sicilian *endecasillabi*, see Sanguineti, 1965.

creased this proportion. Sicily's poets, however, rejected this option, probably for aesthetic reasons. Poems were increasingly being recited rather than sung, and wrenching the strong word stress of Italian in so many lines did not appeal to them. Clearly, something had to go if Italian poets were to employ a line of ten syllables, and that something was the invariable division into 4 + 6.

The alternative models available for the first crafters of *endecasillabi* were the 6 + 4 lines of poems like *Girart de Roussillon* and the experiments of Peire Vidal. The Italian poets' first step towards solving their problem was to combine lines of 4 + 6 with lines of 6 + 4. This was something that French poets had always rejected because it causes phrasal stresses to appear at irregular and unpredictable intervals. But for Italian poets, having two possible places to break the line doubled the chances of finding a word-final stressed syllable. The second step was to balance an extra syllable in the first hemistich by one fewer in the second (as Vidal had done), thereby admitting the host of Italian paroxytons. This produced a line of 5 + 5, or rather 4F + 5, and was so shocking that French critics immediately labeled the balancing act *coupe italienne.*[29]

Even the earliest *endecasillabi* contain both *coupe italienne* and the mixing of 4 + 6 with 6 + 4 lines; for example, those of the poem beginning 'Rosa fresca aulentissima' by the Cielo d'Alcamo, which dates from between 1230 and 1250.[30] The striking difference between the *vers de dix* and the *endecasillabo* can be seen from the following lines, which open a sonnet by the Sicilian poet Giacomo da Lentini (fl. c. 1250).[31] The syllabic formula of each line is given in brackets and Italian syllables lost by synaloepha are in superscript.

(1) Io m'**aggio** **post**^{o} in **cor**^{e} a Dio servire [4M + 6F]
(2) Com'io po**tes**se **gir**^{e} in para**di**so: [6M + 4F]
(3) Al **san**to **lo**co c'**agg**^{io} au**di**to **di**re [4F + 5F]
(4) O' si man**tie**ne sol**la**zo, **gioc**^{o} e **ri**so [6F + 3F]

("I have set my heart on serving God so that I may go to heaven, that holy place where, I have heard said, comfort, and joy and laughter never cease.")

Note that both (1) and (2) rely on synaloepha for their masculine caesuras, and that this merging of vowels blurs the division between the two hemistichs, unifying what in Occitan is a clearly divided line.[32]

Italian metrists describe this line as follows: lines with caesura after 4M and 4F are *a minore* (because their first colon is shorter) and those with caesura after

[29] *Coupe italienne* is also often described as *overflowing caesura*, see Kastner, 1903: 83.

[30] For *coupe italienne* in Cielo's verse, see Fiorentino, 1964: 87–92.

[31] The text is that of Sanguineti, 1965; this is the first of Lentini's poems in that volume.

[32] For synaloepha (Italian: *sinalefe*), see Elwert, 1973: 21–24. Its English equivalent can be seen in phrases like 'many a' when pronounced as two syllables.

6M and 6F are *a maiore*.[33] Modern hierarchical theories of poetic meter represent the alternative structures of the *endecasillabo* as in Figure 1 below.[34] Note that PT would give this meter's correspondence rules as: position size: one syllable (plus an extrametrical syllable in position 10); prominence type: stress; prominence site: colon-final strong positions.

(A) A *maiore* Design

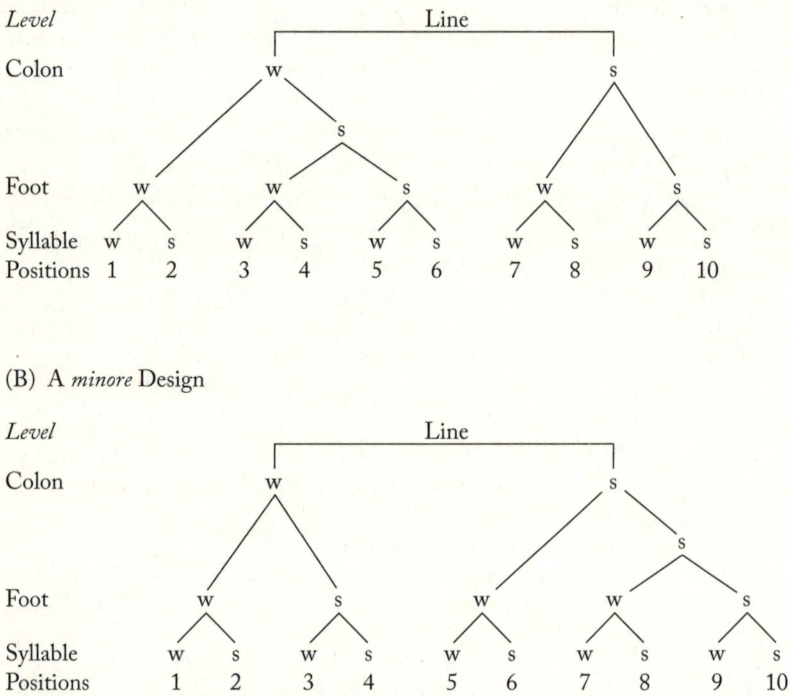

Fig.1 : *Endecasillabo* : Alternative Structures

To French poets the *endecasillabo* has no caesura, no mandatory peak of stress and no word boundary mid-line, but most Italian critics have described the line as having a *cesura mobile* (after 4M, 4F, 6M, or 6F syllables). Some modern Italian metrists have also argued that the *endecasillabo* has no caesura, which would make lines like the following metrical:[35]

(5) Sov-ra-ma-gni-fi-cen-tis-sa-ma-**men**te [accented ?4 ?6 10]

---

33 See Elwert, 1973: 52–54.

34 See Piera, 1980: 46, Hanson, 1996: 61, and Hanson, 2009: 272.

35 For a critique of the concept of caesura, see Bertinetto, 1981: 194–227.

This hypothetical line, however, is unusual in having no obvious mid-line peak of stress (shown by ?4 ?6 in brackets). Almost all actual lines have a phrasal stress in one of these positions 4 and 6, and this combines with the strength of Italian word stress to give the *endecasillabo* a great deal more rhythmic variety than the French *vers de dix*.

Italian *endecasillabi* contain other strong syllables and stressed monosyllables in addition to the phrasal (colon-final) peak in position 4 or 6. Even though the position of this mid-line peak ensures that 85 percent of lines are vaguely iambic, there are many possible stress profiles to the line.[36] This can be seen from the following six examples, lines by Guido Cavalcanti (b. c. 1250–d. 1300):[37]

(6) Che fa tre**mar** di chiari**ta**te l'**â**re	$[4^a\ 8^a\ 10^a]$	(4, 2)
(7) **Allor** si **mi**se nel **mor**to co**lo**re	$[4^a\ 7^a\ 10^a]$	(4, 14)
(8) Che fe' l°' immagi**nar** che mi con**qui**se	$[2^a\ 6^a\ 10^a]$	(23, 8)
(9) I' mi **pos**so blas**mar** di gran pe**san**za	$[3^a\ 6^a\ 10^a]$	(32, 25)
(10) **Mol**to cortese**men**te mi ris**puo**se	$[1^a\ 6^a\ 10^a]$	(30, 37)
(11) Ris**plen**de più che sol **vos**tra fi**gu**ra	$[6^a\ 7^a\ 10^a]$	(2, 3)

("Who makes the air tremble with brilliance;" "Then assumed a deathlike pallor;" "Who made the image that conquered me;" "I can curse great suffering;" "Very courteously answered me;" "Your figure shines brighter than the sun.")

Romance metrists have terms for each of these stress configurations: (6) is a *sapphic* line $[4^a\ 8^a\ 10^a]$; (7) is a *dactylic* $[4^a\ 7^a\ 10^a]$; (8) is a *heroic* $[2^a\ 6^a\ 10^a]$; (9) is a *melodic* $[3^a\ 6^a\ 10^a]$; (10) is an *emphatic* $[1^a\ 6^a\ 10^a]$: and (11) is an *adonic* $[6^a\ 7^a\ 10^a]$.[38] Note that lines of the sapphic and heroic type often have a fourth or fifth accent, making them more iambic, and that this particular example of the adonic is simply a heroic line with a clash of stresses in positions 6 and 7. I have not numbered the first stress in (11) because in many adonic lines such a fourth stress appears in position 1 or 4. The emphatic example has much in common with iambic pentameters with initial inversion, and the dactylic offers a quite different (triple-time) rhythm. The melodic example is like Lentini's line in (4) above: it begins with two anapests; if a fourth stress occurs in such lines it is usually in position 8, giving the line an anapestic opening but an iambic close.

The *endecasillabo* became the favorite long line of the poets at the court of Fredrick II in Palermo, and the verse form the *sonnet* became a favorite in Italy and throughout the world; Lentini may have been its inventor.[39] The sonnet is

---

[36] See Elwert, 1973: 60–68.

[37] For the poems of Guido Cavalcanti, see Cirigliano, 1992.

[38] The many terms that critics have employed for different types of *endecasillabo* (Sp. *endecasílabo*) are listed and defined in Domínguez Caparrós, 2001: 35–45.

[39] For an extensive history of the form in Italian, see Ruschioni, 1974.

rather like a fourteen-line stanza from an Occitan *canso*, but since no *canso* has been discovered with its structure it seems more likely that it was derived from a traditional eight-line Sicilian form known as the *strambotto*, with a six-line coda added.[40] The strongest evidence for this is the rhyme scheme of the earliest sonnets: their octaves rhyme ab ab ab ab like the *strambotto*, and their sestets carry a similar rhyme: cd cd cd. Only as the vogue for the sonnet spread north did poets devise more intricate rhyme schemes for the sonnet, such as octaves rhyming abba abba, and sestets rhyming cde cde.

Approximately 85 percent of Lentini's *endecasillabi* are iambic, almost sufficient for metrists to classify his verse design as stress syllabic, but this figure varies in the lines of later poets.[41] Certainly, the three Italian poets whose work Chaucer knew had very different stylistic preferences in this respect, and I shall examine them in the next section of this chapter.

Metrical Stylistics: Dante, Petrarch, and Boccaccio.

Although it is most unlikely that Chaucer met either Petrarch or Boccaccio on his visits to Italy, he clearly knew some of their works from his reading. *Troilus and Criseyde* could have been composed only with a copy of Boccaccio's *Filostrato* to hand, and the 'Canticus Troili' (*Troilus and Criseyde*, 1: 400–20) is a translation of Petrarch's sonnet beginning 'S'amor non è, ché dunque è ch'io sento?' (*Canzoniere*, Poem 132). Chaucer must also have known something of Dante's *Commedia*: the *House of Fame*, which was a reaction to the success of the Italian celebrity poet, contains an invocation in the best Dantesque manner, and Chaucer employs *terza rima* in one of his shorter poems.[42] Boccaccio delivered a long series of lectures on Dante's poem in Florence during the decade of Chaucer's visits. The English poet may not have attended them, but he had access to some of Italy's best libraries, and he was able to access the work of all three Italian poets.[43]

As the center of gravity of Italian literature drifted northwards in the middle of the thirteenth century a new type of poetry appeared. Dante first described it as a *dolce stil nuovo* (*Purgatorio*, Canto 24) and credited its introduction to three poets, one of whom was Guido Cavalcanti.[44] These poets purged the Occitan troubadour tradition of its grosser aspects (such as preferring other men's wives) and substituted something close to religious worship: a devotion to one woman

[40] See Wilkins, 1959: 29–31.

[41] See Duffell, 1991: 317.

[42] See Chaucer's poem 'A Complaint to His Lady,' lines 24–39.

[43] See Pearsall, 1992: 108.

[44] The other poets to whom Dante attributes the development of the *dolce stil nuovo* were Bonagiunta Orbicciani da Lucca (b. c. 1220–d. c. 1290) and Guido Guinizelli (b. c. 1235–d. 1376).

that could survive death. That woman had to be pure (*pura*), as well as beautiful (*bella*) and unspoiled (*honesta*), and since virgins were in short supply she was often below the modern age of consent.[45] The praises of such a lady had to be sung in the most refined language, with lush metaphors, outrageous hyperbole, and a surfeit of poetic suffering. This way of wooing, and of versifying, was an instant hit with both ladies and poets; Cavalcanti and Dante were among its early adherents and almost a century later Petrarch was still trying to perfect this *dolce stil*, even though it was no longer *nuovo*.

To illustrate the variety of styles in the *endecasillabo* I have selected three 300-line samples for statistical analysis. The first is from Dante's religious epic the *Commedia*, the second from Boccacio's narrative *Filostrato*, and the third from Petrarch's sonnets of what has become known as the *Canzoniere*.[46] The *Commedia*'s strophe design is *terza rima* (aba bcb cdc etc.); *Filostrato*'s is *ottava rima* (ababab cc), and in Petrarch's sonnets the original octave (4 x ab) has become two quatrains (2 x abba) and the sestet often contains a third rhyme. The lines in the Dante sample were composed c. 1310–20; those in the Boccaccio sample date from c. 1345; and the selected Petrarch sonnets were composed at various times between 1340 and 1360.

Since the lines I have chosen are only *samples* taken from the *universe* of all the possible verse instances that the poet's design will generate, I have subjected my results to the standard tests of statistical significance. The comparison in this section will focus on the three features of metrical style where I have found significant differences between the three poets. On other features (such as enjambment, rhyme quality and quantity, and the presence of extrametrical syllables), the differences between the lines of these three poets are minor. The three distinguishing features are the division of the line into cola (the *mobile* Italian caesura), the mechanics of syllable count (more specifically, the merging of adjacent vowels in synaloepha), and the placement of stressed syllables in the line (the accentual rhythms).

Using the definition of traditional Italian metrics (the word-boundary following the principal mid-line stress) a mobile caesura provides the *endecasillabo* with an important source of variety. The following examples demonstrate this: (12) and (13) are the opening lines of Dante's *Commedia*, where an *a minore* line follows an *a maiore*, while in (14) and (15) Boccaccio neatly contrasts a masculine caesura at 'alcun' with a feminine caesura that plays on the same word (*Filostrato*, I: 164–65):

---

[45] The literary worship of earthly ladies was soon eclipsed by the cult of the Virgin Mary, which rapidly spread across Europe; for the most extensive collection of Marian poems in Europe, see Mettmann, 1959–72.

[46] The texts used for my analysis are Petrocchi, 1975 (Dante's *Commedia*), Vianello, 1966 (Petrarch's *Canzionere*), and Windeatt, 1984 (Boccaccio's *Filostrato*).

(12) Nel **mezzo** del cam**min** de **no**stra vita [6M + 4F]
(13) Mi ritro**vai** per **u**na **selv**ª o**scu**ra [4M + 6F]

("In the middle of our life's road I found myself in a dark wood.")

(14) Veg**gend**° al**cun** che **fi**so rimi**ra**va [4M + 6F]
(15) Al**cu**na **don**na **se**co sospi**ran**do [4F + 5F]

("Watching, like any boy who stops and stares at any girl, hiding his tender feelings.")

These examples illustrate the use of this potential for rhythmic variety, and Figure 2 below quantifies the frequency with which the three poets employed each type of line:

Caesura @	Dante %	Boccaccio %	Petrarch %
4M	28	33	42
4F	30	33	14
A Minore	58	66	56
6M	32	20	37
6F	9	11	3
A Maiore	41	31	40
Other	1	3	4
Total	100	100	100

Fig. 2: Comparison of Caesuras

These figures show that Boccaccio employed significantly more *a minore* caesurae than either of the other two poets, and that Petrarch employed mostly masculine caesuras (his M: F ratio is more than 4:1). Petrarch achieves this high proportion in a language where oxytonic words and stressed monosyllables are rare largely by the use of synaloepha on an impressive scale. The colon variety in the *endecasillabi* of *Canzoniere* therefore often takes the form of a contrast between a caesura at 4M and one at 6M, one contrived by synaloepha, and the other by apocope. For example the following lines (7–8) from Poem 248 of the *Canzoniere*:

(16) **Quest**ª, aspet**tat**ª al **re**gno **del**li **dei**, [4M + 6F]
(17) **Co**sa **bel**la mor**tal** **pass**ª e non **du**ra. [6M + 4F]

("This woman long awaited in heaven; beautiful, mortal things pass and endure not.")

All three poets employ synaloepha often, both in total and at the caesura, as can be seen from Figure 3, where the number of synaloephas is expressed as a percentage of the number of lines in the sample:

Synaloephas *Per100 Lines*	Dante %	Boccaccio %	Petrarch %
Total	66	84	121
@ Caesura	33	29	45

Fig. 3: Comparison of Synaloephas

Dante and Boccaccio, like other poets before them, used synaloepha to obtain variety of caesura, making the number of masculine caesuras at least equal to the number of feminine ones, but in Petrarch's versifying both synaloepha and masculine caesuras became obsessions. The combination of the two had an important effect on the verse design: Petrarch was able to make the line a closely welded unit rather than two identifiable components, while drawing attention to the mid-line stressed syllable rather than diminishing it. The extreme use of synaloepha can be seen in the following lines, which open Petrarch's Poem 148:

(18) Non **Te**sin, **Po**, Var^{o}, **Arn**^{o}, A**dig**^{e} e **Tib**ro [2^{a} 5^{a} 6^{a} 7^{a} 8^{a} 10^{a}]
(19) Eu**fra**te, **Tig**re, **Nil**^{o}, **Erm**^{o}, **Ind**^{o} e **Gan**ge [2^{a} 4^{a} 6^{a} 7^{a} 8^{a} 10^{a}]
(20) **Tan**^{a}, **Istr**^{o}, Al**feo**, Garon^{a} e'l mar che **frange** [1^{a} 2^{a} 4^{a} 6^{a} 8^{a} 10^{a}]
(21) Ro**dan**^{o}, Ibero, Ren, **Sen**^{a}, **Alb**^{i}, **Er**^{a}, **Eb**ro [2^{a} 4^{a} 6^{a} 7^{a} 8^{a} 9^{a} 10^{a}]

("Not the" + list of the world's rivers.)

Obviously Petrarch is able to increase the semantic load of a line by squeezing six or seven stressed syllables into it, but he has also achieved something else. In creating monosyllables by synaloepha he has been able to place five primary stresses in odd-numbered positions without impeding a regular duple-time delivery of the lines. 'Varo,' 'Ermo,' 'Tana,' 'Sena,' and 'Era' have all become monosyllabic and lie in what modern generative metrics terms weak positions. In effect, Petrarch discovered the principles behind Kiparsky's monosyllabic constraint: either of two consecutive monosyllables can be made the more prominent in delivery without any threat to meaning, and the second of three consecutive monosyllables is demoted by the two that surround it and becomes an offbeat. Petrarch thus created a new monosyllabic Italian that has more than a passing resemblance to English.

The third feature I shall examine is accentuation: as noted above, even Lentini's early *endecasillabi* are predominantly iambic. This is a function of stress peaks on syllables 4 and 10, or 6 and 10 (and in many lines on 4, 6 and 10). Even so, *endecasillabi* with five stresses in strong (even-numbered) positions are rare: only 6 percent of Dante's and Boccaccio's lines have this stress profile. This figure rises to 12 percent in Petrarch's and the difference is statistically significant. Both Dante and Petrarch seem to have saved such heavily iambic lines for big occasions, as in the final line of the *Commedia*, and also that of Poem 244 in the *Canzoniere*, where Petrarch recalls the first line of Dante's poem:

(22) L'a**mor** che **mov**^{e} el **sol**^{e} e l'**al**tre **stel**le [2^{a} 4^{a} 6^{a} 8^{a} 10^{a}]

("The love that moves the sun and the other stars.")

(23) Per**ché** 'l cam**min** è **lung**^{o} è 'l **temp**^{o} e **cor**to [2^{a} 4^{a} 6^{a} 8^{a} 10^{a}]

("Because the road is long and the time is short.")

The percentages of positions 4 and 6 of each sample that contain stressed syllables differ somewhat: 74 percent of Petrarch's sixth syllables are stressed compared to 63 and 64 percent respectively in the Dante and Boccaccio samples. The accentuation of Petrarch's *endecasillabi* clearly differs from those of his predecessors, and Gasparov describes Petrarch's *endecasillabo* as a meter that is intermediate between syllabic and stress-syllabic.[47] Obviously, such a verse design merits careful examination in this volume, since Chaucer knew some of Petrarch's lines well enough to translate them. I shall therefore submit the *endecasillabi* of all three poets to the test of SMP (and also, where helpful, to that of PT).

According to SMP a pentameter meets the iambic norm if it has no stress maximum in a weak (odd-numbered) position. Several traditional types of Italian line meet this norm, not just the line of five iambs (stresses in 2, 4, 6, and 8), but also the heroic line (stresses in 2 and 6), the sapphic line (4 and 8), and the rare Type A1 (stressed only in 6) and even rarer Type B1 (only in 4). Two other types of line may also meet this definition: the emphatic (stressed in 1) providing its only s in w is line-initial; and the adonic (stresses on both 6 and 7). A stress in position 1 does not violate SMP because it does not have two neighbors, and a stress in position 7 is not a stress maximum if the neighboring position 6 also contains a stress. If we combine all these types under the heading SMP iambic then almost all *endecasillabi* fall into just three rhythmic types. The percentage of each type contained in each of my samples is shown in Figure 4 below:

[47] See Gasparov, 1987: 332.

Accented *Syllables*	*Endecasillabo Rhythm*	Dante %	Boccaccio %	Petrarch %
SMP	Iambic	79	72	83
4–7–10	Dactylic	6	20	0
3–6–10	Melodic	13	8	15

Fig. 4: Comparison of Rhythms (Based on SMP)

These figures show that Boccaccio's design favored dactylic rhythms, and that Petrarch's design eliminated them. They also show that Petrarch's only violation of SMP is the melodic line; but 15 percent is a substantial minority, and so the description of his *endecasillabo* as iambic is not justified. Petrarch chose not iambic rhythm, but rhythmic variety, just as Dante had done, but the chief form of variety Petrarch's design sanctions is an anapestic first hemistich with an *a maiore* caesura. In contrast, lines stressed on syllable 4 and followed by an *a minore* caesura form an overwhelming majority in Boccaccio's poem, features that also allowed him to indulge in his preferred form of variety—triple time.

Petrarch avoided dactylic rhythms: the contrast between their triple time and the prevailing duple time of his lines seems to have been too great. Nevertheless, almost one-in-five of his lines contains a stressed syllable in position 7. In my analysis they are all (58) classified as adonic lines, because in their position 6 forty-nine of them have a lexical stress and nine have a monosyllable, invariably a pronoun. A triple-time delivery of these nine lines that subordinates any stress on the pronoun to the stress in position 7 is not impossible, but it is not inevitable. There is a strong case that the natural emphasis of some phrases promotes a pronoun, as in the final line (246, 14) of the poem in which Petrarch prays that he may die before Laura and says that he does not want ears to hear:

(24) **Sen**za l'**o**neste <u>sue</u> **dol**ci pa**ro**le [1ª 4ª 6ª 7ª 10ª]

("Without <u>Her</u> sweet ingenuous words.")

Promoting the pronoun in this way makes every line of the poem's sestet adonic; since the original description of such a line was a *fragmento adónico*, this seems an appropriate rhythm for Petrarch's subject.[48]

This interpretation of Petrarch's lines with a stress in position 7 is born out by comparing them with Boccaccio's many dactylic lines. Boccaccio very often places amphibrachic words in positions 6–7–8 of such lines in Book 1 of the *Filostrato*: for example, *distrutta* (64), *piacente* (154), *ridendo* (164), *rispetto* (187), and *pelagio* (250). But Petrarch never does this: in his lines with a stress in position

[48] The term *fragmento adónico* (for a line with clashing stresses in positions 6 and 7) appears first in Ferguson, 1981: 66.

7, position 6 always contains a pronoun, as in example (97), or an auxiliary verb: *suo* (247, 12), *mie* (248, 12), *mi* (249, 1), *ch'i* (348, 14), *à* (350, 2), *è* (350, 8), and *che* (352, 1 and 355, 13). From this it is clear that Petrarch was avoiding peaks of stress in position 7; as with his use of multiple synaloepha, he was demoting stressed syllables in weak positions.

The above analysis shows that Petrarch rendered passages of *endecasillabi* much more iambic in rhythm, but there remains in his design a predilection for an anapestic line-opening to provide rhythmic variety, and he employed far more of what modern metrists call *colon-initial inversion* to provide even greater variety. Thus the percentages for emphatic lines (*initial inversion*) and adonic lines (*medial inversion*) in my samples are as follows:

Accented *Syllables*	*Endecasillabo Type*	Dante %	Boccaccio %	Petrarch %
1>—10	Emphatic	26	17	23
>6–7–10	Adonic	9	9	19
>4–5–10	Other	1	1	2

Fig. 5: Comparison of Inversions (Based on PT)

The figures for Petrarch in this table can be compared with those for inversion in the iambic pentameters of English poets: initial inversion is at its highest in Milton's *Paradise Lost* (7 percent of lines), and medial inversion is at its highest in Webster's dramatic verse (8 percent).[49] Petrarch loved duple time, but he sought far more rhythmic variety in it than any English iambic pentameter poet.

To sum up, Chaucer encountered three very different styles of *endecasillabo*: the accentually variable line of Boccaccio, the preponderantly iambic line of Petrarch, and the line of Dante that was in many respects intermediate between the two. But none of these designs were quite English iambic pentameters: the poets' desire for rhythmic variety was too great or, more probably, the language's secondary stresses and tendency to stress-timing are not sufficiently strong. As in so many aspects of poetic meter, the principle of fit was all-important in the development of a particular design.

Epilogue

By 1378, when Chaucer last visited Italy, both Boccaccio and Petrarch were dead, and Italian critics call the century that followed the *secolo senza poesia* (in *vulgare*, that is); this term is an exaggeration, but most Italian writers did return to Latin, doubtless reassured by the higher value that Dante and Petrarch put on

[49] The statistics quoted are from Duffell, 2008a: 240–45.

their Latin works. The next chapter in the history of the *endecasillabo*, therefore, belongs to Pietro Bembo (b. 1470–d. 1547).[50] He was a busy and ambitious cleric who whiled away his spare time by composing sonnets in the manner of Petrarch. When he became a cardinal in 1520 he had the confidence to publish them, and they were an instant success: there followed a vogue, for *l'art de petrarquiser* in France, Spain, Portugal, and England.

The art's English exponents were Sir Thomas Wyatt (b. 1503–d. 1542) and Henry Howard, Earl of Surrey (b. c. 1517–d. 1547), who around 1532 began writing English sonnets.[51] Bembo followed Petrarch's verse design very closely in his own sonnets, and the poets of Spain and Portugal followed Bembo; but French poets employed the *vers de dix* for their sonnets, and Surrey did likewise, while Wyatt patriotically tried to invent his own English meter.[52] Only after Sir Philip Sidney's visit to Italy in the 1570s did English poets rediscover the meter that so attracted Chaucer on his visits in 1372 and 1378. When Sidney sat down to write his own *Canzoniere* (called *Astrophel and Stella*) in 1580, he eschewed the *vers de dix*, ignored traditional English versifying, and retraced Chaucer's steps to the English metrical canon.[53]

---

[50] For the works of Pietro Bembo, see Dionisotti, 1966.

[51] For the poems of Wyatt, see Rebholz, 1978; for those of Surrey, see Keene, 1985.

[52] See Duffell, 2008a: 120–21.

[53] For Sidney's iambic pentameters, see Bullett, 1947: 172–278.

9
The *Décasyllabe* in England

At this point I shall summarize this volume's progress in the study of ME versification. In Chapter 5, I examined briefly the surviving texts in OE, ME, and AN that reveal the native background to Chaucer's versifying. In subsequent chapters I probed more deeply into one type of meter.

In Chapter 6, I showed that the verse designs of a number of ME poems differed from the iambic tetrameter in only two respects: the ME designs allowed headless lines (the omission of an initial offbeat to give a strong trochaic pulse) and lines with epic caesura (the division of the line into two two-beat half-lines). In order to be precise, I described these ME designs as *duple-time four-beat dolniks.* I also examined in detail the most important factor masking the closeness of these ME dolniks to stress-syllabic tetrameters: the extensive para-phonology of ME, compounded by scribal error.

In Chapter 7, I showed that it was John Gower, and not Geoffrey Chaucer, who transformed the duple-time four-beat dolnik into the iambic tetrameter. Gower did this in two languages: in AN by making his *octosyllabes* iambic and in ME by eschewing headless lines and epic caesura. The loss of these two traditional ME features, however, risked rhythmic monotony: four relentless beats preceded by four offbeats. Gower's reluctance to employ initial inversion made this meter less than an ideal for long narratives, which he relieved by incorporating many different stories in *CA.*

In Chapter 8, I examined the verse designs of the Italian *endecasillabi* that Chaucer knew well, and in this chapter I shall examine the emergence of a new longer line in both AN and ME during the last quarter of the fourteenth century. I shall begin by looking at the math of line length and explaining why Chaucer's and Gower's longer line had no precedent in England.

The Math of Line Length

The most obvious advantage a line of ten syllables has over a line of eight is that it can hold more linguistic material—25 percent more to be precise. The second advantage in a language where rhymes are scarce is that longer lines require fewer rhymes, four pairs of rhyme words per eighty syllables instead of five—20 percent fewer. The third advantage in a language where binary contrasts between stressed and unstressed syllables are possible is that there are more permutations of the binary digits *1* (more stress than its neighbor) and 0 (less stress). Since the line-final syllable must always have more stress than its neighbor, the number of permutations in a decasyllable is factorial nine (9!), and the number in an octosyllable is factorial seven (7!). This is an immense difference: a decasyllable can accommodate seventy-two times as many permutations of stress/non-stress (362,880 as against 5,040).

Finally, in a highly monosyllabic language, the difference between the two line lengths in the number of permutations of word-boundary position is in the same ratio—72:1.[1] These calculations show that there is a great deal more potential for variety in the longer line, in semantic content, syntax, accentual profile, and the positioning of lexical boundaries. There must therefore have been a very good reason why English poets before Chaucer ignored such potential riches.[2]

The most obvious reason is that composing approximate octosyllables was easy and composing decasyllables difficult. The poets of England had for centuries counted beats, not syllables, and they have continued to pass this habit onto their children in the form of nursery rhymes and proverbs right up to the present day. Rhythmic beats and the intervals, or offbeats, that divide them, build naturally into fours: the symmetry of 2 + 2 = 4 beats has attracted versifiers in many languages.[3] When the Normans arrived in England their favorite poetic line had eight syllables, which equated to four beats and four offbeats. The traditional French way of counting to eight relied on weak word stress and syllable timing; the English way exploited the potential for producing eight syllables by filling each of the intervals between four beats with a single syllable. This method produced exactly eight syllables if the poet began the line in the most obvious English way, with a grammatical monosyllable. If he did not, it produced a headless line, and if he was forced occasionally to slip two light syllables into an interval, it produced the dolnik. Once AN had acquired the strong word stress of English, and something of its stress-timing, AN poets could do the same. Thus it is that

[1] In English verse monosyllables represent more than 70 percent of words as units; see Duffell, 2002b: 305, table (column 2). Similarly, the proportion of words that are monosyllables in French verse is around 67 percent; see Billy, 1999: 510, note 12.

[2] The popularity of the line of ten syllables has extended to all the languages of Europe; see Thomas, 1904 and Alonso, 1958. For the spread of Western European meters to Central and Eastern Europe see Gasparov, 1996: 166–269.

[3] The four-beat rhythm is common to many verse traditions worldwide; thus, for example, the Old Tamil *kural* meter resembles English common measure; see Alphonso-Karkala, 1972: 293. For beats as the basis of children's verse, see Burling, 1966: passim; four-beat verse is particularly simple because of its generation by doubling; see Attridge, 2013: 150.

many AN political songs have also survived in English versions, and the lines of both texts share the same approximate regularities.[4]

The *octosyllabe* is also relatively easy to adapt because in continental French it is a one-beat line: the stress on every eighth syllable is emphasized by rhyme, and rhymes arrive with great regularity.[5] Introducing three mid-line beats into such lines just converts them from expresses into stopping trains. The conversion was easy, as is evidenced by the many volumes of verse published by the Anglo-Norman Texts Society, and, indeed, by a substantial proportion of the ME verse that has survived. The reason why the *vers de dix* did not cross *La Manche* as easily was that it was too complicated, it was a two-beat line: the first beat (usually in position 4) was supplied by a phrasal stress that did not rhyme, and the second (in position 10) by one that did. Without the precise syllable timing of continental French, English audiences never knew when the next stress would arrive. The eventual solution was to settle for five beats, a prime number with no factors, but it brought with it unforeseen advantages, as I shall demonstrate in the next chapter.

This chapter will be devoted to making the case that, even if the French *vers de dix* was not the model for the iambic pentameter, it provided a springboard from which Gower (in particular) and Chaucer could make the leap to the English stress-syllabic meter. In this chapter I shall plot the trajectory from the *vers de dix* to the pentameter, and show how, and why, in French at least, the leap was not consolidated by subsequent poets. This will involve a comparison between the verse designs of four poets versifying in England in the second half of the fourteenth century and the first half of the fifteenth. They all versified in French, but the first poet obeyed the rules of the French meter as far as his skills allowed, the second chipped away at those rules a little, the third violated them most horribly, and the fourth showed that those rules could outlive the outrage. But before proceeding to tell the story of the *vers de dix* in England I shall recapitulate the metrical rules of the French meter and place them in a modern linguistic setting.

The French Decasyllable: A Constraint-based Approach

In 2005 I joined Dominique Billy in demonstrating that John Gower took a vital step towards creating the English iambic pentameter in the late 1370s, when he began to compose the first AN *vers de dix* and gave them a prevailing iambic rhythm. Our article offered new support for the belief of many scholars in France, and some teachers of French in the USA, that the iambic pentameter is

[4] See Pyle, 1935 and Aspin, 1953.

[5] See Kastner, 1903: 140-42

of French origin.[6] The case for a French origin badly needed support, because the English textual evidence is heavily against it. By the year 1400 both Chaucer and Gower were composing English poetry with a verse design that was very like Petrarch's and very different from Machaut's. This development is more likely to have been led by Chaucer, because he knew Italian, visited Italy, translated Boccaccio, and may even have met Petrarch.

In this chapter I shall present Billy's research and our conclusions for the first time in English. Its core will consist of the research Billy conducted in preparation for two articles, one on Froissart's metrics published in 1999, and the other on our joint publication of 2005. I was privileged to be allowed to assist him on the second and, since he prefers the term *décasyllabe* to *vers de dix*, I shall acknowledge his greater contribution by adopting the former term forthwith.[7] In explaining Billy's analysis, however, I shall introduce some abbreviations of my own that will prove useful in subsequent chapters.

Billy noted that the verse design of the *décasyllabe* contains two distinct *constraints*, the first is *d'ordre accentuelle* and the second *d'ordre morpholigique.*[8] I shall translate these terms loosely, but simply, as a 'stress constraint' and a 'word constraint.' I shall refer to the first as the PS (phrasal stress) constraint, remembering that phrasal stress is the only remaining type in modern French, and the second as the WB (word-boundary) constraint. WB prevents the syllables in positions 4 and 5 of a *décasyllabe* belonging to the same word, and PS causes the line's first phrasal stress to fall in positions 4. An individual decasyllabic line may either observe or violate each of these constraints: that is, it may be +WB or -WB, and +PS or -PS. A given line may also meet the demands of these constraints only by a metrical convention that allows a feminine word or masculine adjective to appear at the caesura. I shall describe lines that preserve a constraint in this way as =WB or =PS.

=WB is achieved in French by elision (rather than the Italian synaloepha): I shall illustrate =WB by one of Machaut's lines scanned in Chapter 4. I have simplified my scansion aids because by the fourteenth century word-stress in Continental varieties of French had weakened to the point where versifiers could ignore it. Thus the only metrically significant stresses in this line are the phrasal ones in positions 4 and 10, and they are the only ones I mark here (by bold typeface or underlining).

---

[6] For an example of unquestioning belief in a French model, see Figg and Palmer, 2001: 31.

[7] Up to this point I have used the terms *octosyllabe*, *vers de dix*, and *alexandrin* to describe the three most popular French meters, hoping that the visual difference between them would aid readers. Since this book's business with the other meters is almost complete this no longer applies.

[8] See Billy and Duffell, 2005: 74.

(1) Quant à vous **pens**^{e} // et je sui entre gent

("When I think of you and I am in company.")

In this line WB is threatened by the post-tonic syllable of *pense*, and then rescued by the elision of that syllable before an initial vowel in the second hemistich. The result of this convention (=WB +PS) is what French metrists call a line with *elided caesura*, and lines with such a caesura represent one of three types found in fourteenth-century *décasyllabes* (but are rare in earlier ones).

The most common type of *décasyllabe*, however, by a large margin, is the line that observes both constraints (+WB and +PS); again I illustrate it by a line from Machaut:[9]

(2) J'aim mieux lan**guir** // en estrange con**tree**

("I prefer to languish in a foreign country.")

This type of line has what is known as a *masculine caesura*, and because it is +WB and +PS is regarded as the prototype of the meter. Note that a variant of it violates the PS constraint. Again I illustrate this with lines by Machaut to show that, while position 4 contains a syllable with word stress, the mid-line phrasal stress has migrated to later in the line (notated by both bold typeface and underlining):

(3) Et la tres grant // dou**ceur** qui en des**cent** $[4^{e}\ \underline{6}^{\underline{e}}\ \underline{10}^{\underline{e}}]$
(4) Et se des biens // de For**tu**ne n'ai **mie** $[4^{e}\ \underline{7}^{\underline{e}}\ \underline{10}^{\underline{e}}]$

("And the surpassing sweetness it engenders;" "And if I am not blessed with fortune's gifts.")

Both 'grant' in (3) and 'biens' in (4) are masculine words, and so these lines qualify as having a masculine caesura, but, although these words bear phrasal stress in other contexts, here they are subordinated in the stress hierarchy to a subsequent syllable: that occupying position 6 in (3) and that occupying position 7 in (4). In terms of constraints these lines are therefore +WB but, at best, can only be described as =PS.

The third type of line that occurs frequently in passages of medieval *décasyllabes* is the line with lyric caesura, and in terms of constraints such a line is +WB and -PS. Again I illustrate this with a line by Machaut :

(5) Et les **goutes** // de **plui**^{e} et de la mer $[\underline{3}^{\underline{e}}\ 6^{e}\ \underline{10}^{\underline{e}}]$ =

("And the drops of rain and of the sea.")

[9] See Chapter 4, examples (33) to (36).

In this line I have also marked the syllable in position 6, because it offers an alternative site for phrasal stress to position 3. This alternative would have been particularly attractive when the line was set to music (assuming that the syllable in position 3 did not coincide with the musical beat).

To sum up this constraint analysis, +WB and +PS (masculine) *décasyllabes* are by far the most common, but other lines were sanctioned by convention: =WB +PS (with elided caesura); +WB -PS (with lyric caesura)); and +WB=PS (which I shall term lines with a *subordinated masculine caesura* because the syllable in position 4 does not carry the final stress of the phrase). The trend between the eleventh and thirteenth centuries was for the WB constraint to strengthen. At the beginning of that period poets employed lines that were -WB and +PS (termed *epic caesura*), like the following line (36) from the *Vie de Saint Alexis:*

(6) Oz mei, pul**ce**[le]! // Celui tien ad es**pus**

("Listen to me, girl, take this man as a husband.")

In lines like this the poet simply treated his *décasyllabe* like a *tetrasyllabe* plus a *hexasyllabe*, each capable of being either masculine or feminine. But such a violation of WB was increasingly avoided and by the thirteenth century had been all but abandoned. By then it was common for 90 percent of the lines in a decasyllabic poem to have masculine caesuras and most of the remainder to have lyric caesuras.[10]

The gradual replacement of epic by lyric caesuras represented a strengthening of the WB constraint at the expense of the PS constraint. Billy relates how this was reversed in the fourteenth century, when poets wishing to place feminine words mid-line began to prefer elided to lyric caesura, that is, they challenged WB (=WB) rather than violating PS (–PS). This is the background, expressed in terms of constraints, to the revisit I shall make to the 1999 and 2005 research into the *décasyllabes* of Froissart and Gower. But before comparing the verse designs of those two poets I shall examine briefly some *décasyllabes* that are even more relevant to the subject of this volume because they may be by Chaucer.

The Poems of 'Ch'

The manuscript MS French 15 owned by the University of Pennsylvania contains a number of poems connected with the English court.[11] It is difficult to date the manuscript precisely, but it contains five ballades by Oton de Granson

[10] See Billy, 1992: 807–9.

[11] See Wimsatt, 1982; the text of these fifteen poems is now on the website given in 'Works Cited.'

(b. c. 1345–d. c. 1397), and this suggests a date in the late 1360s. The manuscript also holds fifteen poems in which the initials 'Ch' appear under the rubric, and James Wimsatt's research into the members of the royal court offers no candidate for these initials other than Chaucer. This raises the question of whether there is any evidence in these poems that the young Chaucer was a metrical innovator, and I shall pursue that question here. The fifteen Poems of 'Ch' comprise ten ballades, four *chançons royales*, and a rondel. My sample for quantified analysis consists of the first nine of the fifteen poems (six ballades and three *chançons*).

The poem and strophe designs of Ch's verse are extremely conventional, as is its content: lovers and ladies pine, sigh, and rejoice, invoking abstract nouns (like Generosity, Danger, and Hope), and dropping classical names (like Helen, Ariadne, and Dido). Stereotypes and cliches abound and the treatment of love and all its tropes shows very little originality. As Pearsall notes, these are exactly the type of poems that young courtiers wrote to prove that they could; and, even if 'Ch' is someone else, Chaucer would have been expected to engage in such feats of versification as part of his life at court.[12] Although Pearsall finds little merit in these fifteen poems it is worth examining the verse design of the Poems of 'Ch' in some detail, because any signs of metrical originality would increase the credibility of the attribution.

Figure 1 below compares the proportion of each type of line in my quantified sample of the Poems of 'Ch' (300 lines) with that in Froissart's ballades, which contain 470 lines in total, as analyzed by Billy.[13]

	Percentages			
	Masc. Caes.	*Lyric Caes.*	*Elided Caes.*	*Other Caes.*
Poems of 'Ch'	75	11	9	5
Froissart: Ballades	89	4	6	1

Fig. 1: Comparison of Ballade caesuras: 'Ch' and Froissart

These statistics show that 'Ch' employed twice the proportion of feminine words at the caesura as did Froissart in the same verse form. They also show that the Poems of 'Ch' contain more lines that do not meet the fourteenth-century *décasyllabe*'s norms (in the column headed *other*). The ways in which they deviate from the norm can be seen from the examples below, where I have noted the irregularity in brackets, whether it is in the accentual pattern or syllable count:

(7) Secours con**for**te // Dangier preste**ment** [4F + 5M] (1.16)
(8) Congnoistre q̣ụẹ // loyau**ment**, sans fauls tour [7^{e} 10^{e}] (2.22)
(9) En jeun^{e} es**ta**[te] // Leesse habandon**ner** [4F + 6M] (8.25)

[12] See Pearsall, 1992: 73–74.

[13] For an analysis of Froissart's lyric verse, see Billy, 1999: 538–41.

(10) [ ] Atro**pos,** // prest^e a me devou**rer** [3M + 6M?] (8.22)
(11) Et l'acort joieuse**ment** // traïc**tier** [6M + 4M] (9.11)

("Help soothes Danger quickly;" "Know that loyally, without deceit;" "in youth to abandon gaiety;" "Atropos ready to devour me;" "and to make sweet peace.")

Example (7) seems to have *coupe italienne*, since *dangier* is usually two syllables in the Poems of 'Ch.' Example (8) has a *weak* masculine caesura, making them +WB and -PS; I mark the monosyllable that lacks phrasal stress with a dotted underline. Example (9) has epic caesura (also -WB and +PS), since *leesse* is always three syllables in these poems. Example (10) is either a syllable short or has lyric caesura and requires hiatus in its second hemistich, displacing the mid-line peak of phrasal stress onto syllable 7. Finally, example (11) has a colon boundary and phrasal stress at syllable 3, but it scans best as a 6 + 4 line of the type found in *Girart de Roussillon*. When lines like example (11) occur in 4 + 6 *décasyllabes*, Billy describes them as having an *enjambed caesura*, but I prefer to reserve that term for lines in which a phrase rather than a word straddles the hemistichs, because that is by far the most common type of enjambment at line ends.[14]

The presence of deviant lines like examples (7) to (11) in the Poems of 'Ch' also arouses a suspicion that there were occasions when the poet found difficulty in expressing his thoughts using conventional forms, and so resorted to archaic types of line that survived more in memory than in current practice.[15] Alternatively, the deviance may be a sign that 'Ch' was metrically challenged, or that he was not working in his mother tongue. The remaining features of 'Ch's metrics are unremarkable: 53 percent of his rhymes are masculine, and he employs elision 23 times per 100 lines. Overall, therefore, there is little in the poems to attract the interest of modern scholars other than the initials 'Ch.'

[14] Remarkably, there is no line in my sample of the poems of 'Ch' where a phrase, but not a word, runs on past position 4, as in examples (3) and (4) above. The absence of such lines suggests that 'Ch' was rather less confident in fitting French syntax to his template than was Machaut, or indeed Froissart, who employed a large number of them. Note that Billy uses Aldo Menichetti's term *formes ancipites* ('ambiguous structures') for the lines that I describe as having an *enjambed caesura*; see Billy and Duffell, 2005: 87.

[15] It is difficult to say whether 'Ch' knew that Occitan poets violated the *décasyllabe's* word-boundary constraint on rare occasions, or whether he was simply stumped for a more regular line.

Froissart's Reforms of the *Décasyllabe*

Jean Froissart spent the years 1361–1369 in England at the court of Queen Philippa, and quickly established himself as a royal favorite, chronicler, and poet. Like his royal patron, Froissart came from Hainault, and his work contains many forms typical of the Picard dialect. Approximately 3,500 of his decasyllables have survived in *dits* ('ditties') and in lyric forms such as *ballades* and *rondeaux*.[16] The longest of his poems, a *dit* entitled *L'Orloge amoureus* (*OA*), dates from c. 1368, and in its 1174 *décasyllabes* Froissart ingeniously compares love to the working of a clock. *OA*'s strophe design, appropriately, is the tick-tock of the rhymed couplet, but its verse design is much more controversial.

As Billy notes, the poem's modern editors have described many of its lines as *extraordinaires* (abnormal), *deféctuosités* (defects), or even *amorphes* (formless).[17] Billy's 1999 analysis addresses these criticisms, and he examines and quantifies the irregularities concerned in a more objective and logically rigorous fashion. His article covers all Froissart's *décasyllabes* and demonstrates that the verse design of *OA* differs significantly from that of his other decasyllabic poems. This shows even from a quick comparison between *OA* and Froissart's ballades: as noted above, 89 percent of the lines in the ballades have a masculine caesura, 6 percent have an elided, and 4 percent a lyric caesura. In *OA*, on the other hand, only 80 percent of lines have a masculine caesura, and elided and lyric caesuras each account for only 6 percent.

The remainder of *OA*'s lines show a variety of departures from the norm, of which the most important are illustrated by the following examples.[18]

(12)	Ce que les **aul**[tres] // instrumens ne font pas	[4F + 6F]	(13)
(13)	Et de lo**yal** // a**mour** les circons**tan**sces	$[4^{e}\ \underline{6}^{\underline{e}}\ \underline{10}^{\underline{e}}]$	(31)
(14)	La roe ḍẹ // **Desir** a ce l'a**tour**ne	$[\underline{6}^{\underline{e}}\ \underline{10}^{\underline{e}}]$	(594)
(15)	Et a ma neccessi**té** // pourfi**ta**ble	$[7^{e}\ \underline{10}^{\underline{e}}]$	(540)
(16)	Toutes fois, **da**me, // que je le vous **die**	[4F + 5F]	(895)
(17)	La premer**ain**ne // **roe** qui y **lo**ge	$[4^{e}\ \underline{6}^{\underline{e}}\ \underline{10}^{\underline{e}}]$	(100)
(18)	Comme le Papil**lon** // a la chan**de**le	$[\underline{6}^{\underline{e}}\ \underline{10}^{\underline{e}}]$	(134)
(19)	Avec Perseve**ranc**^{e} // et Dili**gen**sce	$[\underline{6}^{\underline{e}}\ \underline{10}^{\underline{e}}]$	(432)
(20)	Les heures amou**reu**ses, // au voir **di**re	$[\underline{6}^{\underline{e}}\ \underline{10}^{\underline{e}}]$	(482)

("That which other devices cannot do;" "And the circumstances of faithful love;" "The wheel of desire has turned to this;" "And advantageous to

[16] For Froissart's poetical works, see Scheler, 1870–73; for the text of the *Orloge amoureus*, see Dembowski, 1986.

[17] For a discussion of Froissart's editors' analysis of *OA*'s meter, see Billy, 1999: 511–17.

[18] See Billy, 1999: 510.

my needs;" "The principal wheel that is located there;" "Like a moth at a candle;" "With persistence and diligence;" "To see told the hours of love.")

Four lines in *OA* have epic caesura like example (12); ten lines have an overflowing caesura like example (13); and fifty-two lines have a weak masculine caesura like example (14). Example (15) is a unique line that violates both the WB and PS constraints. Three lines in *OA* have *coupe italienne* like (16) and (17), and the latter has its principal mid-line stress in position 6. Fifteen lines subdivide 6 + 4 with a masculine caesura like example (18); four lines divide 6 + 4 with an elided caesura like (19); and eight lines divide 6 + 4 with a feminine caesura like example (20)

From the above statistics and his close examination of individual instances Billy concludes that the aim of Froissart's metrical reforms was to provide a counterpoint to the many hundreds of standard 4 + 6 *décasyllabes* in this poem.[19] Some 80 percent of *OA*'s lines observe both the meter's constraints, WB and PS, while only 12 percent offer the meter's conventional form of rhythmic variety—the compromise of WB or the violation of PS. Because *OA* was Froissart's longest decasyllabic poem, he set out to increase the level of rhythmic variety substantially, and he did so largely by including lines of the 6 + 4 type. In order to do so, he had to violate WB, PS, or both, and once he had taken this unconventional decision, he experimented with even more unconventional lines. I find Billy's analysis of Froissart's reformed *décasyllabes* as impressive today as when I first read it, and his conclusions on its motivation equally convincing.

Billy discounts any possible Italian connection to Froissart's versifying on the grounds that there is no sign of Italian influence in any other aspect of the poem.[20] This seems very reasonable, since Froissart composed *OA* ten years before his journey to Italy in 1378, when he may have met Petrarch and Chaucer in Milan. Froissart's own sense of rhythm was quite sufficient to enable him to see the advantages of incorporating the counterpoint of the 4 + 6 line, without the aid of an Italian model. The potential for this counterpoint had always existed in the meter, and Italian poets had sensed this in the thirteenth century; it should therefore be no surprise if at least one French poet did the same, unprompted, in the fourteenth.

Billy closed his article by pointing out that this counterpoint is highly appropriate in a poem about a clock, which works by mechanical forms of tension (=as shown by such terms as *movement*, *pendulum*, and *escape mechanism*.[21]

[19] See Billy, 1999: 516–17.

[20] See Billy, 1999: 520 and 523.

[21] See Billy, 1999: 544.

Gower's Deviant Decasyllables

John Gower produced two collections of ballades: his *Cinkant Balades* (*CB*) seem to have been composed at various time between 1377 and 1399, and those in his *Traité* (*T*) probably date from shortly before his marriage in 1397. *CB* contains 55 poems and *T* contains 18, and if incomplete and repeated lines are excluded Gower has left us 1,626 decasyllables (split 1,287 and 339 between the two collections). The article that Billy and I published in 2005 on Gower's *décasyllabes* was the result of a joint project to analyze and compare Gower's (1,626) French and (469) English decasyllables.[22] Since the results of our study of the former were published in French, I shall take this opportunity to bring them to the attention of English-speaking readers, and in the account that follows I shall give prominence to percentages, so that they can be compared with those in other poems analyzed in this chapter.

Our 2005 article showed that Gower's reforms of the *décasyllabe* were much more drastic than those of Froissart in *OA*. In order to set the irregularity of Gower's lines in the context of this chapter, Figure 2 below gives the percentages of each type of line in the Poems of 'Ch,' Froissart's ballades, Froissart's *OA*, and Gower's *CB* and *T* combined, based on the entire corpus with the exception of the Poems of 'Ch,' where I have used my 300-line sample.

	Type of Caesura			
	Masc.	*Lyric*	*Elided*	*Other*
Froissart Ballades	89	4	6	1
Poems of 'Ch'	75	11	9	5
Froissart *OA*	80	6	6	8
Gower *CB* & *T*	71	0*	13	16

Fig. 2: Comparison of Three Poets' *Décasyllabes*

The most obvious difference between Gower's lines and those of the other poets is that he employed fewer of the conventional types of caesura and more of the unconventional: the proportion of his lines in the *Other* column is double that of Froissart's *OA*. Gower also employed double the proportion of elided caesuras and avoided lyric caesuras. Only three of Gower's lines have lyric caesura (fewer than 1 percent), including the following:

(21) Car lors **chan**tont // et Merl^{e} et Pape**gai** [3^{e} 10^{e}] (*CB*, 36: 3)

("For the blackbird and finch sang to them.")

[22] Ours was an e-mail collaboration and we met only when it was complete. Dominique did most of the work on this article and produced the final typescript, while I performed the same task on its companion, which covered Gower's English decasyllables.

Note that position 6 in this line contains a strong syllable, as does one of the other two lines of this type.

Among the 16 percent *Other* are eleven epic caesuras (0.7 percent of total), and they include the following:

(22) Qe mieulx vol**droi**[e] // morir en son ser**vage** [$\underline{4}^{e}$ $\underline{10}^{e}$] (*CB*, 23: 14)

(23) Car qui bien **ai**[me] // ses amours tard ob**lie** [$\underline{4}^{e}$ $\underline{10}^{e}$] (*CB*, 25: R)

("That would rather die in her service;" "for he who loves well is slow to forget his passion.")

Our 2005 article notes that apocope in AN may have regularized some of these lines, particularly those with *dame* at the caesura (for example, *CB*, 2: 23 and *CB*, 19: 20).[23] In Chapters 6 and 7 of this volume, however, I showed that dividing the line at the caesura in this way and allowing a post-tonic syllable in both halves was a common device in ME four-beat verse. Gower may therefore have been taking advantage of an English convention as well as a French one in these eleven lines.

The great majority of the lines in the *Other* category are of two types: those where WB is violated and those where PS is compromised. The largest group consists of 138 lines (8.5 percent of total) that violate the WB constraint and have the same word occupying positions 4 and 5. These 138 subdivide very differently from the comparable lines in Froissart's *OA*, where 29 out of 31 had a phrasal stress in position 6. In Gower's *décasyllabes* only 28 of these lines (1.7 percent of total) have such a 6 + 4 structure, including the following lines: [24]

(24) Si fuisse en para**dis** // ceo beal ma**noir** [$\underline{6}^{e}$ $\underline{10}^{e}$] (*CB*, 5: 21)

(25) O tresgentile **dame** // simpl^{e} et **coie** [$\underline{6}^{e}$ $\underline{10}^{e}$] (*CB*, 9: 33)

(26) Qe nulle medi**cine** // m'est ver**raie** [$\underline{6}^{e}$ $\underline{10}^{e}$] (*CB*, 27: 4)

(27) Al universit**é** // de tout le **monde** [$\underline{6}^{e}$ $\underline{10}^{e}$] (*T*, 18: 22)

("If this fine mansion were in paradise;" "O exalted lady, sincere and Shy;" "Of which no medicine will cure me;" "To the university of life.")

The overwhelming majority of Gower's lines that violate the WB constraint (110 lines, or 6.8 percent of total) have a phrase-final stress in position 4 and must be classed as having *coupe italienne*. They include the following:

(28) Du Provi**dence** // q'est celesti**al** [$\underline{4}^{e}$ $\underline{10}^{e}$] (*CB*, d1: 3)

(29) Henri le **quatre**, // l'oure soit be**noit** [$\underline{4}^{e}$ $\underline{10}^{e}$] (*CB*, d2: 2)

(30) Q'es flour des **autres** // la plus excel**lente** [$\underline{4}^{e}$ $\underline{10}^{e}$] (*CB*, 16: 26)

---

[23] See Billy and Duffell, 2005: 76.

[24] See Billy and Duffell, 2005: 77, 82.

(31) Mais cest ess**am**ple // n'est pas ave**nu** [4ᵉ 10ᵉ] (*CB*, 18: 3)

("Of Providence that is celestial;" "Henry IV, may the hour be blessed;" "Which is the most excellent of all flowers;" "But this example has not actualized.")

Most of the remaining lines classed as *Other* compromise the PS constraint (PS=): fifty lines (3 percent of total) have a subordinated masculine caesura, like the following line:

(32) Ensi com dieus // le voet, ensi se**rra** [4ᵉ 6ᵉ 10ᵉ] (*CB*, 2: 15)

("Just as God wills, so it shall be.")

Note that in AN, with its stronger word stress, the syllables in both positions 4 and 6 would have been made prominent in delivery, giving the line a marked iambic rhythm. A further 110 lines of Gower's lines (5.3 percent of total) have a weak masculine caesura, including the following:[25]

(33) Q'apres dieu et // les saintz de Para**dis** [6ᵉ 10ᵉ] (*CB*, 9: 7)
(34) Au solail, qe // les **her**bes eslu**mi**ne [6ᵉ 10ᵉ] (*CB*, 21: 1)
(35) Pour penser les // **amours** de temps long**tein** [6ᵉ 10ᵉ] (*CB*, 24: 9)
(36) N'ad cure de // ma supplica**cion** [10ᵉ] (*CB*, 35: 12)

("That after god and the saints of paradise"; "in the sun that makes the greenery shine;" "to think of the loves of long ago"; "takes no heed of my humble prayer.")

Note that examples (33), (34), and (35) have phrasal stress in position 6, but example (36) does not; these four lines are thus typical of this group. Overall, lines with phrasal stress in position 6 are about three times as common in Gower's *balades* as in Froissart's *OA*.

The final contribution to Gower's *Other* percentage comes from half a dozen lines that lack a caesura after any of the conventional positions, that is, after 3F syllables (lyric), 4M (masculine), or 4F (epic or *coupe italienne*). These highly irregular lines include the following:

(37) Du fillᵉ au Cal**cas** mesna sa lee**sce** [5ᵉ 10ᵉ] (*CB*, 20: 22)
(38) Deux prestres enbasti**ront** tout le plai [7ᵉ 10ᵉ] (*T*, 10: 18)
(39) Cil rois qui valentini**ans** ot noun [8ᵉ 10ᵉ] (*T*, 16: 5)

("Repaid Calcas's daughter's disloyalty;" "two priests drew up the whole petition;" "The kings who heard Valentinian's name.")

[25] See Billy and Duffell, 2005: 83–86.

Billy offers two possible explanations of these lines: the first is that Gower's abandonment of the word-boundary constraint (after position 4) led naturally to an occasional line of this type; the second is that AN speakers may have shifted the accent in some French words (particularly foreign names) to the normal Germanic syllable for stress.[26] Yet, while '**Cal**cas' and 'Va**len**tinians' are credible AN accentuations 'enbas**ti**ront' is much less so.

From the foregoing analysis it can be seen that there are a large number of deviant lines in Gower's two works, and in 2005 Billy and I offered two hypotheses to explain Gower's decasyllabic verse design. The first of these we labeled the 'accentual' hypothesis, and the second the 'alternative-model' hypothesis. The first assumed that Gower set out to give his lines an overwhelmingly iambic rhythm, like that of ME verse (or, indeed, the octosyllabes of his own *MO*). The second assumed that, like Froissart in *OA*, Gower wished to counterpoint his many lines with phrasal stress in position 4 with a number of lines where that stress was in position 6.

Gower's avoidance of lyric caesura, where the stress in position 3 defies an iambic pulse, obviously supports the first hypothesis. We supported it further in our article with the aid of a series of graphs: these showed clearly the difference between Froissart's and Gower's placement of strong and weak syllables throughout the line.[27] One graph showed that the proportion of post-tonic syllables in Froissart's lines tends to peak only in position 7; another showed that the proportion in Gower's lines peaks in all the odd-numbered positions. Gower's *décasyllabes* are, in fact, 87 percent iambic, if measured by the percentage (12.8) of lines where a stressed syllable occurs in an odd-numbered position (3, 5, or 7).

The decasyllables with a peak of stress in position 3 are the few lines with lyric caesura, like example (21) above, and some of those with a peak in position 5 are very deviant lines like example (37). Most of the lines that have phrasal stress in position 7, however, have a weak masculine caesura in position 4, and some lines with a peak in position 5 may be the result of a weak masculine caesura in position 6, including the following:

(38) Au point quant dan**ger** ṃẹ // respon**de**ra [5^{e} $\underline{6}^{e}$ $\underline{10}^{e}$] (*CB*, 30: 18)
(39) Et pour le boun**té** ḍọṇṭ // vous estes **plei**ne [5^{e} $\underline{6}^{e}$ $\underline{10}^{e}$] (*CB*, 33: 24)

("To the point when danger answered me;" "And for your generosity which overflows.")

Such lines add a twist to our second hypothesis: that Gower, like Froissart in *OA*, wished to include a number of lines dividing 6 + 4 as a sort of counterpoint.[28]

[26] See Billy and Duffell, 2005: 89 and 91.

[27] See Billy and Duffell, 2005: 78–81.

[28] See Billy and Duffell, 2005: 82.

These two examples suggest that Gower went as far as including 6 + 4 lines with weak masculine caesura. Even if these lines are excluded, however, the percentage of lines with phrasal stress in position 6 in Gower's poems is three times that in Froissart's.

More than half of Gower's lines with a peak of stress in an odd-numbered position (7 percent by my calculation) have that peak in position 7, as in the following examples:[29]

(40)	La gentil**esc**^{e} // et la **doul**ce fi**gur**e	[<u>4</u>^{e} 7^{e} <u>10</u>^{e}]	(*CB*, 13: 9)
(41)	Et par par**ol**e // chan**ger** le visage	[<u>4</u>^{e} 7^{e} <u>10</u>^{e}]	(*CB*, 19: 3)
(42)	Ma do**lour** <u>**mont**</u>^{e} // et ma **joie** des**cres**ce	[<u>4</u>^{e} 7^{e} <u>10</u>^{e}]	(*CB*, 20: R)

("The nobility and the sweet form;" "And by words change her expression;" "My grief grows and my joy diminishes.")

Such lines with peaks of stress in positions 4–7–10 have a marked triple-time rhythm, with double offbeats between each of three strong beats. These lines provide a counterpoint to the prevailing iambic rhythm, in the same way that *OA*'s lines with phrasal stress in position 6 provide a 6 + 4 counterpoint to the prevailing rhythm of 4 + 6. Both these examples of rhythmic variety resemble that found in the Latin goliardic meter, which in Chapter 2 I noted was only *predominantly* trochaic (with only 85 percent of lines containing the prevailing trochaic rhythm).[30] Such counterpoint can be seen as a primitive form of the tension found in English iambic pentameters, where colon-initial inversions provide a much more subtle form of rhythmic variety.

In the 2005 article Billy and I concluded that the meter of *CB* and *T* was a natural development of the meter of *MO*: having succeeded in composing *octosyllabes* in AN that were predominantly iambic, Gower simply graduated to the longer line.[31] We also concluded that Gower must have recognized the same potential as Froissart for rhythmic counterpoint in the meter, and that both poets relieved the monotony of stress peaks in position 4 by including lines with peaks in position 6. Gower's more drastic violation of WB we put down to his prioritizing an iambic pulse running throughout the line to a subdivision of 4 + 6, or indeed into any regular subdivision.

We concluded that the AN language was the major factor in the making of Gower's new meter, plus his success in imparting an 'English' rhythm to the *octosyllabe* in *MO*. Two features of the dialect, both derived from its close contact

[29] Our, 2005 article did not focus on position-7 stress, nor did it discuss elision rates or masculine- / feminine-line ratios; my statistics for these are therefore based on a continuous 300-line sample (*Balades* X to XXI, and the unrepeated lines of *Balade* IX'S envoy), chosen because the opening ballades contain many missing and incomplete lines.

[30] For Goliardic meter, see Greene and Cushman, 2012: 574.

[31] See Billy and Duffell, 2005: 89, 92–93.

with English, made it imperative to find a new rhythm for an AN *décasyllabe*: stronger word stress masked the two clear beats that gave the continental French *décasyllabe* its rhythm, and a tendency to stress-timing disrupted the regularity with which those two rhythmic events occurred. Once Gower had decided to compose a longer AN line, an iambic *décasyllabe* was the obvious answer to the problem of how to give it a rhythm that its audience could appreciate.[32] English audiences sense an iambic rhythm in lines like Machaut's, 'Le grant desir que j'ai de vous veoir,' and Gower made that rhythm his staple. Thus we argued that Gower's new meter grew from a combination of the deviant phonology of the French of England and a potential that always existed in the *décasyllabe*. It was, in other words, a natural development, with no discernible outside influence.

We discounted the possibility of Italian influence on Gower's meter for two reasons: there is no sign of Italian influence on the content of Gower's ballades and, as far as we know, Gower could not read Italian. We also discounted Chaucer's influence, because almost all, if not all of his English decasyllables date from after his return from Italy in 1378, while the accepted date for the composition of Gower's first *balade* is 1377.

Since the publication of that article, however, I have had doubts as to whether Gower's *décasyllabe* was a natural progression from his *octosyllabe*. The first of those doubts is based upon the weakness of the chronological evidence: the dates of both Chaucer's and Gower's first decasyllabic poems are far from certain. Many scholars believe that one of Chaucer's shorter decasyllabic poems, the *ABC*, was written for the Duchess of Lancaster in the late 1360s. Pearsall dismisses this belief as the result of editors trying to enhance a negligible poem with a myth of royal patronage, but the editors of the *Riverside Chaucer* cling to it, and the dating is at least worth investigation.[33] In Chapter 11 I shall seek internal, metrical, evidence of the date of *ABC*'s date of composition and also query whether the poem is so bad that it could have deterred Chaucer from using its meter for the best part of a decade.

The date proposed for Gower's first decasyllables as 1377 is also highly questionable: it seems to have been arrived at on two assumptions. The first is that when Gower moved into the Priory of Saint Mary Overys he began writing bal-

---

[32] Although Gower's language contains many continental French forms it is unmistakably AN: for example, *CB*'s *flour*, *hour*, *oels*, and *coer* contrast with *fleur*, *heure*, *yeulx*, and *cuer* in the Poems of 'Ch.' There are also examples of AN word-final schwa deletion in *CB*; for example, the word *comme / come / com* is a monosyllable for Gower, regardless of how he spells it ('come' in *CB*, 12: 26, 13: 9, 15:17, and 18: 27; 'com' five times throughout *CB*, 18). Note that such deletion also appears to have applied to feminine past participles: thus Gower rhymes *durtée* with *loialté* and *fée* with *abandoné* in *CB*, 17. Once again, however, uncertainties of gender in medieval French may be involved.

[33] See the contrasting views expressed in Benson, 1988: 1076–77 and Pearsall, 1992: 83–84.

lades the moment he unpacked.[34] The second is that he is more likely to have composed AN ballades while working on the AN poem *MO* than when he had begun his Latin *Vox clamantis.*[35] But, is it not more likely that his first French ballades offered a respite from his Latin labors in 1379 than that they added to his workload of versifying in AN in 1377 (and, of course, to the chaos of relocating his home)? Since the scholars responsible for the dating had so little to go on, I believe that they made questionable assumptions.

I can find nothing in any *balade* to indicate Gower's ignorance of the events of 1378, except his omission of references to Italian poetry, which so occupied his friend Chaucer on his return to England. This omission, however, could also have another explanation: Gower may have seen the Italian poems Chaucer brought back with him, and discussed their versification, but had been unsure of the meaning of the lines.[36] Moreover, even if Gower's earliest *balade* does date from 1377, Chaucer may well have introduced Gower to the Italian *endecasillabo* at any time after 1372, when the younger poet made his first Italian journey and became an admirer of Dante.

My second reason for doubting the conclusions to which we came in 2005 is wholly metrical: there is a series of small clues that Italian versifying may have influenced Gower, clues that are missing from Froissart's reforms in *OA*. Gower was trying to adapt a compound French meter (with a rhythm of x^1 x^2 x^3 PS // x^1 x^2 x^3 x^4 x^5 PS) to a language with strong word stress, which was just one of the problems that Lentini and the Sicilians had faced over 100 years earlier. Gower may have arrived at the same solution as the Italians independently, but the fact

34 The date of, 1377 was originally proposed by Gower's editor, Macaulay in, 1899, and it was supported by Hagman, 1968 and Cressman, 1986.

35 Gower's biographer favors an even earlier date for the first ballade, although we do not know which one it was (see Fisher, 1964: 99). Fisher wanted to find a plausible audience for Gower's ballades (courtly lyrics could hardly have been recited after supper in the priory's refectory), and therefore suggested that they had been written for performance before a medieval dining club known as the London Pui (active in the early, 1370s); see Dean, 1991. I would suggest an alternative audience: Chaucer and a few other close friends. By the late, 1370s Gower's days were spent preaching public morals first in *MO* and then in *Vox clamantis*; but the love lyrics he composed over the following twenty years were most likely restricted to his closest circle—at least until Gower's reputation for morality and a new marriage transformed them into clever youthful games that he could dare show to a king.

36 Modern cultural studies have identified many examples of a phenomenon termed *stimulus diffusion*, which Fisher describes as follows: "a society need not borrow another society's alphabet or architecture. It may borrow the *idea* of writing or of building in stone. Authors who compose together or who read one another's writings over a period of years need not borrow each other's words, but they are likely to show concern for the same themes and experiment with the same forms" (Fisher, 1964: 234). To that I would add: "such as decasyllables with no fixed caesura."

that the solution was lying in his friend's working papers makes this unlikely. Nothing can be proved, but I give below the metrical clues for readers to make their own judgment.

The first clue is the Gower's use of caesura: the proportion of Gower's lines with elision at the caesura (13 percent) is extremely high for French verse. The second clue is Gower's use of *coupe italienne*: this type of line accounts for less than 10 percent of Froissart's WB violations in *OA*, but it accounts for over 90 percent of Gower's violations. The third clue that Italian versifying may have influenced Gower lies in the fact that the lines of *CB* are less iambic than those of *MO*, composed at least a decade earlier: lines with stress peaks on 4–7–10, make up 7 percent of total in my *CB* sample. In 1378 Chaucer brought back from Italy a copy of Boccaccio's *Filostrato* in which 20 percent of lines have a peak of stress in position 7. Chaucer, eschewed such lines when he wrote *TC*, but Gower may have seen them as precedents for a more rhythmically varied AN line.

From this list of reasons for doubt it can be seen that Chaucer's influence on Gower's *décasyllabe* should not be so easily dismissed. The parallel progress of the two poets towards lines that were regular in both syllable count and rhythm is unlikely to have been a coincidence. While the case for collaboration would not satisfy a criminal court, I believe that the balance of evidence is in favor of an exchange of knowledge and advice on metrical matters between the two poets. In any event, it is important to recognize that French influence was more a negative than a positive factor in motivating Gower's and Chaucer's iambic lines. The continental two-beat line simply would not work in AN or in English: word stress and stress-timing drowned out the rhythm. The two poets therefore resolved to give their decasyllables the same rhythm as their shorter lines, which made the French WB constraint a waste of time—and so they ignored it. And it allowed violations of the PS constraint as well—providing a stress in position 6 rescued the line's rhythm. One of the two friends knew well that Italian poets had faced the same problems a century earlier and had arrived at pretty much the same solution.

Gower's iambic *décasyllabe* became the victim of history. The French king and the English language were the ultimate victors in the Hundred Years War: the *Roi de France* kept the *terroir* and the English people gained a single language.[37] Once the kings of England had begun to use English in public they soon found that it could inspire their troops to imitate the actions of a tiger etc. At the beginning of the fifteenth century English became more popular with each victory, and in the middle of it AN became less fashionable with every defeat. Although men of the law clung to French for some time thereafter, English emerged from the fifteenth century triumphant.

[37] The final, decisive, battles of the Hundred Years War were fought at Remigny (1453) and Chastillon (1455), but most English historians never mention these two names; see Davies, 1999: 434–35.

Thus it was that Gower's *décasyllabe* earned Dominique Billy's description: 'le dernier mètre anglo-normande.' The last significant versifier in AN was undoubtedly the dialect's finest poet, and so AN went out with a bang, not a whimper. It lives now only in numerous entries in the English dictionary, and in the cemetery of forgotten books, but it is very difficult to understand the way that English speakers versify unless we know what was achieved in AN.[38]

The *Décasyllabe* in Captivity

The story of the *décasyllabe* in England does not end with John Gower: in 1415 the fortunes of war brought another French poet to London, and they lodged him in the Tower.[39] Charles, duc d'Orléans (b. 1394–d. 1465), the grandson of one French king and the father of another, remained a prisoner in England until 1440, and by the time he returned to France he had become as fluent in English as in French. He composed a large number of poems in captivity, including a considerable number in English.[40] Apart from the subtlety of its thought, Charles's English poetry is distinguished by its versification: its rhythms are a great deal more regular than those of Hoccleve, Lydgate, or Skelton.[41] Moreover, Charles differed from these three English poets in being able to count syllables; he seems to have benefited from being fluent in two languages and knowing how sharply word stress separates their two rhythms. Also in one of those languages final schwa was still syllabified, which must have helped him understand exactly how Chaucer was versifying more than twenty years earlier. This is reflected in the predominantly iambic rhythms of Charles's English tetrameters and pentameters, which were composed at a time when English schwa deletion was almost complete.

Charles's ability to versify in Chaucer's manner in English might lead us to expect that his French versification might show the influence of Gower, or at least of Froissart. Charles's French design, however, ignores word stress except phrase-finally and observes the word-boundary constraint strictly, while his avoidance of elided caesuras is a stylistic trait of his own, The contrast between Charles's English and French versifying is doubtless related to his double fluency: when he spoke or thought in French, word stress was absent, and so it played no

[38] For the 'Cemetery of Forgotten Books,' see Ruiz Zafón, 2004: 1–6.

[39] At her trial, Jeanne d'Arc declared "Dieu aime bien le duc d'Orléans," and she intended to rescue him from his imprisonment in England if God allowed; see Purcell, 1973: 18.

[40] For Charles's French poems, see Champion, 1907; for his English poems, see Steele, 1941. For a discussion of Charles's authorship of the English poems, see Purcell, 1973: 12–13.

[41] See Duffell, 2008a: 106–14.

part in his French versification; when he wrote in English, on the other hand, he employed the language's word stress to good effect. Gower used AN's word stress in crafting his French lines, because it was there, while Charles had little or no word stress to work with in fifteenth-century Francien, and so he relied on word-boundaries and phrasal stresses to construct his lines in the traditional manner.

In conclusion, I shall demonstrate how Gower's 'dernier mètre anglo-normande' died with that dialect, by giving some vital statistics on the *décasyllabes* of Gower, Froissart (*OA*), Charles, and the sonnets of the most influential poet of sixteenth-century France, Pierre de Ronsard (b. 1524–d. 1585).[42] Figure 3 below shows the percentage of lines in each poet's work that have each type of caesura, and also the percentage with a strong syllable in position 7.

	Caesura				*Strong*
Poet	*Masc.*	*Lyric*	*Elided*	*Other*	*in Pos.7*
Froissart	80	6	6	8	18
Gower	71	0	13	16	7
Charles	84	15	0	1	24
Ronsard	84	0	16	0	30

Fig. 3: Comparison of Features in Four Poets' *Décasyllabes*

These statistics show clearly that Froissart tried to move the *décasyllabe* in a new direction and that Gower sought to do something far more ambitious, but neither was successful in influencing the long-term development of the meter.

There were doubtless linguistic factors in Gower's failure to influence the course of French metrics: the first was that without word stress his rhythms were inaudible to French ears. A second was that AN, with its simplified grammar and different orthography, was never highly regarded in France.[43] In this environment one Englishman's attempt to innovate in the abstruse area of versification had no chance of surviving the dialect's demise. This has not prevented Gower's verse from appearing in French anthologies, or deterred French scholars from esteeming his poetry highly. Although Gower's reputation as a French poet has done rather better than Charles d'Orléans's standing as an English one, there is no entry under Gower's name in the *Concise Oxford Dictionary of French Litera-*

[42] My sample of Charles's *décasyllabes* consists of Ballades LV, LXIII, LXXX, and lxxxv, a Chant royal (1434), and a Complainte (1443) in Champion's edition; my sample of his *octosyllabes* consists of Ballades VIII, XXVII, XXXVII, L, LX, LXIX, LXXII, LXXXII, and CV, and Rondeaux XXXI–XXXIV. For Pierre de Ronsard's *Amours*, see Schmidt, 1964; my sample of Ronsard's *décasyllabes* consists of the first 300 lines of *Amours de Cassandre*.

[43] For the view that by the fourteenth century AN was French gone to ruin, see Vising, 1884: 57.

ture.[44] Once again it seems that chauvinism is shy of the fact that, during the *melee* that was the Hundred Years War, a major French poet was English and a major English poet French.

Finally, to return from the theme of this chapter, French verse composed in England, to the overall theme of the volume, there is no proof that Chaucer was involved in Gower's French metrical experiments, or that Gower influenced Chaucer in the direction of greater regularity, but there is a strong likelihood. Certainly, there is a clear parallel between Gower's frustrated efforts to develop accentually and syllabically regular meters in French and Chaucer's successful innovations in English.

[44] See Reid, 1976: 266, where Napoleon's Marshall, Laurent Gouvion-Saint-Cyr, occupies Gower's place in the alphabet.

10
Metrical Stylistics

The concept of stylistic analysis has come under attack in recent years. Stanley Fish argued that stylistics is never objective, because researchers have to interpret what is significant and should be measured before they research.[1] In his latest book, however, Derek Attridge demonstrates that carefully conducted stylistic analysis adds to our understanding and enjoyment of a poem.[2] In this chapter I shall meet Fish's reservations by selecting features that provide the most striking differences between the metrical styles of two poets: Shakespeare and Milton. Shakespeare's sonnets and Milton's *Paradise Lost* are universally acknowledged to be in *strict* or *canonical* iambic pentameters, yet they differ in many particulars.

From a comparison of the versification of these two disparate works it should be possible to identify the primes of metrical style in this meter. This will enable me to analyze Chaucer's longer line, and measure its stylistic differences from the lines of both Shakespeare and Milton. Choosing these particular poets' work as controls for analysis has a further advantage: Gilbert Youmans and Xingzhong Li have also used them to investigate the meter of Chaucer's longer line.[3] Thus, although their samples and methodology were different from mine, I can correlate my findings with theirs to shed further light on the subject.

Relevant Stylistic Features

The most obvious features of this meter for quantitative analysis are those that I have used to define it in Chapter 3: how far do the lines observe the constraints of SMP, the syllable strength constraint of PT, and the cumulative constraint requiring a stress in either position 4 or position 6.[4] While checking on the

[1] See Fish, 1980, Chapters 2 and 10.

[2] See Attridge, 2013: 128–36.

[3] See Youmans and Li, 2002. For the application of optimality theory to Shakespeare's and Milton's metrics, see Hayes, Wilson, and Shisko, 2012.

[4] These features are also chosen by Tarlinskaja in her 2014 study of the English dramatic pentameter. Her 87 pages of tables cover the versification of more than 130 plays by a variety of Elizabethan and Jacobean authors.

observance of these constraints I shall also measure some things that are no more than norms in the canonical line: the frequency with which inversion occurs, the proportion of strong positions that contain stress, the occasional use of disyllabic substitution, and the way that the uneven number of beats in an English decasyllable subdivide.

The question of subdivision is a controversial one: many traditional, as well as linguistic, analysts of the meter have argued that the iambic pentameter has no caesura. Certainly the English meter has nothing like the WB constraint in the French *décasyllabe*. Nevertheless, in the Hengwrt manuscript of *CT* many lines are subdivided by virgules, vertical lines that may be the scribe's work but could just possibly be Chaucer's.[5] SMP and PT state that inversion may occur only after a major syntactic boundary but, as Shakespeare's 'Never' x 5 line from *King Lear* shows, that includes every position in the line.[6] In their 2002 article Youmans and Li also chose a syntactic definition of the line's major subdivision, and they discovered that Chaucer's verse design allows a mid-line colon boundary in any position.

Nevertheless, Li's figures show that 87 percent of Chaucer's lines have a major syntactic boundary between positions 4 and 8, that is, where almost 100 percent of Italian *endecasillabi* have their *cesura mobile*.[7] My own research suggests that there is one position in this part of the line where Most English poets have avoided placing a word boundary too often: immediately after position 4. The random placement of the words found in English iambic pentameters would give, on average, around 80 percent of lines a word boundary in this position, but the actual percent may be as low as 52 percent.[8] In this volume I shall term lines with such a boundary *pausing lines* and lines without it *running lines*; and, obviously, pausing lines observe the French WB constraint, while running lines violate it. Froissart and Gower were the only poets to compose a significant number of running lines in the *décasyllabe*, but from the first such lines represented a substantial proportion (between a quarter and a half) of all Italian *endecasillabi*.[9] Since an artificial balance between pausing and running lines seems to be a norm of the English iambic pentameter I shall take account of that balance in my analysis.

There is, however, another subdivision of the line that may also be important, a rhythmic one. The first implication of the change from a four-beat to a

[5] For the text of *Hengwrt*, see Lloyd Morgan, 2003.

[6] See Shakespeare, *King Lear*, 5.3.308.

[7] See Youmans and Li 2002: 158.

[8] For mid-line boundaries in Italian *endecasillabi*, see Chapter 8, Figure 2. Marina Tarlinskaja argues that the bipartite division of English iambic pentameters is extremely important (1987: 332).

[9] For details of how the probability of a word boundary immediately after position 4 can be calculated, using the vocabulary of the text concerned, see Duffell, 2002b: 302 n14.

five-beat rhythm is the loss of symmetry: a four is a pair of pairs, but the only way that the human mind can subitize five beats (that is, create and recognize them intuitively) is by subdividing them into either two-plus-three or three-plus-two beats.[10] The alternatives can be seen from the opening lines of Shakespeare's first sonnet:

(1) From **fai**rest **crea**tures // we de**sire** in**crease,** [2 + 3 beats]
(2) That **there**by **beau**ty's rose // might **ne**ver die [3 + 2 beats]

Note that Shakespeare rhymed the noun *increase* in (1) with the verb *decease*, which suggests that the modern stress distinction between *increase* and ***increase*** had not become rigid by the 1590s. Note also that the alternative subdivisions offer a source of variety in the five-beat line that is absent from its four-beat predecessor.

In his most recent book, Derek Attridge describes four-beat verse as having the rhythm of song, and five-beat verse as having the rhythm of speech, which is less symmetrical.[11] But music has proven soporific qualities (which is why the medical profession play it in ultra-sound scanning chambers), and so the five-beat line is the obvious choice of a discerning poet who plans to tell a long series of stories without lulling his audience to sleep. Comparing the page-turning power of Chaucer's *CT* and Gower's *CA* shows clearly which poet got this right. The above examples also show that the natural stress hierarchy of the line effects a subdivision of the line into either 2 + 3 or 3 + 2 beats. For the two types of line that result I shall use the labels *minor* and *major*, derived from Italian metrics. Thus example (1) is a minor line because its first subdivision is smaller than its second, and the (2) is a major line for the converse reason. Again, I shall take account of the balance between major and minor lines in the samples I analyze.

Since the balance between major / minor lines and pausing / running ones seems to have been of concern to English poets, I differ from Youmans and Li in my analysis of the stress hierarchy in this meter. They argue that there is a single norm for the stress profile of the iambic pentameter line, while I would argue for two norms, which poets have to choose between when crafting a line in this meter.[12] The two profiles are shown in Figure 1 below.

---

10 For *subitization*, see page 3 of this volume.

11 See Attridge, 2013: 124.

12 See Youmans and Li 2002: 153.

```
                    x                              x
          x         x              x               x
x    x    x    x    x         x    x    x    x     x
x x x x x x x x x x           x x x x x x x x x x
```

(a) Major Line (b) Minor Line

Fig. 1: Stress Hierarchy in the Iambic Pentameter

I have labeled the major line '(a)' because for centuries European metrists have called it the *Type A line* but Youmans and Li argue that profile (b) best reflects the structure of the iambic pentameter, on the basis of how often position 4 contains stress (in some 90 percent of Chaucer's lines) according to Tarlinskaja (as against no more than 80 percent for any other strong position).

The obvious counter to this argument is that the 90 percent may reflect no more than a stylistic norm, and that this figure varies greatly between the iambic pentameters of different poets, as even Tarlinskaja's crude statistics for the three poets show.[13] Moreover, as I demonstrated in Chapters 4 and 9, a single model with structure (b) is what distinguishes the French 4 + 6 *décasyllabe* from the English long-line canon. Note that example (1) above violates the French WB (word-boundary) constraint and (2) violates both the WB and PS (phrasal stress) constraints.

Since the proportion of lines with profile (a) is one of the chief differences between the iambic pentameters of different poets, it will be one of the features that I shall quantify in the stylistic analysis that follows. I shall once again base my statistics on 300-line samples, in this case on the first 300 lines of Shakespeare's sonnets, Milton's *Paradise Lost* (*PL*), and Chaucer's *General Prologue*, (*GP*). I shall also quantify two other features, which I shall deal with first because they affect a smaller proportion of lines, and are intrinsic to all the definitions of the meter examined in Chapter 3.

The first, and less common, of these two features is polysyllabic *inversion*; that is, the presence of a strong syllable in a weak position. From previous research I know that inversion occurs more than twice as often in Keats's sonnets as in Shakespeare's, and so in this chapter I shall compare inversion in Chaucer

[13] See Youmans and Li 2002: 156. Tarlinskaja has argued that stressed syllables occur most often after syllable 6 in the utterances of normal speech, and that poets who place stress in position 4 of their iambic pentameters do so to emphasize that their discourse is verse not prose (1987: 86). She also shows that iambic tetrameters usually contain as many stresses in positions 2 and 6 as in 4 (1987: 269–72). For audiences used to four-beat verse in English, or knowing something of *décasyllabes* in French, a 'this be verse' marker might well be useful. Tarlinskaja also states controversially that the openings of poems tend to be stricter than their closes (1987: 343).

and my two controls.[14] As noted in Chapter 3, inversion normally occurs in the iambic pentameter after a major metrical or syntactic boundary (the *closure principle*), and on the rare occasions it appears elsewhere foot and word boundaries must coincide (the *bracketing condition*). I shall therefore check for syntactic and foot boundaries when I identify inversions in my three samples. And, finally with regard to inversion, I shall note violations of SMP, that is, stress peaks in positions 3, 5, or 7.

The third feature I shall measure is the converse of inversion: *erosion* or *weak beats*, which I shall define strictly as the presence in strong positions of grammatical monosyllables, which do not receive stress in normal delivery. In examples (1) and (2) above all the syllables in strong (even-numbered) positions have greater stress than their neighbors, and this gives these lines a strong iambic pulse. Many iambic pentameters, however, lack such a peak of stress in one of these positions, weakening but by no means negating, the iambic pulse; for example, the sixth and seventh lines of Milton's *Paradise Lost*:

(3) Sing **Heav'n**ly Muse, // that on the **secret** top [weak third beat]
(4) Of **O**reb, or of **Si**nai, // didst in**spire** [weak second beat]

Erosion in position 4 or 6 produces a line with a more even balance of stress between its two halves: both have two strong beats, almost a return to the rhythmic symmetry of the native English line.

The appearance of a grammatical monosyllable in position 2 is not always synonymous with a weak beat; sometimes it represents a transfer of that beat to the preceding syllable, and it would be better described as monosyllabic initial inversion. The following examples from Shakespeare's sonnets illustrate the two possibilities:

(5) Look in thy glass, // and tell the face thou **view**est (3: 1)
(6) If from thy self // to store thou wouldst con**vert** (14: 12)

Rhythmic theory would identify a beat in the word 'Look' in example (5), making it in PT's terms a monosyllabic inversion (or, in Attridge's terms, a line opening with an implied followed by a double offbeat).[15] In example (6), on the other hand, emphasizing either of the first two syllables in delivery is equally meaningful. In my scansions I shall distinguish between lines like these by underlining, as here, the initial syllable of any that are better classified as monosyllabic inversions.

---

[14] For a comparison of inversion in rhymed iambic pentameters, see Duffell, 2008a: 246.

[15] For double offbeats, see Attridge, 1982: 96–102.

Many canonical iambic pentameter lines contain erosions, or weak beats, and some contain two (*double erosion*). The proportion of lines with erosion in any given position in an individual poets' lines varies: thus, for example, a figure just below 20 percent is the highest I have found for erosion of any one ictus of a poet's iambic pentameters, but this high level occurs in position 6 of Gray's lines and position 8 of Byron's.[16] So erosion is another indicator of metrical style.

Just as PT's closure principle and bracketing condition best explain inversion in the iambic pentameter, so the cumulative constraint best explains the behavior of erosion. In example (3) above the third beat is weak, as is the second beat in (4). The cumulative constraint ensures that if one of these beats is weak the other must be strong, and around 70 percent of iambic pentameter lines have both strong second and third beats. The middle of the line is thus as important to this meter as is the center of the board to the game of chess.[17] Most English iambic pentameters have a strong iambic pulse running from positions 3 to 6, and the others have a minimal pulse provided by one strong and one weak beat. Having generalized, I shall now turn to the particular metrical styles of Shakespeare and Milton.

Shakespeare's and Milton's Poem Designs

Other studies I have published indicate that the line structure of Milton's sonnets differs only a little from that in his blank verse, but it is worth noting the contexts in which my two control samples appear because they are indicative of the poets' attitudes to tradition and metrical innovation.[18] Only Shakespeare had to search for rhymes in my controls, while Milton's challenge was that of giving form to long passages of blank verse. I shall pause briefly to examine how Shakespeare and Milton tackled the architecture of their poems before I compare the mechanics of their meter.

Shakespeare's pentameters appear in a series of poems with a well-established design, but the sonnet was a fixed form with many variations, and Shakespeare chose the simplest of them, and used it monotonously (more than 150 times). As noted in Chapter 8, the sonnet had started life as eight plus six lines with *rimes croisées* (ab ab ab ab : cd cd cd), and in the hands of the *dolce stil novo* poets it became an octave of *rimes embrassées* (abba abba) followed by any of a range of sestets with either two or three rhymes (such as cd cd cd, cde cde, or

[16] For a comparison of erosion in rhymed iambic pentameters, see Duffell, 2008a: 247.

[17] See, for example, Heidenfeld, 1977: 62, or the first advice given in any chess manual.

[18] For the stylistic differences between the iambic pentameters of Milton's sonnets and those of *PL*, see Duffell, 2002b: 299.

cdd ccd).[19] When the sonnet reached Paris in the 1530s, Marot and Saint-Gelais gave it a waist, a rhymed couplet after the octave (abba abba cc deed), and in this format it became known as the *sonnet régulier.*[20]

In their English sonnets, Wyatt and Surrey transferred this couplet to the foot of the poem, which gives it a final flourish that was absent from the French design.[21] Surrey also took the form back to its roots by using mostly *rimes croisées* instead of *embrassées*, but he was an ambitious rhymester: in one of his sonnets he employed only two rhymes (rhyming *springs* eight times, and *vale* six) and he often carried a rhyme forward from octave to sestet. Shakespeare has given his name to Surrey's sonnet but, in fact, the Bard did no more than simplify Surrey's design.

Shakespeare was following a fashion for writing sonnets that was set off by the publication of Sidney's *Astrophel and Stella* in 1590.[22] How simple and single-minded Shakespeare's design is can be seen from a comparison with the designs in Sidney's volume or in Spenser's *Amoretti* (published in 1595).[23] The other two poets use a wide variety of designs, involving both *rimes croisées* and *embrassées*, carrying rhymes forward from one quatrain to the next, and employing only four or five rhymes in any one sonnet. In contrast, Shakespeare's sonnets have seven different rhymes, so that only one rhyme is required for each new line-final word. The task of rhyming is therefore no greater than in Chaucer's couplets. It may be that strophe design did not interest Shakespeare, and that the flexible format of his dramatic verse influenced the versification of his sonnets; certainly he used far more feminine lines in his sonnets than Spenser, while Sidney had used none at all.[24]

All metrical issues interested Milton: he versified in several languages and his metrical range in English included both Petrarchan sonnets and duple-time four-ictic dolniks (in *L'Allegro* and *Il Penseroso*).[25] Milton prefaced *PL* with an explanation of why he chose blank verse for his poem, in which he cited the examples of Homer and Virgil to make it clear that he set himself the very highest

---

[19] See Ruschioni, 1974: 14–22 and Elwert, 1973: 125–34.

[20] Some early French sonnets did not open their sestet with a couplet; the *régulier* rhyme scheme (abba abba ccd ede) became general only in the seventeenth century; see Kastner, 1903: 236–40.

[21] Surrey sometimes maintained the same rhymes through octave and sestet, and also composed a sonnet with *rimes embrassées*; see Keene, 1984: 40–42 and 69.

[22] See Bullett, 1947: 173–225.

[23] Thus, for example, in Sonnet V of the *Amoretti* Spenser finds five rhymes for 'pride' and three for 'honor'; see McCabe, 1999: 390.

[24] For Sidney's and Shakespeare's use of feminine lines, see Duffell, 2008a: 127 and 132.

[25] In his edition Leonard separates Milton's Italian poems published in 1645 (31–36) from his Latin and Greek poems (1998: 512–611); Milton's two surviving Greek poems contain only twenty-seven dactylic hexameters in total (1998: 579–80).

standards of verse craft.[26] Milton, however, did not have available the classical poets' chief sources of metrical variety: they were able to employ lines with between 12 and 17 syllables and could make accent and ictus coincide almost at will. Instead Milton exploited other design features, one of which was analogous to strophe design: almost 40 percent of his lines are enjambed, and this allowed him to build his lines into verse paragraphs, passages where a series of enjambments is followed by a strongly end-stopped line.[27] His other sources of variety were within lines rather than between them, as will emerge from the analysis of verse design that follows.

In summary, Shakespeare seems to have been under the influence of his contemporaries when he composed his sonnets: of Sidney and Spenser but also perhaps even of Surrey who, under French influence, excluded major lines from his sonnets almost completely. The looser meter of dramatic verse might also have been an influence on Shakespeare's versifying; during the 1590s he wrote at least six and perhaps as many as a dozen plays.[28] On the whole, therefore, we might expect Milton's pentameters to show signs of more careful design and execution.

Stylistic Features of Shakespeare's Pentameter

My analysis shows that polysyllabic inversion is relatively rare in my Shakespeare sample.[29] It contains only 14 examples of initial inversion and just 4 of medial; I give below three examples of each:

(7) **Ma**king a **fa**mine // where a**bun**dance lies (1: 7)
(8) **Pro**ving his **beau**ty // by succession thine (2:12)
(9) **Na**ture's be**quest** // gives **no**thing, but doth lend (4: 3)
(10) Be, as thy **pre**sence is, // **gra**cious and kind (10: 11)

[26] In his preliminary note on *PL*'s verse Milton describes rhyme as "no necessary adjunct or true ornament to a poem [. . .] in longer works especially, but the invention of a barbarous age"; see Leonard, 1998: 119.

[27] For an analysis of a Miltonic verse paragraph based on punctuation, see Duffell, 2008a: 150.

[28] My list of Shakespeare's plays composed in the 1590s is taken from Drabble, 1985: 889–91.

[29] The figures given by Tarlinskaja for Shakespeare's sonnets (1987: 71) cannot be correlated with mine because she does not recognize that stress in English lines and utterances is relative (Liberman and Prince, 1977), or a hierarchical feature (Hayes, 1989 and 1995). Nor does she allow for the difference between monosyllabic (phrasal) stress and strength (Kiparsky, 1977 and Hanson and Kiparsky, 1996). As a result, her measurements of stress in weak positions and non-stress in strong positions include inversions, incursions, and erosions in unspecified proportions.

(11) Harsh, **feature**less, and rude, // **bar**renly **per**ish (11: 10)
(12) Your self **again**, // **af**ter your self's **decease** (13: 7)

There are two metrical features worthy of special note in these examples; the first is that Shakespeare does not combine initial inversion with second-foot erosion (the fourth syllable of such lines must be stressed in order to establish an iambic rhythm before the audience think that they are listening to prose). The second is that medial inversion, at least in this sample, occurs only after a major syntactic boundary, and it is more often after position 6 (as in examples (10) and (11), when the final stress quickly reasserts the rising rhythm) than after 4 (as in example (12)).

The above examples also contain a number of erosions (marked by dotted underline): these may occur in any foot except the last, as the following examples of erosion (in first, second, third and fourth foot, respectively) show:

(13) And by ad**di**tion // me of thee de**feat**ed (20: 11)
(14) Till **Na**ture, as she wrought thee, // fell a-**do**ting, (20: 10)
(15) By **add**ing one thing // to my **pur**pose **no**thing (20: 12)
(16) Hast thou, the **Mas**ter // **Mis**tress of my **pas**sion (20: 2)

Each of these locations of a weak beat produces a subtly different modulation of the line's iambic rhythm. As this poem shows, Shakespeare often employed many erosions in the same sonnet, but he employed double erosion in only six lines of my sample (2 percent of total), and none of those double erosions involves the second foot. Thus double erosion affects the first and third feet of example (17) and the first and fourth of (18):

(17) Pluck the keen teeth // from the fierce **ti**ger's jaws (19:3)
(18) Is but the **seem**ly **rai**ment // of my heart (22: 6)

In each of the dozen examples above, numbered from (7) to (18), I have marked with two slashes the syntactic boundary that follows the strongest mid-line stress, and four of those twelve lines qualify as major on that basis (examples (10), (11), (14), and (18)). A very clear majority of Shakespeare's lines are minor (71 percent) and a similar majority (67 percent) are pausing lines. Both these majorities are much slimmer in Milton's poem. The proportions of major and running lines in their verse is, in fact, the biggest stylistic difference between the two poets, but both extremes must be allowed in the definition of the canonical line.

Figure 2 below compares the features of inversion, erosion, and subdivision in my Shakespeare and Milton samples (the symbol * indicates a fraction of 1 percent).

	Features % Lines											
	Inversion				*Erosion*						*Subdivision*	
Sample Foot:	*1*	*2*	*3*	*4*	*1*	*2*	*3*	*4*	*x2*	*Total*	*Major*	*Running*
Shakespeare	5	0	*	1	10	4	12	8	2	34	29	33
Milton	6	*	1	*	10	10	17	12	4	49	47	41

Fig. 2: Comparison of Three Metrical Features

These statistics show that there were important differences between the metrical styles of the two poets, even though most poets, critics, and readers unhesitatingly classify their lines as iambic pentameters.

Stylistic Features of Milton's Pentameter

As shown in Figure 2, Milton employs initial and medial inversion only slightly more often than Shakespeare. Only once in my sample does he employ initial inversion in consecutive lines and, like Shakespeare, never combines initial inversion with a weak second beat. But almost half of his initial inversions are combined with a weak third beat as in the following lines:

(19) **Un**der thy **con**duct, // and in **dread**ful deeds (1: 130)
(20) **Ri**vers or **moun**tains // in her **spot**ty globe (1: 291)

Similarly, weak beats occur in position 6 of lines 30 ('so'), 126 ('but'), 147 ('and'), 158 ('but'), 216 ('and'), and 280 ('on') – all of them beginning with a trochaic polysyllable. Such a weak third beat occurs significantly more often in lines with inversion than in lines without it, and the rhythmic shape of these lines (rather like a dumbbell with two weights at each end) seems to have pleased the poet.

Milton's other inversions are also interesting: he seems to have been anxious not to invert the second foot, and in the following example he employs a Latinate stress shift to avoid such an inversion (which would have been followed by a weak beat):

(21) Who now tri**úmphs**, // and in th'ex**cess** of joy (1: 123)

Most of Milton's few medial inversions follow a major mid-line syntactic boundary, as in:

(22) What shall be right: // **far**thest from him is best (1: 247)
(23) Smote on him sore be**sides**, // **vaul**ted with fire (1: 298)

A few however seem to be better explained by the bracketing condition, including the following line:

(24) To do aught good // **never** will be our task (1: 159)

Milton must have wanted an inversion here to provide rhythmic variety, because he could have achieved a perfect iambic rhythm by transposing '**never**' and 'will.'

Milton's use of erosion, or weak beats, is very different from Shakespeare's: my *PL* sample contains almost half as many weak beats again as my sonnet sample (49 as against 34 per 100 lines). In particular there are more than twice as many weak beats in position 4, including the following:

(25) The **mother** of man**kind**, // what time his pride (1: 36)
(26) And **study** of re**venge**, // im**mor**tal hate (1: 107)

And, unlike Shakespeare, Milton also combines weak beats in the second and fourth feet as well as the first and third, as the following examples show:

(27) He **trusted** to have **e**qualled // the Most High (1: 40)
(28) Shall grieve him, if I fail not, // and dis**turb** (1: 167)
(29) Winged with red **light**ning // and im**pe**tuous rage (1: 175)
(30) Not by the **suff**'rance // of su**per**nal power (1: 241)

The final major difference between the two poet's pentameters is that Milton employs far more major lines: 47 percent as against 29 percent. Milton clearly strove for a more even balance between the two rhythmic templates, but he does not alternate major and minor lines—only 43 percent of lines in my *PL* sample were followed by an unlike line (very far from perfect alternation, which would produce 94 percent). Instead my sample contains blocs of consecutive major lines, the longest of which contains six (1: 53–58):

(31) Con**found**ed though im**mor**tal: // but his doom >>
(32) Re**served** him to more wrath; // for now the thought >>
(33) Both of lost **hap**piness // and **last**ing pain >>
(34) Tor**ments** him; round he throws // his **bale**ful **eyes** >>
(35) That **wit**nessed huge af**flic**tion // and dis**may** >>
(36) Mixed with ob**dú**rate pride // and **stead**fast hate. ////

The chances of a bloc of six major lines occurring by chance are about half the actual occurrence of 1 in 50. My *PL* sample also contains four blocs of five consecutive major lines (odds = 1/45; actual = 1/15). One possible explanation of this clustering is that once Milton had a template in his mind he tended to use it several times before switching to the other template. This passage is a perfect example of the Miltonic verse paragraph, with a long series of enjambments and a final resolution of the wrestling match between syntax and meter in example (36).

Although Milton seems not to have set out to alternate major and minor lines, he made use of a less salient contrast by alternating lines with weak beats in the second and third feet, once again producing a special rhythmic effect:

(37) Here in the heart of Hell // to work in fire (1: 151)
(38) Or do his **errands** // in the **gloomy** deep (1: 152)

Example (37) is a clear case of monosyllabic inversion, as its alliterations of the aspirate emphasize. Although the statistics in Figure 2 mask it, the openings of Milton's lines do differ significantly from those of Shakespeare's. Half of Milton's first foot erosions qualify as monosyllabic inversions compared with only one quarter of Shakespeare's. Thus the total number of inversions of both types in my Milton sample represents 11 percent against the 7 percent of my Shakespeare sample, a difference equal to just over two standard errors.

As my examples show, English iambic pentameters frequently violate the norms of the French *décasyllabe*, which Froissart's *OA* defies on occasion and Gower's *CB* defies much more often, and they do so in the same two ways. Lines like example (38) violate the WB constraint, and lines like (37) violate the PS constraint. Some iambic pentameters, however, violate both, for example the first line of *PL*, where the word 'diso**be**dience' provides two of the line's beats. In this line position 6 contains the primary stress and there is no word boundary between positions 3 and 6. In my *PL* sample 15 percent of lines have this double violation: they are both *running* and *major*; this compares with only 6 percent of lines in my Shakespeare sample. As a result, of this difference 73 percent of my *PL* sample's lines violate the French constraints (by being *running*, or *major*, or both); and this compares with 56 percent lines in my Shakespeare sample.

In my 2000 article I labeled these two types of line, those observing and those violating the constraints, 'French' and 'Italian' (because Italian poets observed neither of them); but in a work that analyzes many lines in these two languages, those terms might be confusing. In this volume, therefore, I shall refer to English lines that observe both French constraints as 'Gallic' lines, and English lines that violate either or both constraints as 'Italic' lines. The Gallic: Italic ratio in my *PL* sample is thus 27:73 and in my Shakespeare sample it is a more even 44: 56. Milton clearly preferred his lines not to emphasize by phrasal stress any division into 4 and 6 syllables, while Shakespeare sought a more even balance. The reasons for Milton's preference can only be surmised, but it is a curious coincidence that his contemporaries in Italy, Spain, and Portugal were moving their line of ten syllables in the same direction.

In summary, the differences measured show Milton to have employed more inversions, many of them monosyllabic. He also employed more erosion, so that his verse offers a pleasing contrast between lightly and heavily stressed lines;

and he used many more major, running, and Italic lines.[30] I have little doubt as to which of these two poets poured most effort and ingenuity into his versifying, but, as George Wright showed, Shakespeare's dramatic experience enabled him to achieve a dazzling array of metrical effects in a language far closer to the rhythms of normal speech than Milton's rhetorical mock-Latin.[31] Shakespeare's proportion of lines with their strongest mid-line stress in position 4 followed immediately by a word boundary was also much closer to the norms of English speech. Milton was thus, as in many other ways, creating a highly artificial medium for his message.

The Norms of Chaucer's Pentameter

Before examining Chaucer's longer-line verse design we should note that soon after 1378 Chaucer changed strophe designs very abruptly. All his early work in shorter English lines is in rhymed couplets, but on returning from Italy he followed Boccaccio's example and employed ballade strophes in narratives. In Chapter 12 I shall present a synopsis of Chaucer's longer-line strophe designs, and here I shall note only that he reverted to the rhymed couplet for most of *CT*, including all of *GP*. This saved him finding extra rhymes and enabled him to divide his narrative at natural points rather than at metrically convenient ones.

The modern consensus is that Chaucer's longer line is a pentameter of some sort, either a crude *proto-iambic pentameter* or the first example of the real thing. Certainly, Barber and Barber have provided convincing evidence that Chaucer's line had a norm of ten syllables, and Youmans and Li have made a strong case that this decasyllable was basically iambic in rhythm. A few voices dissent as far as doubting whether Chaucer's line has all of the features that characterize the canonical meter, most notably the voice of Thomas Cable.[32] In this section I shall

[30] Philip Hobsbaum states that Milton's blank verse differs from Shakespeare's by having heavier stresses (1996: 15), but this conclusion depends on his adherence to the outdated four-level theory of stress. My analysis shows the opposite: Milton's lines have fewer heavy stresses, but his greater use of weak beats makes the remaining beats more salient.

[31] For Shakespeare's dramatic pentameters, see Wright, 1988: 91–107 and Tarlinskaja, 2014: passim, where they are compared with those of other authors.

[32] Cable regards Chaucer's design as less sophisticated than that of the canonical iambic pentameter (hence the 'Folk Poet' in Youmans and Li's title). Cable argues that Chaucer did not employ inversion, and that the apparent examples result from what he calls 'hovering stress,' involving not just in words like '**ho**nour' > ho**nour**' and 'synging' > 'syn**ging**e,' but also words like '**re**dy.' Cable's 'hovering stress' assumes a very wide application of the Move X rule in ME, and the word *increase* in example (1) of this chapter suggests that some stress assignments were still unresolved in Early Modern English. Youmans and Li, on the other hand, argue that only monosyllabic inversion can explain

examine whether Chaucer's lines share the key features of either Shakespeare's, or Milton's, or of both.

The features I have chosen, inversion, erosion, and major lines, are capable of distinguishing the metrical style of Shakespeare from that of Milton, and the quantification of these features in Chaucer's lines will enable me to relate them to the norms of the canonical line. In addition I shall search for features of Chaucer's metrics that are not shared with the other two poets.

My sample from the General Prologue (*GP*) to the *CT* contains a number of apparent examples of polysyllabic inversion, including those in the following lines:

(39) **Re**dy to **wen**den // ọṇ my **pil**grymage (21)
(40) **Syn**gyng^e he was, // or **floy**tyng^e, al the day (91)
(41) **Af**ter the scol^e // of **Strat**ford **at**te **Bo**we (125)

I say 'apparent examples' because many of the disyllabic words concerned had alternative accentuations, as is shown by Chaucer's rhyming: thus he often employed rhymes such as '**li**kynge' / '**sprin**ge.' Although the Move X rule seems to have had a much wider application in ME than in Modern English, this accentuation of 'li**kyn**ge' was poetic license. And the application of Move X to compounds can explain other apparent initial inversions in my *GP* sample, such as 'Cur**teis**' in (99), 'Gre**houn**des' in (90) and 'Som**what**' in (264).

There must also be some doubt also as to whether example (41) is a special case: it opens with a grammatical disyllable with 'weak' (or *débil*) stress, and these exist in every Romance language as well as English: examples include *avec* (French), *para* (Spanish), and *very* (English). They do not become stress peaks in normal speech because their stress is subordinated to that of a following lexical word. If *after* is an inversion in example (41), it may have to be labeled a 'weak inversion.' Remarkably, only one of the lines in my *GP* sample with a grammatical monosyllable in position 2 can be regarded as an inversion:

(42) Bet ṭḥạṇ a **la**zar // ọṛ a beg**ges**tere (242)

So it can be argued many of Chaucer's apparent polysyllabic inversions are doubtful and that he made scant use of inversion of any sort.

For the purpose of the present chapter I shall base my statistics upon apparent inversions, some of which I believe will prove on closer examination to be what they appear. But in the next chapter I shall gather a much larger sample of

---

what they call 'Gascoigne transformations,' that is, the reversed word order in phrases like 'Short was his gowne' (*GP*, 93), where 'His gown was short' would have been more clearly iambic. For other writers who have doubted whether Chaucer's longer line is a canonical iambic pentameter, see Davis, 1988 and Dane, 2009.

apparent inversions from eight different poems in order to address my doubts and revise my statistics accordingly.

My *GP* sample contains only seven apparent examples of inversion that are not line-initial; they include the following inversions in the third or fourth foot:

(43) And f̣oṛ to **fastn**ͤ his hood // **un**der his chyn (46)
(44) A **ye**man **hadd**ͤ he // and **ser**vantz na**mo** (101)

The inversion in example (43) does not follow a major syntactic break, but a subdivision of the line into 6 + 4 syllables; it also involves a grammatical word with weak stress. Example (44) is a little dubious because it is difficult to rule out a French accentuation of 'ser**vantz**,' but as an inversion it observes the bracketing condition.

Surprisingly, my sample contains three second-foot inversions, the least common type of all in the canonical meter:

(45) Of smal **co**ral // a**bout**ͤ hirͤ arm she bar (158)
(46) And heeld **af**ter // the **ne**we world the space (176)
(47) That no **drope** ne **fill**ͤ // **up**on hirͤ brest (131)

These examples also observe the bracketing condition, but again the word '**co**ral' in example (45), as a French derivation, may have been subject to Move X ('cor**al**'). And again the inversion in (46) involves the word *after* with its weak stress contrast; elsewhere Chaucer always rhymes it with words like *laughter*, and never with words like *bokeler*. These three lines can be described as having lyric caesura, like the French *décasyllabe*, or as being imitations of the *endecasillabo melodico*.[33] The second description is more accurate, because all three lines have stress peaks in positions 3–6–10, like the Italian line.[34]

In contrast to his infrequent use of inversion, Chaucer often employed erosion, or weak beats, including those in the following examples, which are given in the order of the foot affected:

(48) And ịṇ his hand he baar // a **myg**hty bowe (108)
(49) And **pyn**nes, f̣oṛ to **ye**ven // **fai**re **wy**ves (234)
(50) In hopͤ to **ston**den // ịṇ his **la**dy grace (88)
(51) And carf bi**forn** his **fa**der // ạṭ the **ta**ble (100)

He also employed double erosion, or weak beats, in the second and fourth feet, as well as in the first and third; examples include those in the following lines:

---

[33] For the use of the *endecasillabo melodico* by poets whose work was known to Chaucer, see Chapter 8, Figure 4.

[34] Two of the three examples of lyric caesura in French noted in Chapter 9 lack stress in position 6: Poems of 'Ch,' 1:43, and Froissart's *OA*, 11.

(52) Bifil that ịṇ that seson // ọṇ a <u>day</u> (19)
(53) Or ịf̣ men <u>smoot</u> it // ẉịṭḥ a **yerde smert**e (149)

Just over 4 percent of my sample's lines have double erosion, evenly divided between erosion in positions 1 + 3, 1 + 4, and 2 + 4.

Chaucer employed many more minor lines than major ones, and a series of three consecutive major lines occurs only four times in my sample (where random distribution would produce such a series twice as often). One such series (lines 77–79) is given below:

(54) <u>For</u> <u>he</u> was **lat**^{e} **ycom**^{e} // from <u>his</u> viage
(55) And **wente** for to <u>doon</u> // his <u>pil</u>gry**mage**
(56) With <u>hym</u> ther <u>was</u> his **sone**^{e}, // a <u>yong</u> squ**ier**

Unlike Milton, therefore, Chaucer seems to have used major lines sporadically to provide variety.

Chaucer thus made use of all three of the exceptional features I have measured, features that offer the canonical line relief from a uniformly iambic rhythm. It is now possible, therefore, to place quantified statistics for his lines alongside those for the other two poets in Figure 3, below.

Features		*% Lines*		
		Chaucer	*Shakespeare*	*Milton*
Inversion:	1st foot	4	5	6
	2nd foot	*	0	*
	3rd foot	*	1	1
	4th foot	*	*	*
Total Inversion		**6**	**7**	**8**
Erosion	1st foot	6	10	10
	2nd foot	8	4	10
	3rd foot	16	12	17
	4th foot	12	8	12
Total Erosion		**42**	**34**	**49**
(of which x2)		(4)	(2)	(4)
Major Lines		26	29	47
Running Lines		31	33	41

Fig. 3: Comparison of Three Poets' Metrical Features

This comparison reveals that Chaucer employed inversion less often than the other two poets and erosion with a frequency somewhere between Shakespeare's and Milton's. Chaucer also employed very similar proportions of major lines and running lines to Shakespeare. Since 8 percent of lines in my *GP* sample are both running and major, Chaucer's proportion of Italic lines is 49 percent, not far behind Shakespeare's 56 percent; both poets thus achieve a fairly even balance between Gallic and Italic lines.

These statistics confirm Youmans and Li's conclusion that Chaucer's lines were well within the norms of the canonical iambic pentameter. In some ways Chaucer's lines are stylistically closer to Milton's, but in others they are much closer to Shakespeare's. Chaucer's verse design clearly embraced all the features of the canonical iambic pentameter, but his verse (as it has come down to us) also contains lines that appear to be syllabically irregular, and which require explanation.

Irregular Lines in Chaucer's *GP*

Most of the lines in my sample that deviate from the decasyllabic norm do so systematically: they lack a syllable, or have an extra one, in certain positions, and they can be conveniently labeled. I have already used those labels ('headless,' 'broken-backed,' 'with double anacrusis,' and 'with epic caesura') in the preceding chapters of this volume because they have a long history in English versifying.

There are five headless lines in my sample, that is, their first hemistichs have an initial *implied offbeat*; they include examples (57) and (58) below:

(57) [ ] Al bis**mo**ter^{e}d // ẉịṭḥ his ha**ber**geon (76)
(58) [ ] **Twen**ty **boo**kes, // clad in blak or reed (294)

Chaucer employed many headless lines in his shorter line and he clung to the practice in his new longer line; they represent almost 2 percent of the lines in my sample. There are also two candidates for broken-backed lines:

(59) Hath ịṇ the Ram // [ ] his half cours y**ron**ne (8)
(60) Hir^{e} **gret**test^{e} **ooth** // [ ] was but by Seint^{e} Loy (120)

Scanned as here, both could be described as having an implied offbeat in the second hemistich; but (59) can be delivered so as to make the word 'half' a beat (instead of 'his'), which makes the implied offbeat non-initial. Some manuscripts of *CT*, however, offer an alternative by adding a word-final schwa to 'half.' Similarly, (60) may be regularized by syllabifying the final schwa of 'Seinte' to give the scansion:

(60)a Hir^{e} **gret**test^{e} **ooth** // was but by **Sein**te Loy (120)

This scansion is just defensible because the disyllable *seinte* is an adjective, meaning 'sainted' or 'holy,' and the term 'Sainted Loy' is not beyond credibility. But in *The Riverside Chaucer* Norman Davis classifies (60) as broken-backed, and the Hengwort manuscript has the reading 'Seint' (without the schwa).[35] The safest thing to say about broken-backed lines in my sample, however, is that they represent less than 1 percent of total.

There are two lines in my sample that I would classify as having double anacrusis in the first hemistich, that is they have an initial double offbeat:

(61) [At that] **tyme**, for // hym **liste ride** so
(62) [With a] **thredbar**ᵉ **cop**ᵉ // as is a povrᵉ **scoler** (260)

Example (61) has an alternative scansion if the schwa of 'tymᵉ' is deleted and 'for' becomes an erosion (giving an unusual caesura after a stressed third syllable). The only alternative to this scansion of (62) is to emend the line by omitting its first 'a.' The result would make adequate sense, but the emendation cannot be justified on the basis of the manuscripts.[36] Editorial interference is also required to regularize two other lines with a double offbeat in the second hemistich:

(63) And by his **syd**ᵉ // a swerd and {a} bo**keler** (112)
(64) He **hadd**ᵉ of gold **ywroght** // a {ful} **curious** pyn (196)

The word 'a' in example (63) can be justified only by subjecting 'bokᵉ**ler**' to syncope, and the word 'ful,' which is one of Youmans's 'metrical fillers,' could be omitted from (64) with little loss to the meaning.[37] The only alternative to emenda-

[35] The Ellesmere manuscript (San Marino, CA: Huntington Library, MS EL. 26. C. 9) dates from no later than 1410; the Hengwrt manuscript (Aberystwyth: National Library of Wales, MS Peniarth, 392D) was copied by the same scribe a few years earlier, but is considerably less regular. The editors of Benson, 1988 base their text of the *Canterbury Tales* largely on Ellesmere (see Benson's note on page xli). It is clear, therefore, that some of the exemplars in circulation even at that early date were much more regular than others.

[36] Eighty-two manuscripts containing at least parts of *CT* have survived and most lines have textual variants; see Manly and Rickart, 1940. The surviving verse in *CT* amounts to almost 20,000 lines, but I know of no study that attempts to collate what Duggan calls 'authorial lines.' There are, however, three good reasons for believing that scribes were more likely to have made Chaucer's line irregular than the reverse. The first is that Duggan found 'authorial' lines in other ME works much more regular than 'scribal' ones. The second is that Gower's *CA* is much more regular than any of Chaucer's four-beat verse, and this may partly result from Gower's personal checking of the copies. The third reason is that Chaucer's meter was new, so that his earliest scribes would have copied works versified on other principles. It is therefore likely that the scribes' understanding of Chaucer's verse design would have been imperfect, and so any difference between exemplar and copy is unlikely to have been the result of good editing.

[37] 'Metrical fillers' are redundant monosyllables; Duggan gives as examples in ME verse 'ful' before an adjective and 'for' before 'to' (1996: 227).

tion is to accept that on rare occasions Chaucer allowed a double offbeat other than hemistich-initially, after the manner of the earlier English poets discussed in Chapters 5 and 6 above.[38]

There are three candidates for epic caesuras in my *GP* sample: they may have an extra post-tonic syllable in position 4, which produces a double offbeat between the second and third beat. In each case, however, there is an alternative explanation: the final schwas of the words *coppe* (in line 134) and *wiste* (line 224) might be deleted, and the word *geten* (line 291) might be reduced to a monosyllable by syncope. Syncope is also required to make seven other lines regular: my scansions include 'crist^{e}ndom' (line 49), 'rid^{e}n' (57), 'wond^{e}rley' (84), 'that ^{i}s (180), 'much^{e}l' (211), and 'o^{v}er' (216 & 249). Similarly, I have treated the initial -e of 'estatlich' (in lines 140 & 281) as a Gallicism that might have been ignored by ME speakers.

In total between 4 and 5 percent of the lines in my sample contain vestiges of traditional modes of versifying in English. In those lines syllables before the first beat in each half-line are treated as anacrusic, or syllables after the last beat in the half-line are treated as extrametrical. There was a good reason for this metrical conservatism: Chaucer's new meter contained more regularity than any of the meters he knew in other languages, because it regulated both syllable number and accent. He therefore needed to balance that excess of regularity by retaining some of the sources of rhythmic variety found in the work of earlier English poets. This decision was part of his overall sense of rhythm: he recognized the need for variety in order to make prolonged regularity more attractive to the ear. Chaucer's metrical conservatism thus served the same function as the much higher levels of inversion in later English pentameters.

The traditional metrical features to which Chaucer resorted for variety have not disappeared from versifying in English. Folk forms, such as proverbs and nursery rhymes, rely upon them, but they can also be found in later centuries' literary works: Shakespeare's dramatic verse, Milton's *L'Allegro* and *Il Penseroso*, Coleridges's *Christabel*, Tennyson's *Maud*, Browning's *The Statue and the Bust*, and Eliot's *The Waste Land*. Few lines in *GP* violate the norms of the strict iambic pentameter, and Chaucer captured even the subtlest features of that meter. His long-line verse is certainly the work of a *littérateur*, not a folk poet; but my analysis casts doubts on the other main conclusion of Youmans and Li's 2002 article, their hypothesis of the iambic pentameter's basic structure. I shall close this chapter by re-examining that hypothesis in the light of the evidence presented above.

[38] See Putter and Stokes, 2014: 7.

The Hierarchical Structure of the Iambic Pentameter

In that article, Youmans and Li did not take sufficient account of the great differences between Shakespeare's and Milton's pentameters, and so they mistook a stylistic feature of Shakespeare's line for a categorical one that applied to all iambic pentameters. There were several reasons for their mistake, and the first was that they used a blunt instrument to measure stress: the four-level theory accepted by Tarlinskaja, which has long been superseded. Many of the stresses in Youmans and Li's statistics are not relative, they do not identify syllables with greater stress than their neighbors; and when their table records a stressed syllable in a weak position we do not know whether they are describing a strong syllable or a monosyllable, inversion or incursion, or just a pronoun like *his*, which is a peak of stress in expressions like 'It's <u>his</u> alone,' but not in phrases like 'To <u>each</u> his <u>own</u>.'

Secondly, Youmans and Li's analysis of primary syntactic boundaries is equally ill-defined: those after positions 1, 2, 3, 8, and 9 are likely to result from sharp enjambments (they are what French metrists term *rejets* and *contre-rejets*);[39] and those after 5 and 7 are almost all divided from the phrasal stress by a post-tonic syllable, although Li does not say so. This just leaves the boundaries after positions 4 and 6, which identify the lines as pausing and running, and major and minor. Thus it is that Youmans and Li discovered only that Chaucer was almost as fond of minor lines as Shakespeare. The most accurate way, therefore, to depict the twin structures that represent every poet's choice in the iambic pentameter is by the diagrams I gave in Figure 1, Chapter 8, of this volume.[40] I repeat it, with English examples, as Figure 4 below, and in the next chapter I shall pursue the question of just how Chaucer came to employ this twin design.

Note that these alternative structures are the same as those for the Italian *endecasillabo* (chapter 8, Figure 1). The correspondence rules of the two meters, however, differ: in the *endecasillabo* the prominence site is colon-final strong positions, which must contain stress; in the iambic pentameter the prominence site is all weak positions, which must not contain strong syllables unless licensed by the closure principle or the bracketing condition. The cumulative stress constraint, however, adds a further refinement to PT: if position 4 does not contain a stressed syllable then position 6 must. It is, therefore, not surprising that F.T. Prince concluded that Milton observed the norms of the *endecasillabo* in *Paradise Lost*.[41]

---

[39] For *rejet* and *contre-rejet*, see Grammont, 1937: 35 and Scott, 1980: 72.

[40] Carlos Piera first proposed this twin structure for the Spanish *endecasílabo*, and Kristin Hanson later argued that it was shared by both the Italian *endecasillabo* and the English iambic pentameter; see Piera, 1980: 46 and Hanson, 1996: 61. Hanson, 2009 sets out her case in greater detail.

[41] See Chapter 3, Note 49.

(A) Major Rythmic Variant

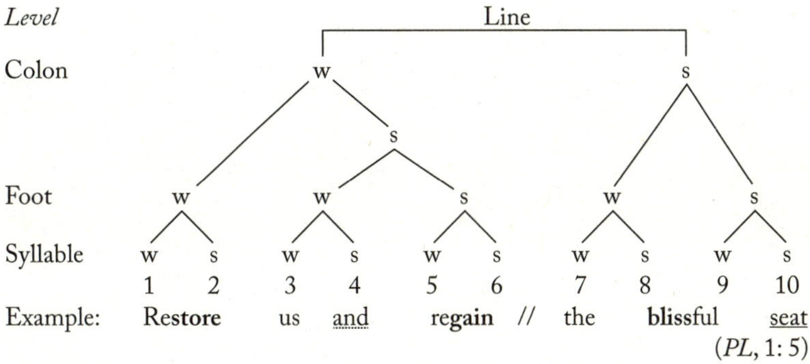

(B) Minor Rythmic Variant

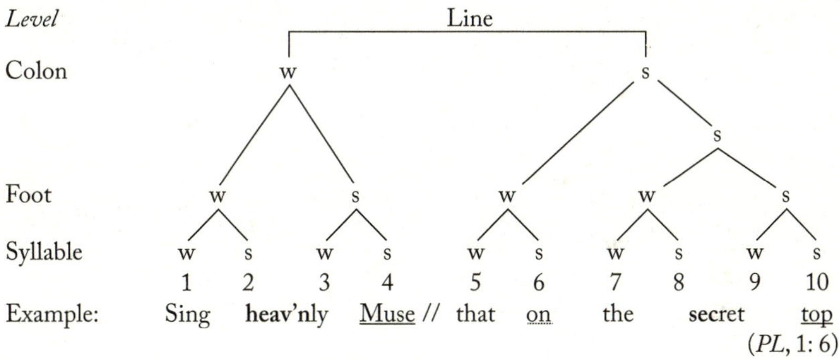

Fig. 4: The Iambic Pentameter: Alternative Structures

11
Chaucer's Pentameters

This chapter will be devoted to a more detailed examination of Chaucer's long-line verse over time and in different works. I have begun by concentrating on features that divide one type of decasyllabic line from another (the *décasyllabe* from the *endecasillabo*) and one poet's work from another's (Shakespeare's from Milton's), but I have kept constant watch for any other metrical features that are not randomly distributed in my samples. I have also increased my sample considerably, to well over 2,000 lines taken from eight poems, which have been chosen to provide verse of a variety of genres (narrative, lyric, argument, and philosophizing), and widely different registers and voices (from learned to aristocratic, and from moralizing to slapstick).[1]

Variation and Change in Chaucer's Pentameters

This analysis will seek evidence of variation and change in Chaucer's iambic pentameter in the following eight works: (1) *ABC*, dating from pre-1369 (according to Benson) or post-1378 (according to Pearsall), (2) *Anelida and Arcite* (*AA*), dating from the late 1370s (3) *The Parliament of Fowls* (*PF*), dating from c. 1380, (4) *Troilus and Criseyde* (*TC*), dating from 1381–86 (5) The General Prologue (*GP*), (6) The Knight's Tale (*KT*), (7) The Reeve's Tale (*RT*), and (8) The Pardoner's Tale (*PT*), from *The Canterbury Tales* (*CT*), dating from between 1387 and 1400.[2] The quantification in this chapter will be based on the whole of *ABC* and the first 300 lines of each of the other poems, making 2,284 lines in total.

These works appear to divide neatly into two chronological groups, which I have labeled 'earlier' (*ABC*, *AA*, *PF*, and *TC*), and 'later' (*GP*, *KT*, *PT*, and *RT*). *KT*, however, is a reworking of *AA* (making it especially valuable stylistically)

[1] The link between poetic form and semantic content is debated at length by Tarlinskaja, 2014: 267–86. In her Chapter entitled 'Meter and Meaning' she establishes quite clearly that poets can use metrical features to reinforce their meaning and add the 'special intensity' that typifies poetic discourse.

[2] My samples for this exercise are all taken from Benson, 1988 to ensure consistency; line numbers in *CT* refer to Benson's fragment numbers.

and, as Gillian Rudd argues, the Tale is probably almost unchanged from an earlier work *Palamon and Arcite*, composed c. 1381.[3] Apart from the dating of *ABC* the chief problem in relating these varied works to a time frame is that we have little idea of the order in which *CT* was composed. There is thus no guarantee that *GP*, as we have it, was an early composition, and Pearsall, who places *RT* among the last tales to be composed, warns against placing too much weight upon his judgment.[4]

There are two advantages of extending my sample of Chaucer's lines. The first is that it should enable me to detect variation and change in his crafting of lines; the second is that it will increase for analysis the number of lines containing rare features, such as inversion, double erosion, headless lines, epic caesura, and more extreme departures from the norm. My methodology remains the same as in my selection and measurement of samples in previous chapters, and therefore I shall begin with a table of results against which readers can check my analysis and conclusions. Figure 1 shows the percentage of lines that contain each of the features that I have shown to be the most obvious departures from the norm. They are: *running* and *major* lines (which violate the French *décasyllabe*'s constraints); *initial* and *medial inversions* (rare in English); *erosions* (common in English); and oxytonic or *masculine lines* (very rare in Italian, but making up the majority of lines in Modern English poetry).

My division of the eight works sampled into earlier (pre-1383) and later (probably post-1382) avoids the problem of dating *ABC*'s composition, which is controversial, but I shall examine the alternatives in detail later in this section. The results of my analysis are shown in Figure 1:

(All figures per 100 lines)

Sample	*Running Lines*	*Major Lines*	*Italic Lines*	*Initial Invers*	*Medial Invers*	*Erosion Total*	*Masc. Lines*
ABC	22	18	35	4	*	36	18
AA	27	19	38	1	*	36	25
PF	23	29	43	1	2	32	26
TC	23	19	35	1	1	36	25
Earlier	25	20	38	1	1	35	24
KT	30	21	45	1	*	49	47
GP	31	26	49	1	*	42	42

[3] See Rudd, 2001: 110.

[4] See Pearsall, 1992: 227.

PT	30	25	43	3	1	40	45
RT	21	26	42	1	*	45	32
Later	28	25	45	2	1	45	41
TOTAL	26	23	42	3	1	40	33

Fig. 1: Chaucer Samples: Various Features

It is reasonably safe to conclude that the first four of my samples were composed pre-1383—unless Chaucer began his translation of *TC* at the end and worked backwards. The dating of the second group, however, is much more tenuous.

KT was Chaucer's third attempt to tell this story from Boccaccio's *Teseida* in English; the first was *AA*; the second, *Palamon and Arcite*, has not survived, but *KT* could well be this lost work with a three-line introduction.[5] Even if this is the case, however, *KT* represents a mature, if not late, piece of versifying: it was open to revision post-1386 if Chaucer had so desired. The surviving version of *GP* was not necessarily composed in 1387 when Chaucer first conceived the idea of a pilgrimage format for a collection of stories. Nevertheless, the gap between the number of stories planned and recorded in *GP*, and the number completed by 1400 suggests that the surviving text was not a late revision.

PT was almost certainly composed after 1386 because it quotes (lines 538–39) the teaching of Pope Innocent III's *De miseria condicionis humanae*: Chaucer was working on a translation of all or part of this treatise between 1387 and 1394.[6] The dating of *RT* is more speculative: Pearsall guesses that it was composed relatively late, and it does seem quite likely that Chaucer took the risk of including bawdy tales only when his reputation was secure. (In the same way, D. H. Lawrence exhibited paintings of pubic hair when Joe Anon would not have dared to do so.)[7] Nevertheless there are counter arguments to Pearsall's case: French *fabliaux* of the type represented by *RT* (but in *octosyllabes*) date from the end of the twelfth century, and Juan Ruiz's *Libro de Buen Amor* and Boccaccio's *Decameron* appeared soon after the plague years, when the constant presence of death undermined sexual morality all over Europe.[8] Chaucer could have decided

[5] Lines 889–91 of the first fragment integrate the story into *CT*; see note 3.

[6] See Pearsall, 1992: 228 and Lewis, 1978: 74.

[7] When Lawrence's pictures went on display in the summer of 1929, London's police removed them but, in recognition of the artist's fame, spared them from destruction on condition that they were deported (to the USA); see Kennedy, 2003.

[8] The composition and circulation of scurrilous stories, or *fabliaux*, began two centuries earlier (see Greene and Cushman, 2012: 477), but the intellectual respectability of pornography increased greatly after the Black Death. The *Decameron* dates from 1348–

that bawdy was intellectually acceptable and reasonably safe at any time after the fame of those two works began to spread.[9]

Nevertheless, the case that my later group was composed after my earlier is a strong one, and it is further strengthened by a number of key metrical features that separate the two groups: strophe design, feminine lines, weak beats, and Italic lines. To take the first of these, the works I have labeled Earlier employed complex ballade designs, *PF* and *TC* are in rhyme royal, *ABC* is in octaves (rhymed abab bcbc), and *AA* consists of a narrative in rhyme royal and a complaint in a mixture of ballade meters. Before his second visit to Italy in 1378 Chaucer had employed couplets for his major works (*BD*, *HF*, and the *Romaunt*), but he found that Italian poets employed complex strophes for narratives (*terza* and *ottava rima*), and even more complex ones for lyrics such as the *sonnet* and *canzone*. Chaucer tried to rival the Italians when he returned: abandoning couplets and four-beat lines along with the unfinished *HF*, he too employed complex strophes for every type of verse. Only after 1386 did he return to rhymed couplets for most narratives, while using more complex strophes more selectively. This change in Chaucer's strophe designing underlies the division of the eight works I have chosen.

Italian poets employed feminine (*piano*) lines almost exclusively, thus exaggerating the paroxytonic bias in the language's lexicon. Before Chaucer's second visit to Italy he had employed an even mixture of masculine and feminine lines (no more biased than 60:40), but on his return this feminine proportion shot to 76 percent, which gave the great majority of his lines a similar trochaic close to that of almost all Italian *endecasillabi*. My sample of lines from later works shows that this Italianate feature did not last: by the late 1380s Chaucer's lines had returned to the more even mix of his early verse, a mix resulting from the composition of the ME lexicon and Chaucer's desire to syllabify word-final schwas in a somewhat old-fashioned way. We know that Chaucer syllabified some schwas at the line end from his rhyming such words in *TC* and *PF* as 'Troye' / 'fro ye,' 'Rome' / 'to me,' 'bowes / enow is,' and 'speres' / 'here is.' Since the difference in the proportion of masculine lines between my earlier and later samples is equivalent to twelve standard errors (12σ), we can be confident that this difference applies to the whole of the works concerned.[10]

The difference between my two sub-samples in the proportion of lines that contain weak beats or erosion is also statistically significant—to six standard

53 and, although the *Libro de Buen Amor* was probably composed in the 1330s, its fame spread across Europe much later; for the possibility that Chaucer may have had access to a translation of the *Libro de Buen Amor*, see Deyermond, 2004.

[9] Licentiousness in times of plague has often fascinated writers of subsequent generations; see Landa, 1990 and Manzoni, 1961.

[10] Note also that 'come' is rhymed with 'to me' in *O & N* 1671–72. For the calculation of standard errors, see Chapter 3, Note 68.

errors (6σ). This also means that we can be confident that the difference applies to the whole of the works concerned. The number and position of Chaucer's weak beats in the earlier group thus ensures that the verse's texture is very similar to that in Shakespeare's sonnets, while in later poems the texture of the verse is closer to that in Milton's *PL*. This suggests that Chaucer was more consciously seeking stresses in crafting the earlier lines and had a clearer grasp of what provided a sufficiently iambic, and more varied, rhythm by the time he composed the later poems.

The final significant difference between my earlier and later samples is that between the proportions of Italic lines in the two groups (to more than 4σ). The earlier group has a proportion of running lines that is very close to the probability analysis for the poems' vocabulary (around 20 percent), while the later group has a percentage that is closer to that in Shakespeare's sonnets (28 versus 33 percent).[11] Milton and most subsequent English poets boosted this proportion even further, but in his mature works Chaucer, like Shakespeare, seems to have preferred a fairly even balance between lines that subdivided 4 / 6 (both in terms of word boundaries and phrasal stresses) and lines that did not. In this respect Chaucer's change in preference is the converse of that found in his use of feminine lines.

Individual 300-line samples, however, show anomalies: *RT* is intermediate between earlier and later groups in the use of feminine lines, and its percentage of running lines is close to that of the earlier group. *AA* relies mainly on running lines for its Italic total, while *TC* relies mainly on major lines. There are also differences, not necessarily statistically significant, between individual works in the later group. The reasons for these anomalies must lie outside chronology: they suggest that other variables affect the percentages, and in Chapter 13 I shall investigate those variables. Here, however, I shall turn to the question of the chronology of *ABC* and review the new evidence offered by the foregoing metrical analysis. On one statistic I shall postpone comment: that of *ABC*'s many initial inversions. I shall deal with this anomaly when I come to examine all Chaucer's inversions later in this chapter.

[11] A probability model based on Chaucer's vocabulary in *TC* and *GP* shows a random expectation of between 19 and 22 percent for running lines; see Duffell, 2002b: 305. Probability modeling is a technique first employed by Gasparov, 1987 as a means of testing whether any feature of a verse text is part of the poet's verse design. It involves comparing how frequently that feature appears in the text with how frequently it occurs in contemporary prose.

The Date of Composition of *ABC*

As noted above, the dating of *ABC* is one of the issues that divide modern scholars. Having conducted a metrical analysis I should like to contribute to that debate by combining metrical and other considerations in my personal judgment.

If *ABC* had been composed c. 1370, its lines would have been the first English decasyllables, and the only decasyllables for a decade to survive. There are a number of reasonable expectations we should have of a 1370-ish ME poem in decasyllables. The first is that it should be in rhymed couplets, like most French *dits* and the other works by Chaucer of this date; the second is that its proportions of masculine and feminine lines should be evenly balanced, as was the case with French *décasyllabes* and Chaucer's own early four-beat verse. The third is that its violations of the French WB constraint (the stronger of the two) should be few, as with Froissart's *OA* (c. 4 percent) and Gower's *CB* (c. 9 percent). All of these expectations are frustrated in the actual poem, and instead its metrical features fit snugly into the group I have identified as dating from 1378–1382. The proportion of lines violating WB, in particular, is what would result simply from a decision to ignore the constraint altogether. There is also another implication of this snug fit: if lines so accomplished had been crafted in 1369, what could have led Chaucer to abandon this daring experiment with disregarding French norms and composing iambic ME decasyllables?

As Pearsall pointed out, a strong argument against a very early date is the weakness of the evidence for it.[12] It was more than a century after Chaucer's death before a connection with John of Gaunt was suggested, and later editors and critics then became enamored of the idea that there was a close relationship between poet and duke, and so repeated that suggestion as if it were fact.[13] Chaucer had a habit of abandoning things (for example, *HF*, *AA*, *LGW*, and some of the Tales in *CT*), but he usually did so for understandable reasons: *HF* was never going to match Dante's *Commedia*, and it was in a meter that no longer attracted; *AA*'s complaint had become too heavy for the narrative; *LGW* was a repetitious imitation of Ovid, and Chaucer suddenly had a better idea for a collection of stories;[14] Chaucer's skill at parodying the metrical romance was proven when he broke off *ST*, and the poet's death cut off *CT*. But the abandonment (for a decade) of the first good, English, iambic pentameters takes some explaining.

---

[12] Although the primary audience of medieval court poets was princes, Chaucer had ambitions to reach a much wider audience; see Pearsall, 1992: 190.

[13] Thomas Speght first linked *ABC* and the Duchess of Lancaster in his 1602 edition; Pearsall argues that this was Speght's invention (1992: 84); for a facsimile of that edition see Brewer, 1969.

[14] For Chaucer's debt to Ovid, see Pearsall, 1992: 114. Ovid's *Heroides* greatly influenced one of Chaucer's favorite genres, the medieval Complaint. For the text of Ovid's *Heroides*, see Showerman, 1914.

A detailed metrical analysis of *ABC* reveals it to be a typical Chaucer product of the years 1378–82. It is not impossible that it was produced ten years earlier and kept in storage, but it is highly unlikely.

Inversion in Chaucer's Pentameters

As noted above, another issue that divides modern scholars is whether Chaucer employed inversion, and whether he observed the same norms for its use as later iambic pentameter poets. The inversions in *ABC* show that Chaucer was no stranger to trochaic line-openings, but there is a good reason for the exceptional number in that poem. *ABC*'s structure requires twenty-three *virtual alliterations*: the first line in each strophe must begin with a word that has the same onset as a letter of the alphabet. Of those 23 alliterations, 7 are of monosyllabic words, 3 are of words stressed on their second syllable ('Al**mighty**,' 'Kalen**de**res,' and '**Redressed**') and 13 are of words that produce apparent inversions. These apparent inversions divide into three groups: (1) names from antiquity, which are particularly subject to Move X in ME verse ('Moises,' 'Xristus,' 'Ysaac,' and 'Zacharie'); (2) French-derived words subject to Move X ('Bountee,' 'Comfort,' 'Purpos,' and 'Virgine'); (3) other words also subject to Move X ('Fleeinge,' and 'Ladi'); and (4) words that almost certainly represent inversion ('**Glori**ous,' '**No**ble,' and '**Tem**ple').

The number of inversions in the 184 lines of *ABC*, however, contrasts with the numbers in my other samples, as Figure 2 illustrates.

(Actual Numbers of Lines)

Sample	*1 Names Move X*	*2 French Move X*	*3 Other Move X*	*4 Firm Invers*	*5 Weak Invers*	*TOTAL INVERS*
ABC	4	6	5	7	2	24
AA	0	1	0	2	3	6
PF	6	1	0	8	2	17
TC	1	2	2	6	0	11
KT	0	2	2	3	5	12
GP	0	3	4	2	3	12
PT	1	4	3	9	0	17
RT	0	3	1	5	1	10
TOTAL INVERS	12	22	17	42	16	109

Fig. 2: Total Inversions by Type and Sample

The apparent inversions in my other samples fall into the same four groups, plus one other mentioned previously: (5) grammatical disyllables with weak stress (in this group I include the words *after*, *under*, *upon*, *other*, and *neither*). One of the advantages of increasing the total number of lines analyzed is that it swells the number of apparent inversions to over 100, and Figure 2 quantifies the result.

The 42 inversions of type 4 (here labeled 'firm') that cannot be accounted for either by Move X or the weakness of the word's stress contrast, include 27 initial inversions of which the following eight lines contain the most obvious examples (I give one from each work):

(1) **Tem**ple de**vout**, // ther God hath his **wo**ninge (*ABC*, 145)
(2) **Sin**gest with vois me**mo**rial // ịṇ the **shade** (*AA*, 18)
(3) **Wo**men i**now**^{e} // of **which**e som^{e} ther **wee**re (*PF*, 233)
(4) **Simpl**^{e} of a**tir** // and debo**nair**^{e} of **che**re (*TC*, I: 181)
(5) **Than**ked be **For**tun^{e} // ạṇḍ hir^{e} **fal**se wheel (*KT*, 925)
(6) **Re**dy to **wen**den // ọṇ my pilgry**ma**ge (GP, 21)
(7) **Nei**ther in ci**tee** // ṇẹ in no vil**la**ge (*PT*, 723)
(8) **Pi**pen he **koud**^{e} and **fissh**^{e}, // and **net**tes **bee**te (*RT*, 3927)

The majority of apparent inversions in my samples, however, are much more dubious; as Cable points out, they could equally well be accounted for by Move X.[15]

The 27 firm examples of initial inversion, however, are in themselves sufficient proof that Chaucer's verse design allowed instances a trochaic opening. This being the case, giving the many lines opening with a Move X disyllable a trochaic opening would have been a licit delivery, and so would giving 20 of ABC's 23 stanza openings a strong alliteration. Chaucer's verse design clearly allowed initial inversion, even though he did not cultivate this form of rhythmic contrast in the way that Shakespeare and Milton did later. Their one line in twenty offers variety; Chaucer's one line in fifty is little more than a permissible exception. Nevertheless, Chaucer must have discovered from his alphabetical exercise how little an initial trochee interferes with the perception of a line's iambic rhythm. Nor could he have been unaware that the *Filostrato* he was translating contained many *enfatico* lines.

In total my samples contain 36 medial inversions (as compared to 73 initial ones) and again only the minority (11 medial inversions) fall into category 4 ('firm'). Most of the firm medial inversions in my samples are like the following:

[15] Although I have preferred the term *Move X*, taken from metrical phonology, rather than Cable's metaphor *hovering stress*, my research confirms the importance of his observations. In order for this phenomenon to account for all Chaucer's inversions, however, Move X would have to apply to many inflected verbs forms, such as 'maketh' (PT, 518) and 'semeth (PT, 553), where the second syllable is so weak that it often suffered syncope in ME.

(9) Redresse me, // mooder, and me chastise (*ABC*, 129)
(10) Non other word // speketh she, moch[e] or lyte (*AA*, 174)
(11) Ryght of a park // walled with grene ston (*PF*, 122)
(12) And ek for me // preieth to God so dere (*TC*, I: 32)
(13) And thurgh thy dronke nos[e] // semeth the soun (*PT*, 553)
(14) Our[e] corn is stoln, // sothly, it is na nay (*RT*, 4183)

All these medial inversions observe the bracketing condition, in that word and foot boundaries coincide; more remarkably, five are third-foot in versions. While examples (10), (11), and (13) cannot be accounted for by the closure principle, they resemble the others in following the strongest mid-line stress. This suggests that Chaucer regarded metrical boundaries as more important than syntactic ones in sanctioning inversion and that he intuitively recognized the boundaries of rhythmic feet.

In Chapter 8 I noted that, when Chaucer translated a Petrarch sonnet in *TC*, he balked at imitating the rhythm of an adonic line (that is, a fourth foot inversion). Most of the fourth-foot inversions in my samples are far less firm than example (13): they also usually involve grammatical words with weak stress. Example (15) below is an exception, but (16) is more typical:

(15) Fond I Venus // and hir[e] porter Richesse (*PF*, 261)
(16) The gretter was ther noon // under the sonne (*KT*, 863)

Note that in (15) the inversion of '**por**ter' observes PT's bracketing condition but not the closure principle. The most likely reason why Chaucer was more tolerant of third-foot inversions than of fourth-foot was that he wanted his verse's iambic rhythm to reassert itself well before the line end, in accordance with the closure principle ('beginnings free/ endings strict').

Finally, there are two firm medial inversions in my samples that do not meet the bracketing condition; they are:

(17) At regard of the hev[e]nes // quantite (*PF*, 58)
(18) And in hir[e] hous // she abood with swich meyne (*TC*, I: 127)

These lines typify the two rhythms that Chaucer found in abundance in Boccaccio's *endecasillabi*, but rejected for his own meter as being insufficiently iambic: the *melodico* line (accented 3–6–10) and the *dactilico* rhythm (accented 4–7–10).[16] It is difficult to tell whether Chaucer tried these two Italian variants just to hear how much they disrupted his chosen rhythm, or whether these lines simply contain primary copyists' errors.

In summary, there is sufficient evidence that Chaucer's design allowed initial inversion, even if he did not use it often enough for it to become a major source of

[16] For Boccaccio's *dactilico* and *melodico* lines, see Chapter 8, Figure 4.

rhythmic variety in his verse. There is also some evidence that Chaucer's favored position for medial inversion was immediately after the colon boundary in Gallic lines (those subdivided into 4 + 6 syllables). The fact that almost all Chaucer's inversions observe the bracketing condition points to his appreciation that reversals of his prevailing iambic rhythm should be limited to the contexts in which Move X mostly operated in ME—within disyllabic words. The Move X rule may thus be the origin of this particular feature of the canonical English iambic pentameter. Chaucer seems to have taken lexical and metrical bracketing into account in his crafting of lines, and if this was the case, it confirms that his design is foot-based. In the next chapter I shall examine the structure of Chaucer's iambic feet and put the whole concept of bracketing under the microscope.

From the foregoing analysis it is clear that inversion is only a minor source of rhythmic variety in Chaucer's verse. In a language where Move X had such widespread application, a few irredeemable trochees disturbed minimally the smooth texture of long passages of iambic verse. For variety to offset this regularity Chaucer relied on other techniques: the number and location of weak beats, the positions of the strongest mid-line stress and principal syntactic boundary, and a few lines that deviate from the iambic pentameter norm in ways that became obsolete. I shall now examine each of these techniques in more detail.

Weak Beats and Linear Subdivisions

Figure 1 shows that in the later group of my samples Chaucer employed significantly more weak beats, and that he achieved a balance between the number of Gallic and Italic lines that is not found in the earlier group. While the differences between earlier and later groups are highly statistically significant, those between individual poem samples are not so clear or consistent. For example, four of the samples show an imbalance within the category 'Italic' of the subcategories 'Running' and 'Major.' My *AA* and *KT* samples contain far more running lines than major ones, while the opposite applies to my *PF* and *RT* samples. These discrepancies point to there being other variables that affect these features besides date of composition. Chapter 13 will look more closely at the texts concerned in the hope of discovering what some of those other variables are, but in this section I shall limit myself to exemplifying the types of line and correlating them with the position of weak beats.

Italic lines, those that violate one or both of the *décasyllabe*'s constraints, can be divided into three sub-types: running lines (those violating only WB), major lines (those violating only PS), and what I shall term *free* lines, which violate both constraints. This more accurate sub-division than the one shown in Figure 1 is shown in Figure 3, which compares the percentage of each of these sub-types of Italic line in my samples with the percentage of Gallic lines:

Line Types	*Earlier Samples*	*Later Samples*
Gallic	62	53
Running	18	22
Major	13	19
Free	7	6
TOTAL	100	100

Fig. 3: Percentage of All Line Types: Eight Samples

These statistics show increases in the proportions of both major lines (those that violate only the PS constraint), and running lines (those that violate only the WB constraint), but not lines that violate both constraints. The increases are obviously balanced by a significant decrease in the proportion of Gallic lines.

Crafting each of these four types of line has linguistic and rhythmic implications that I illustrate below from my samples. Gallic lines are the most common, because in any English text well over 70 percent of words (as items) are monosyllables, and because many more pairs of monosyllables contrast w^s than s^w. Probability modeling shows that a random arrangement of the words in Chaucer's poetry into ten-syllable units would have an 80 percent chance of creating a word boundary immediately after syllable 4 in each unit.[17]

Gallic lines, those with phrasal stress in position 4, immediately followed by a word boundary, can be crafted in three different ways, as the following examples demonstrate:

(19) I wot it wel, // thou wolt ben our^{e} so**cour** (*ABC*, 65)
(20) On hors, on **fot**^{e}, // in al the feld ab**out**e (*AA*, 35)
(21) Saw I **Delyt**, // that stod with Gentilesse (*PF*, 224)

Lines like example (19) are the most common because of the plethora of English monosyllables; lines like (20) are also common because most ME disyllables end in schwa, which can be elided; and lines like example (21) are more rare because iambic disyllables are relatively few (mostly prefixed verbs).

When crafting Gallic lines, poets have to begin by finding a phrase that is four syllables long (to its last stress); this is a much easier task in English than finding a six-syllable phrase, and for this reason Gallic lines will form the majority in any iambic pentameter poem – unless the poet takes care to vary this aspect of line structure for aesthetic reasons. The statistics in Figure 1 show that Chaucer exercised this care in the later, but not in the earlier group of poems. All the lines must be divisible into 4 + 6 syllables in French *décasyllabes*, because the essence of their poetic rhythm is the equal time interval between phrasal stress-

[17] For a detailed explanation of how these odds are calculated, see Duffell, 2002b: 302, note 14.

es. But in Italian *endecasillabi* such monotony would be a luxury, and in English iambic pentameters it is a gross defect. English lines are already burdened with a surfeit of regularity, because they are isodynamic as well as isosyllabic; dividing them all in the same place would be *de trop*.

The chief aesthetic precaution that English poets take is to balance the Gallic lines in a poem by boosting the proportion of Italic ones beyond the 20 percent of running lines that random word-placement would produce. Fortunately, there are more ways than one of crafting an Italic line, and they are listed and illustrated from Chaucer's work below.

The first way is by the use of running lines, where the stress in position 4 followed by a post-tonic syllable makes the language's many trochaic disyllables available without elision. Note that running lines often contain a weak third beat (as in (23) below):

(22) As doth a **hev**^{e}nyssh // **perfit creat**ure (*TC*, I: 104)
(23) She was **ar**isen // and al **red**y dight (*KT*, 1041)

Where a running line's third beat is strong, as in (22), trochees tend to take over the second half of the line, offering a strong rhythmic contrast with the first half and with the passage as a whole. Running lines may also be major lines, when they become what I have termed free lines; for example, instance (25) below; but many major lines are not running lines: instead they contain a weak second beat, like (24), or a second beat that is simply outranked within its phrase, like (26):

(24) That may go thurgh the **go**let // **soft**^{e} and **swoo**te (*PT*, 543)
(25) In all^{e} the **or**dres **four**^{e} // is noon that kan (*GP*, 210)
(26) This **A**leyn al for**gat**, // both^{e} **mel**^{e} and corn (*RT*, 4076)

Chaucer often called on one word to supply both the second and third beats in the line, as in the following examples:

(27) With **thor**nes veny**mous**, // O **hev**^{e}ne queen (*ABC*, 149)
(28) Of **quen**^{e} Ane**lida** // and fals Arcite (*AA*, 11)

Italian poets shun this mid-line placement of polysyllabic words, and Piera argues that this is for intonational reasons (to do with pitch accent in Italian).[18] In English, on the other hand, such placement utilizes secondary stress to make the line even more clearly iambic. ME speakers, like Modern English speakers in the US, employed strong secondary stress, and it often supplied Chaucer and his contemporaries with line-end rhyme.[19]

---

[18] For intonational factors in the *endecasillabo*'s verse design, see Piera, 2001.

[19] My statistics are based on Stubbs's transcription of the Hengwrt manuscript, the text of which is markedly less regular in meter than that of the Ellesmere manuscript on

In my scansions I have underlined the first of two stresses employed in this way and placed the second in bold typeface. This second stress, though often secondary in the modern language, always carries the rhyme in Chaucer's verse, and my notation recognizes it as the end-of-colon marker. Chaucer often placed polysyllabic words in positions 4–5–6; although he may have noticed that Boccaccio never did so, his two priorities were making his pentameters iambic and employing all his language's resources; and secondary stress was an important resource.

In summary, Chaucer's pentameter lacked constraints on word boundaries (+WB) and the position of the strongest mid-line stress (+PS), and this made it a very different meter from the French *décasyllabe*. Moreover, it differed from the Italian *endecasillabo* by always having five beats, whereas some variants of the Italian meter were clearly four-beat lines. The English line's design governed both the number of beats and the number of syllables, but it had other sources of variety: the position of colon boundaries and of mid-line stress peaks, and the number and position of weak beats. Other devices to give the meter's lines variety were therefore almost redundant: the occasional inversion and the rare lines that were vestiges of older modes of versifying are present in Chaucer's long-line verse, but they are peripheral. Since I have enlarged my line sample partly in order to capture more of them, I shall examine those peripheral features in the next section of this chapter.

Before leaving the subject of the sub-division of Chaucer's lines, however, I shall comment briefly on the virgules that divide many of the lines in the Hengwrt manuscript of *CT.* Critics pay little attention to them because they are unlikely to be Chaucer's own notation. My sample for the quantification I give was the first 200 lines of *GP*, and Figure 4 shows the percentage (rounded) of lines with a virgule in each position. The (a) percentage is of all lines, and the (b) percentage of lines with virgules.

All Numbers are Percentages

After:	*4M*	*4F*	*6M*	*6F*	*Other*	*None*
(a) % of all lines	33	17	12	5	10	24
(b) % of lines with Vs	44	22	15	7	12	*

Fig. 4: Position of Virgules in Hengwrt

Note that some lines without virgules contain a full point, sometimes in an inexplicable position.

The percentages in row (b) are very close to those for minor / major lines in my analysis (a ratio of 66:34), but some of Hengwrt's subdivisions appear not to be syntactic, as the following examples show:

---

which Benson, 1988 is largely based.

(29) Aboven alle nacions | in Pruce (*GP*, 53)
(30) In Lectow | hadde he reysed | and in Ruce (*GP*, 54)
(31) At mete | wel ytaught was she with alle (*GP*, 127)
(32) Of grece | whan she dronken hadde hir draghte (*GP*, 135)

The most likely explanation for these virgules is that they are scribal memory aids: the copyist probably used them to ensure that he had to commit to memory no more than eight syllables of the exemplar at a time. 'Pruce,' 'lectow,' and 'Ruce' may be singled out as the only major-category words in their subdivision because they were unusual words requiring care. 'At mete' introduces a sudden change of subject (from what leaves the mouth to what enters it), and 'Of grece' is a *rejet* from the previous line's enjambment. But even if my guesses at the scribe's motivations are wrong, the virgules appear to have only vague structural significance.

Chaucer's Non-Canonical Lines

My samples contain a number of lines that deviate from the norms of the English iambic pentameter, insofar as they violate SMP, PT, or the cumulative constraint governing positions 4 and 6. Headless lines make up the majority of these deviant lines and they occur in all my samples. Examples are:

(33) [V] Bring us to that palais // that is bilt (*ABC*, 183)
(34) [V] Craumpyssheth // her lymes crokedly (*AA*, 171)
(35) [V] Ther^{e} as swetness^{e} // ev^{e}remor^{e} inow is (*PF*, 185)
(36) [V] Of this kynges son^{e} // of which I tolde (*TC*, I: 261)
(37) [V] Of the bodies // and the gret^{e} honour (*KT*, 997)
(38) [V] Senec seith a good word // doutelees (*PT*, 492)
(39) [V] With his typet // wound^{e} about^{e} his heed (*RT*, 3953)

Most headless lines in my samples are enjambed with the previous line, and they are thus the second of a pair of lines (not necessarily rhymed) that has (in Ovid's terms) had 'one foot stolen away.' The full rhythmic effect of this pairing can be seen in the following couplets:

(40) For hym was lev^{e}r^{e} // hav^{e} at his beddes heed
(41) [ ] Twenty bookes, // clad in blak and reed (*GP*, 293–94)
(42) On halyday^{e}s // biforn hir^{e} wold^{e} he go
(43) [ ] With his typet // wound^{e} about^{e} his heed (*RT*, 3952–93)

The fact that this 'Ovidian' effect often involves unrhymed lines, as in (42) and (43), helps give Chaucer's couplets the openness that distinguishes them from those of French narrative verse. Chaucer's syntax flows across boundaries and his metrical devices do the same.

As the first eight examples of this chapter show, Chaucer recognized that an opening trochee interferes minimally with a verse's iambic pulse. In theory this would have allowed him to begin a line with a disyllable ending in schwa, but in practice such lines are impossible to identify with confidence, because they are indistinguishable from schwa-deleted headless lines; thus, for example:

(44) B**a**the the **war**deyn // and our^{e} **fe**law^{e}s **al**le (*RT*, 4112)
(44)a [V] Bath^{e} the **war**deyn // and our^{e} **fe**law^{e}s **al**le

The Northern dialect form 'bathe' is almost certainly monosyllabic, like 'oure' later in the line, and I have counted this line as headless.

Headless lines offered Chaucer an additional source of rhythmic variety, and they made his verse sound more like normal speech. Stress peaks do tend to form on alternate syllables in English, but the alternation is often broken in long utterances, and headless lines produce such a break. It is perhaps surprising that Chaucer did not employ more of them; after all, more than 2,000 lines in Shakespeare's plays lack a syllable.[20] The inclusion of such lines gives dialogue an authenticity that perfectly iambic utterances do not have, and it is clear from my figures that Chaucer clung to the occasional use of this traditional type of tension in ME verse, even in his later compositions, resisting the influence of French and Italian isosyllabism on his versifying.

Very few lines in my samples lack a syllable in any other position than the first in the line. I noted one exception (line (8) of *GP*) in the last chapter; other examples are:

(45) O **womb**^{e}! O **be**ly! [/] O **styn**kyng cod! (*PT*, 534)
(46) Of al hir art // [ ] **count**^{e} I noght a **tare** (*RT*, 4056)

The first of these lines seems to be a reversion to the ME four-beat line, which in its context gives it greater emphasis; and the second is a broken-backed line, with five beats but one implied offbeat, which also adds emphasis; but it is tempting to emend the second half of this line to: "I **count**^{e} it noght a **tare**."

There are also six lines in my sample that would be a syllable short if elision were applied rigorously, and I give two of them below:

(47) For, ạṣ of **trou**the, $_{H}$ is ther noon her **ly**che (*AA*, 76)
(48) The **fai**re $_{H}$ **har**dy **queen**^{e} // of Scithia (*KT*, 882)

The obvious explanation for these anomalies is that Chaucer forgot to elide the word-final schwas of 'trouthe' and 'faire' before the following vowels. It is important to remember that poetic elision was as much a borrowed French conven-

[20] For details of the hypometric lines in Shakespeare's plays, see the tables in Wright, 1988: 292–95.

tion as it was a reflection of contemporary speech habits, because they varied so widely from person to person and from utterance to utterance. In his defense it should be noted that bridge players often forget conventions, and Chaucer wrote more lines than most players have made bids.

Chaucer's lines with extra syllables are far fewer than those that lack a syllable, and they usually have the extra syllable at the caesura. The following lines offer the best candidates for epic caesuras in my samples:

(49) Wer^{e} **bit**ter, **nei**[ther] // in **er**the nor in see (*ABC*, 50)
(50) Whoso thee **lo**[veth], // he shal not **lov**^{e} in vain (*ABC*, 71)
(51) That she him **trus**[ted] // ov^{e}r **any** crea**ture** (*AA*, 91)
(52) That **he** was **ser**[vaunt] // **un**to her **la**dish**ip**pe (*AA*, 191)
(53) As for to **ho**[noure] // hir^{e} **god**des ful de**vou**te (*TC*, I: 151)
(54) Unto the **cra**[del], // and in his hand it **hen**te (*RT*, 4212)

The first thing that strikes the reader about these examples is how many of them have other possible explanations. In (49) syncope could apply to 'neith^{e}r' to make it a monosyllable or the final schwa of 'erth^{e}' could be deleted; syncope could also apply to 'lov^{e}th' in (50) and 'crad^{e}l' in (54), which invites resyllabification of its final '-l' with the following syllable. But if 'servaunt' and 'honoure' must be disyllabic, producing epic caesurae, then why not these other words? Chaucer may have employed this device from French *décasyllabes* and ME four-beat dolniks only rarely, but it seems he did employ it.

For this reason we cannot be sure whether some of the redundant word-final schwas in my samples represent epic caesuras or not; for example, those in the following lines:

(55) Axeth thin **hel**[pe], // thin **hert**^{e} is ay so **free** (*ABC*, 12)
(56) Fro La**ci**do[mye] // to **mak**^{e} hir^{e} al**li**aunce (*PT*, 605)

Here it might be argued that Chaucer forgot that he needed to elide the redundant word-final schwas, but the natural pauses in delivery that these lines invite are so marked that we should probably assume that Chaucer's metrical intention was an epic caesura.

Although eight lines in *ABC* have an extra syllable as a result of a redundant *-e*, we should not take them as indications of a very early date, because such redundant *–e*s are as much a feature of *GP* (post-1387) as *BD* (c. 1369). Other lines in my samples with an extra syllable are very few: in most cases an extra syllable in anacrusis seems the likely explanation (as in *PT*, 500 and 605).

A small number of lines in my samples of earlier works suggest that Chaucer may have had to feel his way towards a cumulative constraint on weak beats. The lines concerned are:

(57) And al was **fal**snes // that she to him **men**te (*AA*, 160)

(58) On Parnas**o** // that ẉịṭḥ thy **sustres** **gla**de (*AA*, 16)
(59) So cryëden // that ṭọ the **sterr**^{e}s hit **wen**te (*AA*, 27)
(60) Ne ḅỵ non ḅụṭ he / **Lo**ves **ser**vaunt be (*PF*, 159)
(61) And **pre**ieth f̣ọṛ hem // ṭḥạṭ ben ịṇ the cas (*TC*, I: 29)

Examples (57) and (60) have two consecutive weak beats, which occur very rarely in later centuries' iambic pentameters. Examples (58) and (59) show that Chaucer regarded secondary stresses as strong enough to create an iambic pulse. His stressing of 'Parnaso' in (57) seems very different from Boccaccio's (and Modern English) 'Parnaso.' Finally, example (61) has three consecutive erosions and violates the cumulative constraint: thus a normal delivery would make 'hem' in position 5 a minor peak of stress. But it is important not to get this exception out of proportion: violations of the cumulative constraint are less common in my samples than inversions that violate both the closure principle and the bracketing condition (as in examples (17) and (18) above).

Chaucer's aim, like that of later English poets, was to give his lines an iambic rhythm, and a peak of stress in either in position 4 or 6 is the key to that endeavor. Grammatical monosyllables in both positions 4 and 6 negate the line's iambic pulse. If the intervening monosyllable (for such it must be) is stressed, then SMP will be violated (because position 5 will contain a peak of stress) and the line's iambic pulse will be arrested. If, on the other hand, the intervening monosyllable is also grammatical, an iambic pulse can only be maintained by artificially stressing one (or both) of its neighbors. Example (61) above requires such artificial stressing: it is a *weak line*, a category that good poets shun. This aversion clearly began with Chaucer, whose weak lines represent less than 0.1 percent of the total in my samples.

The mandatory stress in position 4 or 6 was a feature of Boccaccio's *endecasillabi* that Chaucer could hardly have missed while translating *Filostrato*. But the monosyllabic structure of the language offered temptations to ignore the Italian norm in the crafting of English lines. Chaucer, with very few exceptions, resisted temptation, because he must have recognized the weakening or disruption of the rhythm that resulted. In this respect, also, Chaucer's verse design was very close to that of the modern canon.

Conclusions

My research shows that Chaucer's new English meter was born in panoply: the design of his first lines in the meter, which were probably composed c. 1378 rather than c. 1369, remained almost unchanged in the 1390s. The origins of this new meter lay in the practicalities of verse craft and in Chaucer's social luck: his knowledge of Italian poetry reassured him that the rhythms he sought to give an English line of ten syllables were viable and attractive. He also intuited that those rhythms were the perfect fit for his language.

The influence of French poetry on Chaucer's new verse design was mostly negative: on the one hand it gave him the principle of elision with which to solve the problem of schwa deletion, but on the other it presented a model of what would not work in English. He and Gower both recognized that the two-beat rhythm of the *décasyllabe* was not viable in ME or AN because of their strong word stress, and both poets decided to give their longer lines a five-beat rhythm, a previously untried extension of the four-beats that dominated the poetry of England's two languages. Chaucer and Gower also refused to be bound by the *décasyllabe*'s constraints (+WB and +PS), because those constraints imposed an intolerable burden: they inhibited the use of their language's many trochaic words mid-line.

In Italian poetry Chaucer found a pleasing variety of word boundaries that enabled the poet to make a chosen rhythm flow through the lines, but he also found some of the rhythms in Boccaccio's verse less attractive than others. The triple time of *dactilico* lines in particular must have reminded him of English folk verse and, since he sought something more dignified, he excluded them. Additionally, the mixed rhythm of *melodico* and *adonico* lines probably sounded too much like prose, so they too were excluded. This left Chaucer with the iambic lines he wanted, lines that stylized the natural duple-time rhythm of his language in the most normal way: to achieve this, rather than a trochaic rhythm, Chaucer exaggerated in his lines the tendency in ME prose for utterances to begin with a monosyllable.[21]

Chaucer's confidence in the iamb, based on his Italian models, led him to compose ME lines that violated the French WB and PS constraints far more often than did Gower's AN *décasyllabes*; and they also led him to make those lines more strongly iambic than Gower's: while *CB* contains occasional peaks of stress in odd-numbered positions as a source of variety, Chaucer allowed only small deviations from his chosen rhythm: an occasional line that lacked an initial offbeat, or contained an inversion or an epic caesura. With time, Chaucer learned to derive more rhythmic variety from the use of weak beats in different positions, and he reduced the number of feminine lines (Italian *piani*) with their contrapuntal trochaic closes, and lines ending in schwa, which gave at least a potential for syllabification. Instead he achieved an even stronger counterpoint by boosting the proportion of running lines in his verse because when a trochaic word occupies positions 4 and 5 the remainder of a feminine line becomes trochaic. Chaucer's favoring such lines was what ensured that much of his later verse has

[21] My research into monosyllables was based on Hengwrt, and it showed that over 70 percent of sentences in the Tale of Melibee but over 90 percent of the lines in *GP* begin with a monosyllable.

a balance between Gallic and Italic lines that is similar to the balance in Shakespeare's sonnets.

This chapter has been devoted to the analysis of samples that, in total, are sufficiently large to ensure the statistical significance of some key differences that I have identified.[22] I hope that at some time in the future a computer-based study of Chaucer's whole corpus will ask the same questions and re-examine my conclusions. If nothing else, my analysis offers pointers to the metrical features on which a more exhaustive study should focus. In the meantime I trust that my sample-based data will increase readers' understanding of Chaucer's versifying and help them derive added enjoyment from his work.

In the course of this chapter I have noted how Chaucer's headless lines often have an aesthetic function; in the next two chapters I shall look at some other ways in which Chaucer's verse reveals a mastery of both language and metrical craftsmanship, and I shall try to evaluate his achievement at every structural level.

[22] In total, my Chaucer samples contain approximately the same number of lines (2,000) as Xingzhong Li analyzed for his dissertation; see Li, 1995.

12
Chaucer's Strophes

This chapter and the next will present the case that Geoffrey Chaucer raised the craft of versifying in English to an art, and that in doing so he equaled, and possibly excelled, the achievements of Europe's finest poets in this field. Among the definitions of the word *art* in dictionaries are the following:

> Works produced by skill and imagination. . .branches of creative activity; a skill at doing a specified thing, typically one acquired through practice
>
> OED

Chaucer's versifying qualifies for all these descriptions and does so at three levels: he showed exceptional skill and imagination in his design and execution of (1) strophes, (2) lines containing ten English syllables, and (3) rhythmic units within such a line. Chaucer's versification is, in this way, a major contributor to making his work poetry of the highest order. As noted in Chapter 2, the definition of poetry in most dictionaries goes something like this:

> Literary work in which special intensity is given to the expression of feelings and ideas by the use of distinctive style and rhythm.
>
> OED

Versifying becomes *verse art* when meter and rhythm are sufficiently distinctive to encourage readers to return to a text again and again, and to derive lasting pleasure not only from what the poet has to say, but also from the way that he or she deploys language in the process. In the course of this chapter I shall try to illustrate that Chaucer did the second of these so well that subsequent English poets could only match his achievement by mastering his techniques.

The analysis that follows focuses on each of the three levels of Chaucer's verse art in turn: the crafting of poems from strophes, the crafting of lines, and the crafting of rhythmic feet. This chapter will be devoted to the first of those three. The key variables in the crafting of strophes in which all lines have the same verse design are: (1) the number of lines in the strophe, (2) the number of different rhymes required for each new rhyme word, (3) the interval between the rhyming words, (4) the position of the rhyme within the rhyme word, and (5) the option of using a refrain.

As noted in Chapter 5, even ME folk poets could craft complex strophes that opened with long alliterative lines and closed with short rhyming ones.[1] Rhyme came into English verse from Latin and French and gradually ousted alliteration as the dominant form of phoneme repetition, just as it had replaced assonance in France. With rhyme came a greater potential for strophe construction than varying line length had offered poets of the Classical languages. In Medieval Latin what we term *masculine* rhymes preceded *feminine* ones, although they arrived in pre-Islamic Arabic poetry simultaneously many centuries earlier.[2] In English and in Italian a third type of rhyme occurs naturally within words (like ag**ility** / ab**ility** and *dubito* / *subito*) and is termed *triple* rhyme in English and *rima sdrucciola* in Italian.[3] To create triple rhymes in French, poets need to combine words: thus *mois de mai* rhymes with *bois de mai*, but to French ears they appear contrived and to English ones comic.[4]

The clearest indication that Chaucer intended word-final schwas to be pronounced at line ends is that he uses rhymes like *Rome* / *to me* (*GP*, 671–72). There were thus many more feminine rhymes available to ME poets than to modern ones, and this is reflected in my samples. The frequency with which French and Italian poets employ feminine rhymes is very different: in Italian poetry the feminine *rima piana* is the *rima normale* because the majority of Italian words are paroxytonic and most poets have tended to stylize this feature in their verse; thus there are only a handful of masculine (*tronche*) and triple (*sdrucciole*) rhymes in the works of Dante and Petrarch.[5] The French lexicon, however, divides almost 50:50 between oxytonic and paroxytonic words; as a result poems with only feminine rhymes are rare, as are poems earlier than the sixteenth century that alternate masculine and feminine rhymes.[6] Although the ME lexicon was replete with words of both types, Chaucer could scarcely have missed the fact that the Italian poetry he most admired almost always employed feminine rhymes.

Refrains first appeared in European court poetry in the eleventh century and by Chaucer's time their use was firmly established as a way of linking strophes within a poem.[7] At first sight repeating a line four times in a poem to close its strophes seems a way of simplifying the poet's task, but in fact it complicates it, because at least four rhymes have to be found for the last word of the refrain. 'Ch' then gave his ballades refrains, but his greater rhyming feat was in the use of the

---

[1] See Chapter 5, examples (14) to (19), and Fein, 2000.

[2] For the development of feminine rhymes in European verse, see Brittain, 1937: 197 and Beare, 1957: 288.

[3] For *sdruccioli*, see Elwert, 1973: 88–89.

[4] For artificial rhymes in French, see Kastner, 1903; 56–57.

[5] See Elwert, 1973: 90–91.

[6] For the use of M/F rhyme alternation in French poems earlier than 1600, see Kastner, 1903: 56–57.

[7] For refrains, see Greene and Cushman, 2012: 1151–52.

chançon royal: in his first poem, for example he employs the scheme abab cc dd in five strophes with the same rhymes. He thus had to find ten different words for each of the four rhymes, which was no mean achievement.

As far as rhyme was concerned, medieval French versifying was an art of extremes: composers of lyrics favored highly elaborate strophes with complex rhyme schemes, while composers of narrative verse mostly settled for the simplicity of rhymed couplets. The first reason for the difference was practical: lyrics are generally short and narratives long, so while finding four words with ten rhymes was a practical proposition in French, finding hundreds of words with ten rhymes would have been very difficult. This makes Gower's *MO* a remarkable feat of rhyming: he found six rhyme words for every rhyme he employed over thousands of lines. The second reason for elaborate rhyme schemes in lyrics was aesthetic: the musical setting could ensure that lines with the same rhyme also matched in terms of musical notes.

When Chaucer made his second visit to Italy in 1378 he had composed (or at least begun) three substantial poems: *BD*, *RR*, and *HF*, all narratives of sorts, and all in rhymed couplets. In Italian poetry, however, he encountered far longer narratives with more demanding strophe designs, and he was doubtless impressed. The couplet, as I noted in the last chapter, has the least demanding of rhyme schemes (matched only by the Shakespearian sonnet): the poet has to find just one other rhyme for each new line-final word. In contrast, *terza rima* requires the poet to find two other rhyme words for every new line-final word, and the Petrarchan sonnet requires an average of just over two other rhyme words.[8] Even *ottava rima* requires an average of 1.7 other rhyme words. From the date of his return Chaucer rose to the challenge, as far as he could in English, of mastering this greater level of difficulty. Only after he had proved himself by composing an 8,000-line narrative in rhyme royal and achieving a measure of fame with it did he return to the simple couplet.

Of the key features of strophe design that I listed at the beginning of this section the only one that remains for me to comment upon is the size of the intervals between rhymes. Shakespearian sonnets are a little more complex than couplets in that the rhymes have to be alternated (abab), and Petrarchan sonnets a little more so, because two b-rimes must be inserted between a-rimes and vice versa (abba abba). In *MO* Gower makes his audience wait even longer for the full rhyme scheme to manifest itself (aab aab bba bba).[9] One of the narrative drawbacks of complex strophes is that they can be inconvenient. If poets get to the end of what they want to say half way through a strophe they have to insert padding,

[8] The difficulty varies according to whether the sonnet's sestet has two or three rhymes; see Ruschioni, 1974: I, 18–19.

[9] The French rhyme terms are: *rimes plats* (aa bb), *croisées* (abab), and *embrassées* (abba); see Kastner, 1903: 67–68; the Italian equivalents are *rime baciate*, *alterne*, and *abbraciate*; see Elwert, 1973: 111.

and the longer the strophe, the more padding is required. From his translation of the *Filostrato* it appears that Chaucer recognized padding in some of Boccaccio's *ottava rima* strophes, and the English poet exercised the translator's prerogative: he omitted it from his own poem.

Chaucer learned by experience that couplets interfere least with the momentum of a narrative: they don't play games of "wait and see" with the audience, and they fit the narrative too closely to allow much padding. Chaucer was first and foremost a teller of tales, and when his art began to detract from his narratives he ruthlessly simplified his art. But, like all good narrators, he also tried to bring his characters to life, and in *CT* one of the ways that he did this was letting his most pretentious pilgrims play those strophe-design games. Chaucer undoubtedly took a great interest in the subject of strophe design, and this can be seen clearly from the brief synopsis and review of his many designs that follows.

If a versifying analyst had ever been able to get Chaucer on a couch, the poet would probably have admitted that he found his second visit to Italy traumatic. On his return Chaucer abandoned *HF*, and his shorter line, and the couplet. Whether or not he had ever attempted a decasyllable before, he now threw himself into a frenzy of composing such lines and weaving them into strophes, as he knew the great Italian poets had done. He was a man with a mission, and a meter, and a willingness to experiment with the architecture within which that meter was displayed. This pursuit of excellence and willingness to experiment shine most clearly in the poem and strophe designs of *AA*, one of the first works he composed after his return.

AA begins with three strophes of an invocation (to Mars) and twenty-seven of narrative, all in the seven-line stanza of rhyme royal (abab bcc). Editors and critics disagree on the model for Chaucer's strophe; Fisher offers the simplest answer: Gower. Fisher seeks to date the first of Gower's ballades to earlier than 1377, in order to provide a more credible audience for love lyrics than the residents of Saint Mary Overys, and rhyme royal is one of Gower's favorite strophe designs. If Fisher is correct, Gower introduced the form to England, if he is not, then Chaucer may at least have been a partner in its introduction. Of the sample of *CB* I analyzed in Chapter 9, Balades x, xi, xii, and xiv are in rhyme royal, and the remaining seven are in the eight-line stanza of Chaucer's Monk's Tale (abab bcbc). When Gower dedicated *CB* to Henry IV many years later he did so in two poems, one with each design; and, since the individual poems in *CB* cannot be dated, Gower may even have begun using rhyme royal after Chaucer. If we take into account the wide range of designs available in the French poetry that the two Englishmen had read, it is very difficult to believe that they failed to discuss strophe design.

Another possible hypothesis is that Chaucer derived rhyme royal from Boccaccio's *ottava rim*a by eliminating the fifth line (rhymed a), which would have made his rhyming task easier. The index I have suggested above gives *ottava rima* 1.7 degrees of difficulty to rhyme royal's 1.3, a reduction sufficient to ease the problem of the English language's rhyme poverty. Moreover, since seven English lines contain roughly as many words as eight Italian ones, this transition would have been a logical and helpful step for a translator.

But there is a further possibility: Machaut's favorite ballade strophe contained eight lines rhymed abab ccdd, and the first of the c rhymes introduced a new line length of seven syllables.[10] In his famous ballade with the refrain "Le grant desir que j'ai de vous veoir," however, Machaut simplified this design by omitting the seven-syllable line and rhyming the fifth line b. The result was abab bcc—rhyme royal. From one of the most admired poems of the previous generation, straight to the two friends' poetry was a very small leap, and I am inclined to favor that explanation for its simplicity.

In any event, Chaucer chose rhyme royal for his narrative in *AA*, did so again in *PF*, and after composing 8,000 lines of *TC* gave the meter a new English name—*Troilus meter.*[11] In each of these works Chaucer embedded a lyric poem: in *AA* a long 'compleynt' after the French fashion, in *PF* a brief *rondel*, and in *TC* the "Canticus Troili," a translation and exploration of one of Petrarch's finest sonnets.[12] The rondel was a fixed form, and for the "Canticus" Chaucer employed three strophes of rhyme royal, but for the "Compleynt of Anelida" (*AA*, 211–346) he employed his most elaborate strophe design.

The "Compleynt" consists of fourteen stanzas subdivided as follows: "Proem" (1 stanza), "Strophe" (6 stanzas), "Antistrophe" (also 6), and "Conclusion" (1 stanza), making the poem design a palindrome. The design of the "Proem" and "Conclusion," and all but one of the stanzas in the "Strophe" and "Antistrophe," have nine lines rhymed aab aab bab—with a difficulty index of 3.5 degrees. The fifth stanzas of both "Strophe" and "Antistrophe" contain two line lengths, which I shall notate by giving their number of beats in subscript as follows:

a a a b　a a a b　b b b a　b b b a
4 4 4 5　4 4 4 5　4 4 4 5　4 4 4 5

This design has a difficulty index of 7.0 degrees (compared with Gower's of 5.0 in *MO*), and Chaucer attempts an even higher bar in the second stanza of the "Antistrophe," which he rhymes aaa aaa aaa (index 8.0). In the "Compleynt" Chaucer demonstrated what could be achieved by way of strophe construction

[10] For Machaut's fondness for including a *heptasyllabe* in his eight-line strophes, see Woledge, 1961: 220–26.

[11] Only after James I of Scotland (b. 1394–d. 1437) borrowed Chaucer's *Troilus* meter did the strophe design gain the name *rhyme royal*; for the text of James's poetry, see Mackenzie, 1939.

[12] For a line-by-line comparison between Petrarch's Sonnet 132 (Poem 142) and Chaucer's 'Canticus Troili' (*TC*, I, 400–20), see Windeatt, 1984: 112. For the differences between the French *rondel* and the Chaucerian *roundel*, see Stillman, 1966: 58–60.

in rhyme-poor English; in the *Teseida* Boccaccio boasted that his was the first poem in the vulgar tongue to challenge the classics in portraying feats of the art of Mars.[13] By dedicating *AA* to Mars Chaucer identified with the Italian poet's confidence and ambition.

Pride, however, comes before a fall, and Chaucer never showed off in this way again. In the "Conclusion" he sobs that he is so overcome with emotion that he cannot bear to go on. He adds one last strophe of rhyme royal in a vain attempt to continue the story and then stops. Like a man who has gone fishing from a rowboat and has hooked a whale, Chaucer must have realized that the "Complaint" is too monstrous for the narrative, and he leaves the story from Boccaccio's *Teseida* until he can do it justice in a meter better fitted to long narratives, and without the distraction of a strophe-design extravaganza.

Chaucer also employed rhyme royal for many of his short poems: *The Complaint unto Pity*, *A Complaint to His Lady* (the first two strophes), *Chaucer's Words to Adam His Owne Scriveyn*, *Truth**, *Gentilesse*,* *Lak of Stedfastnesse**, *Lenvoy de Chaucer a Scogan*, *The Complaint of Chaucer to His Purse**, *Against Women Unconstant*, *Complaynt d'Amours*, and *A Balade of Complaint*. The closing line of each strophe is repeated in the four poems I have asterisked, and to the last of these Chaucer added an envoy, rhymed aabba.

In *The Canterbury Tales* the Host's Prologue to *ST* and four pilgrims' contributions are in rhyme royal: The Man of Law's Tale, The Prioress's tale, The Clerk's Tale, and the Second Nun's Tale. This is a piece of clever characterization: the five pilgrims who employ French ballade meters (these four and the monk) are well-educated snobs, and the Host is arrogantly intent on intimidating the author. Although Chaucer had composed some of these tales before he decided on the rhymed couplet as the staple of his collection, the pilgrims to whom he gave them were not chosen at random. The knight, as a man of action, was allotted not only the tribute to Mars, but also the practical couplet. The pilgrims who strove to be "estatlich of manere" or to make their speech "ful of hy sentence" claimed the ballade meters.

The strophe design that Chaucer employed next most often after rhyme royal was Gower's favorite, the octave with three rhymes: abab bcbc. This is rhyme royal with an extra b rhyme, and its difficulty index is thereby raised from 1.3 to 1.7. Chaucer employed it in The Monk's Tale and *ABC* and in four shorter poems: *Lenvoy de Chaucer a Bukton*, *The Former Age*, *To Rosemounde*, and *Fortune*. The poem *To Rosemounde* is a single ballade and *Fortune* a is triple ballade: in both poems Chaucer repeats the final line of each strophe (abab bcbC), and maintains the same three rhymes throughout each ballade. *Rosemounde* has no envoy, but the three ballades of *Fortune* are followed by a seven-line envoy, which resembles rhyme royal, but has only two rhymes (abab bab).

[13] See Pearsall, 1992: 119.

In the *Complaint of Venus* Chaucer translates three of Oton de Granson's ballades and adds to them an envoy, which explains his debt, and pays tribute to the poet he calls "the flour of hem that make in Fraunce,"[14] The strophe design of the three ballades, which is an octave with three rhymes (abab bccB), is Granson's choice, but Chaucer's envoy is longer and more elaborate: its ten lines involve only two rhymes (aab aab baab). Chaucer carries one rhyme, that for *Fraunce*, through the first two ballades (but not the third) and repeats it in the envoy. The envoy turns the authorial-modesty *topos* into boasting by complaining about the scarcity of rhyme in English.

W. A. Davenport pointed out the chief difference between the strophe designs of Chaucer's ballades and those of his French models.[15] French poets carried the same rhymes forward from strophe to strophe, something they were able to do easily because of the plethora of *suffix rhymes* in a language with oxytonic stress. Such grammatical rhymes in French include present and past participles (rhyming in *-ant* or *-é*), finite verb forms (such as those ending in *-ons*, *-ez*, *-ai*, *-oit*), nouns (such as those ending in *-age* and *-ure*), and adjectives and adverbs (ending in *-euse* and *-ment*).

Chaucer must have become very aware of the dearth of grammatical rhymes in English when he translated the *Roman de la Rose*, and in his own verse he takes advantage of many of the French loan words that facilitate rhyme. He also makes use of rhymes on secondary stresses (like Medieval Latin poets), and occasionally rhymes the suffixes of words ending in *-ing* or *-yng*. For the most part, however, Chaucer finds *root rhymes*: these do not lend themselves to protracted rhyming. Davenport regards Chaucer's observation in the *Complaint of Venus* that there is a scarcity of rhyme in English as ironic, but in terms of grammatical rhymes (which may make up more than 60 percent of those on a page of Lorris's *Roman de la Rose*) Chaucer is accurate, and his pride is justified.[16] Finding as many root rhymes as Chaucer does in his ballades is no mean achievement.

In *The Complaint of Mars,* Chaucer employs his favorite rhyme royal for the twenty-two strophes of proem and narrative that open the poem and then uses sixteen nine-lined strophes (rhymed aab aab bcc) for the complaint itself. Many of Chaucer's poems evidence strophe-design shifts simply because their structure is bipartite, background plus complaint; but Chaucer's metrical separation of

---

[14] The date of the Savoyard poet's birth is unknown; he died in a duel in 1397; for the text of Granson's poetry, see Winther, 2010.

[15] See Davenport, 2000: 181.

[16] For doubts on the accuracy of Chaucer's observation, see Davenport, 2000: 183; Davenport concluded that Chaucer 'did not seek the phonetic subtlety' of French rhymes, rather than being hampered by a shortage of rhymes in English (2000: 201). For an example of a passage of Lorris's *Roman de la Rose* with 63 percent suffix rhymes, see Woledge, 1961: 145.

narrative and dialogue may be simply following the French courtly convention of separating *dits* from *chançons* by meter as well as length.

In *A Complaint to His Lady,* Chaucer again separates background from complaint metrically, using two strophes of rhyme royal and an eight-line ballad strophe as the background and eight ten-line strophes rhymed aab aab cddc for most of the complaint. But the poem also includes three different forms: the first (lines 15–23) is a nine-line strophe with two rhymes and three unrhymed lines (axab abyb z); the second (lines 24–39) consists of sixteen lines of *terza rima*, and the third (lines 50–57) is an octave that opens with a monorhyme quatrain (aaaa bccb). Both unrhymed lines (*sueltos*) and monorhyme quatrains (*cuaderna vía*) have a long history in Spanish, and before that in French.[17] Regardless of their origin, however, surviving texts suggest that both were experiments in English that Chaucer never repeated.

Nor did Chaucer return to *terza rima.*His sixteen-line structure seems untidy and unfinished: it requires two lines rhyming with the words *wo* and *drede* to complete the meter's moebius-like symmetry (aba bcb cdc ded efe gag). Pearsall concludes that Chaucer decided he was no Dante halfway through this experimental excursion in the Italian poet's meter.[18] Yet it is equally likely that Chaucer realized *terza rima*'s magic lay in the combination of spiritual content with an endless trinity of lines, and that the absence of the first of these elements made the second merely an undistinguished vehicle for conventional sentiments. The intensity that Chaucer could achieve with his talent for language was not spiritual, it was philosophical: he tells us exactly how the world is and leaves us to enjoy or suffer it. His friend Gower always found a spiritual message in a random universe, but Chaucer left us to find our own.

Womanly Noblesse also employs a nine-line strophe design, and the poem is a *tour de force* of rhyming: its three strophes (rhymed aab aab bab) and its envoy (rhymed abab aa) contain only two rhymes (in *-aunce* and *-esse*). Someone was sufficiently impressed by the strophe design and execution to add the subtitle "Balade that Chaucier made" to a manuscript. *Merciles Beaute* is an equally elaborate metrical artifact, a triple roundel, each of its three parts rhyming AB_1B_2 $abAB_1$ abb AB_1B_2. Poetry, as Anne Birrell reminds us, is a game that poets play.[19] The playing style of Medieval European poets relied heavily on rhyme and strophe design, and Chaucer at his best was clearly a player in the top division.

There is one final piece of strophe design in Chaucer's surviving oeuvre that deserves special mention. In Chapter 8 I examined the verse design of *ST*, noting that Gaylord's description of the meter as 'dainty doggerel' was fully justified.[20] I also showed that the Tale's four-beat lines were as close to iambic tetrameters

---

[17] For *cuaderna vía* and *versos sueltos*, see Domínguez Caparrós 2001: 93 and 490.

[18] See Pearsall, 1992: 112.

[19] For the ludic theory of poetry, see Birrell, 2004: 19–42.

[20] See Gaylord, 1979.

as Chaucer ever came; but *ST*'s strophe design is even more remarkable and must be seen in its context. In this tale, Chaucer took the medieval *topos* of authorial modesty to extremes: the author is more than modest, he is masochistic, and the first hint of this is in the Host's prologue to the tale. This is one of the *Canterbury Tales'* few excursions into the sophisticated French form rhyme royal, and it seems designed to intimidate any pilgrim who wanted to employ a simple native meter. But Chaucer plunges in with a variant of common measure and a well-worn narrative line, and he is suitably humiliated when the Host forces him to cut off this tale in mid-sentence. Lest the reader feel sympathy for the narrator, his tale is made blatantly bad.

The content of *ST* is banal and, superficially at least, its form is equally execrable. The narrative is a stereotype of the tale of chivalry (knight fights giant for elf-queen), its pace is painfully slow, and the story line is cluttered with unwanted detail. The setting is vague (somewhere in fairyland) and is never brought to life; the characters (all two-and-half of them) lack individuality; and the humor lies largely in the absurdity of the detail.[21] To complement the poverty of the content, *ST*'s language is full of cliches and its versification is equally hackneyed: double common measure with tail rhyme. The basic strophe has six lines with a rhyme / beat formula a4 a4 b3 a4 a4 b3, like a half-strophe of *Guy of Warwick*.[22] Chaucer completes thirty-one strophes before being interrupted in the middle of the thirty-second. At first sight, therefore, the parody looks very like its target, and the author is severely punished for his misjudgment.

At a deeper level, however, the form of *ST* is full of meaning: its poem design encapsulates good and evil, and its strophe designs tell a story of their own. *ST*, as interrupted, is divided into three *fits* with the following number of strophes in each: 18, 9, and 4½. This structure is full of numerological significance because all these numbers are functions of the number nine: 2 × 9, 1 × 9, and 9/2; moreover, the sums of their digits are also nine: 1 + 8, 0 + 9, and (4 × 2) + 1. The number 9, like mankind, is both good (the square of the Trinity) and evil (the death card in a fortune-teller's pack). The three numbers (twice nine, nine, and a half of nine) are also entropic: they represent a diminution that can proceed to infinity, but the number nine is also a symbol of regeneration: next comes zero (newly introduced from the East), and after that the series begins again with one.[23] Today we relegate numerology with astrology to a pseudo-science, but

[21] Thus, for example, there seem to be only two reasons for mentioning the knight's nose in line 729 of *ST*: (1) every other feature has been mentioned, and (2) it rhymes with 'rose.'

[22] See Chapter 5, Note 57, above.

[23] The Indian concepts of zero and moving point arithmetic reached Europe in the twelfth century; see Hughes, 1989.

in Chaucer's day it was taken very seriously indeed, not least by men who wrote treatises on the astrolabe.[24]

The strophe design of *ST* also has numerological significance: the strophes of the poem with the basic design (a4 a4 b3 a4 a4 b3) are divided into two groups of thirteen, the number of greatest ill omen. After the first group of basic strophes (I–XIII) Chaucer tries to elaborate the design, and it all goes wrong. First he adds a bob (a single beat line) and introduces a third rhyme, which makes the rhyme / beat formula for strophe XIV: a4 a4 b3 c1 b4 b4 c3. He follows this in XV by an even greater elaboration: he repeats the scheme of the first three lines to produce a strophe of ten lines with a rhyme / beat formula: a4 a4 b3 a4 a4 b3 c1 a4 a4 c3. Strophe XV is the apogee of Chaucer's design experimentation, and I give it in full (lines 797–806) to show its structure and rhythm, and his three verse designs in combination:

(1) **In**to his **sa**[del] // he **clamb** a**non**,
(2) And **pri**keth **o**ver **stil**^{e} and stoon
(3) An **elf**-queen^{e} for t'es**pye**,
(4) Til he so **long**^{e} hath rid^{e}n and goon
(5) That he foond, in a **pry**ve woon,
(6) The **con**tree of Fai**rye**
(7) So **wil**de;
(8) For in that **con**tree was ther noon
(9) That to him **dur**ste **rid**^{e} or goon
(10) [ ] **Nei**ther wyf ne **chil**de;

This elaborate strophe requires six a-rhymes and the Chaucer who is telling this tale is unable to find the sixth, so he repeats 'goon.' The level of rhyming skill displayed falls further in strophes XVI and XVII, in both of which he is forced to introduce a fourth rhyme to complete the ten-line structure. At that point he concedes, and in XVIII he reverts to the simpler design of strophes I–XIII, but with a third rhyme. He tries the elaborate ten-line strophe once more in XXVII, but is forced to admit a fifth rhyme to achieve it, and he finally settles for the easiest of the many designs he has tried: the three-rhyme version of the basic design (a4 a4 b3 c4 c4 b3). The strophic architecture of *ST* is thus a carefully engineered failure: Geoffrey the Rhymer first becomes over-confident, then over-ambitious, and finally admits defeat.

I shall conclude this study of Chaucer's strophe designs with a brief note on enjambment, between lines as well as strophes. Chaucer's longer strophes are almost always self-contained in that he rarely allowed enjambment between them; one notable exception is 'so bright a star / As was Criseyde' (*TC*, I: 175–76); but he often employed enjambment between couplets. Chaucer does not employ the

[24] For a modern study of medieval numerology, see Burge, 2001.

more extreme forms of enjambment: the severance of adjectives from following nouns, or line-final conjunctions. Mostly he severs clause from clause and phrase from phrase, but the sentences that result are often long and encompass several lines. Chaucer sometimes severs single-word subjects from verbs, as in "she // Was whit" (*BD*, 904-05), and verbs from objects as in "she bar // A pair" (*GP*, 158-59); and he sometimes severs anomalous verbs, as in "bigan // To riden" (*GP*, 44-45). Note that all three of these examples are enjambments between couplets.

The percentage of lines that lack a punctuation mark in modern editions is a simple measure of enjambment in a poem, but it is only a rough one, because it depends partly on the poet and partly upon the editors concerned. The editors of the *Riverside Chaucer*, however, seem to have worked to common standards and this makes a comparison of this parameter in Chaucer's rhyme royal strophes and his couplets a useful one. Of the first 300 lines of *TC*'s rhyme royal, 22 percent lack a punctuation mark, and for a similar sample of *GP*'s couplets this figure is 16 percent; the difference is not statistically significant. The comparable figure for the first 300 lines of Shakespeare's sonnets in the Alexander edition is 18 percent, and so Chaucer and Shakespeare seem to have enjambed their lines equally freely.

Milton's decision to dispense with rhyme in *PL* made enjambment easier, and the 42 percentage of lines in Leonard's edition that lack a punctuation mark reflects this. Perhaps a fairer comparison with Chaucer's couplets is Dante's *terza rima*, where 38 percent of lines lack a punctuation mark in Petrocchi's edition. The fact that both Milton and Dante were attempting to compose a work that rivaled Virgil's doubtless affected their cultivation of enjambment.[25] But, to be fair to Chaucer, he employed enjambment far more often than the French decasyllabic norm, and he enjambed between, as well as within, couplets.[26] Finally, he varied his syntax according to whether he was crafting a poetic narrative or making pithy comments about individuals. Therefore, the first ten sentences of Hanna and Benson's text of *GP* in *The Riverside Chaucer* average 6.7 lines in length, while the next ten sentences average only 2.3.

The words that best describe Chaucer's talents as a strophe designer are *versatility* and *discretion*. He tried many different designs and he derived them from everywhere he knew: France and Italy were the most obvious sources but he was equally able to show his skill in an English popular form like tail rhyme. At his most ambitious he attempted the Doric architecture of Pindar: the strophe and antistrophe in *AA* want only an epode to rival the most brilliant creations

[25] For Virgil's use of enjambment and verse paragraphs, see Jackson Knight 1944: 181–84.

[26] Enjambment is common in French *octosyllabes* but rare in *décasyllabes*; see Kastner, 1903: 107–8.

of ancient Thebes.[27] In that poem Chaucer also tried mixing line lengths, but did not repeat the experiment, probably because that form of variety works best in a language where duration is the foundation of rhythm, as it was in Ancient Greece and medieval France.

Chaucer showed discretion when and where he used different strophe designs: he proved that he could make complex strophes work well for long narratives, as the best Italian poets had done; and he chose a form that interfered little with the narrative flow, rhyme royal. However, for most of his best stories he returned to the form that advanced the action by natural steps, the open couplet, with its enjambment between strophes as well as lines. Chaucer embraced variety in his strophes, but his design shifts are always for a good reason. Chaucer's *Complaints* are rather like opera: when the plot has reached its conclusion the sad lady starts to sing, and the intensity Chaucer has shown in the expression of ideas, is replaced by an intensity of feeling, which is all the more effective for being carried in someone else's words. Ovid had sensed the power of vicarious female emotion more than a millennium earlier, and the popularity of heroines like Mimi, Violetta, Aida, and Butterfly today shows that such outpourings have not lost their appeal.[28]

[27] The Pindaric Ode was essentially triadic and its third element, or *Epode*, was invariably in a different meter; see Howatson, 1989: 578–79.

[28] For the importance of this emotion to modern opera, see 'Music in Italy,' in Hindley 1977: 351–58.

13
Chaucer's Half-Lines and Feet

As a designer of strophes, Chaucer was extremely competent, and in the last chapter I argued the case for his versatility and discretion in crafting strophes. The magnitude of Chaucer's achievement in the crafting of lines is clear from the analyses presented in Chapter 11. Probably with the aid of his friend John Gower, and certainly inspired by the Italian poets he venerated, Geoffrey Chaucer invented the verse design that would dominate the poetry of the English language for the next 500 years. To list the poets who followed in the self-confident steps of Chaucer's five iambic feet would require a volume larger than the present one; and major poems in Chaucer's meter continue to be read and studied all over the world. Nevertheless, I would question whether Chaucer's verse craftsmanship is sufficiently appreciated or its intimate details are clearly enough understood. I shall therefore summarize the main findings of the research presented so far before attempting a more ambitious linguistic analysis of the way that his longer line works.

The Crafting of Lines

Chaucer's longer-line verse design is the canonical iambic pentameter because it observes all the norms that define that meter: in traditional terms, the norm of his lines is five accentual iambs, five rhythmic feet of the type now labeled w^s. In the terms of Attridgean metrics, Chaucer's lines consist of five beats separated by single offbeats, and any double offbeats they contain are carefully balanced by adjacent implied offbeats. Beats are provided by single syllables with stress, or exceptionally by unstressed monosyllables (a feature I term *weak beats*); and offbeats are provided by the weak syllables of polysyllabic words or by monosyllables of any type. In order to maintain a sufficiently strong iambic pulse throughout the line stressed syllables must provide either the second and fifth beats, or the third and fifth beats.

In the terms of Halle and Keyser and SMP, Chaucer maintains an iambic pulse in his lines by excluding syllables with more stress than their neighbors from odd-numbered positions. In the terms of Hanson and Kiparsky and PT, Chaucer's template has ten right-strong positions, the size of which is one syllable, and the strong syllables of polysyllabic words are constrained from appearing in weak positions except after a major syntactic boundary. Other inversions are rare and are restricted to situations where word and metrical boundaries coincide. Finally, either positions 4 and 10 or positions 6 and 10 must contain a stressed syllable.

Stylistically, Chaucer's pentameter is closer to Shakespeare's than Shakespeare's is to Milton's. Chaucer's line contains an even balance between Gallic and Italic lines, and its proportion of weak beats is intermediate between the proportions in the verse of those two poets. Chaucer also employs a more even balance of masculine and feminine lines than either of these later poets, and fewer inversions. Chaucer compensated for his parsimonious use of inversion by his adherence to other forms of tension, vestiges of an older mode of versifying in English such as headless lines, epic caesuras, and double initial offbeats. Later Shakespeare would restrict his use of these features of the native dolnik to his dramatic verse, while Milton would cultivate one of them (the headless line) in two youthful poems to display his virtuosity.[1] But Chaucer was assured of an audience long used to these ancient forms of tension and used them as frequently as he did inversion.

Chaucer invented the iambic pentameter, and the data gathered in the preceding chapters of this volume enable modern readers to identify key factors in the creative process. The first was Chaucer's resolve to compose decasyllables in English: his wide knowledge of the poetry of other languages must have taught him the advantages of the longer line. It could carry a heavier semantic burden and accommodate more complex syntax. It was also more economical in its use of rhyme and, perhaps most importantly for an ambitious narrator, its rhythm was more like normal speech and less like song. Nor could the native English long line, with its clattering alliterations and wildly irregular length, offer the polished and ample vehicle for English poetry that Chaucer required.

Chaucer's resolve to compose English decasyllables was matched by Gower's to compose *décasyllabes* in AN. The two friends had already followed parallel paths in regularizing AN and ME octosyllabics when they turned their attention to the longer line, and again their solutions to its problems were remarkably similar. There may be a little exaggeration in describing the two poets as having a joint program to reform the craft of versifying in England – but not much. Given Chaucer's literary preoccupations, it is difficult to believe that the subject of Dante's verse (and later Boccaccio's) did not figure in the two men's conversation. Could Chaucer have become so riveted by Gower's description of the world's ills, or Gower so entertained by Chaucer's account of its delights, that the two poets ignored the beauty of "l'amor che mov'il sol' e l'altre stelle"? At the point where

[1] For deviant lines in Shakespeare's dramatic verse, see Wright, 1988: 105–7; for Milton's variable tetrameter, see Duffell, 2008a: 150–51.

academic research meets common sense the answer to these questions has to be 'No.'

Another key factor in Chaucer's creative process must have been his realization that the rhythm of the French *décasyllabe* was not viable in English (or, indeed, in AN). The intervening word stresses and the lack of precision in timing the delivery of syllables in the two languages of England masked the French meter's primary rhythm. Both poets, therefore, decided to give their longer line a native rhythm, a complex secondary rhythm that stylized the alternate peaks and troughs of stress in the Island's languages. It may have occurred to the two poets spontaneously that such a rhythm freed their lines from the twin tyrannies of the canonical *décasyllabe*, the constraints that fixed the position of a mid-line word boundary and most salient peak of stress, but Chaucer could hardly have missed the fact that Dante's versifying rejoiced in that freedom. In any event, what I have termed running and major pentameters were the result.

Where the French two-beat line was relentless and risked monotony, Chaucer's (and Gower's) new line was capable of many modulations: not only could pausing pentameters be relieved by running ones, and minor by major, but any of the first four beats (or combination of two non-consecutive ones) could be weak, giving the line its own distinctive micro-rhythm. The two poets' resolve to compose iambic decasyllables must have been strengthened by the success of Italian poets in the same endeavor. The majority of Dante's lines are vaguely iambic and a minority perfectly so; and the iambic rhythm of Petrarch's lines is even more marked.[2] Moreover, a secondary-stress habit carried over from English would have facilitated Chaucer's detection of an iambic pulse in the *endecasillabo*. What is perhaps surprising is that Gower's longer AN line allowed the less common Italian rhythms, while Chaucer excluded the dactylic, melodic, and adonic variants almost completely.

The iambic pentameter, like the *endecasillabo*, is capable of embracing great rhythmic variety, and in Chapter 11, I showed that Chaucer seems to have realized this. His later pentameters are more varied than his earlier in three ways: he found a more even balance between masculine and feminine lines; he employed more weak beats in a variety of positions; and he found a more even balance between Gallic and Italic lines. The first of those changes can be seen as a reaction to having tried too hard to make the earlier lines sound like *endecasillabi*, with their inevitable trochaic closes. The other two changes, however, are likely to be the result of trial and error: the gradual discovery that variety within this new regular pattern pleased the ear.

The use of weak beats is the more obvious source of variety: as noted in Chapter 10, it is one of the features that most clearly distinguish Milton's pentameter from Shakespeare's. There are four places where a weak beat can modify

[2] For iambic *endecasillabi*, see Chapter 8, Figure 4.

the line's rhythm, plus three combinations of non-consecutive places where weak beats amplify the contrast between one syllable (that with the strongest stress) and the rest of the line, so the variety of micro-rhythms produced by weak beats is very considerable. Thus when Chaucer increased the proportion of weak beats in the works that make up my later sample he increased the rhythmic variety found in his verse.

Within the proportion of Italic lines in my samples, however, there is a variance between individual works that suggests other factors may be involved besides a chronological quest for greater rhythmic variety. One factor that springs to mind is semantic: does Chaucer favor either Gallic or Italic lines for particular subjects or genres? Another is lexical: do Italic lines offer the poet an opportunity to employ a wider vocabulary, either in a passage or in a whole poem? I shall begin by exploring the semantic hypothesis.

Increasing the proportion of Italic lines obviously increases the rhythmic variety in an iambic pentameter poem, and I have shown elsewhere that the proportion of running lines in English pentameters increased steadily between Milton and Keats. This probably represented a growing aesthetic preference for a more even balance of the two rhythms. A preference for rhythmic variety, however, would also lead the poet to avoid long passages in which all the lines were either Gallic or Italic. Nevertheless, sequences of lines in which one type of line preponderates are common in Chaucer's verse, and I shall briefly examine whether this preponderance has any semantic significance.[3] I term passages with a preponderance of Gallic lines *+Gallic* and those with a preponderance of Italic lines *+Italic*, and it is noteworthy that Italic lines in +Gallic passages usually have an alternative syntactic boundary after the fourth syllable, while the Gallic lines in +Italic passages usually have an alternative boundary after the sixth (or post-tonic seventh). I shall mark these alternative boundaries with a single slash in my scansions.

I shall begin by examining the openings of *AA* and *KT*, two works that tell essentially the same story, but in different words and different strophe designs. In both, however, there is a change of genre after line 210, where in *AA* the chivalric narrative pauses and Anelida's complaint begins. This break is also marked by a change of strophe design, from rhyme royal to more complex designs that are probably experimental, because Chaucer does not persevere with any of them for long.

[3] Tarlinskaja 2014: 267–86 presents strong evidence that poets use meter to reinforce meaning. In a section on what she terms *rhythmical italics* she shows that inversions often serve this purpose in sixteenth- and seventeenth-century English poetry (2014: 269–78). Her only references to what I term *major* and *minor* lines take the form of statistics for the position of the strongest mid-line stresses and word boundaries in plays by many different authors (2014: 287–374).

The three opening strophes of *AA* consist of an invocation of the deities of war; they derive from Boccaccio, and before him from Sallust, and Chaucer adds a third source of his own invention to dignify the work still further.[4] Strophe 1 runs as follows, and I append the letters {G} to Gallic and {I} to Italic lines:

(1) Thou **ferse** god of **armes**, // Mars the **rede**, {I} (*AA*, 1–7)
(2) That in the **frosty contre** // **called Trace**, {I}
(3) Within thy **grisly temple** // ful of **drede** {I}
(4) **Honoured** art // as **patroun** / of that **place**; {G}
(5) With thy **Bellona**, // **Pallas**, / ful of **grace**, {I}
(6) Be **present** and my song //contynu^{e} and **guye**; {I}
(7) At my begynnyng // thus to the I **crye** {I}

This strophe has a heavy concentration of Italic lines, which may reflect the amount of Classical name-dropping that Chaucer employs, and the social pretensions of his oeuvre. When he begins his story, a tale of princes, queens, and knights, the concentration of Italic lines remains relatively high, around 42 percent over the next 200 lines.

Anelida's complaint contains a significantly lower proportion of Italic lines (29 percent) and within it there are further contrasts; thus when the heroine complains in highly conventional terms Italic lines take over briefly:

(8) **Alas**! Wher is **becom**^{e} // your gen**tilesse**, {I} (*AA*, 247–50)
(9) Your^{e} **wordes** ful of **plesaunc**^{e} // and hum**blesse**, {I}
(10) Your^{e} **ob**servaunces // in so low **manere**, {I}
(11) And your **awayting** // and your be**synesse** {I}

But, when she comes to the particular charges and her personal feelings, Anelida's song becomes more lyrical, and also contains only pausing lines, in which the first and most important syntactic boundary is after syllable 4:

(12) My **swete** foo, // why do ye so, / for **shame**? {G} (*AA*, 272–78)
(13) And **thenke** ye // that **further**^{e}d be / your **name** {G}
(14) To **lov**^{e} a **new**^{e} // and ben un**trewe**? / Nay! {G}
(15) And **putte** yow // in **sclaunder** now / and **blame**, {G}
(16) And do to me // **adversite** / and **grame**, {G}
(17) That **lov**^{e} yow most //—God, wel thou wost—**alway**?{G}
(18) Yet **com**^{e} **ayein**, // and yet be pleyn / som day, {G}
(19) And than shal this, // that now is mys, / be **game**, {G}
(20) And al **foryiv**^{e}, // whil^{e} that I **live** / may. {G}

[4] Chaucer is clearly bluffing when he cites 'Corynne' (*AA*, 21): the only candidate for this reference is a woman poet who is reputed to have defeated Pindar in a poetry contest, but whose works have not survived; see Di Marco's introductory note in Benson 1988: 375.

Remarkably, seven of these lines contain rhymed tetrameters with an extra foot; in this passage, it might be argued, the five-beat meter of speech bursts with song.

In *KT* Chaucer also begins with 210 lines of chivalric narrative, and he shows off the rhythmic variety of his new meter in the tale of heroes, knights, and ladies. Descriptions of the heroine (now named Emily), in particular, bring Chaucer out in a rash of Italic lines, with rhymes as feminine as the subject, and they lead to a climax as ethereal as her voice:

(21) And in the **gardyn**, // at the **sonn**^{e} upriste, {I} (*KT*, 1052–56)
(22) She **walketh** up and doun, // and as hir^{e} **liste** {I}
(23) She **gad**^{e}reth **floures**, // **party whit**^{e} and **rede**, {I}
(24) To **mak**^{e} a **subtil gerland** // for hir^{e} **hede**; {I}
(25) And as an **aungel** // hev^{e}nyss**hly** she soong. {I}

The rhythm of these lines, with their many polysyllables and mostly feminine caesuras, helps Chaucer paint a delightful picture.

The last 90 lines of my *KT* sample differ from those in *AA* by being not song, but dialogue, a spirited altercation between the two rival knights. And, appropriately, the two hostile halves of every line scowl at one another across a barrier in which +PS reinforces +WB in the fiercest French manner:

(26) This Pa**lamon**, // whan he tho **wordes her**de, {G} (*KT*, 1123–31)
(27) Dispi**tously** // he **looked** and answ**erde**, {G}
(28) 'Wheith^{e}r **seistow** this // in **ernest** or in pley?' {G}
(29) 'Nay,' quod Ar**cit**^{e}, // 'in **ernest**, by my fey! {G}
(30) God help^{e} me so, // me list ful yvel^{e} **pleye**.' {G}
(31) This Pa**lamon** // gan **knytt**^{e} his **browes tweye**' {G}
(32) 'It ner^{e},' quod he, // 'to thee no greet ho**nour** {G}
(33) For to be fals, // ne for to be trai**tour** {G}
(34) To me, that am // thy **cosyn** and thy **brother** {G}
(35) Ysworn ful **dep**^{e}, // and ech of us til **oother**,' {G}

To summarize, the quoted passages from these two works suggest that Chaucer showed a marked preference for Italic lines in chivalric narratives, or conventional courtly discourse, but an even stronger preference for Gallic lines in song or lively dialogue.

Another genre that seems to draw Chaucer to Italic lines is the sermon or Biblical exemplum. Thus the pardoner begins his tale in sententious fashion and employs a balance that favors Italic lines:

(36) Adam our^{e} **fader**, // and his wyf **al**so, {I} (*PT*, 505–11)
(37) Fro Pa**radys** // to **labour** / and to wo {G}
(38) Wer^{e} **driven** for that **vic**^{e}, // it is no **drede**. {I}
(39) For whil that Adam // **fasted**, as I **rede**, {I}

(40) He was in Paradys; // and whan that he {I}
(41) Eet of the fruyt // deffended / on the tree, {G}
(42) Anon he was cast out // to wo and **peyne**. {I}

But this unctuous metrical style changes when the *riotoures* begin their quest and an urchin brings a sense of stark realism to the tale:

(43) 'Go bet,' quod he, // 'and **axe** redily {G} (*PT*, 667–74)
(44) What cors is this // that **passeth** heer forby {G}
(45) And look^{e} that thou // **report**^{e} / his **name** weel.' {I}
(46) 'Sir^{e},' quod this boy, // 'it **nedeth** nev^{e}r-a-**deel**; {G}
(47) It was me toold // er ye cam heer two **houres**. {G}
(48) He was, par**dee**, // an old felaw^{e} of **youres**, {G}
(49) And sodeyn**ly** // he was yslayn to-**nyght**, {G}
(50) For**dronk**^{e}, as he // sat on his bench up**right**.' {G}

Later in the tale a mysterious old man introduces a quite different register of speech, and a different balance of Italic and Gallic lines, when he tells the *riotoures*:

(51) I **knokke** with my staf, // both^{e} **erl**^{y} and **late** {I} (*PT*, 730–36)
(52) And **seye** '**Leeve mooder**,' // leet me in! {I}
(53) Lo how I **vanyssh**^{e}, // flessh, and blood, and skyn! {I}
(54) **Allas**, whan shul / my **bones** // been at **reste**? {I}
(55) [ ] **Mooder** with yow // **wold**^{e} I **chaung**^{e} my **cheste** {?}
(56) That in my **chambre** // **longe tym**^{e} hath be, {I}
(57) Ye, for an **heyre** clowt // to **wrappe** me!' {I}

Note that example (55) is probably a headless line, although '**chaunge**' could be two syllables and thus a rare inversion sanctioned by PT's bracketing condition.

Of the later works represented in my samples *RT* has the lowest proportion of Italic lines (42 percent), and once again the early and more genteel part of the narrative contains a higher proportion (47 percent) than the remainder of the tale (where it is 37 percent). The following sequence of Italic lines describes the rascally miller and his snobbish wife dressed up for church, and affecting respectability:

(58) And she cam **after** // in a **gyt**^{e} of reed; {I} (*RT*, 3954–60)
(59) And **Symkyn hadde** // **hosen** / of the same. {I}
(60) Ther **dorste** no wight // **clepen** hir^{e} but '**dame**'; {I}
(61) Was noon so **hardy** // that went^{e} by the **weye** {I}
(62) That with her **dorste rag**^{e} // or **ones pleye**, {I}
(63) But if he **wolde** be //slayn of Sym**kyn** {I}
(64) With **panad**^{e}, or with knyf, // or boi**dekyn**. {I}

The last two lines carry the menace beneath the outward show, as if to warn the reader that this will not be a tale of chivalry and courtly love.

When the action starts, however, the lines become almost entirely Gallic: the tricked clerks chase their freed horse in its lust for the mares of the fen with scarcely a running line to speed them. Chaucer reminds us that males are constantly on heat in this episode, and when the time for the clerks' sexual revenge arrives Gallic lines take over both narrative and dialogue:

(65) 'And **gif** that he // out of his sleep **abreyde**, {G} (*RT*, 4189–96)
(66) He **myghte** doon / us **bath**^{e} // a vileynye.' {I}
(67) **Aleyn** answerd^{e}, // 'I **count**^{e} hym nat a **flye**,' {G}
(68) And up he rist, // and by the **wench**^{e} he **crepte**. {G}
(69) This **wenche** lay / upright^{e} // and **faste slepte**, {I}
(70) Til he so ny / was, // er she **myght**^{e} espie, {I?}
(71) That it had been // to **late** for to **crie**. {G}

The tricking of the miller's wife that follows is described in coarser language, and in lines with even more brutal Gallic caesuras

(72) Soon^{e} **after** this // the wyf hir **rowtyng** leet {G} (*RT*, 4213–18)
(73) And gan **awak**^{e}, // and **went**^{e} hir^{e} out to **pisse** {G}
(74) And cam **agayn**, // and gan her **cradel mysse** {G}
(75) And **groped** heer / and ther, // but she foond noon {I}
(76) '**Allas**!' quod she, // 'I **hadd**^{e} **almoost** mys**goon**, {G}
(77) I **hadd**^{e} al**moost** / goon // to the **clerkes** bed. {I}

The male chauvinism of the *fabliau* ensures that the two women are suitably grateful, and that the clerks return to Cambridge victorious. With the ex-carpenter's revenge on the miller, equilibrium, if not peace, is restored among Chaucer's group of pilgrims.

To summarize, the presence, and combination, of Gallic and Italic lines in Chaucer's verse may have helped him achieve artistic effects: a choice of line structure could help convey *the fragrance of flowers and the flutter of ladies' lashes* (in the case of Italic), or *the rat-tat-tat of street talk* and the *short, sharp, shock of illicit sex* (in the case of Gallic). This interpretation of the clustering of Gallic and Italic lines, however, needs to be checked by further research, and there are other, simpler explanations of the increase in Italic lines in Chaucer's later pentameters.

The first explanation is lexical: running lines offer the opportunity to include a trochaic word in positions 4–5, and such words represent the majority of the polysyllables in ME. In my samples, therefore, the average Italic line contains more polysyllabic words than the average Gallic one. Chaucer's increase in Italic lines thus enabled him to deploy a greater proportion of his lexicon. The increase may well represent an increasing confidence in his versifying in this meter. This is a subject to which I shall return in my examination of the foot-structure of Chaucer's lines later in this chapter.

A second alternative explanation of the increase in Italic lines is rhythmic and aesthetic. The two types of line offered a pleasing source of variety: this was in addition to the variety provided by weak beats and masculine rhymes, and the retention of the archaic feature of headless lines. Variety was important to Chaucer: by making his lines iambic throughout he ran the risk of making them so regular that they became boring, and monotony was the chief weakness of the two-beat *décasyllabe* that he knew from his youth and shunned in his maturity.

In the Italian *endecasillabo* Chaucer found a surfeit of variety and he was very selective in imitating it: he embraced the variety offered by Gallic and Italic lines, but he rejected the triple time that characterized both Boccaccio's dactylic and Petrarch's melodic and adonic variants. Triple time was something of a joke to educated Englishmen (and in limericks it still is today): combined with heavy alliteration, it provided the verse rhythm of ME tradesmen's pantomimes.[5] Chaucer therefore took the risk of composing exclusively duple-time decasyllables; this proved to be a sound judgment, because the secondary stresses and stress-timing of the English language makes its speakers much more tolerant of accentual regularity than their Continental neighbors. Chaucer's confidence in an iambic decasyllable was probably reinforced by his friend Gower, who was experimenting with the same rhythm's dominance in AN. And the beauty of Dante's and Petrarch's many iambic lines would have been further encouragement.

There are clearly advantages for crafters of decasyllabic lines to have no constraints on word boundaries or phrasal stresses, but there are also disadvantages. French poets had a relatively easy task expressing their thoughts in a series of fours and sixes: it was a rhythm that was easy for poets to create and easy for audiences to recognize. Since ten syllables are too many for humans to count rapidly and intuitively (as the virgules in Hengwrt confirm), Chaucer also probably composed his pentameters one colon at a time rather than as unbroken entities.[6]

The Crafting of Half-Lines

The problem of crafting lines from two cola of varying lengths had occupied Italian poets and critics more than a century earlier, and their analysis, which is preserved in modern Italian works on metrics, was broadly as follows.[7]

[5] For the meter of ME mystery plays, see Chapter 4, Note 32.

[6] For subitization and the perception of numbers of stimuli, see Chapter 1, Notes 7 and 9.

[7] For the Italian description of the *endecasillabo* as a combination of two rhythmic units (such as a *quinario tronco* + a *settenario piano*), see Elwert, 1973: 55–57.

In lines of ten syllables poets combine an *opening* hemistich phrase with a *closing* one and I shall illustrate each in English from the Chaucer's *GP*. Opening hemistichs, whether in *endecasillabo* or pentameter, are of four lengths, and here I show the grouping of English syllables into metrical feet by bracketing:

(a) Thann^{e} **longen** folk // [w^s] [w^s] (*GP*, 12)
(b) To **ferne halwes** // [w^s] [w^s] w (*GP*, 14)
(c) So **priketh** hem **natur**^{e} // [w^s] [w^s] [w^s] (*GP*, 11)
(d) The **hooly blisful martir** // [w^s] [w^s] [w^s] w (*GP*, 18)

These openings have 4M, 4F, 6M, and 6F syllables, respectively, and the final syllables of (b) and (d), which have feminine endings, could be regarded as extrametrical, like line-final post-tonic syllables. For each of these openings there is a close that completes the metrical set of 10M/F, and these could be scanned as independent entities:

(a) // to goon on **pil**grimages [w^s] [w^s] [w^s] w (6F syllables)
(b) // **kowth**^{e} in **sondry londes** [s^w] [s^w] [s^w] (5F)
(c) // in hir **corages** [w^s] [w^s] w (4F)
(d) // for to **seke** [s^w] [s^w] (3F)

In these closes I have re-bracketed the syllables to show that the closes of (b) and (d) in themselves have a trochaic rhythm, which becomes emphasized when the rhyme is feminine, as in all these examples.

Running lines like (b) and (d), therefore, offer a sort of trochaic counterpoint to the dominant iambic rhythm of Chaucer's pentameters and help save it from monotony. Or, to choose another metaphor, many of Chaucer's lines have a trochaic undertow that runs against the iambic tide of his verse. This, I believe, is one of the reasons that Chaucer was attracted to increasing the proportion of Italic lines in his later works. I shall also find other reasons when I look deeper into the structure of his lines in the next section.

The Crafting of Feet

When Chaucer made his decasyllables iambic he solved a problem that had defeated ME (and AN) poets for generations: how to count ten syllables quickly and intuitively. Chaucer's solution was to count five pairs of syllables, which would divide into either 2 + 3 or 3 + 2 pairs, offering the same desirable variety as the *endecasillabo*. But Chaucer's method of line construction involved more than bolting two cola together in either the Gallic or Italic manner; it also involved the bracketing of pairs of syllables with a potential for stress contrast, termed *binary feet* by modern linguistics. Most of these feet contained a [w^s] contrast, giving the lines a predominantly rising rhythm and justifying the name iambic pentameters.

English syllables, however, are already linked and contrasted—in polysyllabic words (like *meter*) and *clitic* groups of monosyllables (like *the meat*). I have already noted that the majority of English polysyllabic words are trochaic like *meter* [s^w], while the majority of clitic pairs of monosyllables are iambic like *the meat* [w^s]. Thus lines of English verse involve two types of bracketing, lexical (in words) and metrical (in feet). And one way of describing the crafting of English lines is as the processing of raw materials (words) into finished products (poetic feet).

In order to elucidate this production process I shall draw on two pieces of research that I published with an interval of a dozen years. The first was a word audit of the opening of passages of poems by sixteen different English poets, ranging from Chaucer to Keats.[8] Figure 1 below gives the results for two of my samples: it shows the percentage of each possible word configuration found in the first 1,000 words of *GP* and the first 1,000 words of Shakespeare's sonnets. I excluded from my count of syllables any lost by syncope, apocope, or elision, but I included line-final schwas, which may have been syllabified, as Chaucer's punctilious rhyming suggests.

Types of Word	*Percentage of Words as Units*	
	Chaucer	*Shakespeare*
Monosyllables	72	76
Trochaic Disyllables (s-w)	16	14
Iambic Disyllables (w-s)	5	6
Trisyllables (s-w-s)	3	2
Trisyllables (w-s-w)	2	2
Tetrasyllables (w-s-w-s)	<1	<1
Tetrasyllables (s-w-s-w)	<1	<1

Fig. 1: Word Audit: Samples from Two Poets' Pentameters

From these figures it is clear that monosyllables and trochaic disyllables are the bricks and mortar with which English poets work, and that words of other configurations play only a minor part in the crafting of lines. The role of these ancillary raw materials is greatest in the line endings of *GP*: thus in the 300-line samples analyzed in Chapters 10 and 11 of this volume iambic disyllables (5% of total words) provided 10 percent of the rhyme words, and polysyllables (7% of total) provided 32 percent of the rhyme words. Heidi Kurtz first pointed out this eccentric distribution in her 2012 study of etymology in four of Chaucer's Tales.[9]

[8] See Duffell, 2002b.

[9] See Kurtz, 2012.

In my samples 90 percent of tetrasyllables and more than half of all trisyllables are line-final. Another of Kurtz's observations was of a concentration of trochaic words immediately before the caesuras of Chaucer's lines.[10]

To investigate how my research for this volume correlated with Kurtz's I counted how frequently trochaic words occurred other than line-finally in four of my Chaucer samples from Chapter 10 (I took the first 75 lines of each type in each of the later works for this purpose). The 300 Gallic lines contained 243 trochaic words that were not line-final, while the 300 Italic lines contained 478, almost twice as many. The difference between the contents of the two samples in this respect was thus statistically significant to 18σ, and it cannot be attributed to sampling error. One purpose served by Chaucer's increase in the use of Italic lines, therefore, was to accommodate more trochaic disyllables, the most common type of polysyllabic word found in ME texts.

Evidence of the ability of Italic lines to accommodate more trochaic words appears in the examples I have employed earlier in this chapter. To take the extreme case, when Chaucer wanted to use five trochaic words in the same line, the only way he could do so was as in the following examples, where three elisions help pack ten such words into two lines:

(23) She **gad**^{e}reth **flou**res, // **par**ty **whit**^{e} and **re**de,
(24) To **mak**^{e} a **sub**til **ger**land // f̣oṛ hir^{e} **he**de;

Since lexical trochees make up more than three-quarters of the disyllables in Chaucer's text, and well over half of the polysyllables, their role is pivotal in the construction of his iambic pentameters. And running lines are the key to deploying effectively a substantial portion of the English lexicon.

The combination of Gallic and Italic lines in Chaucer's verse thus serves three functions: it offers rhythmic variety in a meter with an overriding iambic pulse; it enables Chaucer to tell his tales (and make his characters speak) in different registers; and it renders the meter a better fit for his language, admitting a large stock of important words. The last of these functions also helps explain the increased proportion of Italic lines in Chaucer's later works: as he gained confidence in his new meter he was able deploy a more representative selection of his language's lexicon, and in doing so he achieved a more even balance of the two types of line.

My second piece of research that sheds light on the process of crafting iambic pentameters was published only recently and was an audit not of word con-

[10] Kurtz's computer-based analysis of the words that close Chaucer's lines and half-lines covered their etymology, as well as their rhythm, and it highlighted the rhythmic contrast between sequences of trochaic words in these positions and the iambic verse design.

figurations, but of the constituents of binary feet in Chaucer's *GP.*[11] This analysis identified seven types of binary foot in Chaucer's lines, and they are as follows. The first type is the lexical iamb, and examples from the opening of *GP* include [a**non**], [re**soun**], and [bi**gan**]. But Figure 2 shows this word configuration to be relatively rare, even if the number is boosted by polysyllabic words like [y**fal**le] and [de**vy**se] which open with an iamb, and words like [o**pi**ni**on**] that produce two lexical iambs.

The converse of the lexical iambic foot is the *lexical trochee*; lexical trochees are by far the most common type of disyllable in English but they are strongly disruptive of an overall iambic rhythm and, as noted in Chapter 3, they are mostly confined by English poets to colon initial positions (by the closure principle). In Chapter 9 I also noted that many of the lexically trochaic feet in in *GP* consist of grammatical words like [*after*] and [*under*], which are less salient in the line's stress profile because their first syllable rarely carries phrasal stress.

A much more common type of binary foot is the *clitic iamb:* examples from the opening lines of *GP* include [*the droght*], [*of Merche*], [*a day*], and [*at night*]. These are much more numerous than lexical iambs in both Middle and Modern English, and they are also more common than *clitic trochees,* like [*hath in*], [*kaught in*], and [*Noon of*], which constitute another of the binary foot types. Many pairs of monosyllables, however, do not have a clear orientation; for example, in the combinations [*that in*], [*whan that*], and [*and of*] there is no clitic bracketing to aid versifiers, and any stress contrast between them depends on context; in an iambic context many performers will give them a rising rhythm, but that rhythm is a feature of a particular delivery instance, not of the verse instance. In this, these *neutral pairs* are quite different from the pyrrhics of quantitative verse. They may weaken the passage's prevailing rhythm, but they are variables rather than constants.

A further refinement of iambic regularity in the English long-line canon is the presence of another type of binary foot, the *phrasal* iamb. Traditional metrics knows this feature as *incursion*, because it regards it as the insertion of an extra stress in the line. A phrasal iamb is produced when two major-category monosyllables words (nouns, adjectives, verbs, and adverbs) are metrically bracketed. The foot so produced, however, is an iamb (not a spondee), because the rules of phrasal stress in English make the second syllable more prominent in delivery than the first. In verse composed in the East Midland dialect of ME phrasal iambs were rare because most adjectives retained a final schwa to separate the two potential stresses. There are many more examples in Early Modern English verse, for example [*mak'st waste*] in Shakespeare's first sonnet, [*fair child*] in his second, and [*lives sweet*] in his fifth.

[11] See Duffell, 2014.

Because trochaic disyllables like *insight* outnumber iambic ones like *incite* by more than 3:1, the final type of binary poetic foot is of overwhelming importance to poets crafting iambic verse in English. This is the *bracketing mismatch*, or the division of a trochaic word between two poetic feet. This importance is increased by the fact that such a mismatch helps form not one but two iambic feet, as in the phrase [*A wor*]-[*thy man*], and longer words like *pilgrimage* (s^w s^w) can create two bracketing mismatches in an iambic line if they are preceded by a monosyllable.

Figure 2 below gives percentages for the occurrence of the seven types of binary foot in the first thousand feet of *GP* and of Shakespeare's sonnets.[12]

Foot Type	*percent (rounded)*	
	Chaucer	*Shakespeare*
Lexical Iambs	12	12
Clitic Iambs	19	25
Phrasal Iambs	2	3
Neutral Pairs	13	12
Bracketing Mismatches	52	44
Lexical Trochees	1	2
Clitic Trochees	1	3

Fig. 2: Structure of Chaucer's and Shakespeare's Poetic Feet

These percentages show that the most common method of creating iambic feet in English (a trochaic language) is by bracketing mismatches, and that neutral pairs provide as many poetic feet in this meter as do right-strong words. The difference between the Chaucer and Shakespeare figures for bracketing mismatches is highly statistically significant, as is the difference between the figures for clitic iambs. I shall return to the subject of the first of these differences, but the second suggests that Shakespeare handled monosyllables with greater confidence than Chaucer, since far more of them reinforce the line's iambic rhythm.[13] Finally, the difference between the figures for both types of trochee confirms an observation made in Chapter 10: Shakespeare employed inversion more often than Chaucer, who balanced this by employing other sources of rhythmic variety, the headless line and the epic caesura.

[12] Duffell 2014: 158 gives the statistics in this table for Chaucer to one place of decimals. For this research I used the text of Hengwrt because one of my concerns was the significance of virgules in that manuscript. Headless lines and lines with epic caesura in Hengwort were not included in the sample.

[13] I noted Shakespeare's skillful use of monosyllabic lines in Chapter 3, but it could be that Chaucer employed more bracketing mismatches for two other reasons: his personal, polyglot, lexicon contained a larger stock of polysyllables, and many of Chaucer's polysyllables had become monosyllables in early Modern English.

In Chapter 11 I noted that Chaucer increased the proportion of weak beats in his later verse to the same end, to increase rhythmic variety. The majority of Chaucer's iambs result from placing the strong syllables of his language's many trochaic words in even-numbered positions. In particular, he used one device to precipitate a series of bracketing mismatches in the remainder of the line: he exaggerated in his verse the tendency for ME sentences to begin with a monosyllable. Thus, for example, 74 percent of sentences in the prose Tale of Melibee begin with a monosyllable, but 94 percent of lines in *GP*.[14] Moreover, as noted above, increasing the proportion of running lines in his later verse also helped Chaucer create bracketing mismatches, while increasing the proportion of major lines enabled him to accommodate more polysyllables in the first half of the line.

More generally, the statistics in Figure 2 show that Chaucer's crafting of iambic pentameters shared all the features of Shakespeare's. The difference between their designs was of degree and not of quality, and the many small differences I have detected are stylistic, like those between Shakespeare's and Milton's pentameters. All poets composing iambic pentameters in English face the same task: they have to forge iambic lines from a trochaic language. Chaucer, with his plethora of bracketing mismatches, showed them the easiest way to do it. Initial monosyllables and running lines are invaluable resources in converting the natural, trochaic, rhythm of the English language into a highly polished, iambic, poetic rhythm.

Later English poets used these same techniques: for example, Keats crafts an iambic pentameter from the trochaic tetrameter "**Beau**ty is a joy for **e**ver" by prefacing it with the words "A thing of"; and Gray does the same with "**plough**man **home**ward plods his **wea**ry" by giving it a monosyllabic head ('The') and tail ('way').[15] In Gray's case the line's trochaic core is even marked by alliteration, so that within the foreign-inspired pentameter lies a more primitive native line. All these nuances were present in the first English iambic pentameters and Chaucer handled them as skillfully as any later poet.

When Chaucer decided to craft an English decasyllable he had many choices open to him; each had its advantages and pitfalls, but one was a perfect fit for the English language and offered numerous opportunities to enhance the impact of his semantic material. It could serve as a suitable vehicle for invocations, songs, and sermons, and for high ideals and low comedy. Chaucer's meter is word-dancing that can still delight us today as it helps convey his wit and wisdom

---

[14] This figure is based on a sample consisting of the first 300 lines / sentences of each work.

[15] For *Endymion*, Book I, see Stillinger, 1978: 103–32; for Gray's *Elegy*, see Reeves, 1973: 61–66. Note that in the early thirteenth century Orm and Nicholas of Guildford were the first poets to give four-beat lines an iambic rhythm in this way.

to modern audiences.[16] Ezra Pound argued that Chaucer understood a great deal more about life than Shakespeare, and a great deal more about the learning of his age.[17] One of the reasons why the breadth of Chaucer's understanding is manifest is that his crafting of lines and feet, and all that comes between, is of so high a quality. Chaucer got so many things right first time, and that is the mark of a great craftsman and a great artist.

Geoffrey Chaucer, courtier, diplomat, bureaucrat, and politician, found time to revolutionize the craft of verse in Europe. Half a millennium later the poets of his language were still paying him the compliment of writing their finest poems in his meter. Superficially, the line he invented was heavily regulated: its syllables, accents, beats, and offbeats were all numbered; but beneath the surface his lines teemed with variety, so that each could be refreshingly different from its neighbors. His meter was a perfect fit for its language, finding a place for every shape and size of word in the English lexicon. It was also capable of reinforcing his meaning: his lines could be dressed for court, or street, or prison cell, or wench's bed, and their nuances helped bring his fictions to life. At the opening of the *Parliament of Fowls* Chaucer gave a new twist to the Latin motto *Ars longa vita brevis*, and he worked steadily thereafter to join his hero Dante in raising "the craft so long to lerne" into an art.

[16] A full range of CDs in which modern scholars read Chaucer's Middle English verse can be purchased from Professor Paul Thomas, The Chaucer Studio, 484 East 2100 North, Provo, Utah 84604–1834, USA.

[17] See Pound, 1961: 99–103.

14
The English Chaucerians

Chaucer went one better than Gower even in death: Chaucer's bones lie in Westminster Abbey (near the seat of government), and Gower's in Southwark Cathedral (in the medieval red-light district). His blindness prevented Gower seeing eight years of the fifteenth century, but he had a scriptorium full of people to read to him and to take dictation, and a wife to tend his needs. A year before Chaucer's death in 1400, Gower presented their new master, Henry IV, with poetic offerings in three languages, Latin, AN, and ME. The English contribution was a 385-line ME poem entitled *In Praise of Peace* (*IPP*), which was in rhyme royal strophes containing lines of ten syllables and five beats. Gower had long employed rhyme royal and iambic decasyllables in AN, and in the 1380s he had composed a brief "Complaint" (*CA*, viii: 2217–2300) in ME with similar metrical features. The success of *Troilus and Criseyde* had doubtless influenced Gower's decision to compose in English, and the growing reputation of the *Canterbury Tales* gave him the confidence in the longer ME line to use it to address his king.

I shall begin this chapter by offering a structural analysis of Gower's longer line in order to highlight its distinctive features.

Gower's Iambic Pentameters

In this section I shall recapitulate the main findings of Duffell and Billy, 2004 and add to them some new data on the metrical features that I have identified in Chapters 11 to 13. While the 2004 study covered both of Gower's longer-line poems, the new data, for consistency, is based on a sample of the first 300 lines of *IPP*.[1] This has the additional advantage of demonstrating how close the figures are for the sample and for the entire surviving corpus of Gower's 469 longer ME lines.

The chief conclusions reached in 2004 were: (1) Gower's verse design met the definition of the canonical English iambic pentameter; (2) Gower's longer lines

[1] See Duffell and Billy 2003–04: 383–401. The text analyzed was that of Macaulay, who based his text of *CA* on the Fairfax MS in the Bodleian Library, Oxford, and that of *IPP* on the Trentham Ms owned by the Duke of Sutherland.

were more regular in both rhythm and syllable count than Chaucer's; and (3) Gower merited more credit for having pioneered the stress-syllabic system that dominated English versifying between the sixteenth and nineteenth centuries. The last of these conclusions was reinforced by the study of Gower's AN verse.[2] A number of detailed findings led to these conclusions. The first was that barely 1 percent of Gower's lines contained other than ten syllables to the final stress, a figure quite likely to result from scribal accuracy (error was doubtless minimized in the first instance by Gower's careful checking of work emanating from his own scriptorium). Another finding was that Gower had been slightly more consistent than Chaucer in the deletion of word-final schwas, both by elision and in his treatment of common words ending in schwa as monosyllables. A third was that Gower's longer-line verse contained fewer deviant or exceptional lines.[3]

The possible lyric caesuras in *IPP* involve words like *wisdom* (line 31), *tiraunt* (48), *vengance* (49), and *reson* (60), which are more likely to be examples of the wider application of Move X in ME than in modern English; and the two possible examples of epic caesura involve the words *bataile* (66) and *heven* (79). Since the first of these words is sometimes disyllabic in Chaucer (see, for example, *GP*, 61) and the second is often reduced to *hev^{e}n* by syncope in the English of all eras, it is reasonable to assume that Gower's design excluded both lyric and epic caesura.

There are two consecutive lines in my *IPP* sample that lack a syllable in the Trentham MS, but which Macaulay emended; more recent editors have allowed them to stand as:[4]

(1) [ ] Pes is ọf̣ al charité the **keie** (90)
(2) Which hath the lif and soul [ ] **forto weie** (91)

Although example (1) scans well as a headless line, the syntax of the passage would be improved by the initial conjunction 'for,' especially since without emendation this would be Gower's only headless line. Similarly, (2) could be scanned as broken-backed, but the word 'soule' has a final schwa almost everywhere in Chaucer's work, and the word is derived from the OE disyllable *sawol*; emendation therefore seems justified. Another line also presents problems in scansion:

(3) Whiche helpples as in balance hongen (263)

Only syllabifying both word-final schwas can give this line ten syllables; it is an ugly pentameter, and runs more smoothly as a tetrameter with two unusual eli-

---

[2] See Billy & Duffell 2005: 75 and 82–93.

[3] See Duffell and Billy 2003–04: 395–96.

[4] For the text of Gower's *In Praise of Peace*,' see Forni, 2005.

sions. The problem is compounded by the fact that *balance* seems to be left-strong in *CA,* v: 4553.

Gower's pentameters are almost as regular in rhythm as in syllable count, and possible inversions in my sample from *IPP* fall into the same categories as those identified in Chaucer's verse (Chapter 11, Figure 2). They involve names, like 'Henry' (line 1) and 'Ector' (281); words of Romance origin, like 'govern^{e}' (3), 'justice' (8), and 'tenetz' (295); Germanic words with two possible stress assignments, like 'wisdom' (31) and grammatical words with weak stress, like 'undir' (39 and 215) and 'aftir' (160 and 232). And, just outside my sample, the word 'uppon' appears in s^w positions three times (302, 315, and 324). Almost all of Gower's inversions can thus be accounted for by either Move X or weak stress.

Also outside my sample lies the only initial inversion of a lexical word in Gower's pentameters (the adverb 'Pleinly' in *CA*, VIII: 2247), but there is one initial inversion of a grammatical word in *IPP*:

(4) Aftir reson // yit tempre thi corage (160)

Because of the word's French origin, Move X can account for the stressing of 'reson' in this line, but the position of 'Aftir' suggests that Gower pronounced it with little stress. Although Chaucer's experience with *ABC* may have taught him to tolerate initial inversion, Gower seems to have avoided it as carefully as he did headless lines.

Note that all Gower's weak inversions, like his Move X inversions, observe the bracketing condition, with one exception:

(5) Let men ben armed // agein hem to fighte (251)

This is a discordant line, which invites a dactylic delivery ([s-w-w] [s-w-w] [s-w-w] [s-w]), and it resists editorial emendation, Gower seems to have sacrificed his iambic rhythm to his meaning on this occasion.

There is also one inversion in Gower's poem that cannot be explained by either Move X or weak stress:

(6) Of God what thing // him was levest to crave (30)

Unless Cable's "hovering stress" (Move X) applies even to inflexions, this can only be explained as an inversion licensed by the bracketing condition.[5] From the poverty of my examples it is clear that Cable's view that Chaucer did not employ inversion in the canonical fashion could be applied with more justification to Gower. Also, the fact that Gower does so many unusual things just once in this poem could mean simply that they represent lapses in an old man's concentration.

---

[5] For Cable's 'hovering stress,' see Chapter 10, Notes 32.

The 2004 article in *The Chaucer Review* did not measure the frequency with which weak beats, major lines, or masculine lines occur in Gower's pentameters, at least not in the same way that I have measured them in this volume. It did, however, note that weak beats occur in position 4 in just 6 percent of Gower's lines in the two poems, and that running lines account for 23 percent of total. The figures for these features in my 300-line sample of *IPP* show no significant differences from those for both poems given in 2004, but the new data amplifies this information so as to provide a picture of the role played in the rhythm by weak beats in total, and also by the postponement of the strongest mid-line stress to position 6. Figure 1 below compares the frequency of key features in my *IPP* sample and in Chaucer's earlier and later pentameters, as discussed in Chapter 11.

The table in Figure 1 shows that there are major stylistic differences between the two poets' pentameters, which time (in Chaucer's case) served to increase. The first of these is in the proportion of running lines: Gower's 21 percent is what a probability analysis based on his vocabulary would lead us to expect. Gower neither avoided nor sought such lines but allowed them to happen at the dictate of the words that came to him. He observed no word boundary constraint but simply crafted iambic lines with whatever words came to mind: achieving a balance between lines that closed with rising and others that closed with falling rhythms was thus no part of his agenda.

(All Figures are Percentages of Lines)

Sample	Running Lines	Major Lines	Italic Lines	Weak Beats	Masculine Lines
Earlier Chaucer	25	20	38	35	24
Later Chaucer	28	25	45	45	41
Gower *IPP*	21	14	27	32	15

Fig. 1: Comparison of Chaucer's and Gower's Pentameters

The second difference shown in this table is in the proportion of major lines: Gower observed no constraint on phrasal stress, and when he required more than half the line to complete his opening phrase, its boundary and the peak of stress that went with it were postponed accordingly. The proportion of major lines in Gower's ME verse (14 percent) is little different from the proportion of his AN *décasyllabes* with phrasal stress in positions other than 4.[6] From this I would argue that Gower had no WB or PS constraint, but neither did he show any interest in balancing different micro-rhythms; his pentameters are therefore

[6] See Chapter 9, Figure 2.

overwhelmingly of the type I have labeled Gallic: 73 percent of his lines divide clearly into phrases of four syllables and six.

Moreover, three of the forty-three strophes in my *IPP* sample contain only Gallic lines, including the following (ll. 43–49):

(7) Bot ṭḥog̣ḥ it fel // at **thil**ke **time** so
(8) That A**lisandr**^{e} // his **axing**^{e} hath a**chie**ved,
(9) This **sin**ful world // was al pai**e**ne tho,
(10) Was non which hath // the **hi**he God be**lie**ved.
(11) No **won**dir was // thogh **thil**ke world was **grie**ved:
(12) Thogh ạ **ti**r**aunt** // his **pour**pos **myh**te **win**ne,
(13) Al was **venganc**^{e} // and infor**tun**^{e} of **sin**ne.

This strophe contains thirty-five relentless iambs, all with their strongest stresses in the same position, and each group of five divided into a pair and a trio by a wholly predictable word and phrase boundary. This unrelenting rhythm easily becomes monotonous, and the strophe's creaky syntax and repetitive diction do nothing to help enliven the point that Gower is making. Although a wide knowledge and a deep concern for his fellow humans generally underlie Gower's moralizing, they are not evident here.

The proportion of beats in Gower's pentameters provided by grammatical monosyllables (32 percent) is slightly lower than that found in Chaucer's earlier works. Hence *IPP* lines with five full stresses are not balanced evenly with three- or four-stress lines, which shows that Gower did not fully exploit the potential for rhythmic variety that this contrast offers. Another source of variety that his longer lines lack is that to be derived from masculine/feminine rhyme contrasts. Only 15 percent of *IPP*'s rhymes are masculine, and examples (1) to (13) above are representative of the whole poem in this respect. Even more remarkably, all eighty-four pentameters of the "Complaint" in *CA* have feminine rhymes, and this imbalance is difficult to explain. It is as if Gower regarded the pentameter at first as an Italianate curiosity and he hesitated to naturalize its rhyme scheme to the norms of his own AN and shorter-line ME verse.

In summary, Gower's pentameters are considerably less varied than Chaucer's. Gower obviously mastered the craft of composing iambic pentameters, and superficially his lines resemble Chaucer's, but Gower missed the subtleties of the meter. He did not exploit the opportunities to build a pleasing variety within the regularity of his lines, opportunities that Chaucer took, and which help qualify his verse craft for the term *artistry*.

Nevertheless, it is clear that Gower invented the modern iambic canons, both the pentameter and the tetrameter, and the difference between his and Chaucer's verse designs can be expressed neatly in terms of optimality theory. Gower raised the constraint to fill each weak position with a single syllable to a higher rank than it had been accorded in the verse design of any English poet before him.

Hoccleve's Decasyllables

After the deaths of Chaucer in 1400 and Gower in 1408, another duo of Englishmen claimed to be their poetic heirs. The first was Thomas Hoccleve (b. c. 1369-, d. c. 1426), whom most of the critics of subsequent centuries have regarded as no more than a poor imitator of Chaucer. Certainly, Hoccleve advertised his debt to both Chaucer and Gower in his poetry: he claimed both poets as his 'maysters' in *The Regiment of Princes* (composed between 1411 and 1412).[7] He probably thought he was complying with the medieval convention of authorial modesty when he included the following lines (2077–86):[8]

(14) My **de**re **may**ster // (god hys **sow**le **quy**te) {I}
(15) And **fa**der, **Chau**cer, // fayn wold^{e} hav^{e} me taught; {I}
(16) But y was **yong**^{e}, // and **le**ryd lyt^{e}l or naught. {G}
(17) **A**las, my **wor**thy **mais**tyr // honorable, {I}
(18) Thys **lan**dys **ver**ray **tre**sour // and richesse, {I}
(19) Deth, by thy deth, // hath **harm**^{e} irreper**a**ble {G}
(20) Un**to** us don. // Her **ven**geable dur**es**se {G}
(21) Dis**poi**led hath // thys **lond**^{e} of the swett**nes**se {G}
(22) Of reto**ryk**^{e}. // For **un**to Tullius {G}
(23) Was **ne**ver man // so **le**ke $_{H}$ a**mong** us. {G}

Many subsequent critics have taken example (16) at its face value, and have extended it to all of Hoccleve's work.[9] But examples (17) to (22) are fine poetry, a tribute elegant enough to carve on a tomb.

Moreover, the whole passage is skilfully crafted after Chaucer's own practice: it opens with four Italic lines and a Gallic line fused by elision; it closes with five Gallic lines where the French constraints (both WB and PS) are emphasized by major syntactic boundaries and strong stresses mid-line. As the subject shifts from veneration to separation and back to lofty comparison, the micro-rhythms change. But, typically of Thomas Hoccleve, the last line spoils the aesthetic effect: in example (23) an ugly hiatus and the untimely inversion of a grammatical word bring a lame ending to this eloquent tribute. The poet treats the stress of 'among' as variable (like that of 'unto' in examples (20) and (22)), and only hiatus and Move X can maintain the passage's undulating iambic rhythm.

---

[7] For a critical edition of Hoccleve's work, see Furnivall, 1897.

[8] All references and quotations in this chapter relate to the text of O'Donoghue 1982.

[9] See Saintsbury, 1906: I, 232, and Hammond 1927: 55.

Hoccleve's poetry is moral, in the same sense as Gower's, but Gower knew how to enhance his lessons with spicy stories and the best thinking of his age. Hoccleve, in contrast, digresses and becomes repetitive. Thus the action in this, his only major poem, is delayed for almost 2,000 lines by his introduction of an old man, who reminds us of the one in Chaucer's *PT*, but who stays around long enough to bore the reader.[10] *The Regiment of Princes* was composed for the future King Henry V, but Hocccleve received no more royal commissions and spent the rest of his life in poverty without a patron for his muse. Jerome Mitchell and Bernard O'Donoghue were among the first modern critics and editors to see originality and merit in Hoccleve's poetry.[11] O'Donoghue, in particular, argued that Hoccleve was ahead of his time in making poetry of his private concerns, and revealing his emotions in a most un-medieval way.[12]

Another modern champion of Hoccleve is Judith Jefferson, who analyzed his versification in great detail.[13] She demonstrated that Hoccleve's first priority in crafting his lines was syllable count: he adopted the same French conventions as Chaucer and Gower for dealing with word-final schwa and always sought a line of ten syllables to the final stress. (My own analysis of a sample from *The Regiment of Princes* showed that 94 percent of its lines have exactly that number).[14] Jefferson argued that a predominantly iambic rhythm was his secondary aim, something he gave to his ten syllables whenever he could. She described Hoccleve's rhythmic intentions as 'avoidance strategies': he may not have been able to ensure that his lines were delivered with a regular iambic rhythm, but he did take care that no series of lines lapsed into triple time. Given the changes that were taking place in fifteenth-century English, this was probably the best that he could do to capture Chaucer's and Gower's rhythm.

---

[10] The old man appears in line 120 of *The Regiment of Princes* and concludes in line 2016; see O'Donoghue 1982: 76–95.

[11] See Mitchell, 1968: 103–9.

[12] See O'Donoghue 1982: 9–14.

[13] See Jefferson, 2000.

[14] See Duffell, 1991: 483–88. My sample was the first 300 lines of *The Regiment of Princes* in Furnivall's edition. Jefferson takes Hoccleve's adherence to a strict syllable count as a given (2000: 203); the remainder of her article demonstrates how few of Hoccleve's lines fail to meet PT's definition of an iambic pentameter. Many of her examples, however, reveal Hoccleve's stylistic weakness: he placed far too many unstressed monosyllables in strong positions for modern tastes.

Lydgate's Dolniks

In contrast to the dismal failure of Hoccleve's poetic career, Chaucer's other English heir, John Lydgate (b. c. 1370–d. 1450), was a resounding success. He rarely lacked patrons, from city corporations, who generally paid their bills, to the country's nobility, who often did not; and he produced a vast quantity of English verse in the course of his long life.[15] Lydgate was a farm boy, adopted by the Church, taught Latin (at which he excelled), and was introduced to the highest in the land. For political reasons England's rulers at that time were keen to capture in English the wealth of Continental literature; and John Lydgate was the ideal man to supply this market. Had he been paid a good celebrity rate, by the word, he would have become a rich man. As it was, he never experienced Hoccleve's poverty, and he became the most famous poet of his age. Thus the giants on whose shoulders Shakespeare's and Milton's generations thought they were standing were not Chaucer and Gower, but Chaucer and Lydgate.[16]

Lydgate's earlier poems are those most obviously inspired by Chaucer and his later ones are the most voluminous. To the first group belong *The Complaint of the Black Knight* (indebted to Chaucer's *BD*), *The Temple of Glas* (indebted to *HF*), and *The Floure of Curtesy* (indebted to *PF*). To the second group belong his translations: *The Troy Book* (30,000-lines, composed 1412–20), *The Pilgrimage of Man* (24,000 lines, composed 1426–30), and *The Fall of Princes* (36,000 lines, composed 1431–38).[17] Modern critics regard Lydgate's shorter poems as his best, but there is an enormous disparity between Lydgate's standing in his own time and his valuation by most modern readers.[18] This is partly because intellectual fast food, provided first by novels and short lyrics, and more recently by Hollywood, television, and computers, has left neither time nor appetite for long heavy reads, but mostly it is because Lydgate's metrics are badly understood.

Two heavyweight critics, one on each side of the Atlantic, led the modern assault on Lydgate's reputation. George Saintsbury (b. 1845–d. 1933), whose knowledge of English poetry was so vast that he was incapable of organizing his thoughts upon it, castigated Lydgate in 1906 as "a doggerel poet with an insensitive ear."[19] As a specialist in French literature, Saintsbury found it particularly galling that Lydgate either could not, or chose not to, count his syllables; and as a patriot in a period on the brink of war, he greatly resented the attention that

[15] For Lydgate's poems and patrons, see Norton-Smith 1966: xiii–xv; for a full discussion of the Lydgate canon, see Schirmer, 1961.

[16] See Drabble, 1985: 595.

[17] For the text of Lydgate's minor poems, see MacCracken, 1911; for that of *The Troy Book*, see Edwards, 1998.

[18] See Norton Smith 1966: x–xi.

[19] For Lydgate and 'doggerel,' see Saintsbury, 1906: I, 223. Saintsbury's three volumes are a maze of chapters, summaries, inter-chapters, and summaries of inter-chapters.

his German contemporaries had paid to Lydgate, and to English literature in general.[20] Eleanor Prescott Hammond (b. 1864–d. 1933) was even more scathing in the second of her two great volumes on medieval English literature: in 1927 she wrote: "The study of Lydgate's mentality may not be worth the student's candle."[21] This seems a harsh judgment on a mind that had raised its owner from plough-boy to laureate, but Hammond was far more intelligent than most of the men who impeded her career, so she should be forgiven for not being more generous.

In the course of the twentieth century Saintsbury's and Hammond's views of Lydgate became the established wisdom, and Lydgate's case was not helped by the fact that the sort of poetry he wrote doesn't fit well into anthologies; consequently, more readers, especially teachers and students, read his critics than read his poetry.[22] Hammond's conclusion, based on long hours of study, could easily be read as "Don't bother with Lydgate," and I suspect that many students in the generations that followed read it that way. Hammond's opinion of Lydgate continued to be reflected in handbooks on English literature for the remainder of the century, and it is still held by many teachers of English today.[23]

After the deaths of Saintsbury and Hammond in 1933 more objective critics soon made their voices heard. C. S. Lewis and Fitzroy Pyle were among the first of these and by the time that Walter Schirmer and Alain Renoir published their books on Lydgate, just after World War II, the bias in Saintsbury's and Hammond's judgments was more clearly recognized.[24] In particular, the post-war scholars questioned whether Lydgate could have been so highly rated in his own time if his mind and his meter had been so poor. And Hammond's evidence that every poet writing between Hoccleve and Surrey had followed Lydgate's example was an even more telling point against the view that his long line was no more than a failed iambic pentameter.[25] Finally, the deeper study of linguistic change in ME led to a more realistic assessment of how difficult it was in the fifteenth century to craft lines in the same way that Chaucer had done in the fourteenth.[26]

Although Lydgate followed Chaucer and Gower's choices of strophe design, the open couplet and rhyme royal, he made major changes to their verse designs

[20] Saintsbury resented the intrusion of German scholars in his field; not only did they describe, count, and classify lines before they reached opinions, but they got their books out first (Sievers in 1885, Schick in 1891, and Schipper in 1896). For the animosity this aroused, see Saintsbury, 1906: I, 219–34.

[21] See Hammond, 1927: 152.

[22] Thus Lydgate's name does not appear in either Palgrave 1964 or in Gardner 1972.

[23] This conclusion is based on views I collected at the annual conferences of the *New Chaucer Society* in the 1990s.

[24] See Pyle, 1937, Lewis 1938, Schirmer 1961, Renoir 1967, and Pearsall 1970.

[25] See Hammond, 1927: passim.

[26] See Minkova, 1990: 321–30 and 1991: passim.

for his own work. Lydgate returned to the native four-beat dolnik for his shorter line, and for his longer he converted Chaucer's pentameter into a five-beat meter with the same flexibility in the size of its offbeats.[27] Lewis described Lydgate's shorter lines as "good enough octosyllabics," carefully using the term for the four-beat ME dolnik then current.[28] But Lydgate's shorter lines, as found in poems like *Mumming at London* (1427), are clearly constructed on the same principles as his longer. They show the same variability in both syllable count and rhythm: barely 60 percent meet the norms of the iambic tetrameter or pentameter.[29] And the lines in both Lydgate's meters deviate for the same reason: although they always contain the correct number of beats, their offbeats may be implied or double. So his verse has frequent lapses into triple time and many stress clashes, and his shorter line differs only in having fewer offbeats to vary; hence Lewis's greater tolerance of the shorter lines.

This section will concentrate on Lydgate's longer-line verse design, because it was the more innovative, and will begin with a short assessment of the part played by linguistic change in Lydgate's conversion of Chaucer's pentameter into a five-beat dolnik. Fifteenth-century poets and readers had problems with Chaucer's meter because of the further decline and eventual loss of word-final schwas, and the gradual adoption of a single, Germanic, accentuation of French loan words (which brought a severe restriction of Move X). For Lydgate, in the short term, this was a problem of inconsistency: different readers treated word-final schwas and the stressing of French-derived disyllables differently. I shall illustrate this by scanning two very different delivery instances of the same lines, both likely to have been current in the fifteenth century. One is a *cool* performance, with the schwa deletion and accentuation of French loan words more typical of Early Modern English; the second is an *un-cool* performance, which preserves Chaucer's and Gower's practice. I label the un-cool performance (a), because it is the older, and the cool (b). The lines are *GP*, 8, 14, 46, and 74.

The rhythmic profile of each delivery is given in parentheses after the line; and, instead of Attridge's symbols *B* and a variety of *o*s, I use the digit *1* to represent each beat (except the last, marked *5*), and *o* for each single, *oo* for each double, and [] for each implied offbeat:[30]

(24)a Hath ịṇ the Ram // his half cours y**ron**ne (*o 1 o 1 o 1 [] 1 o 5 o*)
(24)b Hath ịṇ the Ram // his half cours ^{y}**ronn**^{e} (*o 1 o 1 o 1 [] 1 [] 5*)

---

[27] Schipper included both Chaucer's and Lydgate's longer lines under the heading 'Rhymed Five-Foot Verse'; see Schipper, 1910: 209–16,

[28] See Lewis, 1938: 28.

[29] For statistical tables comparing Lydgate's longer and shorter lines, see Duffell, 2000: 249.

[30] For Attridge's notation, see Chapter 3, examples (19) and (20).

(25)a To **ferne** **hal**wes // **kowth**^{e} in **son**dry **lon**des   *(o 1 o 1 o 1 o 1 o 5 o)*
(25)b To fern^{e} halw^{e}s // kowth^{e} in **son**dry lond^{e}s   *(o 1 [] 1 [] 1 o 1 o 5)*

(26)a **Trouth**^{e} and hon**our**, // fre**dom** and curteisie   *(1 oo 1 o 1 o 1 o 5 o)*
(26)b Trouth^{e} and **ho**nour, // **fre**dom and curtei**si**^{e} *([] 1 o 1 o 1 oo 1 o 5)*

(27)a His hors wer^{e} **goo**de // þ̣ụṭ he was not gay   *(o 1o 1 o 1o 1 o 5)*
(27)b His hors wer^{e} good^{e} // þ̣ụṭ he was not gay   *(o 1 o 1 [] 1 o 1 o 5)*

The first thing to note is that, as a result of the deleted schwas, the cool deliveries have an irregular number of syllables: eight in (24)b and (25)b, nine in (27b), and ten in (26)b. But this is only one of the ways that the cool performer has made Chaucer sound like Lydgate.

Example (24)a is Lydgate's license to include implied offbeats, rare occurrences in Chaucer, but an essential element in Lydgate's design, and (25)b and (26)b include two of them, which makes them sound to modern ears more like an iambic tetrameter than a pentameter; this is because we tend to demote the words 'cours' and 'halwes' to offbeats. Example (26)a has an initial monosyllabic inversion but in (26)b the falling rhythm persists for most of the line. And finally, example (27)b has a *broken back* (an implied offbeat between the second and third beats), another feature that is rare in Chaucer but is found in abundance in Lydgate's verse.

Lydgate's reform of Chaucer's longer line was aimed at giving his lines a rhythm that would be regular in both cool and un-cool performances. In order to achieve this he reverted to an older tradition of versifying in English, one that produced strongly divided lines with a primary rhythm based on counting beats and not syllables.[31] From Chaucer, however, Lydgate had learned some of the advantages of five beats over four (listed in "The Math of Line Length" in Chapter 9). Since he knew the *décasyllabe* well and the *endecasillabo* not at all, he divided his lines almost invariably into 2 + 3 beats. Thus Pyle calculated that 97.5 percent of Lydgate's lines are divided this way.[32]

Back in 1891 Josef Schick had produced a detailed analysis of the ways in which Lydgate's longer line differed from Chaucer's, but Saintsbury, with typical chauvinism, had dismissed Schick's work on the grounds that he was German and not an Oxford man.[33] Yet Schick had shown that Lydgate's line was not only very different from Chaucer's, it was systematically different. In 1970 Dudley Hascall conducted the first modern linguistic analysis of Lydgate's verse design, and the analysis that follows strongly confirms both Schick's and Hascall's con-

[31] Although he attributes Saintsbury's unfavorable views, at least partly, to poor manuscripts, Pearsall still concludes that Lydgate's syllabic irregularity can only be intentional; see Pearsall, 1970: 60–62.

[32] See Pyle, 1937: 30.

[33] See Saintsbury, 1906: I, 222.

clusions.[34] It places more emphasis, however, on the two-part structure of Lydgate's lines and the way that he crafted them, and it sums up Lydgate's design in a diagram form that is indebted to Attridge and also to Hanson and Kiparsky.

Lydgate's template has ten positions, each representing either a beat or an offbeat; if we denote the beats by arabic numerals, the offbeats by the roman alphabet, and the mandatory mid-line word boundary by a slash, the design looks like this:

a 1 b 2 / c / 3 d 4 e 5

Beats are normally realized by stressed syllables or, in the case of beats 1 to 4, exceptionally by unstressed monosyllables; offbeats are realized by between zero and two syllables of any sort. Note that there are two possible positions for the mandatory mid-line word boundary: if offbeat *c* is realized by a single syllable, it may be a post-tonic syllable (part of the same word as beat 2); this gives the first half-line a *feminine cadence*; or it may commence a new word giving the first half-line, giving a *masculine cadence.* If *c* is realized by two syllables it gives the line an *epic caesura*; if it is realized by zero (making it an implied offbeat) it makes the line *broken-backed.*

In this way, Lydgate reformed Chaucer's meter to meet the prevailing (although transitional) linguistic conditions, and for more than 100 years English poets preferred Lydgate's design, and even performed Chaucer's lines as if they were in Lydgate's meter. His line of five beats with variable intervals, a five-ictic dolnik, was a perfect fit for a language in which the syllabification of word-final schwa was optional, and when those schwas disappeared Lydgate's design lost its chief reason for existence. Many of his lines are good iambic pentameters, simply because alternate peaks and troughs of stress are very common in English speech.[35] So iambic pentameters, in all their variants, lie within the possibilities of Lydgate's five-beat line, and this was the great strength of his meter: it allowed both smooth iambic lines and rougher ones with a variety of other rhythms.

Recently, Maura Nolan made a study of how Lydgate's lines should be performed in order to convey their poetic rhythm, and she concluded that Lydgate sometimes made good use of this smoother / rougher contrast.[36] The question

---

[34] See Hascall, 1970.

[35] Just as full rhyme is a special case of assonance, so the iambic pentameter is a special case of the five-ictic dolnik. In Chapters 6 and 7 I was careful to distinguish between dolniks and strict iambic verse, so-called because it regulates the size of intervals more strictly. Nevertheless, English dolnik poems usually contain some regularly iambic lines, because of the frequency with which stressed and unstressed syllables alternate in the language. However, I doubt whether a 'pairing condition' (of double and implied offbeats; see Attridge, 1982: 175–86) played any part in the development of strict iambic verse.

[36] See Nolan, 2013.

of how to perform Lydgate's lines, on which she focuses, leads to another: how to scan them. Seymour Chatman redefined a *verse instance* as the common denominator of all *delivery instances* – but what if performers vary in their delivery of some unstressed syllables, as I have argued was the case in fifteenth-century England?[37] In that case the only common denominator of the delivery instances will be five beats; but in examples (24) to (27) I have shown that it is possible to scan individual delivery instances, and that is what I shall do in the analysis of Lydgate's longer-line verse that follows. The performance I shall scan is hypothetical: it is relatively cool for the year 1434, when the poem concerned was written. This performance deletes all word-final schwas except those of weak adjectives (as suggested by Pearsall), and those that prevent the line from having a final implied offbeat (which my own study of Lydgate's lines that lack word-final schwa suggests was his normal practice).[38] My analysis is based on half-lines because, as I shall demonstrate, Lydgate seems to have based his versifying upon them. My quantifications are based upon a 300-line sample from Book II of Lydgate's *Life of Our Lady* (*LOL*).[39]

The overwhelming majority of Lydgate's lines have one of only two possible configurations of first hemistich; both configurations contain two beats (notated by *1*) and most often only single offbeats (notated by *o*):

(a) o 1 o 1 / (b) o 1 o 1 o /

Note that hemistich (a) is iambic ([o 1] [o 1]), and hemistich (b) is ambivalent: it is either iambic with an extrametrical syllable ([o 1][o 1] o), or trochaic with a syllable in anacrusis (o [1 o][1 o]). In my sample 67 percent of lines open with hemistich (a) and 21 percent with hemistich (b). Two configurations also account for the vast majority of second hemistichs; the first is iambic, the second trochaic:

(a) [o 1] [o 1] [o 1] (o) (b) [1 o] [1 o] [1 (o)]

Lydgate's lines in which both hemistichs are either (a) or (b) are iambic pentameters; (a) + (a) lines are pausing lines, and (b) + (b) lines are running lines. What makes Lydgate's lines very different from Chaucer's is the proportion of lines that are either (a) + (b), that is, broken-backed, or (b) + (a), that is, have epic caesura. Figure 2 below shows the percentages of lines in my *LOL* sample.

---

37 See Chatman, 1965: 96.

38 See Duffell, 2000: 243, esp. Note 37.

39 These lines are numbered 1–300 in Norton-Smith 1966: 35–43; I have cited the original line numbers in MacCracken 1911.

Combinations	*Percentages*
(a) + (a): pausing iambic pentameters:	34
(b) + (b): running iambic pentameters	12
(a) + (b): broken-backed lines	28
(b) + (a): lines with epic caesuras	9
Lines containing other configurations:	17

Fig. 2: Types of Line in *LOL*

Most of the other configurations (six for each hemistich) contain one or more double or implied offbeats; no other configuration is particularly common. Some 5 percent of lines have one regular hemistich, (a) or (b), and one irregular. Lydgate therefore crafted the great majority of his lines from just four accentual configurations, that is, fewer than the number of different hemistich types I identified in the iambic pentameter or the *endecasillabo*.[40]

The main types of lines identified in Figure 2 above can be illustrated by the following examples from *LOL*, II; beats are indicated by bold typeface when provided by strong syllables, and underlining when provided by monosyllables:

Pausing Iambic Pentameters = (a)+(a)
(28) The grace of God, // **amydde** the **lyly** white (559)
(29) So as the flees // of **Gede**on was wette (576)
(30) Right so hathe Godde // in hir his **grace** shewed (580)

Running Iambic Pentameters = (b)+(b)
(31) She was the **castell** // ọf the **crystall** wall (547)
(32) To make hir **whitest**, // ạṣ in ho**lynesse** (744)
(33) And he that **causith** // **foule3** ịṇ the eyre (764)

Lines with Broken Backs= (a)+(b)
(34) **Only** to vs // **forto** sig**nifye** (534)
(35) Wheche stoode ay clos; // ịṇ conclu**sion** (572)
(36) That **neuer man** // **entre** shall ne pace (573)

Lines with Epic Caesura = (b)+(a)
(37) **Into** hir **closet** // the **Faders** sa**pience** (524)
(38) And ọṇ this **auter** // she made hir sac**rifice** (603)
(39) **Withoutyn brekyng** // or **any** vi**olence** (658)

Other Types of Line
Headless Trochaic = (-1)+(b)
(40) **Entrede** is // **withoutyn** vi**olence** (525)

[40] See the list of Chaucer's four 'opening' and four 'closing' hemistichs, both labeled (a) to (d), in Chapter 12.

Double Anacrusis = (a+1) + (a)
(41) Withe the **Ho**ly Goste // when she was al bydewed (581)

Four-beat Alternative = (a) + (a-2))
(42) That **neuer** man // myght yet vn**close** (548)

Note that my 'cool' performance syllabifies the word-final schwa of '**gra**ce' in example (30), in order to produce a line-final single offbeat. Note also that example (42) can be delivered more rapidly as a four-beat line by demoting ('might'), and that such demotion was how later poets avoided stress clashes. One of Lydgate's most distinguished editors, H. N. McCracken, suggested that Lydgate mixed four-beat lines with his five-beat ones, and some performances of *LOL* doubtless had this feature.[41] Many later English poets have also mixed the two line lengths, and it is tempting to deliver examples (29) and (42) in this way, making them the second lines of a perfectly iambic 5-beat + 4-beat couplet.

These examples illustrate the two advantages over the iambic pentameter that Lydgate's longer line had in the fifteenth century. The first was that it was performer-proof: its underlying five-beat primary rhythm allowed readers to perform the line in different ways. The second advantage was that it contained a variety of secondary rhythms ranging from the perfectly smooth (because five-ictic dolniks include iambic pentameters) to the much rougher (lines with implied and double offbeats). This meter's other advantage over the four-beat line was thus that of resembling speech rather than song. Lydgate could sing as well as narrate, and he employed both line lengths with equal facility.

Maura Nolan goes further in her appreciation of Lydgate's versifying: she argues that he consciously chose broken-backed lines for their aesthetic value: for example, they helped convey a certain register or an individual's speech habits.[42] The sudden changes of the interval between beats that he allowed his readers gave his verse its character and variety, which it is still possible to enjoy. Modern readers can, with a little effort, find the same pleasure in Lydgate's rhythms that his patrons did. But, above all, we should remember that this rhythmically varied style was how readers performed Chaucer's lines for several hundred years, until the resurrection of word-final schwa.[43] Thus, had Lydgate tried to write regular iambic verse, his audience would have been treated to the same irregular performances; and this was doubtless why the foremost poet of fifteenth-century England did not waste his time composing it.

One of the dolnik's advantages was that performers could choose their own treatment of word-final schwas without threat to the poet's primary rhythm, which was based on beats. Roughly 40 percent of Lydgate's longer lines have no

[41] See MacCracken, 1911: viii.
[42] See Nolan, 2013: 110–12.
[43] See Chapter 16.

such schwas and roughly 60 percent of those have ten syllables and are iambic in rhythm.[44] Thus, of his lines in total, roughly one in four is a perfect iambic pentameter, regardless of how word-final schwa is treated; and it is not difficult to treat the word-final schwas of his poems in such a way as to make the majority of lines equally iambic. Nevertheless, many of Lydgate's lines resist such regularization, and the result is verse in which iambs play a large part, but which has considerably more rhythmic variety at the syllable level than Chaucer's line. In short, it was more like normal speech, and Lydgate could be forgiven if he, and his patrons, and the English poets who followed, believed that his meter was an improvement.

To summarize, Lydgate was never short of customers because he piled his lines high and sold them cheap, and anyone could perform them without fear of losing the rhythm. This interpretation of Lydgate's meter explains his success and fame, which were a mystery to Saintsbury and Hammond. Lydgate was not the dimwit envisaged by Hammond, but a man of considerable practical intelligence. He recognized that the dolnik was a better fit for his language (at that point of time) than Chaucer's (rhythmically) or Hoccleve's (syllabically) regular verse.

When fifteenth-century English patrons wanted translations, adaptations, or celebratory verse, they queued for the services of Practical Jack, the Monk of Bury.[45] His patrons were impressed, rather than appalled, when he paraded his knowledge of French and Latin literature, and dropped many pearls of wisdom for the first time in English. The mayor of a dirty and verminous English borough could find nobody better than John Lydgate to dignify his town's celebrations with talk of Troy, Athens, and Rome, of Achilles, Hector, and Alexander, and such great names as these.

Although he could be eloquent when he spoke of the love of his life, the Virgin Mary, there is no case that Lydgate was a great poet. Nevertheless, the high esteem as a scholar and versifier that he enjoyed for a century was hard-earned. He did his best to share all that he knew with his countrymen, and he coped ingeniously with the linguistic uncertainties of his times.[46] Consequently, he fills an important place in the history of versifying in English.

[44] See Duffell, 2000: 247–48.

[45] Norton-Smith lists more than a dozen patrons, ranging from sheriffs to kings, over a period of 37 years (see Note 15 above).

[46] Lydgate's reform of the English tetrameter and pentameter can be seen as a turning back of the clock. In terms of optimality theory, Lydgate gave the constraint to fill each weak position with a single syllable a much lower rank in the hierarchy of his designs than had Chaucer. And until schwa deletion reached the stage that typifies Early Modern English this was a perfectly sensible position for it to occupy: it allowed for the vagaries of contemporary speech.

15
The Scottish Chaucerians

This chapter will be much shorter than the last because Chaucer's early Scottish admirers, paradoxically, understood his meters better than did his English disciples, and they reproduced them proficiently in their own dialect. The Scottish scholars who produced the best poetry in fifteenth-century Britain did not get bogged down in attempts to revive the custom of counting beats and working in half-lines. I shall begin by trying to resolve the paradox.

Both Hoccleve and Lydgate were around thirty years old when Chaucer died, and C. S. Lewis wondered why poets who appreciated that Chaucer's lines were iambic when word-final schwas were pronounced did not simply compose iambic pentameters with such schwas deleted.[1] But Lewis underestimated the problems of versifying in periods that are transitional between two norms for syllabification. He also forgot what had happened in French: 300 years after their word-final schwas had been deleted all French poets continued to count them, and French actors still time their performance of lines so as to take the missing schwas into account.

In the twentieth century, Portuguese has provided an even closer parallel to Middle English, as most Peninsular speakers now delete many of the language's final vowels.[2] That is why old people, Brazilians, and tour guides pronounce the name of my favorite fishing village as 'Monte Gordo,' while its inhabitants prefer 'Mont^{e} Gord^{o}.' Portuguese poets still count this name as four syllables in regular verse and, to complicate matters, professional performers will whisper the final vowels in order to get the timing of the line right.[3] This was the enigma that confronted Lydgate's generation in England, but in Scotland, where word-final

---

[1] See Lewis, 1938: 28.

[2] See Parkinson, 1988; for the most recent developments in Portuguese, see Liberman, 2012 on the website given in Works Cited

[3] Two possible solutions to the problem of disappearing vowels can be seen in the work of Fernando Pessoa (b. 1888–d. 1935); he carried on counting syllables in the traditional way when writing under the heteronym Ricardo Reis, but employed free verse (*verso libre*) when writing as Alvaro de Campos. For the poems of Reis, see Fagundas Duarte 1994; for the poems of Campos, see Berardinelli, 1990; for Pessoa's metrics, see Ferrari, 2012.

schwa disappeared earlier, poets had an advantage. Saintsbury noted this, saying vaguely that it was somehow easier for foreigners to compose lines like Chaucer's, but he did not go into detail.[4]

By 1400 speakers of *Ynglis*, as the ME of Scotland was called, deleted almost all final vowels, but educated Scots (and a few, like Barbour, were graduates of Paris as well as Oxford) must have known well that Sassenachs pronounced word-final schwas in a somewhat chaotic manner. When they performed Chaucer's lines, therefore, they did the opposite of English readers: they made them more regular, syllabifying word-final schwas when it helped improve the iambic smoothness of the line, and ignoring them when it did not. Thus it was that Scottish imitators of Chaucer composed as Lewis said people should: they sought, and for the most part achieved, an iambic rhythm in their own schwa-deleted dialect.

The four most important of Chaucer's Scottish disciples were: King James I (r. 1424–70), who was for long held prisoner in London; Robert Henryson (b. c. 1420–d. ?1506), a Dunfermeline schoolmaster; William Dunbar (b. ?1456–d. ?1513), a favorite of the Tudor Queen Margaret of Scotland; and Gavin Douglas (b. ?1475–d. ?1522), Bishop of Dunkeld. These poets represent four different generations, so the iambic pentameter had the continuous history in Scotland that it lacked in England. The chief influence upon these poets' versifying was undoubtedly Chaucer, but there were other influences, too. It is also worth noting that the poetry of France was read and admired in Scotland throughout the fifteenth century, while that of Italy (then undergoing its *secolo senza poesia*) was not.[5] Modern critics have thought highly of all four of these poets, even as they decried Lydgate, but the extent to which the Scottish poets' lines resemble Chaucer's varies.[6]

James I of Scotland

James composed love poems in the latter part of his captivity (c. 1415–24) and gathered them in a book known as *The Kingis Quair*.[7] His use of Chaucer's favorite ballade meter gave rhyme royal its modern name, and his lines have a more obvious iambic rhythm than Lydgate's. James seems to have spoken an English in which word-final schwas were deleted except when they were *eurhythmic;* that is, when they prevented clashing stresses. This can be seen from the following examples, the first two from the poem entitled 'Cantus' (*C*), and the second two from that entitled 'Stanzas' (*St*):

[4] See Saintsbury, 1906: I, 300.

[5] Medieval French poets were known as *faiseurs*, cognate with the Scottish *makars*; for French influence on Scottish poetry, see Scott, 1967: 14.

[6] See, for example, Fox 1966.

[7] For the poems of James I, see Mackenzie, 1939.

(1) There was no **ta**kyn // ịṇ hir **sue**te face (*C*, 56)
(2) And **ther**fore, **mer**ci, // suete! sen it is so (*C*, 77)
(3) En**brou**din all // with **fre**sche **flou**ris gay (*St*, 3)
(4) The **ly**oun king, // and his fere lyo**nesse** (*St*, 22)

Clearly, whether the adjectives 'suete' and 'fresche,' and the noun 'fere' (modern 'partner') count as one syllable or two depends on whether their word-final schwa prevents stress clash. If this eurhythmic principle is followed, then 90 percent of James's lines are both decasyllabic and iambic.

James had spent his childhood in Scotland, where schwa deletion was further advanced than in London, and deleting the schwas in his lines usually makes them more regular. Some of James's lines, however, become decasyllabic only if a word-final schwa is syllabified, as for instance in the following two examples where the schwa occurs before a vowel:

(5) That ịṇ the **son**ne $_{H}$ // ọṇ thair **sca**lis bryght (*St*, 13)
(6) The **ny**ce $_{H}$ ape; // the **wer**^{e}ley porpa**py**ne (*St*, 26)

Example (6) reflects the fact that pre-vocalic adjectives in ME were the last to lose their word-final schwa, but it is clear that James did not follow Chaucer's (and Gower's) French convention in treating such vowels, and modern readers may be over-generous in regularizing his lines. James did follow Chaucer, however, in allowing both headless and broken-backed lines, for example:

(7) [ ] **Wor**shippe ye // that **lov**^{e}ris bene, this May (*C*, 1)
(8) Ane **ug**ly pit // [ ] depe as **o**ny helle (*St*, 72)

One of the reasons that the versification of *The Kingis Quair* appeals to modern ears is that only 3 percent of its lines are broken-backed, compared with Lydgate's 28 percent.[8] Such lines, however, can be very effective; in (8), for example, the second half-line seems to hurl the reader into the ugly pit as the rhythm suddenly stops and drops, and iambs yield to trochees.

Also like Lydgate, James includes a few lines that invite an alternative four-beat delivery; for example, the following, which I scan as four-beat lines:

(9) A round place **wal**lit // have I found (*St*, 51)
(10) That sem^{y}t to me // of **di**vers **he**wis (*St*, 58)

Demoting 'place' in the stress hierarchy and syncopating 'sem^{y}t' makes both lines excellent iambic tetrameters. James was, of course, surrounded by Englishmen when he wrote these lines, and perhaps that is why some of his lines are so like Lydgate's most irregular ones. But there are also signs in James's iambic pen-

[8] This calculation is based on the two poems given by Scott 1967: 37–43.

tameters of the refinements detected in Chaucer's later works. Although schwa deletion renders almost 100 percent of James's lines masculine, the frequency of weak beats in *The Kingis Quair* (43 per 100 lines) is closer to that in Chaucer's later verse (45) than that in his earlier (35). On the other hand, only 17 percent of James's lines are running (a figure that random deployment of the poem's word configurations would produce), and he includes some sequences of 20 consecutive pausing lines.

Overall, James's versifying is closer to Chaucer's than either Hoccleve's or Lydgate's, and he produced some very charming passages of regular iambic pentameters. For the immediate future Chaucer's metrical legacy would be better preserved in Scotland than in England.

Robert Henryson

Nothing is known about Henryson except that he was a graduate of Glasgow University and a schoolmaster.[9] The Nobel laureate Seamus Heaney, better known for his free verse, paid Henryson's iambic pentameters the compliment of retaining them in a translation for modern readers.[10] Heaney qualified the statement that Henryson is a thoroughly medieval poet by saying:

> Yet he belongs in the eternal present of the perfectly pitched, a poet whose knowledge of life is matched by the range of his art, whose constant awareness of the world's hardness and injustice is mitigated by his irony, tenderheartedness, and ever-ready sense of humour. ("Introduction," vii)

Among Henryson's poems are two in native meters: "Sum Practysis of Medecyne" employs the traditional alliterative meter in thirteen-line strophes; and his short tale of rural romance "Robene and Makyne" is in common measure. But most of his surviving verse is in pentameters, including *The Testament of Cresseid* and *Fables* (both in rhyme royal), and *Orpheus and Eurydice*, which begins in rhyme royal and closes in couplets.

The Testament of Cresseid begins where *Troilus and Criseyde* left off. As Henryson tells us in lines 39–42:[11]

(11) To cut the **win**ter nicht // and mak it schort

[9] See Scott, 1967: 177; for the little information that can be gleaned about Henryson from his work, see Bawcutt and Riddy 1992: ix–xii.

[10] See Heaney, 2009.

[11] The quotations from poems by Henryson in this article are from Bawcutt and Riddy 1992: 1–122; my statistics are based upon the first 300 lines of Henryson's *Testament of Cresseid* given in Bawcutt and Riddy's selection. For Henryson's other works, see Fox, 1981.

(12) I tuik ane quair //—and left all **u**ther sport—
(13) **Writ**tin by **wor**thie **Chau**cer // glo**rious**,
(14) Of fair Cres**seid** // and **wor**thie Troy**lus**

The repetition of the word 'worthie' may offend purists, but the versification reproduces some of Chaucer's most subtle effects: two running and major lines alternate with two very strongly divided lines, and the passage's complex syntax is embellished by an initial inversion.

Composing what Hollywood now calls a *'sequel'* to Chaucer's poem contributed to the preservation of Henryson's work, but his poems that modern readers most enjoy are his retellings (often with a twist) of the Fables of Aesop. Henryson's versifying is much more highly rated by critics than Lydgate's because far fewer of his pentameters are broken-backed, but many of the Scottish poet's lines are not strictly iambic. Thus they contain many lyric caesuras, which prevent an iambic delivery, and some epic caesuras, which stop them from being decasyllabic. The lyric caesuras in the *Fables* include those in the following lines:

(15) To grit **lor**dis // thocht thow be leif and deir (89)
(16) Was gild **bro**ther // and made ane fre bur**ges** (172)
(17) As pure **pyl**gryme // scho **pas**sit owt of town (181)
(18) I have **hou**sis // a**new** of grit de**fence** (250)

It is possible that Move X was applied more widely in fifteenth-century Scotland than in England and all these words at the caesura could be stressed on their second syllable, but it is more likely that these are imitations of the French practice.

The same word categories that occupy positions 3–4 in examples (15) to (18) are also found in positions 4–5 of Henryson's pentameters, sometimes producing epic caesuras because they are not balanced by a trochaic second half-line. The following examples are taken from *The Testament of Cresseid*:

(19) **Doc**tour in **phi**[sick], // cled ịṇ ane **skar**lot goun (250)
(20) **Wrin**gand his **han**[dis] // of**tymes** he said al**lace** (374)

In Henryson's verse the plural inflection *-is* and the past inflection *-it* need to be ambivalent in order to regularize syllable count and rhythm: they must sometimes be syllabified and sometimes not. Our allowing this flexibility makes his lines seem smoother than Lydgate's, and modern readers are also inclined to give the Scotsman the benefit of the doubt on possible examples of Move X; but if we are less lenient there are as many inversions in Henryson's lines as in Hoccleve's.

There are also a few lines in Henryson's poems where either the syllable count or rhythm is in peril. In some cases where either is doubtful, syncope can help regularize the line; these examples are again from the *Fables*:

(21) That ar not con**tent** // with small possessi**oun** (372)
(22) With that the cok // ov^{e}r ṭḥẹ feild^{i}s tuke his flicht (584)
(23) And ịṇ at the **we**dow^{i}s **le**wer // couth he licht (585)

Example (21) has a double anacrusis; in (22) the syncope of 'over' makes the line's only irregularity a weak third beat (demoting 'feilds' before 'tuke'); and (24) has an uncompensated double offbeat after its first beat. If these were Hoccleve's lines, Jefferson would judge that the poet's "avoidance strategies" had broken down.[12]

In summary, although Henryson's avoidance of broken-backed lines suits modern tastes, his pentameters are not strictly iambic. His use of lyric and epic caesuras is probably the result of French influence, but the first kills the line's iambic pulse and the second destroys its syllabic regularity. Moreover, some of his lines easily lend themselves to other rhythms than the iamb. Finally, he does not balance Gallic and Italic lines in his verse as Chaucer did in his later work. The 17 percent of running lines in the samples I have analyzed is no more than the figure that a random arrangement of his words would produce. The alternation of running and pausing lines in examples (11) to (14), therefore, is very much the exception, and many of Henryson's rhyme royal strophes contain only pausing lines.

William Dunbar

Dunbar surpassed Henryson in both his poetic range and his metrical versatility. Dunbar was a court poet and composed verse for many different occasions: his oeuvre includes religious poetry, allegories, narratives, satires, love lyrics, and humorous poems, and he had a range of meters to suit each subject.[13] His strophe designs included rhyme royal (as in *The Thrissill and the Rois*), a variety of ballade meters (including the nine-line stanzas of *The Goldyn Targe*), monorhyme quatrains, and strophes with Latin heads and tails. His verse designs are always appropriate to their subject: thus the four-beat lines of the religious poem *Rorate, celi, desuper* are iambic tetrameters, while those of the humorous poem "Sir John Sinclair Begowthe the Dance" are dolniks. When Dunbar composed a poem beginning "Now lythis of a gentill knight," he employed the meter of Chaucer's *ST*, but he was wise enough to keep the poem short. Dunbar was his own critic and censor, and his confession that "*Timor mortis conturbat me*" is convincing.[14]

[12] See Jefferson, 2000: 223–25.

[13] For a critical edition of Dunbar's poems, see Mackenzie, 1932.

[14] The quotations from poems by Dunbar in this chapter are from Bawcutt and Riddy 1992: 123–209; my statistics are based upon Dunbar's *The Goldyn Targe* and *The Thrissill and the Rois* in Bawcutt and Riddy's selection.

One of Dunbar's most interesting poems metrically is *The Twa Mariit Wemen and the Wedo.* As befits a mock-folk poem, it is in the native alliterative meter, and most of its lines contain five beats, subdivided 3 + 2, as the following examples (lines 311–12) show:

(24) For thocht I say it my self, // the **sev**[e]rance wes **mek**le
(25) Bet**wix** his **bas**tard blude // and my birth **no**ble

The alliterative pattern is a very intricate one, which involves both beats and offbeats, and although his editors describe the poem as unrhymed, the weak rhyme on the final post-tonic syllables of these lines occurs often in the poem. In this manner, Dunbar anticipated the twentieth century vogue for more subtle forms of phoneme repetition than full rhyme.

The verse design of the *The Twa Mariit Wemen and the Wedo* is somewhat more complex than that of most ME alliterative poems. Some of Dunbar's lines have a potential for delivery with additional weak beats; for example, lines 24 and 259, for which I give alternative scansions:

(26) Thair **man**till[is] grein wer as the gres // that grew in May **ses**soun
(26)a Thair **man**till[is] grein wer as the gres // that grew in May ses**soun**
(27) Be **con**stant in your governance // and **coun**terfeit gud **ma**ner[is]
(27)a Be **con**stant in your **go**vernance // and counterfeit gud **ma**ner[is]

In (26)a and (27)a, the alliterations fall on natural peaks of stress and their iambic rhythm is more attractive to modern ears, and perhaps to Dunbar's.

Certainly, Dunbar's finest metrical achievements were his iambic pentameters, the best since Chaucer's. In the following strophe, which opens his most famous ballade, "To a Lady," he employs the contrasts between running and pausing lines to great effect:

(28) Sweit rois of **ver**tew // and of gen**til**nes,
(29) **De**lyt**sum lyl**[lie] // of **ev**[e]rie lustynes,
(30) **Rich**est in **bon**tie // and in **bew**tie cleir
(31) And **ev**[e]rie **ver**tew // that is {wenyt} deir,
(32) Ex**cept on**lie // that ye ar mercy**les**.

Note that I have emended (31), as does Scott (who inserts 'held most'), but Bawcutt and Riddy leave this as line as a tetrameter, which is probably a mistake, as neither of the strophes that follow has a shorter fourth line.[15]

In this strophe Dunbar follows Chaucer in using running lines when paying courtly compliments. This enables him to deploy an average of three polysyllabic words per line, but the flow of those running lines is broken brutally (like the

[15] See Scott, 1967: 116 and Bawcutt and Riddy 1992: 175.

poet's heart) in the fifth line, which has lyric caesura. This line may be delivered (using Move X) to open with two consecutive trochees, or it may be delivered with the stress clash as I have scanned it. But in either case the line opens with a slap in the face that echoes the lady's rejection of the poet. The metrics of this strophe is equally merciless: no poet could have done more to make his form fit his content. The initial inversion of 'Richest' also offers a felicitous change of rhythm, and the three weak beats in five lines serve to soften the poem's implicit reproach. Dunbar brought the *dolce stil novo* to Scotland in this poem, and he did so with the elegance of Petrarch.

Gavin Douglas

Like Dunbar, Douglas was a graduate of St Andrews but, as the third son of an earl, he went on to study in Paris and achieved the high office that evaded his elder contemporary. Although two other surviving poems have been attributed to him, Douglas is best known for his translation of Virgil's *Aeneid*, which Ezra Pound greatly admired for its vigor.[16] Certainly, when Douglas describes a storm at sea, his readers can imagine themselves on board his ship. Tom Scott, however, described Douglas as "a scholar-poet" (like Virgil), "a man of intellect rather than genius," and "a great versifier rather than a great poet."[17] Douglas's learning embraced not only the Classical Languages but also the English poetry of his own and the preceding century; thus he described Chaucer as "sans peir," Gower as "moral," Lydgate as "a monk musing him alone," and Dunbar by the grudging "yit undeid."[18]

There can be little doubt that Douglas aspired to versify like Chaucer rather than Lydgate, but his poetry shares the latter's weakness for digression, literary references, and astrological detail. Douglas also employed alliteration, but usually gave only two, or at the most three words in any line the same onset. Almost all of Douglas's lines can be performed as iambic pentameters, but many modern readers need more than one attempt at choosing which inflections to syllabify before doing so. For example, the following lines (*Prologue to Book* VII, 63–66 and 77–78) require careful preparation before performance:[19]

---

[16] For the text of Douglas's translation of the *Aeneid*, see Kendal, 2011; for critical comment, see Pound, 1961: 115–23.

[17] See Scott, 1967: 180.

[18] The passage in Douglas's poem *The Palice of Honour* that describes these poets (II, xvii) is quoted by Scott 1967: 128.

[19] The quotations from Douglas's poem in this article are taken from Scott 1967: 128–34. In deference to Douglas's insistence that his language was Scottish, and not English, I append my translations to these quotations.

(33) The grond stud **bar**rant, // **wid**der^{i}t, dosk or gray,
(34) Herb^{i}s, flowr^{i}s, and **ger**sis // wal**lowyt** a**way**.
(35) **Wod**dis fo**rest**^{i}s, // with **na**kyt **be**wis blowt,
(36) Stude **strip**yt of thar weid // in **ev**^{e}ry howt.
(37) The **sil**ly scheip // and thar **li**til hyrd **gro**mys
(38) Lurk^{i}s **un**der le // of **ban**kis, wodd^{i}s, and **bro**mys

("The ground lay barren, deserted, dark or grey; herbs, flowers and grasses overgrew. Trees and shrubs, left with naked branches, stood stripped of their foliage in every wood. Both the dumb sheep and their lowly keepers huddle under the shelter of banks, trees, and bushes.")

Assuming para-phonology of plurals (like '**ban**kis' and 'wodd^{i}s') and past participles (like '**wid**der^{i}t' and '**strip**y't) makes these lines good iambic pentameters.

In some of Douglas's lines, however, he tempts the reader to sense triple time; for example, in lines 135–36 of the same Prologue; I give them as examples (39) and (40), with the triple-time alternatives in (39)a and (40)a:

(39) The dew **drop**pis // con**gel**^{i}**t** on stibb^{i}ll and rynd
(39)a The dew **drop**pis con**ge**lit // on **stib**bill and rynd
(40) And scharp hail**sta**nys // mortfun**deit** of kynd
(40)a And scharp hail**sta**nys // mort**fun**deit of kynd

(rynd: "margin"; mortfundeit: "benumbed")

As Scott points out, no English poet can paint winter in words as well as a Scots poet, and no Scots poet could do it better than Douglas, the first to call his language 'Scottish' (a term previously reserved for Gaelic).[20]

The English poets Surrey and Dorset, working later in the sixteenth century, probably knew Douglas's *Aeneid*, but whether it helped them on their way to the iambic pentameter is an open question.[21] Douglas was concerned to make his poem a national statement, and Scott argues that the Scottish language began to decline the moment it was named.[22] Many traces of it remain in the modern variety of English spoken in Scotland, the dialect of modern English that the people of England esteem most highly. It has carried much fine poetry over the centuries.

[20] For the Scottish language and its middle period (1424–1603), see Scott, 1967: 21–23, 186, and 191–203.

[21] For Surrey and Dorset, see Chapter 16.

[22] See Scott, 1967: 24.

Conclusion: The Chaucerians

To sum up the last two chapters, Gower eventually embraced the English language, and the iambic pentameter, but his line lacked a number of the subtler features of Chaucer's. He shunned the native license of headless lines and lines with epic caesura, and he employed almost no initial inversions. Nor did he boost the proportion of running or major lines in his verse in the way that Chaucer had in his later works. But Gower was faced with the same state of the English language as Chaucer and he used the same artifices, from elision to bracketing mismatches, to mold it into sequences of five iambs. Hoccleve attempted to do the same, and he succeeded in crafting lines of ten syllables, but his rhythms sometimes strayed from the iambic. For the next 100 years the versifiers of England and Scotland went their different ways.

The fifteenth century was the best of times and the worst of times for the English language. French was being rolled back in England as surely as the English armies were being rolled back in France, but the English language (like those armies) was in no state to sustain a conquest. It had to resolve some differences between individual deliveries before its poets could establish a new mode of versifying. In England, ME was in the last throes of schwa deletion and of deciding how to stress French loan words. Until these processes were complete poets could not predict how their lines would be delivered: the number of syllables in the line and the position of its stress peaks both varied from performance to performance. Lydgate found a solution to this problem, by reverting to the native mode of versifying, crafting half-lines and counting beats. For a century, the poets of England followed his practice and raised him in esteem to be Chaucer's equal, and since they delivered Chaucer's lines with fifteenth-century syllabification and accentuation, this did not seem unjust.

The Scots had lost most of their schwas much earlier, and so in Scotland what I have described as the modern Peninsular Portuguese enigma did not apply. The only barriers to five Scottish iambs were Move X and some wee inflections (*–is* and *–it*). Since the Move-X problem was of French making, Scots poets found a French solution: lyric caesura. And they left the wee inflections for the wits of Scottish performers to work out for themselves; they also gave them some alliterations to grind their teeth on as good as those in contemporary Scottish alliterative meters.

Scottish readers also knew that Sassenachs peppered their speech with word-final schwas, so they performed Chaucer's lines with such schwas to match those without them, which makes his verse even more regularly iambic. Some cheeky performers may even have used spurious schwas to heal the broken backs of Lydgate's lines. Thus it was that the iamb became Scottish currency while the English counted beats. Henryson and Douglas composed verse that was more rhythmically regular than that of their English contemporaries, but Dunbar was the poet who captured Chaucer's meter (as he caught many others) with all its subtleties. It would be more than half a century before England produced a versifier of his caliber.

The story of the late-medieval Scottish *makars* ends in 1513, when James I's great-grandson and the Scots lords perished, like flowers of the forest, on the battlefield of Flodden.[23] The last mention of Dunbar's name dates from that summer, and Douglas, who had just completed his *Aeneid*, chose that moment to lay down his pen. He then devoted himself to politics and the Church and, as exiled Bishop of Dunkeld, he died of the plague in London in 1522. Thereafter the development of Chaucer's meter lay mainly in English hands. The last of Chaucer's descendants had died in 1459, but in 1517, the English victor of Flodden, Thomas Howard, fathered a poet who would lead the way back to the iambic pentameter.[24]

---

[23] For the Battle of Flodden (or Flodden Field), see Davies, 1999: 375–79; the lament *Flowers of the Forest*, which commemorates Flodden, is the slow march of the Scots Guards.

[24] For the fate of Chaucer's descendants, see Pearsall, 1992: 276–84.

16
Epilogue

In 1513 John Skelton (b. ?1460–d. 1529), former tutor to the young King Henry VIII, was the most celebrated poet in England. Skelton was a scholar of international repute who did not wear his learning lightly; he was also a courtier who used his poetry to attack men and ideas that annoyed him.[1] His poetic reputation sank later in the sixteenth century and rose again only in the twentieth, when free verse accustomed readers to lines that contrasted rather than matching.[2] Skelton's metrics has therefore played a disproportionate role in the critical appreciation of his poetry.

Skelton's longer lines resemble Lydgate's in being based on beats and dividing readily into two units. They differ, however, in that the division is not always into 2 + 3 beats; in Skelton's long-line verse, either or both subdivisions may contain 3 beats; and, more rarely, both may contain 2 beats. Skelton's longer-line verse therefore includes balanced lines (2 + 2 and 3 + 3 beats) and unbalanced lines (2 + 3 and 3 + 2).[3] Since his lines also contain far fewer implied offbeats than Lydgate's, and far more double ones, Skelton's lines vary widely in length. There are also marked differences between Skelton's poems: thus almost all the lines of *The Bowge of Courte* (1498) have five beats, while those of *Speak Parrot* (1521) have between four and six. Because *Speak Parrot*'s lines also contain many more double offbeats, they are noticeably longer (up to fourteen syllables), and they include some lines that are in triple time throughout.[4]

Although the iambic pentameter was a not infrequent visitor to Skelton's verse, he did not allow it to outstay its welcome. He sought a variety of rhythms such as he found in Continental verse, and his 2- and 3-beat hemistichs and im-

[1] For Skelton's works, see Henderson, 1931; for a prime example of Skelton's flaunting his erudition, see the poem 'Speak Parrot.'

[2] For a modern critical evaluation, see Thwaite, 2008: vii–xviii; the quotations in these notes from *Speak Parrot* are taken from pages 64 to 84 of that volume.

[3] Lines of 3 + 3 beats include: 'That **peer**less pome**gra**nate, God save her **no**ble grace' ('Speak Parrot,' line 37); lines of 2 + 2 beats include: 'Ne **tro**po **san**no, ne **tro**po **ma**to' (tr. 'Not too sane and not too mad'; 'Speak Parrot,' line 63).

[4] Triple-time lines include: 'The red rose in **ho**nour to **flou**rish and spring' and 'Some be too **chur**lish, and some be too kind' ('Speak Parrot,' lines 35 & 77).

plied and double offbeats gave him just that. Skelton seems to have despaired of achieving regularity in English verse: English ears could count neither syllables nor moras, and English poets delighted in the coarser effects of rhyme and alliteration.[5] Skelton employed alliteration heavily, but not systematically, and he was an ingenious rhymester. He therefore gravitated towards a verse form that would maximize his talents, and it still bears his name, *Skeltonics*, today. Instead of combining 2- and 3- beat hemistichs, he promoted them to separate lines and rhymed them.

Skeltonics gave free rein to their inventor's love of variety: lines of different lengths and with different rhythms (or no rhythm) follow one another in a rush of rhyme. The rhymes are skilful and often funny, but they reject any scheme or order. When Skelton felt a rhyme coming he just let it out and lived with the consequences, which were often a change of direction in his meaning. Skelton's short-line meter is densely and unpredictably rhymed free verse.[6] Unfortunately, his century craved more order than Skelton's unruly ego could tolerate, and when his successors rediscovered the subtle ways of adding variety to regularity that Chaucer had pioneered, Skelton's innovations became a curiosity that nobody wanted to copy.

After Skelton's death in 1529 two poets, Sir Thomas Wyatt (b. 1503–d. 1542) and Henry Howard, Earl of Surrey (b. ?1517– d. 1547) took up the story of versifying in England. Both men travelled on the Continent, where they discovered the sonnet and Petrarchism, the *art de pétrarquiser*, which had spread from Rome to Paris and was the latest vogue.[7] Simultaneously (as far as we can tell), Wyatt and Surrey set to work on the first English sonnets, but their experience of the form had been different, and the meters in which they chose to compose their sonnets were equally so.[8] Surrey had been a hostage at the French royal court and knew the sonnets of Marot and Saint-Gelais; Wyatt, a career diplomat, had travelled more widely and encountered sonnets in Italy and Spain as well as France.[9] And, since Surrey was only twelve when Skelton died, Wyatt must also have had a better appreciation of the English laureate's verse.

---

[5] Skelton gave his opinion of English as a language in which to versify in the poem 'Philip Sparrow,' and he admitted that his short-lines were rhymed doggerel in the poem 'Colin Clout'; see Thwaite, 2008: x–xi and xiv.

[6] Robert Graves's poem about Skeltonics, in Skeltonics, is a great deal more regular in both rhythm and rhyme scheme than was Skelton's norm; see Thwaite, 2008: viii. For Skelton's list of great, but unlearned English poets, and for his own ingenious Latin versifying, see Graves, 1959: 34 and 95–96.

[7] For *l'art de pétrarquiser*, see Chapter 8, Note 63, above.

[8] See Duffell, 1991: 548–67 and 2008a: 119–23.

[9] Mellin de Saint-Gelais (b. 1487–d. 1558) and Clément Marot (b. 1497–d. 1554) introduced the sonnet into French in the 1530s; Garcilaso de la Vega (b. 1501–d. 1536) and Juan Boscán (b. ?1492–d. 1542) composed the first Spanish sonnets in the same de-

Wyatt's longer-line meter has puzzled modern critics: about 60 percent of his lines are decasyllabic and iambic, and this is in contrast to his shorter lines, most of which are impeccable iambic tetrameters.[10] One of his editors, Rebholz, described Wyatt's longer line as a *flexible pentameter*, which is an alternative term to Tarlinskaja's *five-ictic dolnik* or Fabb and Halle's *loose iambic pentameter*.[11] But this term does not cover lines with four and six beats, which form a conspicuous minority in Wyatt's sonnets. In fact, Wyatt followed Skelton in including balanced lines (of 2 + 2 and 3 + 3 beats) among his pentameters (of 2 + 3 and 3 + 2).[12] Also like Skelton, he included many triple-time half lines, as well as giving some lines irregular rhythms. As his iambic tetrameters demonstrate, the syllabic and rhythmic irregularity of Wyatt's longer lines was a conscious aesthetic choice. While the iambic pentameter was his favorite longer line, he wanted far greater variety in his lines; he found a mixture of rhythms both in Skelton, and in the Italian *endecasillabo*, and he found them pleasing. Wyatt was not ready to settle for the subtle sources of variety that Chaucer had developed, but which Lydgate and Skelton had drowned out with louder and more violent contrasts between lines.

Surrey encountered the sonnet in French, where it had acquired a rhymed couplet in its rhyme scheme, and French poets composed their sonnets in canonical *décasyllabes* of 4 + 6 syllables with just two phrasal stresses.[13] Surrey was far more devoted to the iamb than Wyatt, and so he composed his English sonnets largely in iambic *décasyllabes*: almost all his lines observe both the constraints of that meter and are also iambic.[14] Surrey's lines are not all iambic throughout, because he employed lyric caesura, and they are not entirely canonical *décasyllabes*, because 4 percent of them violate the WB constraint (the same percentage as in Froissart's *OA*). Surrey's design of two iambs separated by a word boundary from three more, a standardized pausing line, had a weakness: it made it difficult to employ trochaic disyllables, which are by far the most common polysyllabic words in English, mid-line; and so Surrey's sonnets are among the most monosyllabic poems in the English language. Only very occasionally did he remedy this weakness by including a running line.

---

cade, but they were not published until after Boscán's death. Wyatt visited Italy in 1527, where he may have encountered Pietro Bembo (b. 1470–d. 1547), the first exponent of *l'art de pétrarquiser*.

[10] For examples of Wyatt's strict iambic tetrameters, see his epigram on 'Anna' (Poem LIV), in Rebholz 1978: 96.

[11] Rebholz 1978: 44–55.

[12] By my calculation 59 percent of Wyatt's longer lines contain exactly 10M/F syllables, 19 percent contain fewer, and 21 percent contain more (see Duffell, 2008a: 120). For Wyatt's 'balanced' lines, see Endicott, 1963: 62–72.

[13] For the verse design of the earliest French sonnets, see Jasinski, 1970: 50.

[14] For Surrey's sonnets see Keene, 1985: 40–43, 51, and 59–60.

Surrey was well aware of the difference between Wyatt's longer-line meter and his own, because he parodied Wyatt's meter in a poem dedicated to his friend and versifying rival.[15] Surrey also seems to have wearied of the relentless subdivision into 2 + 3 beats, and of the monotonous monosyllables that resulted, because when he came to render two books of Virgil's *Aeneid* into English he employed a far higher proportion of both polysyllables and running lines.[16] He also made the bold decision that the iambic accentual feet of his poem represented sufficient regularity, and he followed Virgil in dispensing with rhyme. The result was the smoothest and most attractive long line Surrey ever produced (and he had experimented with more than one).[17] Surrey's *Aeneid* has only about a third of the proportion of running lines that we find in Chaucer's *GP*, but the father of English poetry's metrical artistry was on its way back. When the invention of blank verse and the English sonnet form are taken into account, Surrey emerges as a major figure in the history of English metrics.

Wyatt died of overwork in his royal master's service in 1542, but the king's second and most glamorous wife seems to have been among the poet's compensations.[18] Surrey was beheaded in 1547 for being a descendant of Edward the Confessor while his monarch was the son of a usurper with no such pedigree. In the thirty years that followed England's poets tried to versify like Surrey with varying success. The best versifier among them was another aristocrat, Thomas Sackville, later Earl of Dorset (b. 1536–d. 1608); his "Induction" and "The Complaynt of Henry Duke of Buckingham" in the 1563 version of *The Mirror for Magistrates* contain some of the best iambic pentameters since Dunbar's.[19] The frequency with which Sackville used running lines in these poems is comparable with Surrey's practice in his *Aeneid* rather than that in his sonnets.

Sackville was even more metrically innovative when he wrote for the stage: in 1562 the play *Gorboduc*, his collaboration with Thomas Norton (b. 1532–d. 1584), was performed before the queen, and it initiated a craze for drama that could entertain both the high and low in the land.[20] These two playwrights realized that Surrey's blank verse was the meter that came closest to normal English speech and was the best medium for dramatic dialogue. They also recognized

[15] See Poem 24, in Keene 1985: 58–59.

[16] For the pentameters of Surrey's translation of Virgil's *Aeneid*, see Keene, 1985: 2–39

[17] For his use of *poulter's measure* (iambic couplets with lines alternating 12 and 14 syllables), see Poems 15 and 21–23, in Keene 1985: 45–47 and 50–57.

[18] For two unmistakable references to Ann Boleyn, see Poems XI and LXXX, in Rebholz 1978: 77 and 116.

[19] For The *Mirror for Magistrates*, see Campbell, 1938. Saintsbury, with his prejudice against the Scots and anything he regarded as foreign, describes Dorset's two poems as 'the finest piece of versification in English between Chaucer and Spenser' (1906: I, 333).

[20] For the text of *Gorboduc* see Tydeman, 1992.

that running lines were important for carrying the sort of vocabulary their more elevated characters would use, and so running lines reach 30 percent of total in both parts of the play, that attributed to Sackville and that attributed to Norton.[21]

Later playwrights modified this dramatic pentameter further to make it even more like normal speech: they included feminine lines as well as masculine; they increased the amount of enjambment and inversion; they included trisyllabic substitutions (double offbeats); and they raised the proportion of running lines to around 36 percent. Christopher Marlowe (b. 1564–d. 1593) took the first steps in all these directions; William Shakespeare (b. 1564–d. 1616) took the process to its artistic peak; and, finally, John Webster (b. ?1578–d. ?1532) crafted lines so like normal speech (or prose) that he was forced to retreat in the direction of the strict iambic pentameter.[22] When T.S. Eliot revived Webster's mode of versifying in the twentieth century, however, there was no retreat, and free verse resulted.[23]

Away from the theater, two highly educated Elizabethan poets were also working their way towards Chaucer's meter with all its refinements. Sir Philip Sidney (b. 1554–d. 1586) and Edmund Spenser (b. 1552–d. 1599) were friends who, like Chaucer and Gower, differed in that one had spent time in Italy while the other had not. Sidney therefore knew what Petrarch and Tasso had accomplished in the *endecasillabo*, while Spenser had assiduously mastered every type of English meter. Both were also aware that Du Bellay and Ronsard had moved from *décasyllabe* to *alexandrin* in their sonnets.[24] Thus when Sidney composed *Astrophel and Stella* c. 1580 and Spenser composed *The Faerie Queene* they included both iambic pentameters and hexameters.[25] The shorter line proved a better vehicle for English verse because of its potential for rhythmic variety (2 + 3 or 3 + 2 beats, versus the alexandrine's relentless 3 + 3). Hence, Sidney composed only a few sonnets in the longer line before abandoning it, and Spenser relegated the alexandrine to the close of his *Spenserian stanzas*.

Sidney, impressed by the uniform 10F formula of the *endecasillabo*, gave his pentameters exactly10M lines, but by 1595, when Spenser's sonnets in the *Amoretti* were published, the feminine line was established as an alternative.[26] The practice of playwrights like Shakespeare, no doubt, played a part in this,

---

[21] See Duffell, 2008a: 141–42.

[22] See Lucas, 1927: IV, 250–60.

[23] See Duffell, 2012: passim.

[24] Sidney travelled on the Continent between 1572 and 1575, visiting both Paris and Venice (where he spent a whole year); see Drabble, 1985: 902.

[25] For Sidney's alexandrines in *Astrophel and Stella*, see his Poems I, VI, and VIII, in Bullett 1947: 173–76. The final line in each stanza of Spenser's *Fairie Queene* is an alexandrine; see Hamilton, 1966: 78–547.

[26] For feminine rhymes in Spenser's *Amoretti*, see Sonnets II, V, and IX, in McCabe 1999: 388–92.

but influence also flowed in the opposite direction: when Shakespeare came to compose sonnets he made their lines the strict iambic pentameters of Sidney and Spenser, far different from the meter of his plays.[27] Although John Donne (b. 1572–d. 1631; an actor manqué who had his picture painted in shroud and coffin) tried to inject some of the dramatic pentameter's irregularities into his erotic and religious poetry, Chaucer's meter, with its position size of one syllable, became the canon.[28] Until the advent of free verse the strict iambic pentameter's standing remained unassailable, and generation after generation of poets cultivated its subtle mixture of regularity and variety.

Meanwhile, what of its inventor? By the end of the sixteenth century Chaucer's lines, pronounced without word-final schwas or French stress assignments, seemed rough and irregular, not only compared with Sidney and Spenser, but even with Wyatt and Surrey. Perhaps fortunately, rising literacy reduced the number of occasions in which Chaucer's verse was read aloud and his work was left more and more to specialists. In 1598 Thomas Speght produced the first edition of Chaucer's works to tackle the problem of language change when he included a glossary for general readers.[29] It was 1775 however before another editor, Thomas Tyrwhitt, focused attention on Chaucer's meter. Tyrwhitt, who saw the Italian *endecasillabo* as Chaucer's model, concluded that Chaucer had counted syllables, but Tyrwhitt vacillated between ten and eleven as the intended number, and lines of other lengths he attributed to faulty copying. [30]

In 1863 the American scholar Francis Child revived Tyrwhitt's hypothesis and presented it more cogently.[31] Child argued that Chaucer syllabified word-final schwas unless he could elide them in the French fashion, that his lines were intended to contain ten syllables to their final stress, and that they were predominantly iambic. This hypothesis placed the Father of English poetry at the head of a glorious tradition, linking his verse craft with that of Shakespeare, Milton, and all England's other great poets. One by one, the big names of Victorian and Edwardian literary criticism confirmed their support for Child's view: Walter Skeat in 1872, Bernhard ten Brink in 1882 and 1901, and George Saintsbury in 1906. That Chaucer's longer line was based upon ten syllables and five stresses became the orthodoxy of the twentieth century. Subsequent editors, however, tended to

[27] For the differences between Shakespeare's two pentameter styles, see Duffell, 2008a: 131–35, 142–44, and 240–43

[28] Donne's most irregular poems are his *Satires*; see Smith, 1971: 155–75.

[29] For Speght's editions, see Brewer, 1969, which includes supplementary material from the editions of 1542–1602.

[30] The oldest copy of Tyrwhitt's work dates from 1798; the text is more easily available in the USA as Tyrrwhitt 1973.

[31] See Child, 1863. For European support for Child's hypothesis, see ten Brink 1893 (first published in German in 1877).

minimize discussion of Chaucer's meter, and left deeper discussion of the subject to specialists.[32]

There was much to discuss because, while the hypothesis of Tyrwhitt and Child regularized the great majority of Chaucer's lines, it failed to account for a sizeable minority. The irregular lines raised a number of issues: some were linguistic (they concerned stress and syllabification in Chaucer's ME); others involved the problem of transmission (there were a vast number of manuscripts and variant readings); and still others were stylistic (every poet composes lines that deviate from the norm). In the first half of the twentieth century most critics worked on these problems while remaining within the orthodoxy, but in the second half an alternative hypothesis, which came to be known as *the four-beat heresy,* arose to challenge that of Tyrwhitt and Child.

The arch-heretic was the English scholar James Southworth, who in 1957 argued that Chaucer's longer lines were not iambic decasyllables but "verses of cadence": by this he meant that word-final schwas were irrelevant and that Chaucer was simply counting beats and allowing the intervals between them to vary.[33] The most controversial part of his proposal, however, was that Chaucer was counting the traditional English four beats, not five. Southworth thus reclaimed Chaucer's longer lines from Schipper's category "foreign," and placed them firmly among "native meters."[34] In 1962 Southworth published a second volume supporting his hypothesis, and Ian Robinson enlarged on it further in 1971.[35] Most scholars in the USA, however, were sceptical of the four-beat heresy, and a spirited exchange of views followed, with Southworth steadily losing ground.[36]

At the root of Southworth's hypothesis was his misunderstanding of the nature of English stress: we now know it to be hierarchical, which means that

---

32 Thus Norman Davis covers versification in a little over two pages in Benson 1988. Davis's account is commendably concise but contains inaccuracies: Chaucer's longer line is not 'a line of five stresses' (see the discussion of weak beats in Chapters 10 and 11 above); the French *décasyllabe* did not 'suggest ten syllables,' but four plus six syllables, and only two stresses (which is why English poets up to and including Chaucer ignored its suggestions; see Chapter 9 above); Chaucer's line 'lacks a caesura' only according to the French definition (according to the Italian definition it has a *cesura mobile*; see Chapter 8 above); an epic caesura involves not 'a light syllable before a natural pause,' but a post-tonic syllable before a colon boundary (see Chapters 6, 11, and 12 above).

33 See Southworth, 1957.

34 See Schipper, 1910: 126–50 and Lewis 1898: passim.

35 See Southworth, 1962 and Robinson 1971. Robinson argued that the English tradition of counting beats, not syllables continued uninterrupted between *Beowulf* and Wyatt.

36 For the argument against the 'four-beat heresy,' see Donaldson, 1948 and 1974.

among any five stress peaks one will be stronger and another weaker than the others.[37] The first line of Keats's *Endymion* demonstrates this:[38]

```
                      5
      2          4    x
  1   x          x    x
  x   x      3   x    x
x x x x x    x x x  x x x
A thing of beauty    is a joy forever
```

One possible delivery of this line demotes the minor peak of stress marked 3 so that it becomes part of a (trisyllabic) offbeat; the line is then a "verse of cadence" with four beats. A similar delivery could be imposed on all of Keats's' lines, but this would have nothing to do with the poet's verse design; Southworth's proposal for Chaucer's verse design is therefore no more than a description of one individual's performance—Southworth's own.

In 1972, M. L. Samuels pointed out that the problem of whether Chaucer counted unelided word-final schwas was easily resolvable: if those schwas counted as syllables there would be an inverse correlation between their number and the number of other syllables in the line.[39] It was almost twenty years before anyone checked this out on a large corpus of lines. In 1990 Nicholas and Charles Barber were able to bring a computer to the task, and they proved that there was, indeed, a very strong inverse correlation.[40] A year later their analysis yielded more valuable information: for example, that in some words, like *come* and *oure*, the final *-e* was habitually deleted (thus *com* and *our* were probably Chaucer's doublets rather than scribal errors); they also showed that in another list of words Chaucer sometimes counted the final *-e* and sometimes did not.[41] The Barbers' research convinced most modern critics that Chaucer's metrical intention was basically decasyllabic, and subsequent research, such as that of Youmans and Li, has confirmed that it was also predominantly iambic.[42]

Any description of Chaucer's longer-line as basically decasyllabic and predominantly iambic is, however, a gross simplification. In this volume I have tried to demonstrate that, although five iambs were a radical departure from what went before, they were only part of the story of Chaucer's verse art. Chaucer's versifying was unique in the context of medieval European poetry: he absorbed influences from many quarters; and he gauged the strengths, weaknesses, and fit

[37] See Hayes, 1995: 26–45, discussed in Chapter 2.

[38] For *Endymion*, see Stillinger, 1978: 103–220.

[39] See Samuels, 1972.

[40] See Barber and Barber 1990.

[41] See Barber and Barber 1991.

[42] See Youmans & Li 2002: 156–57, discussed in detail in Chapter 10.

for Middle English of a variety of techniques of verse craft. I have attempted to unravel the linguistic, transmission, and stylistic factors in Chaucer's metrical irregularities, but the elements of his versifying that have stood the test of time are his regularities, and his recognition that some sources of rhythmic variety are required in a regular metre.

Chaucer cultivated variety, in many forms, in order to balance the excessive regularity of the new meter he invented. It was unlike the other meters of Europe in that both syllable and accent marched to its drum, but the music of Chaucer's lines is subtler than drumbeats. He never abandoned the headless line with its riffle of trochees (although he didn't indulge it to excess, like Milton in *L'Allegro*); he also used inversion sparingly (in this respect avoiding the excesses of Keats); and he did not banish the double and implied offbeat entirely to Lydgateland. Chaucer learned to seek out weak beats so as to throw their neighbours into higher relief (if not quite as often as Milton in *Paradise Lost*). He wielded monosyllables appropriately (if less dramatically than Shakespeare at the sonnet's finale), and he entertained a convivial mixture of masculine and feminine rhymes (unlike Sidney, when he rediscovered Chaucer's metre). Additionally, Chaucer made his lines run or pause, and varied their mid-line stress peaks between early and late, as skillfully as did the greatest poets who followed him. There was great variety in Chaucer's variety, and his readers should take pleasure in it.

The *Rig Veda* sings that all meters were created at the same moment as the universe.[43] Thus five iambs were waiting for us among the stars, but it was Geoffrey Chaucer who first caught them in a net and brought them down to earth.

[43] For the *Rig Veda*, X. xc. 9, see Zaehner, 1966: 9.

Works Cited

Adams, John Quincy, 1840, "Defence of the *Amistad*'s Captives before the US Supreme Court," ID 294, at www.digitalhistory@uh.edu.

Aelfric, see Skeat, Walter W; also: http:archive.org/stream/aelfricslivesofs01aelfuoft.

Afonso o Sábio, see Mettmann, Walter.

Aitchison, Jean, 1978. *Linguistics* (London: Teach Yourself).

Alexander, Peter, ed., 1958. *William Shakespeare: The Complete Works*, 4 vols (London: Collins).

Alkire, Ti, and Carol Rosen, 2010. *Romance Languages: A Historical Introduction* (Cambridge: Cambridge Univ. Press).

Allen, Rosamund, 1992. "Introduction," in *Lawman: Brut*, trans. Rosamund Allen (London: J. M. Dent), xiii-xxxvi.

Allen, Rosamund, 2002. " 'Nv Seið mid Loft-Songe': A Reappraisal of Lawman's Verse Form," in *Laȝamon: Contexts, Language, and Interpretation*, ed. Rosamund Allen et al. (London: Kings College London Centre for Late Antique and Medieval Studies), 251–79.

Allen, W. Sidney, 1973. *Accent and Rhythm: Prosodic Features of Latin and Greek: A Study in Theory and Reconstruction* (Cambridge: Cambridge Univ. Press).

Allott, Stephen, 1974. *Alcuin of York: His Life and Letters* (York: Sessions).

Alonso, Damaso, 1958. "Elogio del endecasílabo," in his *De los siglos oscuros al de Oro: notas y artículos a través de 700 años de letras españolas* (Madrid: Gredos), 178–82.

Alphonso-Karkala, J. B., ed., 1971. *An Anthology of Indian Literature* (Harmondsworth: Penguin Books).

Amours, F. J., ed., 1897. *Scottish Alliterative Poetry in Rhyming Stanzas* (Edinburgh: Blackwood).

Andrew, Malcolm, and Ronald Waldron, ed., 1987. *The Poems of the Pearl Manuscript: Pearl, Cleanness, Patience, and Sir Gawain and the Green Knight* (Exeter: Univ. of Exeter).

Armstrong, E. C., et al., ed., 1937. *The Medieval French "Roman d'Alexandre,"* II, *Version of Alexandre de Paris: Text* (Princeton: Princeton Univ. Press).

Aroui, Jean-Louis, and Andy Arloe, ed., 2009. *Towards a Typology of Poetic Forms: From Language to Metrics and Beyond*, Proceedings of a Conference held in Paris, April 2005 (Amsterdam: John Benjamins).

Aspin, Isabel S. T., ed., 1953. *Anglo-Norman Political Songs* (Oxford: Blackwell).
Aspland, C. W., ed., 1979. *A Medieval French Reader* (Oxford: Clarendon Press).
Attridge, Derek, 1974. *Well Weighed Syllables: Elizabethan Verse in Classical Metres* (Cambridge: Cambridge Univ. Press).
Attridge, Derek, 1982. *The Rhythms of English Poetry* (London: Longman).
Attridge, Derek, 2013. *Moving Words: Forms of English Poetry* (Oxford: Oxford Univ. Press).
Auden, W. H., 1966. *Collected Shorter Poems, 1927–1957* (London: Faber and Faber).
Avalle, D'Arco Silvio, 1963. *Preistoria dell' endecasillabo* (Milan: Ricciardi).
Avalle, D'Arco Silvio, ed., 1960. *Peire Vidal, Poesie*, 2 vols (Milan: Ricciardi).
Ayres, Pam, 2008. *The Works: The Classic Collection* (London: BBC Books).
Baehr, Rudolf, 1970. *Manual de versificación española* (Madrid: Gredos).
Barber, Charles, 1993. *The English Language: A Historical Introduction* (Cambridge: Cambridge Univ. Press).
Barber, Nicholas, and Charles Barber, 1990–91. "The Versification of the *Canterbury Tales*: A Computer-Based Statistical Study," *Leeds Studies in English*, 21: 81–103 and 22: 57–84.
Barbour, John, see Gray, J. M.
Bawcutt, Priscilla, and Felicity Riddy, ed., 1992. *Selected Poems of Henryson and Dunbar* (Edinburgh: Scottish Academic Press).
Beadle, Richard, and Pamela King, ed., 1984. *York Mystery Plays: A Selection in Modern Spelling* (Oxford: Clarendon Press).
Beare, William, 1957. *Latin Verse and European Song: A Study in Accent and Rhythm* (London: Methuen).
Bede, see Rowley, Sharon M.
Behaghel, Otto, see Best, Karl-Heinz.
Bembo, Pietro, see Dionisotti, Carlo.
Bennett, J. A. W., see Gray, Douglas.
Benson, Larry E., ed., 1988. *The Riverside Chaucer* (Oxford: Oxford Univ. Press); first published by Houghton and Mifflin in 1987.
Beowulf, see Wrenn, C. L.
Berardinelli, Cleonice, ed., 1990. *Poemas de Álvaro de Campos* (Lisbon: Imprensa Nacional-Casa de Moeda).
Bernhart, Sarah, 1907. *Ma double vie: mémoires de Sarah Bernhardt* (Paris: Champion et Farquelle).
Bertinetto, Pier Marco, 1981. *Strutture prosodiche dell'italiano* (Florence: L'Accademia della Crusca).
Best, Karl-Heinz, 2007. "Otto Behaghel (1854–1936)," *Glottometrics*, 14: 110–42.
Billy, Dominique, 1992. "L'analyse distributionelle des césures dans la lyrique française et occitane du moyen âge," in *Contacts de langues, de civilizations et intertextulaité* (Montpellier: Institut d'Études occitanes), 805–28.

Billy, Dominique, 1999. "Le Décasyllabe rénové de Jean Froisart," *Romania*, 117: 507–54.

Billy, Dominique, and Martin J. Duffell, 2005. "Le Décasyllabe de John Gower ou le dernier mètre anglo-normand," *Revue de Linguistique Romane*, 69: 73–95.

Birrell, Anne, 2004. *Games Poets Play: Readings in Medieval Chinese Poetry* (Cambridge: McGuinness China Monographs).

Boccaccio, Giovanni, see Rossi, Aldo, Windeatt, B. A., and Wallace, David.

Boecis, see Lavaud, René.

Bonghi, Giuseppe, ed., *Ritmo cassinese*, at: http://www.classitaliani.it;

Boni, Marco, ed. 1954. *Sordello: Le Poesie* (Bologna: Il Mulino).

Bownas, Geoffrey, 1964. "Background of Language and Prosody," in *The Penguin Book of Japanese Verse*, ed. and trans. Geoffrey Bownas and Anthony Thwaite (Harmondsworth: Penguin Books), xxxix-lvii.

Bowra, Maurice, 1963. *Primitive Song*, (New York and London: Mentor Books).

Brewer, D. S., ed., 1969. *Thomas Speght: Geoffrey Chaucer: The Works 1532*, facsimile (London: Scolar Press); this volume includes supplementary material from the editions of 1542–1602.

Bridges, Robert S., 1921. *Milton's Prosody, with a Chapter on Accentual Verse and Notes*, revised final edition (Oxford: Clarendon Press).

Brink, Bernhard ten, 1893. *History of English Literature* (London: Bell); first published in German (Berlin, 1877).

Brittain, F., ed., 1937. *The Medieval Latin and Romance Lyric to AD 1300* (Cambridge: Cambridge Univ. Press).

Browning, Robert, see Jack, Ian; also recording at: www.poetryarchive.org/poetryarchive/singlepoet.

Bullett, Gerald, ed., 1947. *Silver Poets of the Sixteenth Century* (London: J. M. Dent & Sons; New York: E. P. Dutton & Co.).

Burge, J., 2001. *Medieval Numerology* (London: Institute of Materials).

Burger, Michel, 1957. *Recherches sur la structure et l'origine des vers romans* (Geneva: Droz).

Burling, R, 1966. "The Metrics of Children's Verse: A Cross-Linguistic Study," *American Anthropologist*, 68.6: 1418–41.

Cable, Thomas M., 1974. *The Meter and Melody of "Beowulf"* (Urbana: Univ. of Illinois Press).

Cable, Thomas M., 2002. "A Rejoinder to Youmans and Li," in Minkova and Stockwell 2002: 177–82.

Cabré, Miriam, 1999. "Italian and Catalan Troubadours," in Gaunt and Kay, 1999: 127–40.

Cædmon, see Mitchell, Bruce.

Campbell, Lily B., ed., 1938. *The Mirror for Magistrates* (Cambridge: Cambridge Univ. Press).

Campos, Alvaro de, see Berardinelli, Clarice.

Casas Homs, José María, ed., 1956. *"Torçimany" de Luis de Averçó: tratado retórico gramatical y diccioniaro de rimas, siglos* XIV–XV, 2 vols (Barcelona: CSIC) .
Cavalcanti, Guido, see Cirigliano, Marc.
Champion, Pierre, ed., 1907. *Le manuscript autographe des poesies de Charles d'Orléans* (Paris: Honoré Champion).
Chant sur la mort de Guillaume le Conquérant, see Du Méril, Edélestand.
Charles d'Orleans, see Champion, Pierrre, Steele, Robert, and Purcell, Sally.
Chatman, Seymour, 1965. *A Theory of Meter* (The Hague: Mouton).
Chaucer, see Benson 1988, Brewer 1969, Lloyd Morgan 2003, Windeatt 1984, and Manly and Rickart 1940.
Chaucer Studio, see Thomas 2013.
Child, Francis J., 1863. "Observations on the Language of Chaucer (Based on Wright's Edition of the *Canterbury Tales*)," *Memoirs of the American Academy of Arts and Sciences*, NS, 8: 445–502 and 9: 265–314.
Chomsky, Noam, 1957. *Syntactic Structures* (The Hague: Mouton).
Cirigliano, Marc, ed. and trans., 1992. *Guido Cavalcanti: Complete Poems* (New York: Italica Press).
Clarke, Dorothy Clotelle, 1964. *Morphology of Fifteenth Century Castilian Verse* (Pittsburgh, PA: Duquesne Univ. Press).
Cole, Thomas, 1969. "The Saturnian Verse," *Yale Classical Studies*, 21: 1–73.
Contini, Gianfranco, ed., 1960. *Poeti del Duecento* (Naples: Ricciardi).
Contini, Gianfranco, 1972. "Equivalenza e permutabilità delle basi metriche nella poesia del Duecento," in *La métrica*, ed. Renzo Cremante and Mario Pazzaglia (Bologna: Il Mulino), 247–56.
Cornulier, Benoît de, 1995. *L'Art poétique: notions et problèmes de métrique* (Lyons: Presses Universitaires de Lyon).
Cressman, R. R., 1986. "Gower's *Cinkant Balades* and French Court Lyrics," PhD thesis, Univ. of N. Carolina at Chapel Hill.
Crystal, David, 1985. *A Dictionary of Linguistics and Phonetics* (Oxford: Blackwell with André Deutsch).
Crystal, David, 2004. *The Stories of English* (London: Allen Lane).
Crystal, David, 2012. *Spell It Out: The Singular Story of English Spelling* (London: Profile Books).
Cuddon, J. A., 1977. *A Dictionary of Literary Terms* (Harmondsworth: Penguin).
Dane, Joseph, 2009. "Towards a Description of Chaucer's Verse Forms," *Studia Neophilologica*, 81: 45–52.
Dante Alighieri, see Petrocchi, Giorgio.
Davau, Maurice, Marcel Cohen, and Maurice Lallemand, 1972. *Dictionnaire du Francais vivant* (London: Harrap).
Davenport, W.A., 2000. "Ballades French, English, and Chaucer's Scarcity of Rhyme," in Kennedy 2000a: 181–201.
Davies, Norman, 1996. *Europe: A History* (Oxford: Oxford Univ. Press).
Davies, Norman, 1999. *The Isles: A History* (London: Macmillan).

Davis Norman, 1988. "Language and Versification," in Benson 1988: xxv-xli.

Davis, Norman, et al., ed. 1979. *A Chaucer Glossary* (Oxford: Clarendon Press).

Dean, James, 1991. "Gower, Chaucer, and Rhyme Royal," *Studies in Philosophy*, 88: 251–75.

Defoe, Daniel, see Landa, Louis.

Dell, Francis, and John Halle, 2009. "Comparing Musical Settings in French and English Songs," in Aroui and Arloe 2009: 63–78.

Dembowski, P. F., ed., 1986. *Jean Froissart: Le Paradis d'amor, L'Orloge amoureus* (Geneva: Droz).

Des Périers, Bonaventure, *Oeuvres recueils*, at: www2.lib.Virginia.edu/rmds/portfolio/gordon/literary/desperiers.

Deyermond, Alan, 2004. *The "Libro de Buen Amor" in England: A Tribute to Gerald Gybbon-Moneypenny* (Manchester: Manchester Spanish and Portuguese Studies).

Dictionnaire du Francais vivant, see Davau, Maurice.

Dionisotti, Carlo, ed., 1966. *Pietro Bembo: Prose, Rime* (Turin: Unione Tipografico Editrice Torinese).

Domínguez Caparrós, José, 2001. *Diccionario de la métrica* (Madrid: Alianza).

Donaldson, E. Talbot, 1948. "Chaucer's Final –e," *PMLA*, 63: 1101–24.

Donaldson, E. Talbot, 1974. "The Manuscripts of Chaucer's Works and Their Use," in *Writers and their Backgrounds: Geoffrey Chaucer*, ed. Derek Brewer (London: Bell), 85–108.

Donne, John, see Smith, A. J.

Dorsten, J. van, ed., 1966. *Sir Philip Sidney: A Defence of Poetry* (Oxford: Oxford Univ. Press).

Douglas, Gavin, see Kendal, Gordon, and Scott, Tom.

Drabble, Margaret, ed, 1985. *The Oxford Companion to English Literature* (Oxford: Oxford Univ. Press).

Dragonetti, Roger, 1960. *La Technique poétique des trouvères dans la chanson coutoise* (Bruges: De Tempel).

Dryden, John, see Hammond, Paul.

Du Méril, Edélestand, ed., 1843. *Poésies populaires latines antérieures au douzième siècle* (Paris: Brockhaus and Avenarius).

Duffell, Martin J., 1991. "The Romance (Hen-) decasyllable: An Exercise in Comparative Metrics," PhD thesis, Univ. of London.

Duffell, Martin J., 1999. "Accentual Regularity in the *Sainte Eulalie*," *Rivista di Studi Testuali*, NS, 1: 81–107.

Duffell, Martin J., 2000. "Lydgate's Metrical Inventiveness and His Debt to Chaucer," in Kennedy 2000a: 227–49.

Duffell, Martin J., 2002a. "Old Words for New Ideas in Metrics," review article, *Hispanic Research Journal*, 3: 175–79.

Duffell, Martin J., 2002b. "The Italian Line in English after Chaucer," *Language and Literature*, 11: 295–305.

Duffell, Martin J., 2003. "French Symmetry, Germanic Rhythm, and Spanish Metre," in *Chaucer and the Challenges of Medievalism: Studies on Honor of H. A. Kelly*, ed. Donka Minkova and Theresa Tinkle (Bern: Peter Lang), 105–27.

Duffell, Martin J., 2004. "The Typology and Origin of Accentual Verse," *Rhythmica*, 2: 67–86.

Duffell, Martin J., 2005. "Some Phonological Features of Insular French: A Reconstruction," in *Studies on Ibero-Romance Linguistics Dedicated to Ralph Penny*, ed. Roger Wright and Peter Ricketts (Newark: Juan de la Cuesta), 103–25.

Duffell, Martin J., 2007. *Syllable and Accent: Studies on Medieval Hispanic Metrics* (London: Queen Mary, University of London).

Duffell, Martin J., 2008a. *A New History of English Metre* (London: Maney and Modern Humanities Research Association).

Duffell, Martin J., 2008b. "Some Observations on English Binary Metres," *Language and Literature*, 17: 5–20.

Duffell, Martin J., 2010. "The Principles of Free Verse in English," *Rhythmica*, 8: 7–36.

Duffell, Martin J., 2012. "Design and Rhythm in T. S. Eliot's *The Waste Land*," *Rhythmica*, 10: 45–76.

Duffell, Martin J., 2014. "Chaucer's Pentameter: Linguistics, Statistics, and History," *Chaucer Review*, 49:135–60.

Duffell, Martin J., and Dominique Billy, 2003–04. "From Decasyllable to Pentameter: Gower's Contribution to English Metrics," *Chaucer Review*, 38: 383–401.

Duggan, Hoyt N., 1986. "The Shape of the B-Verse in Middle English Alliterative Poetry," *Speculum*, 61.3: 564–92.

Duggan, Hoyt N., 1996. "Libertine Scribes and Maidenly Editors: Meditations on Textual Criticism and Metrics," in McCully and Anderson 1996: 29–37.

Duggan, Hoyt N., and Thorlac Turville Petre, ed., 1989. *The Wars of Alexander* (Oxford: Oxford Univ. Press).

Dunbar, William, see Mackenzie, Mackay, and Bawcutt, Priscilla.

Edwards, Robert R., ed., 1998. *John Lydgate: Troy Book* (Kalamazoo, MI: Medieval Institute Publications).

Einhorn, E., 1974. *Old French: A Concise Handbook* (Cambridge: Cambridge Univ. Press).

Elcock, W. D., 1960. *The Romance Languages* (London: Faber and Faber).

Ellesmere manuscript (San Marino, CA: Huntington Library, MS EL. 26. C. 9), see Manly, John Matthews, and Edith Rickart.

Elwert, W. Th., 1973. *Versificazione italiana dalle origini ai giorni nostri* (Florence: Le Monnier).

Endicott, Annabel M., 1963. "A Critical Study of the Metrical Effects in the Poetry of Sir Thomas Wyatt, with Reference to Analogous Effects in Elizabethan Poetry," MA diss., Univ. of London.

Epstein, Edmund L., and Terence Hawkes, 1959. *Linguistics and English Prosody* (Buffalo: Univ. of Buffalo; now NY State Univ.).

Ewert, Alfred, 1943. *The French Language*, (London: Faber and Faber).

Fabb, Nigel, 2001. "Weak Monosyllables in Iambic Pentameter Verse and the Communication of Metrical Form," *Lingua*, 111: 771–90.

Fabb, Nigel, 2002. *Language and Literary Structure: The Linguistic Analysis of Form in Verse and Narrative* (Cambridge: Cambridge Univ. Press).

Fabb, Nigel, and Morris Halle, 2008. *Meter in Poetry: A New Theory* (Cambridge: Cambridge Univ. Press).

Fagundas Duarte, Luiz, ed., 1994. *Poemas de Ricardo Reis* (Lisbon: Imprensa Nacional-Casa de Moeda).

Farren, Martin, ed., 2008. *George Gascoigne: A Packet of Poems and Certain Notes of Instruction* (Warwick: Greville).

Fein, Susanna Greer, 2000. "The Early Thirteen-Line Stanza: Style and Metrics Reconsidered," in Kennedy 2000a: 97–126.

Ferguson, William, 1981. *La versificación imitativa en Fernando de Herrera* (London: Tamesis Books).

Fernando Pessoa, see Reis Ricardo and Campos Alvaro de.

Ferrari, Patricio, 2012. "Meter and Rhythm in the Poetry of Fernando Pessoa," PhD thesis, Univ. of Lisbon.

Ferrers-Howell, A. G., trans., 1973. *Dante: De vulgari eloquentiâ* (London: Rebel Press).

Figg, Kristen N., and R. Barton Palmer, 2001. "Introduction," in *Jean Froissart: An Anthology of Narrative and Lyric Poetry*, ed. Kristen N. Figg and R. Barton Palmer (New York: Routledge), 1–33.

Fiorentino, Luigi, 1964. *Storia della letteratura italiana* (Milan: Mursia).

Fish, Stanley, 1980. *Is There a Text in This Class? The Authority of Interpretive Communities* (Cambridge Mass: Harvard Univ. Press).

Fisher, John H., 1964. *John Gower: Moral Philosopher and Friend of Chaucer* (New York: New York Univ. Press).

Forni, Kathleen, ed., 2005. "John Gower: *In praise of Peace*," in *The Chaucerian Apocrypha: A Selection* (Kalamazoo, MI: Medieval Institute Publications).

Fox, Denton, 1966. "The Scottish Chaucerians," in *Chaucer and the Chaucerians: Critical Studies in Middle English Literature*, ed. D. S. Brewer (London and Edinburgh: Nelson), 164–200.

Fox, Denton, ed., 1981. *The Poems of Robert Henryson* (Oxford: Clarendon Press).

Frank, István, 1953–57. *Répertoire métrique de la poésie des troubadours*, 2 vols (Paris: Champion).

Froissart, Jean, see Scheler, A. and Dembowski, P. F.

Fry, Stephen, 2005. *The Ode Less Travelled: Unlocking the Poet Within* (London: Hutchinson).

Furnivall, F. J., ed., 1897. *Hoccleve's Works: The Regiment of Princes and fourteen minor poems*, EETS, ES 72 (London: Kegan Paul).

Gardner, Helen, ed., 1972. *The New Oxford Book of English Verse, 1250–1950* (Oxford: Clarendon Press)

Gascoigne, George, see Farren, Martin.

Gasparov, M. L., 1987. "A Probability Model of Verse (English, Latin, French, Italian, Spanish, Portuguese)," trans. Marina Tarlinskaja, *Style*, 21: 322–58.

Gasparov, M. L., 1996. *A History of European Versification*, trans. G. S. Smith and Marina Tarlinskaja, ed. G. S. Smith with L. Holford-Strevens (Oxford: Clarendon Press).

Gaunt, Simon, and Sarah Kay, ed., 1999. *The Troubadours: An Introduction* (Cambridge: Cambridge Univ. Press).

Gaylord, Alan T., 1976–77. "Scanning the Prosodists: An Exercise in Metacriticism," *Chaucer Review*, 11: 22–82.

Gaylord, Alan T., 1979. "Chaucer's Dainty 'Dogerel': The 'Elvyssh' Prosody of Sir Thopas," *Studies in the Age of Chaucer*, 1: 83–104.

Gaylord, Alan T., ed., 2001. *Essays on the Art of Chaucer's Verse* (New York and London: Routledge).

Getty, Paul, 2002. *The Meter of Beowulf: A Constraint-Based Approach* (Berlin and New York: Mouton de Gruyter).

Giegerich, Heinz J., 1980. "On Stress-timing in English Phonology," *Lingua*, 51: 187-221.

Gildersleeve, B. K., and González Lodge, 1953. *Gildersleeve's Latin Grammar* (London: Macmillan).

Gill, Stephen, ed., 1984. *William Wordsworth (The Oxford Authors)* (Oxford: Oxford Univ. Press).

Girart de Rousillon, chanson de geste, see Hackett, W. Mary.

Gómez Bravo, Ana, 1998. *Repertorio métrico de la poesía cancioneril del siglo XV* (Madrid: Univ. de Alcalá).

Gower, John, see Macaulay G. C., Peck, Russell, and Forni, Kathleen.

Grammont, Maurice, 1937. *Le vers français: ses moyens d'expression, son harmonie* (Paris: Delagrave).

Granson, Oton de, see Winther, Joan Grenier.

Graves, Robert, ed., 1957. *English and Scottish Ballads* (London: Heinemann).

Graves, Robert, 1959. *The Crowning Privilege* (Harmondsworth: Penguin Books).

Gray, Douglas, ed., 1986. *J. A. W. Bennett: Middle English Literature* (Oxford: Clarendon Press).

Gray, J. M., ed., 1935. *Scottish Poetry from Barbour to James VI* (London: Dent).

Gray, Thomas, see Reeves, James.

Greene, Roland, and Richard Cushman, ed., 2012. *The Princeton Encyclopedia of Poetry and Poetics* (Princeton: Princeton Univ. Press).

Griffiths, Paul, 2006. *The New Penguin Dictionary of Music* (London: Penguin Books).

Guillaume de Machaut, see Hoepffner, Ernst; also at: www1.cpdl.org/wiki/index.php/De_toutes_Flours;

Guy of Warwick, see Wiggins, Alison; also at: http:/www.lib.rochester.edu/camelot/teams/guywtxt.htm.

Gybbon-Monypenny, G. B., ed., 1988. *Arcipreste de Hita: Libro de Buen Amor* (Madrid: Castalia).

Hackett, W. Mary, ed., 1953–55. *Girart de Rousillon, chanson de geste*, 3 vols (Paris: Picard).

Hagman, L. W., 1968. "A Study of Gower's *Cinkant Balades*," PhD thesis, Univ. of Detroit.

Halle, Morris, and Samuel J. Keyser, 1966–67. "Chaucer and the Study of Prosody," *College English*, 28: 187–219.

Halle, Morris, and Samuel J. Keyser, 1971–72. "Illustration and Defense of a Theory of the Iambic Pentameter," *College English*, 33: 154–76.

Hamer, Richard, ed., 1970. *A Choice of Anglo-Saxon Verse* (Faber and Faber).

Hamilton, A. C., ed., 1966. *The Selected Poetry of Edmund Spenser* (New York: New American Library).

Hamlin, Frank R., Peter T. Ricketts, and John Hathaway, 1967. *Introduction à l'étude de l'ancien provençal* (Geneva: Droz).

Hammond, Eleanor Prescott, 1927. *English Verse between Chaucer and Surrey* (Durham, NC: Duke Univ. Press, 1927; reprinted New York: Octogon, 1965).

Hammond, Michael, 1997. "Optimality Theory and Prosody," in *Optimality Theory: An Overview*, ed. Diana Archangeli and D. Terence Langdon (Oxford: Blackwell), 33–58.

Hammond, Paul, and D. Hopkins, ed., 2005. *The Poems of John Dryden*, 4 vols (London: Longman).

Hanson, Kristin, 1995. "Prosodic Constituents of Poetic Meter," *Proceedings of the West Coast Conference on Formal Linguistics*, 13 (Stanford: CSLI Publications), 62–77.

Hanson, Kristin, 1996. "From Dante to Pinsky: A Theoretical Perspective on the History of the English Iambic Pentameter," *Rivista di Linguistica*, 9: 53–97.

Hanson, Kristin, 2009. "Metrical Alignment," in Aroui and Arloe 2009: 267–86.

Hanson, Kristin, and Paul Kiparsky, 1996. "A Parametric Theory of Poetic Meter," *Language*, 72: 287–335.

Hartley, Derek, 2007. *Teach Yourself Tap Dancing* (London: Teach Yourself).

Harvey, Ruth, 1999. "Courtly Culture in Medieval Occitania," in Gaunt and Kay, 1999: 8–27.

Hascall, Dudley, 1970. "The Prosody of John Lydgate," *Language and Style*, 3: 122–46.

Hayes, Bruce, 1983. "A Grid-based Theory of English Meter," *Linguistic Inquiry*, 14: 357-94.

Hayes, Bruce, 1995. *Metrical Stress Theory: Principles and Case Studies* (Chicago: Chicago Univ. Press).

Hayes, Bruce, and Margaret McEachern, 1998. "Quatrain Forms in English Folk Verse," *Language*, 74: 473–507.

Hayes, Bruce, Colin Wilson, and Anne Shisko, 2012. "Maxent Grammars of the Metrics of Shakespeare and Milton," *Language*, 88:4: 691–731.

Heaney, Seamus, trans., 2009. *Robert Henryson: The Testament of Cresseid and Seven Fables* (London: Faber and Faber).

Heidenfeld, Wolfgang, 1977. "Centre," in *The Encyclopedia of Chess*, ed. Harry Golombek (London: Batsford).

Henderson, Harold H., ed. and trans. 1958. *An Introduction to Haiku: An Anthology of Poems and Poets from Basho to Shiki* (New York: Doubleday).

Henderson, Philip, ed., 1931. *The Complete Works of John Skelton, Laureate* (London: Dent).

Hengwrt manuscript (Aberystwyth: National Library of Wales, MS Peniarth, 392D), see Lloyd Morgan, Ceridwen, and Manley, John Matthews.

Henry, Albert, 1953. *Chrestomathie de la litterature en ancien français* (Berne: Francke).

Henryson, Robert, see Fox, Denton, Bawcutt, Priscilla, and Heaney, Seamus.

Hindley, Geoffrey, ed., 1977. *The Larousse Encyclopedia of Music* (London: Hamlyn).

Hirtzel, F. A., ed., 1900. *P. Vergili Maronis Opera* (Oxford: Clarendon Press).

Hobsbaum, Philip, 1996. *Metre, Rhythm and Verse Form* (London: Routledge).

Hoccleve, Thomas, see Furnivall, F. J., Mitchell, Jerome, and O'Donoghue, Bernard.

Hoepffner, Ernst, ed., 1908. *Oeuvres de Guillaume de Machaut* (Paris: Société des Anciens Textes Français).

Hogg, James, see Mack, Douglas, F.

Hogg, Richard, and Christopher B. McCully, 1987. *Metrical Phonology: A Course Book* (Cambridge: Cambridge Univ. Press).

Holt, Robert, ed., 1878. *Ormulum* (Oxford: Clarendon Press).

Hopper, Vincent Foster, 2003. *Medieval Number Symbolism: Its Sources, Meaning and Influence on Thought and Expression* (Mineola, NY: Dover Publications).

Howard, Henry, Earl of Surrey, see Keene, Denis.

Howatson, M. C., ed., 1989. *The Oxford Companion to Classical Literature* (Oxford: Oxford Univ. Press).

Hughes, Barnabas B., ed., 1989. Robert of Chester's Latin Translation of Al-Khwarizmi's Al-Jabr: A New Edition (Wiesbaden: F. S. Lanier Verlag).

Hurford, James R., 1987. *Language and Number: The Emergence of a Cognitive System* (Oxford: Blackwell).

Hutchinson, Thomas, ed., 1935. *The Complete Poetical Works of Percy Bysshe Shelley* (London: Oxford Univ. Press).

Itsumi, Kichiro, 2009. *Pindaric Metre: The Other Half* (Oxford: Oxford Univ. Press).

Jack, Ian, ed., 1970. *Robert Browning: Poetical Works, 1833–1864* (London: Oxford Univ. Press).

Jackson Knight, W. F., 1944. *Roman Vergil* (London: Faber and Faber).

Jakobson, Roman, 1960. "Linguistics and Poetics," in Sebeok 1960: 350–77.

James I of Scotland, see Mackenzie, Mackay.

Jasinski, Max, 1970. *L'Histoire du sonnet en France* (Geneva: Slatkine).

Jay, Peter, trans., 2009. *A Greek Garland: Poems from the Greek Anthology* (Warwick: Greville).

Jefferson, Judith, 2000. "The Hoccleve Monographs and Hoccleve's Metrical Practice: More than Counting Syllables?" in Kennedy 2000a: 203–26.

Jonson, Ben, see Donaldson, Ian.

Kastner, L. E., 1903. *A History of French Versification* (Oxford: Clarendon Press).

Kay, George, 1958. *The Penguin Book of Italian Verse* (Harmondsworth: Penguin Books).

Keats, John, see Stillinger, Jack.

Keene, Denis, ed., 1985. *Henry Howard, Earl of Surrey: Selected Poems* (Manchester: Carcanet).

Kelly, Henry A., 1986–87. "Pronouncing Latin Words in English," *Classical World*, 80: 33–37.

Kendal, Gordon, ed., 2011. *Gavin Douglas's Translation of the "Aeneid"* (London: Modern Humanities Research Association).

Kennedy, Maeve, 2003. "Lawrence's 'Obscenities' Finally Get a Showing"; *The Guardian*, 22 November.

Kennedy, Ruth, 1999. "New Theories of Constraint in the Metricality of the Strong-Stress Long Line as Applied to the Rhymed Corpus of Late Middle English Alliterative Verse," in *Métriques du Moyen Âge et de la Renaissance*, ed. Dominique Billy (Paris: L'Harmattan), 131–44.

Kennedy, Ruth, ed., 2000a. *Medieval English Measures: Studies in Metre and Versification*, special ed. of *Parergon*, 18.1 (July).

Kennedy, Ruth, 2000b. "Strong-Stress Metres in Fourteen-Line Stanza Forms," in Kennedy 2000a: 127–56.

Kenney, E. J., ed., 1961. *P. Ovidius Naso: Amores, Medicamina faciei feminiae, Ars amatoria, Remedia amoris* (Oxford: Clarendon Press).

Ker, W. W., 1898. "Analogies between English and Spanish Verse (*Arte mayor*)," *Transactions of the Philological Society* (London: Kegan Paul, Trench, and Trubner), 113–28.

Kerkhof, Maxim P.A.M., ed., 1995. *Juan de Mena: Laberinto de Fortuna*. (Madrid: Castalia).

King, Martin Luther, 1963. *I Have a Dream* (speech), at: www.youtube.com/watch?v=smEqnnklfYs.

Kiparsky, Paul, 1973. "The Role of Linguistics in a Theory of Poetry," *Daedalus*, 102: 231–44.

Kiparsky, Paul, 1977. "The Linguistic Structure of English Verse," *Linguistic Inquiry*, 8: 189–247.

Kiparsky, Paul, 2009. "Review of Nigel Fabb and Morris Halle (2008), *Meter in Poetry*," paper prepared in the Department of Linguistics, Stanford University.

Koster, W. J. W., 1929. "Versus Saturnius," *Mnemosyne*, NS, 57: 267–46.

Kurtz, Heidi, 2012. "Stress, Etymology, and Metre in Four Canterbury Tales," DPhil thesis, Oxford University.

La Vie de Saint Alexis, see Meunier, J-M.

Laȝamon, see Allen, Rosamund.

Landa, Louis, ed., 1990. *Daniel Defoe: A Journal of the Plague Years* (Oxford: Oxford Univ. Press).

Langlois, Ernest, ed., 1914. *Le roman de la rose par Guillaume de Lorris et Jean de Meun, publié après les manuscrits* (Paris: Société des Anciens Textes Français).

Laude, at: http://www.rm.unina.it/didattica/strumenti/petrocchiDuecento/testi.

Lavaud, René, and Georges Machicot, ed., 1950. *Boecis: poème sur Boèce: le plus ancien texte littéraire occitan*, (Toulouse: Institut d'Études Occitanes).

Legge, M. Dominica, 1963. *Anglo-Norman Literature and Its Background* (Oxford: Clarendon Press).

Lemprière's Classical Dictionary, see Wright, F. A.

Leonard, John, ed., 1998. *John Milton: The Complete Poems* (London: Penguin Books).

Leonetti, Pasquale, 1934. *Storia della tecnica del verso italiano* (Naples: Morano).

Lewis, C. S., 1938. "The Fifteenth-Century Heroic Line," *Essays and Studies*, 24: 28–41;

Lewis, Charlton M., 1898. *The Foreign Sources of English Versification* (New York: H. Holt).

Lewis, Robert E., ed., 1978. *Pope Innocent II: De miseria condicionis humane* (Athens, GA: Univ. of Georgia Press).

Li, Xingzhong, 1995. "Chaucer's Meters," PhD thesis, Dept of English, Univ. of Missouri, Columbia.

Liberman, Mark Y., and Alan Prince, 1977. "On Stress and Linguistic Rhythm," *Linguistic Inquiry*, 8: 249–336.

Liberman, Mark, 2012. "Portuguese is Disappearing One Vowel at a Time," *Language Log*, 12 December; available on the internet at: http://languagelog.ldc.upenn.edu/hll/?p=4366.

Liddell and Scott, 1968. *An Intermediate Greek Lexicon Founded upon the Seventh Edition of Liddell and Scott's Greek Lexicon* (Oxford: Clarendon Press).

Lloyd Morgan, Ceridwen,ed., 2003. *The Hengwrt Chaucer*, CD ROM containing Estelle Stubbs's text of Hengwrt (Leicester: Scholarly Editions).

Lord, Robert, 1974. *Comparative Linguistics* (London: Teach Yourself).

Lote, Georges, 1939. "Les Origines des vers français," *Annales de la Faculté des Lettres d'Aix*, 21: 219–415.

Lotz, John, 1960. "Metric Typology," in Sebeok 1960: 135–48.

Lucas, F. V., ed., 1927. *The Complete Works of John Webster*, 4 vols (London: Chatto & Windus).

Lydgate, John, see Edwards, Robert R., MacCracken, H. N., and Norton-Smith, John.

Macaulay, G. C., ed., 1899–1901. *The Complete Works of John Gower*, 4 vols (Oxford: Clarendon Press).

MacCracken, H. N., ed., 1911. *The Minor Poems of John Lydgate*, I, *The Lydgate Canon and Religious Poems*, EETS, ES 107 (London: Oxford Univ. Press).

Machaut, Guillaume de, see Hoeppffner, Ernst; see also the ballade that is available on the internet at: www1.cpdl.org/wiki/index.php/De_toutes_Flours.

Mack, Douglas, F., ed., 1970. *James Hogg: Selected Poems* (Oxford: Clarendon Press).

Mackenzie, Mackay, ed., 1932. *The Poems of William Dunbar* (London: Faber and Faber).

Mackenzie, MacKay, ed., 1939. *The Kingis Quair* (London: Faber and Faber).

Magnuson, Karl, and Frank G. Ryder, 1969–70. "The Study of English Prosody: An Alternative Proposal," *College English*, 31: 789–820.

Manly, John Matthews, and Edith Rickart, ed. 1940. *The Text of the Canterbury Tales, Studied on the Basis of All known Manuscripts*, (Chicago: Chicago Univ. Press).

Manzoni, Alessandro, 1961. *I promessi sposi*, 2 vols (Milan: Rizzoli).

McCabe, Richard A., ed., 1999. *Edmund Spenser: The Shorter Poems*, (London: Penguin Books).

McCarthy, John J., and Alan S. Prince, 1993. "Prosodic Morphology, I: Constraint Interaction and Satisfaction," Ms., Univ. of Massachusetts, Amherst, and Rutgers Univ., New Brunswick, N.J.

McCully, C. B., and J. J. Anderson, ed., 1996. *English Historical Metrics* (Cambridge: Cambridge Univ. Press)

McCully, Chris, and Sharon Hilles, 2005. "OE Metrics," in their *The Earliest English: An Introduction to Old English Language* (London: Pearson Education), pp. 143–185.

McGann, Jerome J., ed., 1980–86. *George Gordon, Lord Byron: Complete Poetical Works*, 7 vols (Oxford: Clarendon Press).

Meillet, P. J. Antoine, 1923. *Les Origines indo-européennes des mètres grecs* (Paris: Presses Universitaires de France).

Mena, Juan de, see Kerkhof, Maxim.

Merrilees, Brian, 2012. "Gower's French Vocabulary," at: http://homes.chass.utoronto.ca/-merilee/2003/gower.vocab.html.

Mettmann, Walter, ed., 1959–72. *Afonso o Sábio*: *Cantigas de Santa Maria*, 4 vols (Coimbra: Univ. de Coimbra).

Meunier, J-M., ed., 1933. *La Vie de Saint Alexis, poème français du XIe siècle* (Paris: Droz).

Migliorini, Bruno, 1966. *The Italian Language*, abridged and recast by T. Gwynfor Griffith (London: Faber and Faber).

Migne, J. P., ed., 1844. *Gautier de Châtillon: Alexandreis*, in *Cursus Patrilogiae Latinae*, 209: cols 459–74.

Miller, George A., 1956. "The Magical Number Seven Plus or Minus Two," *Psychological Review*, 63: 81–97.

Milton, John, see Leonard, John.

Minkova, Donka, 1987. "The Prosodic Character of Early Schwa Deletion in English," in *Papers from the 7th International Conference on Historical Linguistics*, ed. Anna Giacalone Ramat, Onofrio Carruba, and Giuliano Bernini (Amsterdam: John Benjamins), 445–57.

Minkova, Donka, 1990. "Adjectival Inflexion Relics and Speech Rhythm in Late Medieval and Early Modern English," *Papers of the 5th International Congress on Historical Linguistics*, ed. Sylvia Adamson et al. (Amsterdam and Philadelphia: John Benjamins), 313–36.

Minkova, Donka, 1991. *History of Final Vowels in English* (Berlin and New York: Mouton de Gruyter).

Minkova, Donka, 2009. "On the Meter of Middle English Alliterative Verse," in Aroui and Arloe 2009: 209–28.

Minkova Donka, and Robert Stockwell, ed., 2002. *Studies in the History of the English Language: A Millennial Perspective* (Berlin: Mouton de Gruyter).

Mitchell, Bruce, and Fred C. Robinson, 1982. *A Guide to Old English, Revised with Prose and Verse Texts and Glossary* (Oxford: Basil Blackwell).

Mitchell, Jerome, 1968. *Thomas Hoccleve: A Study in Early Fifteenth-century Poetic* (Urbana, IL: Univ. of Illinois).

Mitchie, Graeme, ed., 1925. *The Buik Of Alexander* (Edinburgh: Blackwood).

Moore, Marianne, 1967. *The Complete Poems of Marianne Moore* (New York: Macmillan).

Navarro (Tomás), Tomás, 1974. *Métrica española* (Madrid: Guadarrama).

Nolan, Maura, 2013. "Performing Lydgate's Broken-Backed Meter," in Yager and Morse-Gagné 2013: 97–114.

Norberg, Dag, 1958. *Introduction à l' étude de la versification latine médiévale* (Stockholm: Almqvist and Wiksell).

Norton, Thomas, see Tydeman, William.

Norton-Smith, John, ed., 1966. *John Lydgate: Poems* (Oxford: Clarendon Press)

O'Connor, J. D., 1973. *Phonetics* (Harmondsworth: Penguin Books).

O'Donoghue, Bernard, ed., 1982. *Thomas Hoccleve: Selected Poems* (Manchester: Carcanet).

Orm, see Holt Robert.

Osberg, Richard, 1996. "The Prosody of the Middle English *Pearl* and the Alliterative Lyric Tradition," in McCully and Anderson 1996: 150–74.

Ovid (P. Ovidius Naso), see Showerman, Grant, and Kenney, E.J.

Palgrave, Francis Turner, ed., 1964. *The Golden Treasury, with a fifth book selected by John Press* (London: Oxford Univ. Press).

Palmer, L. R., 1954. *The Latin Language* (London: Faber and Faber).

Palmer, L. R., 1980. *The Greek Language* (London: Faber and Faber).

Paris, Gaston, ed., 1875. *Les Plus Anciens Monuments de la langue française (IXe et Xe siècles): Album* (Paris: Firmin Didot).

Parkinson, Stephen, 1988. "Phonology," in *The Romance Languages*, ed. Martin Harris and Nigel Vincent (London: Routledge), 131–69;

Pearsall, Derek, 1970. *John Lydgate* (London: Routledge and Kegan Paul).

Pearsall, Derek, 1992. *The Life of Geoffrey Chaucer: A Critical Biography* (Oxford Blackwell).

Pearsall, Judy, ed., 1998. *The New Oxford Dictionary of English* (Oxford: Oxford Univ. Press).

Peck, Russell, ed., 1980. *John Gower: Confesssio Amantis* (Toronto: Univ. of Toronto Press in association with the Medieval Academy of America).

Pensom, Roger, 1982. *Literary Technique in the "Chanson de Roland"* (Geneva: Droz).

Pensom, Roger, 2000. *Accent and Metre in French: A Theory of the Relation between Linguistic Accent and Metrical Practice in French* (Bern: Peter Lang).

Petrarch, see Vianello, Nereo.

Petrocchi, Giorgio, ed., 1975. *Dante Alighieria: "Commedia" secondo l'antica volgata* (Turin: Einaudi).

Piera, Carlos José, 1980. "Spanish Verse and the Theory of Meter," PhD thesis, Univ. of California, Los Angeles.

Piera, Carlos José, 2001. "Intonational Factors in Metrics," in *Linguistic Approaches to Metrics*, ed. Christine Michaux and Marc Dominicy, special issue of *Belgian Journal of Linguistics*, 15.1: 205–28.

Pighi, Giovanni Battista, 1970. *Studi di ritmica e metrica* (Turin: Bottega d'Erasmo).

Pindar, see Itsumi, Kichiro.

Pinsky, Robert, 1998. *The Sounds of Poetry: A Brief Guide* (New York: Farrar, Straus and Giroux).

Poema Morale (Bibliotheca Augustana text) at: http://ww2.hs-augsberg.de/~harsch/anglica/Chronology/12thC/Poema Morale.

Poems of "Ch," see Wimsatt, James I; and at: www.lib.Rochester.edu/camelot/teams/wjch1t.htm.

Potter, D. D., et al., 2003. "Perceiving Rhythm Where None Exists," *Cortex*, 45: 103–09.

Pound, Ezra, 1961. *ABC of Reading* (London: Faber and Faber).

Press, Alan R., ed. and trans., 1971. *Anthology of Troubadour Lyric Poetry* (Edinburgh: Univ. Press).

Prince, Alan S., 1989. "Metrical Forms," in *Phonetics and Phonology, I: Rhythm and Meter*, ed Paul Kiparsky and Gilbert Youmans (San Diego, CA: Academic Press), pp. 45–80.

Prince Alan S., and Paul Smolensky, 1991. "Optimality," talk given at the Arizona Phonology Conference 3, Univ. of Arizona, Tucson.

Prince, F. T., 1954. *The Italian Element in Milton's Verse* (Oxford: Clarendon Press); in the 1962 edition of this book Prince contradicted his 1954 conclusions.

Purcell, Sally, 1973. "Introduction," in *Selected Poems of Charles d'Orléans*, ed. Sally Purcell (Manchester: Carcanet).

Purczinsky, Julius, 165–66. "The Germanic Influence in the *Saint Eulalia*," *Romance Philology*, 19: 271–75.

Putter, Ad, Judith Jefferson, and Myra Stokes, ed., 2007. *Studies in the Metre of Alliterative Verse*, Medium Aevum Monographs, 25 (Oxford: Society for the Study of Medieval Languages and Literature).

Putter, Ad, and Myra Stokes, ed., 2014. *The Works of the "Gawain" Poet* (London: Penguin Books).

Pyle, Fitzroy, 1935. "The Place of Anglo-Norman in the History of English Versification," *Hermathena*, 39: 22–42.

Pyle, Fitzroy, 1937. "The Pedigree of John Lydgate's Heroic Line," *Hermathena*, 50: 26–59;

Raby, F. J. E., 1934. *A History of Secular Latin Poetry in the Middle Ages*, II (Oxford: Clarendon Press).

Rebholz, R. A., ed., 1978. *Sir Thomas Wyatt: The Complete Poems* (Harmondsworth: Penguin Books).

Reeves, James, ed., 1973. *The Complete English Poems of Thomas Gray* (London: Heinemann).

Reid, Joyce M. H., ed., 1976. *The Concise Oxford Dictionary of French Literature*, (Oxford: Clarendon Press).

Reis, Ricardo, see Fagundas Duarte, Luiz.

Renoir, Alain, 1967. *The Poetry of John Lydgate* (London: Routledge & Kegan Paul).

Riad, T., 2010. "Review of Nigel Fabb and Morris Halle (2008), *Meter in Poetry: A New Theory*," *Phonology*, 27: 54–51.

Ricketts, Peter T., 2001. *Concordance of Medieval Occitan* (Turnhout: Brepols).

Rig Veda, see Zaehner, R.C.

Ritmo cassinese, see Bonghi, Giuseppe.

Roach, Peter, 1982. "On the Distinction between 'Stress-timed' and 'Syllable-timed' Languages," in *Linguistic Controversies: Essays in Honour of F. R. Palmer*, ed. David Crystal (London: Edward Arnold).

Robinson, Ian, 1971. *Chaucer's Prosody: A Study of the Middle English Verse Tradition* (Cambridge: Cambridge Univ. Press).

Roman d'Alexandre, see Armstrong, E. C.

Roman de la rose, see Langlois, Ernest,

Ronsard, Pierrre de, see Schmidt, Pierre Marie.

Rossi, Aldo, ed., 1982. *Giovanni Boccaccio: Decameron*. (Bologna: Cappelli).

Rowley, Sharon M., 2011. *The Old English Version of Bede's "Historia Ecclesiastica"* (Cambridge: D. S. Brewer).

Rudd, Gillian, 2001. *The Complete Critical Guide to Chaucer* (London and New York: Routledge).

Ruiz Zafón, Carlos, 2004. *The Shadow of the Wind*, trans. Lucia Graves (London: Weidenfield and Nicholson).

Ruiz, Juan, see Gybbon-Monypenny, G. B.

Ruschioni, Ada, 1974. *Morfologia e antologia del sonetto*, 2 vols (Milan: CELUC).

Russom, Geoffrey, 1987. *Old English Meter and Linguistic Theory* (Cambridge: Cambridge Univ. Press).

Russom, Geoffrey, 1998. *"Beowulf" and Old Germanic Meter* (Cambridge: Cambridge Univ. Press).

Sackville, Thomas, Earl of Dorset, see Campbell, Lily B., and Tydeman, William.

Saintsbury, George, 1906–10. *A History of English Prosody from the Twelfth Century to the Present Day*, 3 vols (London: Macmillan).

Samuels, M. L., 1972. "Chaucerian Final –E," *Notes and Queries*, 217 (1972): 445–48.

Sanguineti, Edoardo, ed., 1965. *Sonetti della Scuola Siciliana* (Turin: Einaudi).

Savage, Anne, ed. and trans., 1983. *The Anglo-Saxon Chronicles* (London: Heinemann).

Scheler, A., ed., 1870–73. *Oeuvres de Froissart, Poésies*, 3 vols (Brussels: Victor Devaux).

Schick, Josef, ed., 1891. *Lydgate's "Temple of Glas,"* EETS, ES, 60 (London: Paul, Trench, and Tubner).

Schipper, Jakob, 1910. *A History of English Versification* (Oxford: The Clarendon Press).

Schirmer, Walter F., 1961. *John Lydgate: A Study in the Culture of the Fifteenth Century*, trans. Ann E. Keep (London: Methuen).

Schmidt, Pierre Marie, ed., 1964. *Pierre de Ronsard: Amours* (Paris: Gallimard).

Scott, Clive, 1980. *French Verse Art: A Study* (Cambridge: Cambridge Univ. Press).

Scott, Tom, ed., 1967. *Late Medieval Scots Poetry* (London: Heinemann).

Sebeok, Thomas A., ed., 1960. *Style in Language* (Boston: MIT Press).

Shakespeare, William, see Alexander, Peter.
Shelley, Percy Bysshe, see Hutchinson, Thomas.
Showerman, Grant, ed. and trans., 1914. *Ovid: "Heroides" and "Amores"* (London: Heinemann, and Cambridge MA: Harvard Univ. Press).
Sidney, Sir Philip, see Bullett, Gerald, and Dorsten, J. van.
Sievers, Eduard, 1885. "Zur Rhythmic des germanischen Alliterationsverses," *Beiträge zur Geschichte der deutschen Sprache und Literatur*, 10: 209–314 and 451–545.
Skeat, Walter W., ed., 1869. *Langland: Piers the Plowman* (Oxford: Clarendon Press).
Skeat, Walter W., ed., 1881. *Aelfric's Lives of the Saints* (London: Trübner).
Skeat, Walter W., 1898. "On the Scansion of English Poetry," *Transactions of the Philological Society*, 484–503.
Skelton, John, see Henderson, Philip, and Thwaite, Anthony.
Smith, A. J., ed., 1971. *John Donne: The Complete English Poems* (Harmondsworth: Penguin).
Smith, A. S. D., and E. G. R. Hooper, 1972. *Cornish Simplified* (Camborne, UK: An Lef Kernewak).
Smith, Barbara Herrnstein, 1968. *Poetic Closure: A Study of How Poems End* (Chicago: Univ. of Chicago Press).
Smith, G. S., 2000. "Russian Poetry: The Lives or the Lines," *Modern Language Review*, 95.4: 29–41.
Sordello, see Boni, Marco.
Southworth, James G., 1957. *Verses of Cadence: An Introduction to the Prosody of Chaucer and His Followers* (Oxford: Blackwell).
Southworth, James G., 1962. *The Prosody of Chaucer and His Followers: Supplementary Chapters to Verses of Cadence* (Oxford: Blackwell).
Speght, Thomas, ed., 1598. *The Works of our Antient and Lerned English Poet, Geffrey Chaucer, newly Printed*, see Brewer, D. S.
Spenser, Edmund, see McCabe, Richard A., and Hamilton, A. C.
Stanley, Eric, ed., 1972. *The Owl and the Nightingale* (New York: Barnes and Noble).
Steele, Robert, ed., 1941. *The English Poems of Charles d'Orléans* (London: Oxford Univ. Press).
Stillinger, Jack, ed., 1978. *The Poems of John Keats* (London: Heinemann).
Stillman, Frances, 1966. *The Poet's Manual and Rhyming Dictionary* (London: Thames and Hudson).
Stockwell, Robert, and Donka Minkova, "The Prosody of 'Beowulf'," in *A "Beowulf" Handbook*, ed. Robert Bjork and John D. Niles (Lincoln: Univ. of Nebraska Press, 1997), 55–83.
Tarlinskaja, Marina, 1976. *English Verse: Theory and History* (The Hague: Mouton).

Tarlinskaja, Marina, 1987. *Shakespeare's Verse: Iambic Pentameter and the Poet's Idiosyncrasies* (New York and Frankfurt: Peter Lang).

Tarlinskaja, Marina, 1993. *Strict-Stress Meter in English Poetry Compared with German and Russian* (Calgary: Univ. of Calgary Press).

Tarlinskaja, Marina 2014. *Shakespeare and the Versification of the English Drama, 1561–1642* (Farnham, Surrey and Burlington, VT: Ashgate).

Tennyson, Alfred, 1965. *Poems and Plays* (London: Oxford Univ. Press); also recording at: www.poetryarchive.org/poetryarchive/singlepoet.

The Buik Of Alexander, see Mitchie, Graeme.

The Concise Oxford Dictionary of French Literature, see Reid, Joyce M. H.

The Larousse Encyclopedia of Music, see Hindley, Geoffrey.

The Mirror for Magistrates, see Campbell, Lily B.

The New Oxford Book of English Verse, see Gardner, Helen.

The New Oxford Dictionary of English, see Pearsall, Judy.

The New Penguin Dictionary of Music, see Griffiths,Paul.

The Owl and the Nightingale, see Stanley, Eric.

The Oxford Companion to Classical Literature, see Howatson, M. C.

The Oxford Companion to English Literature, see Drabble, Margaret.

The Penguin Book of French Verse, see Woledge, Brian.

The Penguin Book of Italian Verse, see Kay, George.

The Penguin Book of Japanese Verse, see Bownas, Geoffrey.

The Princeton Encyclopedia of Poetry and Poetics, see Greene, Roland,

The Song of Ullikummi, see West, M. L.

Thomas, Paul, 2013. *The Chaucer Studio Recordings*, catalogue available at: http://creativeworks.byu.edu.chaucer.

Thomas, Walter A., 1904. "Le Décasyllabe roman et sa fortune en Europe: essai de métrique comparée," *Travaux et Memoires de la Université de Lille*, Nouvelle Série, I, Droit, Lettres, fasc. 4 (Lille: Lille Univ. Press).

Thwaite, Anthony, ed., 2008. *John Skelton: Selected Poems* (London: Faber and Faber).

Trager, G. L., and H. L. Smith, 1951, *Outline of English Structure* (Normanton, OK: Battenburg Press).

Turville-Petre, Thorlac, 1977. *The Alliterative Revival* (Cambridge: Brewer).

Tydeman, William, ed., 1992. *Two Tudor Tragedies: "Gorboduc" and "The Spanish Tragedy"* (Harmondsworth: Penguin Books).

Tyrwhitt, Thomas, ed., 1798. *The Poetical Works of Geoffrey Chaucer: to which are added an essay on his language and versification and an introductory discourse together with notes and a glossary, by the late Thomas Tyrwhitt* (Oxford: Clarendon Press).

Tyrwhitt, Thomas, ed., 1973. *An Essay on the Language and Versification of Chaucer* (Folcroft, PA: Folcroft Library Editions).

Utrera Torremocha, M. Victoria, 2010. *Estructura y teoría del verso libre* (Madrid: CSIC).

Vergil (P. Vergilius Maro), see Hirtzel, F. A.

Verrier, Paul, 1932. *Le vers français: formes primitives, développement, diffusion*, II, *Mètres* (Paris: Henri Didier).

Vianello, Nereo, ed., 1966. *Francesco Petrarca: Canzionere* (Basiano: Bietti).

Vidal, Peire, see Avalle, D'Arco Silvio.

Vising, Johan, 1884. *Sur la Versification anglo-normande* (Uppsala: Almqvist and Wiksell).

Volkoff, Vladimir, 1978. *Vers une métrique française* (Columbia SC: French Literature Publications Co.).

Wallace, David, trans., 1991. *Giovanni Boccaccio: Decameron* (Cambridge: Cambridge Univ. Press).

Walpole, Arthur Summer, ed., 1922. *Early Latin Hymns* (Cambridge: Cambridge Univ. Press).

Walter of Chatillon, *Carmina*, at www.thelatinlibary.com/walter.html; see also Migne, J. P.

Webster, John, see Lucas, F. V.

West, M. L., 1973. "Indo-European Metre," *Glotta*, 51: 161–87.

Whinnom, Keith, 1994. *Medieval and Renaissance Spanish Literature: Selected Essays*, ed. Alan Deyermond, W. F. Hunter, and Joseph Snow (Exeter: Univ. of Exeter Press).

Whitney, William Dwight, 1962. *Sanskrit Grammar* (Delhi: Banarsidass).

Widmaier, Eric P., Herschal Raff, and Kevin T. Strang, 2010. *Vander's Human Physiology: The Mechanics of Body Functions* (New York: McGraw Hill).

Wiggins, Alison, ed., 2004. *Stanzaic Guy of Warwick* (Kalamazoo, MI: Medieval Institute Publications).

Wilkins, Ernest Hatch, 1959. *The Invention of the Sonnet and Other Studies in Italian Literature* (Rome: Edizioni di Storia e Letteratura).

Williams, Gwyn, ed. and trans., 1973. *Welsh Poems: Sixth Century to 1600* (London: Faber and Faber).

Wimsatt, James I., 1982. *Chaucer and the Poems of 'Ch' in University of Pennsylvania MS French 15* (London: Brewer; Lanham MD: Rowman and Littlefield).

Wimsatt, W. K., 1969–70. "The Rule and the Norm: Halle and Keyser on Chaucer's Metrics," *College English*, 31: 774–88.

Windeatt, B. A., 1977. " 'Most conservatyf of soun': Chaucer's *Troilus* Metre," *Poetica* (Tokyo), 8: 44–60.

Windeatt, B. A., ed., 1984. *Chaucer: Troilus and Criseyde* (London: Longman); parallel text with *Boccaccio: Filostrato*.

Winther, Joan Grenier, ed. 2010. *Oton de Granson: Poésies* (Paris: H. Champion).

Woledge, Brian, ed. and trans., 1961. *The Penguin Book of French Verse: To the Fifteenth Century* (Harmondsworth: Penguin Books).

Wordsworth, William, see Gill, Stephen.

Wrenn, C. L., and W. F. Bolton, ed., 1988. *"Beowulf" with the "Finnesburg Fragment"* (Exeter: Univ. of Exeter).

Wright, F. A., 1984. *Lemprière's Classical Dictionary* (London: Bracken Books).

Wright, George A., 1988. *Shakespeare's Metrical Art* (Berkeley CA: Univ. of California Press).

Wright, Roger, 1982. *Late Latin and Early Romance in Spain and Carolingian France* (Liverpool: Cairns).

Wright, Roger, 1994. *Early Ibero-Romance* (Newark DE: Juan de la Cuesta, 1994).

Wyatt, Sir Thomas, see Rebholz, R. A.

Yager, Susan, and Elise E. Morse-Gagné, ed., 2013. *Interpretation and Performance: Essays for Alan Gaylord* (Provo, UT: The Chaucer Studio).

Youmans, Gilbert, and Xingzhong Li, 2002. "Chaucer: Folk Poet or *Littérateur*," in Minkova and Stockwell 2002: 153–75.

Zaehner, R. C., ed. and trans., 1966. *The Hindu Scriptures* (London: Dent).

Zonneveld, Wim, 2000. "The *Ormulum* and the *Lutgart*: Early Germanic Iambs in Context," in Kennedy 2000a: 27–52.

Glossary of Technical Terms Employed in This Volume

accent, dynamic: phonological contrast based on stress
———, *melodic:* phonological contrast based on change in pitch
alexandrin: French line of 6 + 6 syllables to the final stress
alexandrine: English line of six iambs
alliteration: repetition of phoneme at syllable onset
———, *rate of:* average number of alliterating onsets per line in a text
———, *zero-consonant:* convention whereby all vowels alliterate with one another
altercatio: debate poem
amphibrach: ternary foot contrasting w-s-w
anacrusis: optional syllable(s) before the first rhythmic beat
anapest: ternary foot contrasting w-w-s
Anglo-Norman: the dialect of French that was the official language of England from 1066 to 1362
anisosyllabism: irregularity in the number of syllables in line
assonance: repetition of syllable nucleus
a-verse: first half of OE or ME alliterative line
avoidance strategies: the avoidance of stress clashes and sequences of triple time; Hoccleve's metrical intention (Jefferson)
ballade: poem (usually a lyric) with elaborate rhyme scheme; most French *ballades* repeat the same rhyme scheme in each strophe, have a refrain, and close with a shorter strophe (envoi)
beat: prominent rhythmic event (Attridge)
———, *unrealized:* suppressed final beat in some lines of ictic verse (Attridge)
bob: single-beat line separating the alliterative opening of ME strophe from the rhymed wheel that follows
Book: major subdivision of a long poem
bracketing: involvement of two syllables in a special relationship
——— *condition:* inversion allowed when lexical and metrical bracketing coincide (Kiparsky)
———, *lexical:* inclusion of syllables within the same word
———, *metrical:* inclusion of syllables within the same foot
b-verse: second half of an OE or ME alliterative line
cadence, favored: most common rhythm at close of ME alliterative line
caesura: mid-line word boundary of structural significance
———, *elided:* elision of word-final vowel before the caesura
———, *enjambed:* grammatical run-on beyond caesura

———, *epic:* metrical indifference to the presence of a post-tonic syllable immediately before the caesura of a French *vers de dix* or *alexandrin*; by analogy, metrical indifference to a post-tonic syllable following the second beat in English tetrameter or pentameter

———, *lyric:* inversion at syllables 3-4 of phrasal stress in French *vers de dix*; inversion of word stress in positions 3-4 of English iambic pentameter (in imitation of the French convention)

canso: (lit. 'song') Occitan lyric poem with elaborate rhyme scheme

canto: subdivision of poem (esp. Dante's *Commedia*)

canzone: Italian lyric poem with elaborate rhyme scheme

cauda: close or tail of stanza

cesura mobile: optional (four positions) placement of principal mid-line word boundary and stress in Italian *endecasillabo*

chanson de geste: Old French epic poem of chivalry

chant (chançon) royal: poem of sixty lines with five strophes rhymed abab ccdd edE followed by an envoy rhymed ddedE

choriamb: Greek quantitative foot resembling a trochee + an iamb

clash of stress: two adjacent stressed syllables that can both become prominence peaks only by inserting a pause

closure principle: norm that openings are laxer and endings more strict (Smith)

cluster: a sequence of adjacent consonants

coda: optional final phoneme (consonant) of syllable

colon, -a: principal subdivision of sentence or line

compensation: principle that double offbeats must be balanced by implied offbeats (Attridge)

complexity, metrical: measure of deviance from metrical norm (Halle and Keyser)

consonance: repetition of phoneme in syllable coda

consonant: optional less sonorous phoneme in syllable

constraint: norm observed whenever a higher-ranked norm doesn't conflict with it (OT)

———, *cumulative stress:* norm that syllables 4 and 6 of iambic pentameter may not both lack stress

———, *monosyllable:* norm that monosyllabic stress can occur in weak positions

———, *on w positions:* norm that only w positions in the line are affected (PT)

———, *Phrasal-Stress (PS):* norm that syllable 4 in French *vers de dix* should have phrasal stress (Billy)

———, *Word-Boundary (WB):* norm that syllables 4 and 5 of French *vers de dix* should not be in same word (Billy)

constraint ranking: ranking of norms in OT, which determines output when norms conflict

contrast, binary: division of metrical unit into two unlike elements

———, *rhythmic:* division into weaker and stronger elements

———, *stress:* contrast based on dynamic accent

contre-rejet: the words severed from the remainder of their phrase that close the first of two enjambed lines

convention, logographic: traditional, non-phonetic, spelling, e.g., 'Leicester' pronounced 'Lester'

counting, anti-rhythmic: including syllables after the final stress in the count

———, ***rhythmic:*** counting syllables up to the last stress in the line or hemistich
coupe italienne: rare caesura after a post-tonic fifth syllable in *décasyllabe*
couplet: minimum strophe of 2 lines
———, ***elegiac:*** Classical couplet in which a line of 5 dactyls follows a line of 6
———, ***closed:*** couplet allowing enjambment only between its constituent lines
cuaderna vía: Castilian meter: monorhyme quatrain of alexandrines
cynghanedd: combination of alliteration and rhyme employed by Welsh bards
dactyl: ternary foot contrasting s-w-w
décasyllabe: French line usually with 10 syllables to final (phrasal) stress
———, ***4 + 6:*** *décasyllabe* with caesura after syllable 4
———, ***6 + 4:*** *décasyllabe* with caesura after syllable 6
———, ***a césure médiane:*** *décasyllabe* with caesura after syllable 5
———, ***unified:*** *décasyllabe* with no uncounted syllables mid-line
———, ***iambic:*** *décasyllabe* with strong syllables positioned as in iambic pentameter
decasyllable: line of 10 syllables to the final stress in any language including English
delivery: the performance of a line
———, ***natural:*** delivery observing norms of word and phrasal stress
———, ***scanning:*** delivery emphasizing the verse design
delivery design: poet's intended performance of the lines
delivery instance: any meaningful performance of a line
diphthong: two vowels in combination
dip: un-prominent element in OE or ME line
———, ***expanded:*** dip containing more than one syllable
distribution, normal: the usual spread of individual items about a median
disyllable: word of two syllables
dit: Old French narrative poem
dodécasyllabe: French line of twelve syllables; see also *alexandrin*
doggerel: verse with irregular rhythm; poorly crafted verse
dolce stil nuovo: Italian convention emphasizing the perfection of a *bella donna* and delicacy of feeling in the poet's love
dolnik: line with a fixed number of beats, and with offbeats containing between 0 and 2 syllables
———, ***four-ictic***: dolnik with four beats
doublet, monosyllabic: alternative pronunciation as one syllable, as in 'over' and 'o'er'
downbeat, musical: accented beat in music
elision: deletion of word-final vowel before a following word-initial vowel
———, ***rate of:*** number of elisions per 100 lines in a text
endecasillabo: line of ten syllables to the final stress, which is usually followed by a post-tonic syllable in Italian(ate) verse
———, ***a maiore:*** *endecasillabo* with principal mid-line stress in position 6
———, ***a minore:*** *endecasillabo* withe principal mid-line stress in position 4
———, ***adonic:*** *endecasillabo* with peaks of stress in positions 6 and 7
———, ***dactylic:*** *endecasillabo* with peaks of stress in positions 4 and 7
———, ***emphatic:*** *endecasillabo* with peak of stress in position 1
———, ***heroic:*** *endecasillabo* with peaks of stress in positions 2 and 6
———, ***melodic:*** *endecasillabo* with peaks of stress in positions 3 and 6
———, ***sapphic:*** *endecasillabo* with peaks of stress in positions 4 and 8

end-stopping: grammatical and metrical boundaries coinciding
enjambment: syntax overflowing metrical boundaries
erosion: relatively weak form of tension provided by placing a syllable without stress in a strong position
———, *double:* two erosions occurring in the same line
error, sampling: failure of a sample to reflect the behavior of a population because the sample is atypical
———, *scribal:* copyists' mistake
———, *standard:* measure of deviance from the median in samples
event, rhythmic: repeated stimulus (such as drumbeat, syllable, or stress)
———, *inter-linear:* event repeated in each of a series of lines
———, *intra-linear:* event repeated within a single line
fabliau: racy French tale, often of dubious provenance
Faiseurs: school of medieval French poets
fillers, metrical: words that add to the syllable count or regularize the rhythm, but add little to the meaning
fit: subdivision of a poem somewhere between *book* and *strophe*
fit, principle of: hypothesis that meters evolve so as to accommodate the language's entire lexicon (Hanson & Kiparsky); hypothesis that meters evolve to fit the phonology of the language concerned (argued in this volume)
foot: combination of two or more elements; rhythmic unit larger than syllable, smaller than a colon or hemistich
———, *accentual:* combination of stressed and unstressed elements
———, *binary:* foot with two elements (a single w^s or s^w contast)
———, *degenerate:* single mora not footed with a second mora
———, *maximal:* largest possible combination of elements (three in accentual verse)
———, *monosyllabic:* foot in which moras present the only (internal) contrast
———, *overlapping:* foot extended to a half-line in OE verse (Russom)
———, *poetic:* linguistic unit chosen by poet for rhythmic purposes
———, *metrical:* unit of the poet's chosen rhythmic structure
———, *syntagmatic:* hypotheses that syntagms should be regarded as feet (Skeat)
———, *ternary/trisyllabic:* foot with three elements, usually syllables
formes ancipites: lines offering two possible structural analyses (Billy)
Francien: The dialect of the Ile de France employed by the French court, which gradually became the national language
French, Insular: The French of England, but not the Plantagenet court; see AN
genre, epic: poetic text (often traditional) narrating the deeds of a hero
———, *lyric:* poetic text of a type originally set to music
———, *narrative:* poetic text telling a story
group, clitic: adjacent words of which one is structurally dependent upon the other, as in 'the^boy', or 'put^on'
hemistich: half-line, colon
hexameter, dactylic: Classical meter with lines containing six quantitative feet of 4 moras
hexasyllabe: French line of six syllables
hiatus: stop or stutter that occurs when both of two adjacent vowels in separate words are pronounced

hierarchy, constraint: ranking of norms that may conflict in the order that they are more likely to determine output

———, ***metrical:*** structural diagram showing line or utterance divided into hemistichs, feet, syllables, and sometimes moras

———, ***prosodic:*** table of phonological units in descending order of size

iamb: foot contrasting w^s

———, ***clitic:*** monosyllabic foot contrasting w^s, e.g., 'the boy'

———, ***lexical:*** polysyllabic foot contrasting w^s, e.g., 'in**cite**' or 'facili**tate**'

———, ***phrasal:*** the w^s contrast between two lexical monosyllables as in 'black bird' (iamb) versus **black**bird (trochee)

ictus: beat, rhythmic event in utterances

index, of enjambment: number of enjambments per 100 lines of a text

———, ***of rhyme difficulty:*** average number of rhymes required for each new rhyme word

intention, metrical: the poet's choice of designs (poem, strophe, and verse)

interval, inter-ictic: period of time or linguistic material between beats

———, ***rhythmic:*** period of time between events

inventory, foot: list of possible foot patterns in OE alliterative meter (Russom)

inversion: strong form of tension consisting of including a trochee (s^w) in iambic (w^s) verse or an iamb in trochaic verse

IPA: (International Phonetic Alphabet): system for representing the sounds of all languages accurately

italics, rhythmical: metrical features that highlight specific words in a poem (Tarlinskaja)

jongleur: professional performer of troubadour's compositions

kural meter: Old Tamil four-beat meter

l'art de petrarquiser: composing poems after the style of Petrarch, a fashion started by Pietro Bembo in the 1520s

laisses, assonating: (Old French) strophes of irregular lengths linked by assonance

language, analytic: language in which syntax does not depend on affixes to roots

———, ***moraic trochaic:*** language in which moras normally alternate s^w

———, ***syllabic-trochaic:*** language in which syllables normally alternate s^w

———, ***syllable-timed:*** language in which syllables are perceived as occupying the same length of time to utter

———, ***stress-timed:*** language in which stressed syllables are perceived as occurring at regular intervals

———, ***synthetic:*** language in which syntax depends on affixes to roots

langue d'oc: the dialects of Southern France in which 'oc' meant 'yes'

langue d'oïl: the dialects of Northern France in which 'oïl' (later 'oui') meant 'yes'

lift: prominent (stressed) element of OE or ME foot

line: numerically regulated poetic unit, stretching from where counting begins to where it ends (Fabb)

———, ***authorial:*** line that is more likely to be as the poet composed it because it is the same in all witnesses (Duggan)

———, ***broken-backed:*** ME line lacking a syllable between positions 4 and 6, thus producing a stress clash

———, ***expanded:*** OE line where a foot is expanded to a half-line or a half-line to a line

———, ***feminine:*** paroxytonic line

———, *four-beat:* line with four strong positions, found in many of the world's literatures
———, *'Gallic':* a minor and pausing iambic pentameter line
———, *headless:* ME line lacking an initial unstressed syllable; line with an implied initial offbeat (Attridge)
———, *Italic:* a major and / or running iambic pentameter line
———, *major:* an iambic pentameter with its principal mid-line stress in position 6
———, *masculine:* oxytonic line
———, *maximum undivided:* line of eight or nine syllables (traditional French metrics)
———, *minor:* an iambic pentameter with its principal mid-line stress in position 4
———, *pausing:* iambic pentameter with a word boundary between positions 4 and 5
———, *running:* iambic pentameter with no word boundary between positions 4 and 5
———, *scribal:* line involving copying errors because it varies between witnesses (Duggan)
makar: traditional Scottish crafter of verses
matra: Sanskrit term for mora
measure, phrasal: poetic meter based on phrases
meter: rhythm produced by the moraic structure of the language;
———, *accentual:* poetic meter involving the regulation of dynamic accent
———, *alliterative:* poetic meter in which stressed syllables alliterate
———, *Goliardic:* Medieval Latin meter in which three accentual lines were followed by a quantitative line
———, *poetic:* the abstraction underpinning the composition of lines of verse; verse design (Jakobson)
———, *Saturnian:* Old Latin meter with disputed parameters
———, *amphibrachic:* verse based on foot with two contrasts (w-s-w); not found in Classical quantitative poetry
———, *foreign:* English poetic meters imitated from verse in the Romance languages (Schipper)
———, *native English:* English poetic meters derived from Germanic verse (Schipper)
mètre, dernier, anglo-normande: the iambic *décasyllabe* (Billy)
metrical set, completion of: hypothesis that monosyllables in English verse are flexible and may fit any verse template (Chatman)
metrics, generative: linguistic theory that attempts to derive a series of rules that can generate all the lines in a meter (Halle & Keyser)
———, *linguistic:* analysis of poetic meter derived from the modern discipline of linguistics (Jakobson)
———, *quantitative:* versifying that employs the contrast between heavy and light syllables
métrique de syllabes indifférenciées: metrics based on undifferentiated syllables, e.g., Japanese and French (Cornulier)
metron: Greek quantitative measure divisible into two identical feet
mismatch, bracketing: non-coincidence of lexical and metrical boundaries
mode, Aeolian: type of Greek versification in which the lines contain an equal number of syllables
———, *Ionic:* type of Greek versification in which the lines contain an equal number of moras

modesty topos: medieval convention of authorial humility
molossus: Greek quantitative foot with three heavy syllables
monosyllable: word of one syllable
———, *grammatical:* function word such as article or preposition
———, *lexical:* word carrying semantic burden, such as noun or verb
———, *one-mora:* feature limited to function words in English
mora: minimum duration of a syllable
———, *un-footed:* mora that forms no part of a s^w contrast in normal speech
Move X: see rule, rhythm
nebenton: clearly discernible secondary stress, a feature of Germanic languages
non-ictus: linguistic material occupying the interval between beats / ictuses
non-repetition: lack of repetition of onset, nucleus, or coda in two syllables
nucleus: essential core of syllable (vowel or diphthong)
number, magical: 7 ± 2: maximum number of gradations that humans can learn to distinguish (Miller)
octave: eight-line strophe, first sub-unit of sonnet
octosyllabe: French line of eight syllables up to and including the final stress
offbeat: weak element contrasting with beat; equivalent of musical upbeat
———, *double:* offbeat consisting of two syllables
———, *implied:* offbeat of zero syllables
onset: optional initial (consonantal) element in syllable
orientation: whether the positions of a template contrast s^w (left-strong) or w^s (right-strong); parameter of PT
OT (Optimality Theory): hypothesis that linguistic outputs result from a hierarchy of constraints (Prince & Smolensky)
ottava rima: Italian strophe design rhyming ababab cc
pair, neutral: pair of monosyllables that can be contrasted either s^w or w^s, according to metrical context, e.g., 'good news' (both lexical) and 'in a' (both grammatical)
parallelism, multi-phrase: *parallelismus membrorum* involving more than two *membra*
parallelismus membrorum: poetic meter based on parallel phrases, which may match, contrast with, or complement one another
parameter: one of five universal variables in verse design (PT)
para-phones: alternative performances of the same word as in 'never / ne'er'
para-phonology: the presence of para-phones in a language
pararhyme: imperfect repetition of a phoneme in rhyme as in 'tomb / worm' (Dylan Thomas)
pattern, alliterative: alternative positions for alliteration in OE and ME verse
peak, prominence: syllable of greater stress than its neighbors in any utterance
pentameter, canonical: common denominator of the iambic pentameter verse designs of the greatest poets of the English language
———, *dramatic:* iambic pentameter of Elizabethan and Jacobean drama
———, *flexible:* iambic pentameter allowing trisyllabic substitution and stress clash; loose iambic pentameter (Fabb and Halle)
———, *iambic:* line with template of five iambs (PT); line of five beats in which implied offbeats compensate for double offbeats (Attridge)
———, *proto-iambic:* five-beat line that has most, but not all, of the features of the canonical iambic pentameter (Cable)

performance: the delivery of a line whether aloud in public or silently in the reader's head
———, *cool:* delivering lines using the latest pronunciation of the words they contain
phoneme: smallest unit (segment) of the speech chain
phrase: meaningful grouping of words
poem: a single independent poetic composition
———, *prose:* poem in which irregular speech rhythms are employed
poem design: poet's intention regarding overall structure of a poem
poetry: literary texts in which the author attempts to achieve special intensity in the expression of thoughts or feelings by the use of style and rhythm
position number: number of positions in verse template (parameter of PT)
position size: maximum amount of linguistic material in a verse instance that may represent a position (parameter of PT)
poulter's measure: English strophe design in which lines contain 3-3-4-3 rising feet; in its most regular form the strophe contains 6-6-8-6 syllables
probability model: the analysis of control samples of prose to decide whether any feature of a poem is metrical or linguistic
prominence site: positions constrained by verse design, strong, weak, or final (parameter of PT)
prominence type: phonological feature constituting prominence in verse; e.g., stress, strength, or weight (parameter of PT)
PT: (Parametric Theory): hypothesis that five key variables (parameters) characterize all meters (Hanson and Kiparsky)
pyrrhic: quantitative foot consisting of two light syllables
quatrain, monorhyme: strophe design rhyming aaaa
quinario tronco: Italian line of four syllables of which the fourth is stressed; hemistich with the same configuration
refrain: line repeated at the close of every strophe
regularity: the occurrence of a feature at predictable intervals
———, *accentual:* regularity in the number of accented syllables in each line
———, *syllabic:* regularity in the number of syllables in each line
regulation, numerical: the artificial crafting of language so as ensure that a given feature occurs either the same number of times (regular verse) in each line, or a perceptibly different number of times (free verse)
rejet: the words severed from the remainder of their phrase that open the second of two enjambed lines
repetition, full: repetition of an entire syllable (onset, nucleus, and coda)
resolution: the substitution of two weak syllables for one or of a stressed and heavy syllable for two syllables
rhyme: combination of the nucleus and coda of a syllable; more commonly, the repetition of the phonemes in that combination
———, *alternation of:* French convention alternating masculine and feminine rhymes
———, *grammatical:* the rhyming of morphs or inflections
———, *index of:* measure of difficulty: the average number of rhymes for each word required by a strophe design
———, *mixed:* the rhyming of stressed syllable with an unstressed
———, *reverse:* repetition of syllable onset and nucleus, e.g., 'same' / 'safe'
———, *strong:* rhyming of stressed syllables

———, *suffix:* see rhyme, grammatical
———, *weak:* rhyming of unstressed syllables
rhyme royal: strophe rhyming abab bcc
rhythm: the repetition of an event in time
———, *biological:* rhythms such as respiration and heartbeat
———, *complex primary:* repetition of groups of the same event
———, *complex secondary:* repetition involving two or more events
———, *foot-based:* poetic rhythm in which the events are combinations of contrasting elements such as moras or stress and non-stress
———, *free:* poetic rhythm in which the number of events varies from line to line
———, *ictic:* poetic rhythm in which the events are ictuses
———, *interior:* poetic rhythm in which the events are semantic, syntactic, or lexical
———, *lexical:* poetic rhythm in which the events are specific words
———, *linear:* poetic rhythm in which the events are the lines themselves, either matching or contrasting with their neighbors
———, *linguistic:* pattern of s and w moras or syllables: a given for any language
———, *moraic:* repetition of s and w moras within utterances
———, *non-phonic:* poetic rhythm based on things other than sound (e.g., syntax)
———, *phonic:* poetic rhythm in which the events are sounds
———, *phrasal:* poetic rhythm in which the events are phrases
———, *poetic:* repetition of events chosen by poet
———, *secondary moraic:* repetition of groups of s and w moras
———, *semantic:* poetic rhythm in which the events are thoughts or ideas
———, *simple primary:* repetition involving a single type of event and a single interval duration
———, *syllabic:* poetic rhythm in which the events are syllables
———, *syntactic:* poetic rhythm in which the events are grammatical units
———, *verbal:* poetic rhythm in which the events are words
rima normale (It.): *rima piana* (because most Italian words are paroxytonic)
——— *piana (It.):* paroxytonic, or feminine, rhyme, e.g., '**gen**te / **men**te'
——— *sdrucciola (It.):* proparoxytonic, or trisyllabic, rhyme, e.g., 'du**ra**bile / a**ma**bile'
——— *tronca (It.):* oxytonic, or masculine, rhyme, e.g., 'an**cor** / caccia**tor**'
rime abbraciate (Fr. rimes embrassées): the rhyme scheme abba
——— *alterne (Fr. rimes croisées):* the rhyme scheme abab
——— *baciate (Fr. rimes plats):* the rhyme scheme aa bb
——— *riche:* (Fr.) full repetition (of onset as well as nucleus and coda)
———, *simple:* repetition of nucleus and coda
rise: see lift
rondel: Old French strophe design rhymed ABba abAB abb aAB2
rule, metrical: output resulting from the poet's choice of meter and not the structure of the language concerned
———, *rhythm:* stress shift as in 'sweet six**teen**' and '**six**teen tons'
———, *universal:* rule that applies to all languages
rules, correspondence: assumed rules (based on poet's practice) governing the type of linguistic material in verse instances that may correspond to the units of the template
salience: striking prominence (non-metrical)

schwa: reduced vowel like the 'o' in 'sailor'
schwa, eurhythmic: schwa pronounced to prevent stress clash
schwa deletion: loss of schwas in evolution of language or by elision
senarius: Latin line of six feet
septenarius, iambic: Latin line of seven iambic feet
sequence, Latin: medieval verse form, a series of rhymed couplets of varying lengths
sermo illustre: dialect fit for elevated speech (Dante)
sestet: six-line strophe; second sub-unit of sonnet
settenario doppio: line of 2 x 7 syllables, Italian equivalent of *alexandrin*
settenario piano: line or hemistich of 6F syllables
Sievers Type: one of five configurations of stress that between them account for 85 % of OE lines
sirventes: Occitan political poem usually in *vers de dix*
Skeltonics: verse in very short, rhymed, but irregular lines
SMP: (Stress Maximum Principle): hypothesis that a syllable of greater stress than both its neighbors in the same syntactic constituent must not occur in a weak position
sonetto: fourteen-line poem design invented in Sicily c. AD 1250
sonnet régulier: French sonnet with rhyme scheme beginning abba abba cc. . .
speech stream: continuous flow of sound produced in normal utterances
spondee: quantitative foot consisting of two heavy syllables
stanza: belated (medieval It.) term for strophe
stichic: verse in which lines are not grouped in sub-units
stimulus diffusion: the spread of a general practice from one culture to another that does not involve detailed imitation
strambotto: traditional Sicilian verse form with 8 lines rhymed ab ab ab ab
stress: dynamic accent, the acoustic correlates of which are duration, volume, and pitch change
———, *débil:* the weak stress found in grammatical words like '**o**ver' (Eng.) 'a**vec**' (Fr.), and '**pa**ra' (Sp.)
———, *hovering:* extensive application of the rhythm rule (Cable)
———, *phrasal:* extra stress accruing to the final stressed syllable in a phrase
———, *relative:* level of stress of a syllable compared to that of its neighbors
———, *secondary:* lesser stress given to a syllable other than the strongest syllable in a polysyllabic word
——— *grid:* diagram to illustrate the hierarchical structure of stress
——— *hierarchy:* s^w or w^s relationship applied to prosodic levels
——— *maximum:* syllable with more stress than both its neighbors
——— *tree:* branching diagram used as an alternative to stress grid
strophe: group of lines with a structure that repeats itself within a poem
strophe design: the structure of the strophe, usually involving a repeated line length and / or rhyme scheme
strophic: verse in which lines are grouped in sub-units (strophes)
stylistics, metrical: the identification of metrical features that distinguish the versification of a particular poem or poet
stylization: a variation with special characteristics signaling its use for a particular purpose

subitization: instant recognition of small numbers up to three (in some individuals four)
subset (of phoneme repetition): type of repetition that occurs by chance when another type is systematic, e.g., occasional rhymes found in assonating verse
substitution, trisyllabic: replacement of single unstressed syllable by two
sueltos: Spanish unrhymed verse
suprasegmental: phonological feature other than a segment (phoneme)
syllable: suprasegmental feature of language employing phonemes as onset (optional), nucleus, and coda (optional)
———, ***extrametrical:*** syllable that is ignored in determining the rhythm of a line or language
———, ***heavy:*** syllable with branching rhyme; two-mora syllable
———, ***ictic:*** syllable that provides the beat
———, ***light:*** syllable of one mora
———, ***non-ictic:*** syllable that forms part of offbeat
———, ***post-tonic:*** syllable after final stress within word or line
———, ***tonic:*** syllable with stress in polysyllabic word
syllable length: now usually referred to as syllable weight, see 'syllables, light and heavy' and 'theory, moraic'
synaloepha: merging of the final vowel of one word with the initial vowel of the next so as to produce a single syllable
syncope: deletion of an unstressed vowel within a word, reducing its length by one syllable
template: blueprint for creating verse instances; it can usually be inferred only from an analysis of the text concerned
tension: deviation from norm licensed by correspondence rules; source of variety to prevent metrical regularity becoming monotonous
tension metric: refinement of SMP to take account of norms and deviations from them (Halle & Keyser)
terza rima: Italian strophe design rhyming aba bcb cdc etc.
tetrameter: line of four feet
———, ***iambic:*** line of four iambs: w^s w^s w^s w^s
———, ***trochaic, catalectic:*** masculine line of four trochees, the last of which lacks its final (post-tonic) syllable: s^w s^w s^w s^
tetrasyllabe: French line of four syllables
tetrasyllable: English line of four syllables
theory, ludic: hypothesis that poetry is a game played by poets (Birrell)
———, ***moraic:*** hypothesis that syllables are composed of moras and that this accounts for the metrical properties of language
———, ***optimality:*** see OT
———, ***parametric:*** see PT
———, ***reference:*** hypothesis that most lines of OE verse have one of a limited number of stress configurations
time, duple: complex secondary rhythm provided by filling all the intervals between beats (prominent syllables) with a single syllable
———, ***triple:*** complex secondary rhythm provided by filling all the intervals between beats (prominent syllables) with two syllables

trios, grammatical: singular, dual, and plural; 1st, 2nd, and 3rd persons; past, present, and future tenses
triphthong: combination of three vowels
trisyllable: word of three syllables
trochee, moraic: two moras contrasting s^w
———, *syllabic:* two syllables contrasting s^w
———, *clitic:* pairs of interdependent monosyllables in which the first is strong, e.g., 'talk with' / 'walk with'
———, *lexical:* disyllabic words with s^w contrast, e.g., '**tro**chee'
Troilus meter: original term for rhyme royal in English
tropes: Latin verse inserted into the service of the Mass
universe (statistical): an entire population, e.g., all the fish in the sea, contrasted statistically with a sample, e.g., today's catch
upbeat, musical: note preceding the beat
utterance: highest level of the prosodic hierarchy, a unit of language with no syntactic relation to what precedes or follows
variety, rhythmic: mixture of duple and triple time, as in normal English speech
vers de dix: *décasyllabe*, French line with ten syllables to final stress
verse: numerically regulated language (Lotz)
———, *blank:* unrhymed iambic pentameters
———, *free:* verse of which lines may contrast instead of matching
———, *loose:* iambic verse that includes dolniks (Fabb & Halle)
———, *stress-syllabic:* verse that regulates both the number of syllables and the number and position of stress peaks in the line
———, *syllabic:* verse that regulates the number of syllables; in French it also regulates phrasal stresses
———, *syllabo-tonic:* stress-syllabic verse (Gasparov)
———, *transitional:* English verse in which 80-95 per cent of ictic intervals contain a single syllable (Tarlinskaja)
———, *tumbling:* predominantly triple-time meter with lines that contain four beats
verse design: the poet's template and correspondence rules (Jakobson)
verse instance: an actual line of text based on a verse design (Jakobson)
verses of cadence: four-beat dolniks (Southworth)
verso brusco/tronco: Italian oxytonic line
———*fluctuante:* Spanish verse where isosyllabism is only approximate (Navarro Tomás)
———*piano:* Italian paroxytonic line
———*sdrucciolo:* Italian proparoxytonic line
virgule: mark found mid-line in some lines of Hengwrt manuscript
vulgaria: the vernacular dialects of early Italian
wheel: group of shorter lines closing ME strophe, rhyming baba where bob is rhymed a
word, lexical: content word as contrasted with grammatical word, e.g., 'boy' or 'stood' as compared with 'on' or 'the'
word audit: the counting and classification of words involved in forming poetic feet
word stress: the primary stress of polysyllabic words and the stress of lexical monosyllables
word-foot: foot that coincides with stress configuration of an OE word (Russom)

Index

[N. B. Titles of all poems (including short ones) in italics.]